Fortran IV Programming for Engineers and Scientists

Fortran IV Programming

for Engineers and Scientists

Second Edition

PAUL W. MURRILL

and

CECIL L. SMITH

Louisiana State University

1817

HARPER & ROW, PUBLISHERS, New York
Cambridge, Philadelphia, San Francisco,
London, Mexico City, São Paulo, Sydney

FORTRAN IV PROGRAMMING FOR ENGINEERS AND SCIENTISTS, Second Edition

 For information address Harper & Row, Publishers, Inc., 10 East 53d Street, New York, NY 10022.

Library of Congress Cataloging in Publication Data

Murrill, Paul W.
Fortran IV programming for engineers and scientists.

1. FORTRAN (Computer program language)
3. Electronic digital computers–Programming.
I. Smith, Cecil L., joint author. II. Title
QA76.73.F25M87 1973 001.6′424 73-1689
ISBN 0-7002-2419-X

Contents

3 Simple Fortran Programs 45

4 Transfer of Control 67

5 Introduction to DO Loops and to Subscripted Variables 87

6 Multidimensional Arrays and Nested DO Loops 129

Preface to the Second Edition

Since the publication and broad acceptance of the First Edition of this book, many significant changes have occurred in the computing industry and in Fortran instruction. As a result the authors have revised their own approach to the teaching of certain topics. The combination of these factors led to the decision to publish this Second Edition, which the authors think has the following advantages over the First Edition:

1. Since the appearance of the First Edition, time-sharing systems have become progressively more popular, and therefore, discussion of time-sharing systems has been included at several points in the text, especially in Chapters 1 and 3. However, it is the authors' experience that time-sharing systems have not achieved the level of standardization of card-oriented systems, so the instructor will need to supplement the text with material describing operation of the terminal (sign-on, sign-off, program saving, etc.), if one is used.
2. One advantage of the First Edition was that students could begin writing programs at an early stage. This edition incorporates a discussion of format-free input-output such as is available in WATFIV, so that the student's first programs can be written even earlier and without the trauma of format. Early discussion of format has been retained, of course, for those systems that require its use. The authors have been very successful in permitting students to write their first three or four programs without format, and then requiring its use thereafter. At present, no course on Fortran can be considered complete without a coverage of format.
3. Material has been included on the WATFIV in-core compiler and its error messages, but not to the extent that the text becomes usable only to those with access to WATFIV.
4. The material on subprograms (Chapter 9) has been revised extensively. This was probably the weakest point in the First Edition, and we hope this has been corrected.
5. The number of exercises—which was generous in the First Edition—has been increased.

6. We have concluded that the presentation of DO loops and subscripted variables can be accomplished best as follows: DO loops first, single-subscripted arrays second, then nested DO loops, and finally multiple-subscripted arrays. In effect, more meaningful exercises can be formulated that use DO loops but not subscripted variables, whereas it is very difficult to formulate an exercise using subscripted variables that does not require a DO loop or the equivalent counter. Therefore, the preferred order of presentation is incorporated into this Second Edition.
7. The discussion in Chapter 7 of manipulation of character data has been revised extensively and, we think, for the better.
8. The First Edition implied that mixed-mode arithmetic was taboo. Students quickly learned, however, that the compiler would accept it, and they used it without understanding what might happen if they were not careful. The Second Edition addresses this point in a more direct fashion.
9. The introductory chapter has been revised to improve discussion of computer characteristics, compilation, operating systems, and the role of Fortran.

The authors wish to express their sincere thanks to all of those who took the time to point out the strengths and weaknesses of the First Edition. These thoughtful comments were sincerely appreciated, and we would appreciate similar comments on the Second Edition. As in the First Edition, we certainly owe our thanks to our ever-smiling secretaries, Mrs. Jo Ann Caillouet and Miss Verma Dotson.

Preface to the First Edition

This book is intended to serve as both a text for an introductory course in Fortran IV programming and a reference manual for those with prior programming experience. It is primarily aimed toward engineers, scientists, mathematicians, or anyone with a very elementary background in college-level mathematics.

The primary objective of the text is to introduce undergraduate students to Fortran IV programming, and this objective was the prime consideration in selecting the order of presentation of the subject matter. It is felt that most of the included material can be easily understood by freshmen, but enough advanced problems are included to make it appropriate for those who are further along in their studies. Basically, the material is appropriate for any first course in programming.

This text arises from the authors' experience in teaching a one-semester-hour course on Fortran programming for the past five years. With only one hour of lecture per week it is imperative that the student quickly begin to write programs. This requirement is reflected in the text by the introduction of complete Fortran programs in Chapter 3. Since the common thread among the students involved in the course is applied mathematics, it is emphasized in the exercises and examples.

The advantages of this text are (1) a simple introduction in the first chapter to the characteristics and method of operation of digital computers, (2) an organization that allows the students' programming ability to progress at a steady rate, (3) a wealth of examples and exercises for students at all levels, and (4) inclusion of the more recent Fortran options available on computers such as the IBM System/360.

The authors wish to express their thanks to Professor Warren H. Thomas, Department of Industrial Engineering, State University of New York at Buffalo, and to Professor Mary McCammon, Department of Mathematics, Pennsylvania State University, for their very helpful reviewing of the manuscript. Equal thanks are also due to the faculty of LSU's College of Engineering and to countless students for their valuable suggestions. Finally, but certainly not least, our thanks to the smiling secretaries, Mrs. Carol Houston, Mrs. Ruth Albright, and Miss Hazel LaCoste, of the Department of Chemical Engineering, who did most of the work.

Fortran IV Programming for Engineers and Scientists

1

Introduction to Digital Computers

The steam engine and other devices for doing work gave man an extension of his physical capabilities and brought about the Industrial Revolution. In a very similar manner, electronic computers are providing man with tools with which he can process quantities of information and solve problems that otherwise would be impossible to handle. These computers are producing an *informational revolution* that will have more impact on each of our everyday lives than any other aspect of modern technology—even atomic energy. The purpose of this book is to assist you, as a student of science or engineering, in learning to utilize these computers in your day-to-day work.

1-1. Digital-Computer Characteristics

Modern electronic computers are of two basic types—digital and analog. The entire content of this book is directed toward understanding and programming digital computers, and no attention is devoted to the study of analog computers or combinations of analog and digital computers (hybrid computers).

Digital computers can be appreciated best by first considering some of their characteristics. Understanding these characteristics will help us to appreciate their usefulness.

One of the most prominent characteristics of digital computers is their truly incredible *speed*. Although they only work one step at a time, i.e., *sequentially,* they perform their tasks at rates that are beyond the comprehension of the novice. As an example, some large machines are capable of adding together several hundred thousand 16-digit numbers in less than a second. These tremendous speeds make it possible for the machine to do work in a few minutes that might otherwise require years of time.

Not only is the digital computer capable of working very rapidly, but it also has a perfect *memory.* It has virtually instantaneous "recall" of both data and instructions that are stored inside, and it never forgets or loses the accuracy of the information which it has within its memory.

A digital computer is an extremely *accurate* device. In most machines numbers are handled with seven, eight, or nine significant digits, and twice this accuracy can usually be obtained by the programmer. This means that a machine would have no difficulty multiplying 2782.4362 times 40.127896 and obtaining the product correct to eight or sixteen significant figures.

Coupled with the significant characteristics already listed, the digital computer does its work *automatically*. It can accept instructions from its operator, and then execute these instructions without need for human intervention. This implies that the machine can be given a problem; then while you attend a movie, it will do your work with incredible accuracy and at fantastic speeds. Learning to use such a tool should require no further motivation.

Additional characteristics of the digital computer will be noted later, but for the present it will be more advantageous to see how the machine works.

1-2. How the Digital Computer Works

The digital computer is basically a device to accept *data* and a set of instructions as to how to manipulate these data in order to produce a set of answers. The set of instructions is called the *program*, and these are prepared by a *programmer* (you). (See Figure 1-1.) This book is primarily concerned with the preparation of programs. Sometimes the data may be contained within the program, but more often the data are entered into the computer after the program.

In general, the computer may be thought of as being composed of three main sections: the memory, the central processing unit (CPU), and the input/output processor. The computer *memory* is used for storing data, instructions, intermediate results, and final answers; the *central processing unit* performs all the necessary manipulations of the data; and the *input/output processor* communicates with the outside world. (See Figure 1-2.) Transfer of instructions and data among these units takes very little time— in some machines less than one millionth of a second.

All information and signals in transit inside the computer are handled as electrical signals (usually pulses), and in memory this information is stored in magnetic cores,

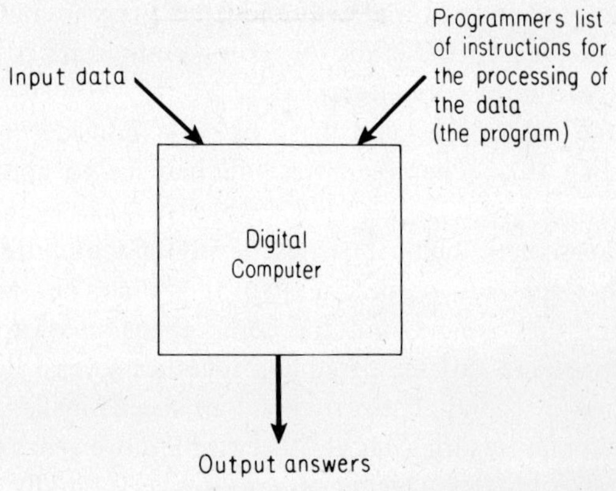

Figure 1-1. Functional role of the digital computer

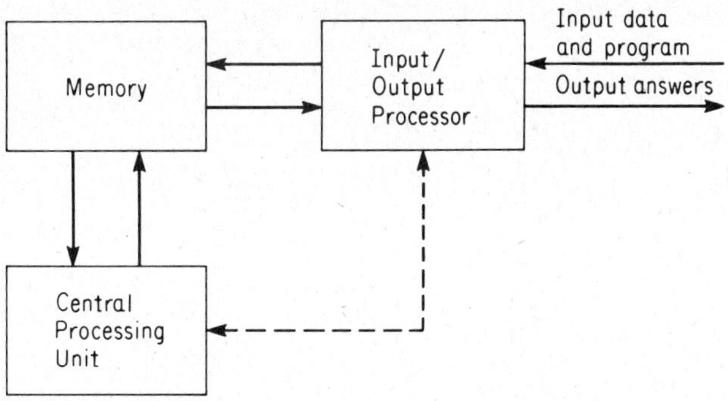

Figure 1-2. Relation of memory unit, arithmetic unit, and control unit (Solid arrows represent information flow, dashed arrows represent control signals.)

switches (flip-flops), and/or as magnetized spaces on drums, discs, and tapes. All of these devices are designed to exist in only one of two states which we may associate with the symbols 0 and 1. (See Figure 1-3.) These two states may be considered as *binary digits* or *bits* (a contraction of "*bi*nary digi*ts*") and are used to represent information. Thus the number system employed is basically binary, but it is usually more convenient for instructions and addresses to be "represented" in the octal or hexadecimal number systems. Nonnumeric information (alphabetic and special symbols) in a computer is represented in a binary code, and numbers are represented in one of two ways: in a *binary-coded decimal system* (each digit coded in a fixed number of bits) or the decimal numbers are converted into the *binary number system* (used in most computers primarily designed for scientific work).

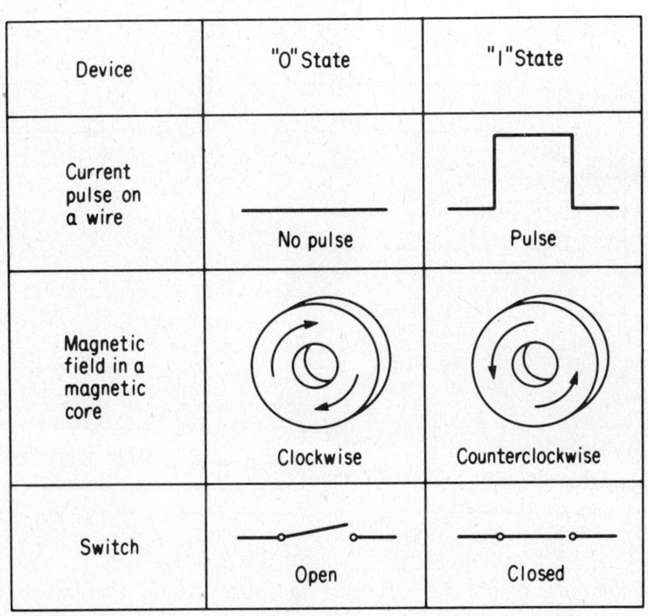

Figure 1-3. Examples of binary devices

1-3. Control and Operation of the Computer

While it is not necessary to understand such topics as binary arithmetic, the electronics of digital circuits, or other topics fundamental to the design of digital computers in order to learn to program in Fortran, a superficial understanding of the general operation of digital computers will easily reveal the origins of certain rules and conventions incorporated into the Fortran language. In reality, Fortran reflects basic machine characteristics to a greater extent than most other languages.

The general schematic diagram of the computing system in Figure 1-2 is shown in a little more detail in Figure 1-4. As pointed out in the last section, this system is broadly divided into three units: central processing unit, memory, and input/output processor. The central processing unit is further divided into two subunits: the arithmetic unit and the control unit. The *arithmetic unit* is responsible for performing operations such as additions, comparisons, etc., on the information in memory. The *control unit* is responsible for interpreting the instructions sequentially in memory and directing the arithmetic unit and input/output processor to perform the appropriate operations.

The concept of storing both the instructions (i.e., the program) and the data in the same memory unit has been of utmost importance in the development of computing machines. The very earliest computers employed hand-wired programs which made them inconvenient to use. The brilliant mathematician John von Neumann proposed the stored program concept which, coupled with the remarkable advances in electronics technology, led directly to computing machines as we know them today.

Since the central memory plays such an important role in the operation of the computer, a clear view of the organization of this memory is essential. Perhaps the most vivid way of visualizing the memory of the computer is as a set of mailboxes called memory cells, memory locations, or storage locations. This analogy is quite appropriate. In each individual memory cell only one word of information may be stored at any one time. This word of information may be either data (numerical or nonnumerical) or

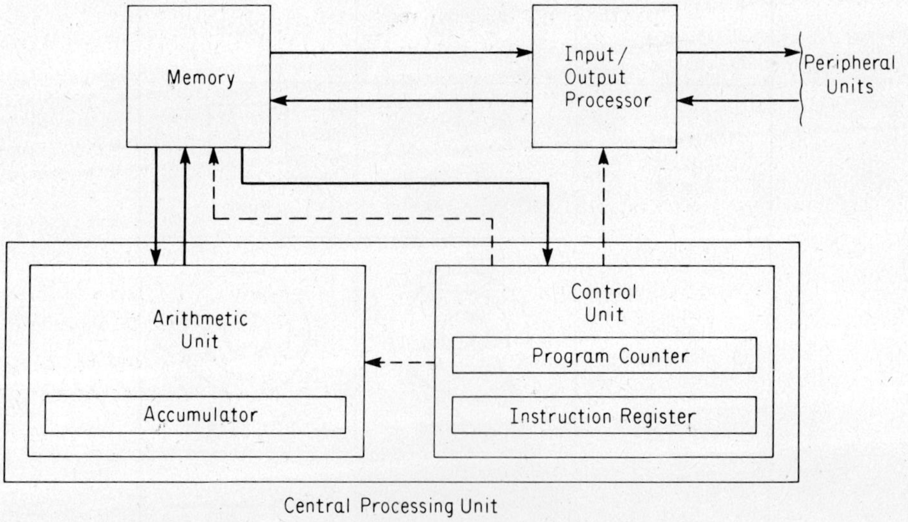

Figure 1-4. Schematic diagram of a simple computer (Solid arrows represent information flow; dashed arrows represent control signals.)

computer instructions. Each memory cell has its own individual address, and it is common to refer to memory cells by their addresses. The word contained in the memory cell appears as a binary number, and by superficial inspection there is no way to identify whether this word is data or whether it is an instruction. The computer must be told explicitly which memory cells contain instructions and which contain data. The control unit of the computer will treat the contents of a memory cell (a word) as though it were an instruction, and the arithmetic unit of the computer will treat the contents of a memory cell as though it were data. Each individual memory cell (or word) contains a fixed, preset number of digits, and that number of digits will limit the amount of significant information that can be stored in that memory cell. The instructions that are used by the computer for the processing of information are constructed so that they deal with memory-cell addresses.

As pointed out in the first section of this book, the digital computer is a sequential machine. Its operation is a sequence of cycles, each of which consists of two phases: a *fetch* phase and an *execute* phase. The fetch phase uses two registers in the control unit: the *program counter* and the *instruction register.* The program counter is often referred to by the more descriptive name of *instruction address register*, and it always contains the address of the next instruction to be executed. At the beginning of the fetch phase, the contents of the location in memory whose address is currently in the program counter is loaded into the instruction register. Therefore the contents of this memory location will be treated as an instruction. At the completion of the fetch phase the program counter is incremented by one, so that it now points to the next instruction to be retrieved from memory.

At the start of the execution phase, the control unit decodes the instruction and issues specific commands to the various elements of the arithmetic unit. In performing its operations, the arithmetic unit utilizes a register called the accumulator to contain the data on which it is to operate. For example, a typical instruction might be to add the contents of a specific storage location in memory to the current contents of the accumulator. The instruction itself contains the address of the memory location involved and a group of bits (called the *operation code*) whose pattern indicates that addition is to be performed. The control unit relays the address to the memory addressing circuits in order to retrieve the contents of the storage location, and activates the "add" circuit in the arithmetic unit to achieve the desired result.

To illustrate the sequence of operations, suppose we examine the instructions required to add the contents of two storage locations (specifically, at addresses 2749 and 1398) and store the result in a third storage location (specifically, at address 1972). Three instructions are required

Instruction	*Explanation*
LW,2749	"Load Word" copies the contents of the storage location at address 2749 into the accumulator.
AW,1398	"Add Word" adds the contents of the storage location at address 1398 to the current contents of the accumulator.
STW,1972	"STore Word" copies the contents of the accumulator into the storage location at address 1972.

In the above explanations, note the use of the word "copies." The instruction LW, 2749 in no way alters the contents of the storage location at address 2749. Similarly, the instruction STW, 1972 does not alter the contents of the accumulator, but does obliterate whatever was previously contained in the storage location at address 1972. Although not specifically mentioned, the instruction AW, 1398 does not alter the contents of the storage location at address 1398. These points can be summarized by the following rule: Read operations on memory are nondestructive; write operations on memory are destructive. Fortran follows this rule exactly.

To further illustrate the sequence of operations, suppose the three instructions are stored in the memory locations at addresses 1027, 1028, and 1029. If the program counter initially contains 1027, the sequence of operations is as follows:

1. The contents of the storage location at address 1027 are copied into the instruction register.
2. The program counter is incremented by 1, giving 1028.
3. The contents of the storage location at address 2749 are copied into the accumulator.
4. The contents of the storage location at address 1028 are copied into the instruction register.
5. The program counter is incremented by 1, giving 1029.
6. The contents of the storage location at address 1398 are added to the contents of the accumulator.
7. The contents of the storage location at address 1029 are copied into the instruction register.
8. The program counter is incremented by 1, giving 1030.
9. The contents of the accumulator are copied into the storage location at address 1972.

Many current computers could perform all these operations in less than ten millionths of a second.

Of course, current computers offer far more features than illustrated by the previous example, but their operations are basically straightforward. The examination of these other features is inappropriate for a manual on Fortran.

1-4. Programming Languages

In the above section we discussed how the computer would execute a program; in this section we want to examine the preparation of a program.

Writing a program directly in instructions, as described in the previous section, is said to be programming either in assembly language or in machine language. While this approach is relatively straightforward, it becomes tedious, especially for large programs. In essence the available instructions comprise the computer's language, which we could learn to speak but would rather not. Of course, the best solution would be for the computer to speak our native language, which for most readers of this book would be English. Unfortunately, this goal has not yet been achieved, although progress is being made.

The current solution is to use an intermediate language that has some of the characteristics in which problems are naturally expressed, but a language that is sufficiently rigorous to permit the computer to perform the translation from the program written in the programming language to the instructions that comprise the computer's natural language. This situation is illustrated in Figure 1-5. The programmer must translate the statement of the problem into statements in the programming language. Using a program known as a *compiler*, the computer translates the statements in the programming language into machine-executable instructions, a process referred to as *compilation*.

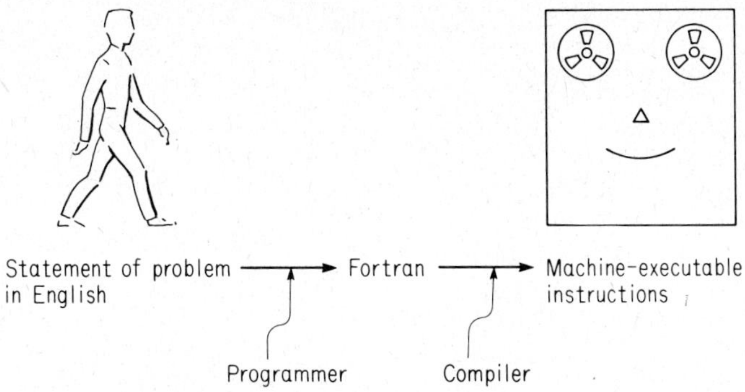

Figure 1-5. Role of Fortran

Since the statement of problems tends to differ from discipline to discipline, several different programming languages have appeared, each with special characteristics that make one language more attractive to some fields and disciplines than to others. In the business field, COBOL (COmmon Business Oriented Language) has dominated, primarily because its features enable large files of data to be manipulated readily. In science areas, Fortran (FORmula TRANslator) has dominated, primarily because algebraic expressions can be readily implemented. However, Fortran has enjoyed some use in business circles. The last decade saw the introduction of several new languages, some of which are easier to learn than Fortran, some of which are more powerful than Fortran, and some of which accomplish objectives (text editing, for example) that Fortran was never designed to accomplish. Nevertheless, Fortran continues to enjoy widespread use, and it will probably continue to do so for the foreseeable future.

Since its introduction in the mid-1950s, Fortran has gone through an evolutionary process that has enhanced its utility as a programming language. The last major extension of the language occurred in the early 1960s. At that time, most operational versions of Fortran were referred to as Fortran II. So many new features were added to the language at that time that the name was changed to Fortran IV. Although the Fortran available on some current machines is closer to Fortran II than Fortran IV, the bulk of the manufacturers have implemented Fortran IV. Therefore, this text will be devoted almost exclusively to Fortran IV.

Although the American National Standards Institute (ANSI) has adopted a standard for the Fortran IV language, the implemented versions available on commercial computers normally contain some (usually) minor variations or extensions. In a text such as this, we shall tend to present what we, at least, feel are the more common implementations. However, at many points these discrepancies force us to use "double-talk" or to insert hedging words such as *generally* or *usually*. Any uncertainties can be clarified by consulting the manuals provided by the computer manufacturer, but these are written for the experienced programmer rather than for the beginner.

A very simple example of a Fortran program is shown in Figure 1-6. This program computes the surface area a of a cylinder with diameter d and height h, the appropriate equation being

$$a = \pi dh$$

In the program in Figure 1-6, the first two statements assign numerical values to variables D and H. The third statement embodies the equation given above with the asterisk (*) denoting multiplication. The fourth statement instructs the computer to print the

```
D=14.25
H=22.5
A=3.1416*D*H
PRINT,'AREA =',A
STOP
END
```

(a) Program

```
AREA =      0.1007275E 04
```

(b) Output

Figure 1-6. Example of a Fortran program

characters AREA = followed by the numerical value of A. The fifth statement, the STOP statement, terminates execution of the program. The END statement informs the compiler that there are no more statements in the program. We shall dwell on the distinction between the STOP and the END statements in more detail in Chapter 3.

In Fortran, the statements in the program are executed sequentially, starting with the first statement and continuing until a STOP statement is executed. The output from the program in Figure 1-6 is written in exponential notation with E standing for "10 to the power." That is, the notation .1007275E04 actually means $.1007275 \times 10^4$ or 1007.275.

1-5. Compilation

The statements in the programming language are translated into an equivalent set of machine-executable instructions by programs known as compilers. Since this must occur

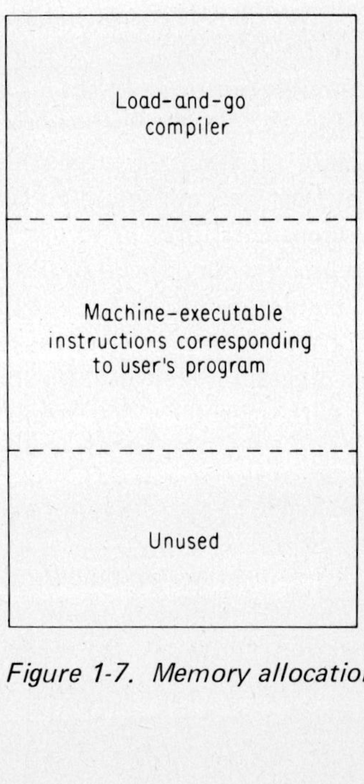

Figure 1-7. Memory allocation for a load-and-go compiler

prior to the performance of any operation specified within the program, this act of translation is generally referred to as the *compilation phase.*

Compilers come in two "styles," one of which is referred to as a load-and-go compiler. A *load-and-go* compiler reads the statements in the program, generates the corresponding machine-executable instructions, and places them directly into another area of memory (see Figure 1-7). During this process, the CPU is executing the set of instructions that comprise the compiler. After processing the last statement in the program, and storing the last machine-executable instruction in memory, the compilation phase is completed. An instruction in the load-and-go compiler then directs the CPU to the first instruction in the set of instructions generated from the user's program, and the *execution phase* begins. The CPU executes this set of instructions until all operations called for by the user's program have been completed. For any logical termination point in the user's program (such as a STOP statement in Fortran), the load-and-go compiler generates instructions that direct the CPU to return to a predetermined location within the compiler itself. When these instructions are executed at the end of the execution phase, the CPU is directed to return to the compiler, thus terminating the execution phase. At this point the user's program has been completed, and the compiler can instruct the computer to proceed to the next program to be run.

Instead of storing the generated instructions directly into memory, many compilers produce the set of machine-executable instructions on punched cards, magnetic tape, or other medium suitable for subsequent reentry of the information into the computer. The sequence of phases is as follows (refer to Figure 1-8):

1. *Compilation phase.* The compiler is entered into memory, followed by the statements written in the programming language (these statements are called the *source program*). The compiler generates the machine-executable instructions on some medium from which they can be subsequently reentered into the computer. This set of instructions is generally referred to as the *object deck*.
2. *Load phase.* Before the set of instructions can be executed, they must be entered into memory. The *loader* is a small program that reads the instructions and places them in memory. Since the compiler's task has been completed, these instructions can be placed in the same area of memory that was used for the compiler.
3. *Execution phase.* Upon completion of the load phase, the loader directs the CPU to the first instruction in the user's program.

As for the relative advantages of the two types of compilers, the following observations are pertinent:

1. Although we will not consider errors in detail until a later chapter, load-and-go compilers are generally able to provide the programmer more information concerning errors, especially during the execution phase. Compilers that produce object decks are poorer in this respect.
2. The load-and-go compiler resides in memory during the execution of the program. Compilers that produce an object deck need not reside in memory past the compilation phase, freeing this memory for use by the program. Thus, larger programs can be run.
3. If the same program is to be executed several times, an object deck can be saved and the compilation phase avoided in all except the first run. Since a load-and-go compiler produces no object deck, the compilation phase must be repeated. However, compile time for load-and-go compilers is generally short.

Although a number of other observations could be made, for small- to medium-scale programs a load-and-go compiler has definite advantages, particularly with respect to the

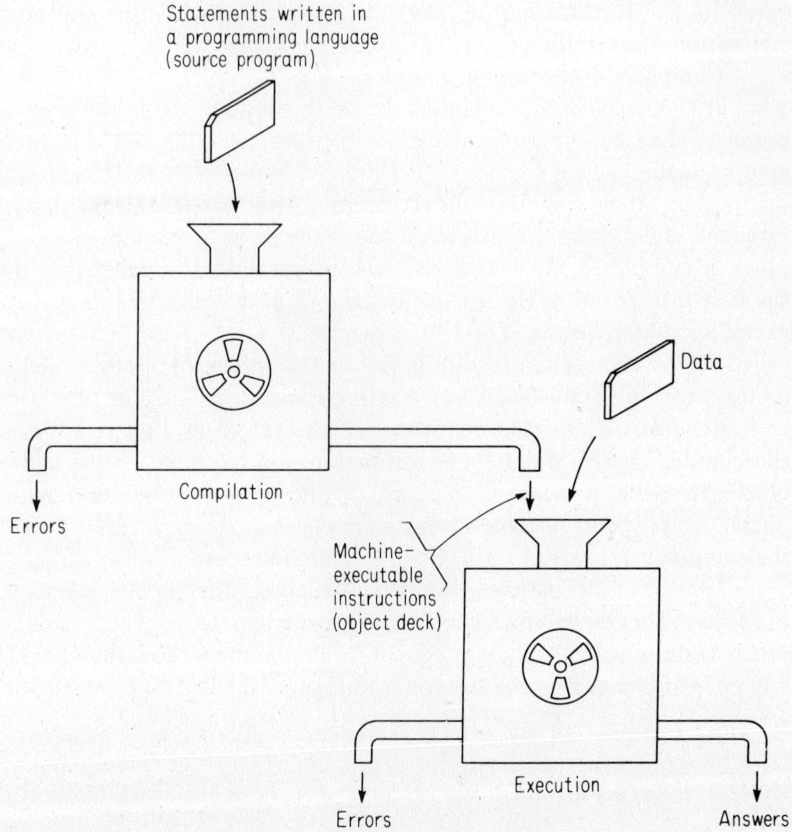

Figure 1-8. Schematic representation of compilation and execution phases for a compiler that generates an object deck

error messages generated. Large users and programmers in production-oriented centers prefer compilers that produce an object deck.

1-6. Batch Processing Systems

Computing systems can be divided into two broad categories with respect to orientation toward users: batch processing systems versus conversational time-sharing systems. Since batch processing appeared first chronologically, we shall consider it before considering conversational time-sharing.

As the operational complexity of general-purpose computing systems continued to increase, centers began to use professional computer operators to operate the machines instead of permitting individual programmers to operate them. Furthermore, the load at most centralized facilities is such that some jobs are almost always waiting to be run. The programmer brings his program to the center, leaves it to be run by the professional operators, and returns for it at some later time. The term *turnaround* encompasses these steps. How long he has to wait (referred to as the *turnaround time*) depends upon a number of factors: the current load on the center, the priority of his work, the running time and memory requirements of his program, etc. The number of times he can have his program run during a day is determined by the turnaround time. Centers at which the

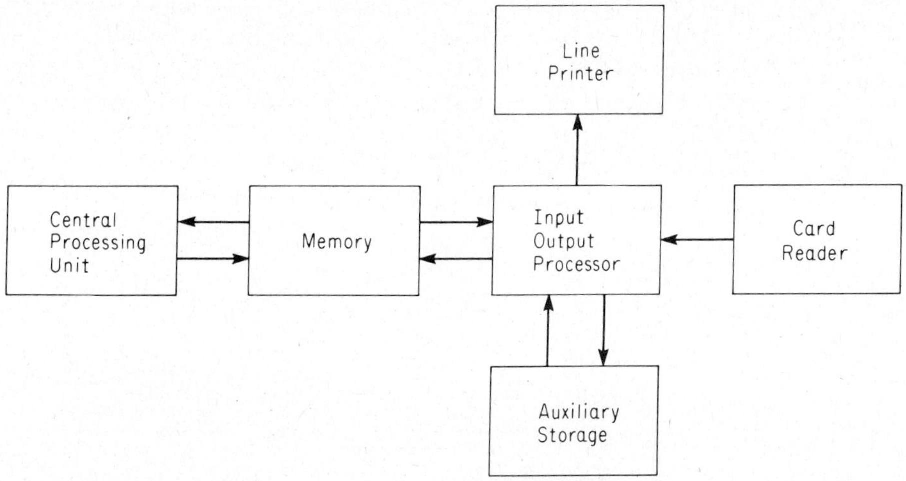

Figure 1-9. System configuration for batch processing

programmer is limited to four turnarounds or less per day are not unusual, although many centers do considerably better.

In explaining the batch processing mode of operation, we shall use the system in Figure 1-9 as the basis of our discussion. This is a relatively minimal configuration, but it will suffice for our purposes.

In the system of Figure 1-9, programs are submitted in the form of punched cards such as the one illustrated in Figure 1-10. This is the so-called Hollerith card, named after Dr. Herman Hollerith who developed the concepts basic to this type of punched card for use in the compilation of the 1890 census. (The 80-column card itself dates back to the 1930s.) The punched card is a cheap and versatile type of input/output medium. It has 80 vertical columns and can hold 80 characters of information—either letters, numbers, or punctuation. The standard card contains ten "number" rows for representing any number from 0 to 9. The ten number rows have above them two zone rows, 11 and 12. The

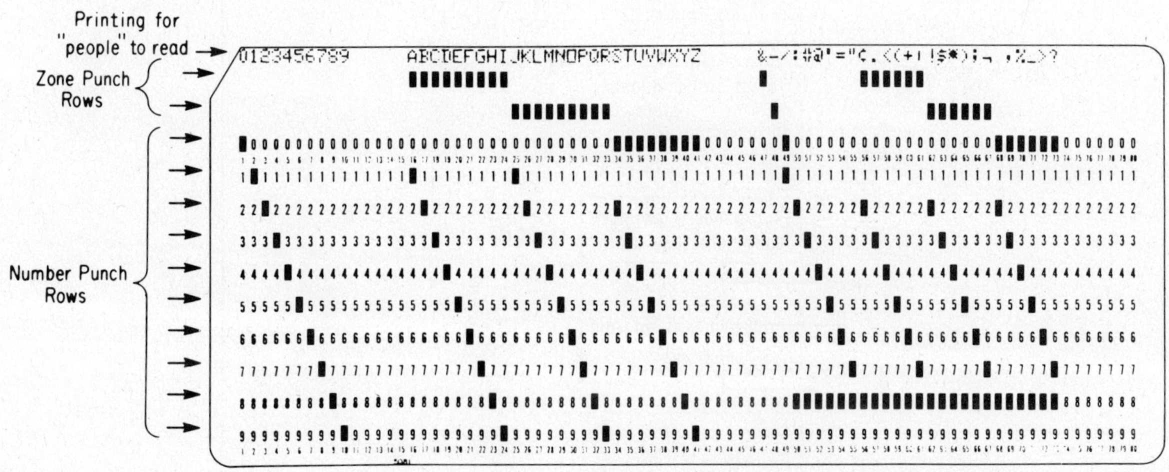

Figure 1-10. A typical punched card shows typical Fortran character code. This punched code varies slightly, depending on the specific computer.

punched card is arranged so that a punch in a single number column will represent digit; by making two or three punches in a single column it is possible to represent any letter of the alphabet or one of the special characters. This is seen vividly in Figure 1-10. The symbolic language of the punched card is automatically translated by the computer into binary information for its internal use.

In a batch processing environment, a supervisory-type program often referred to as the *operating system, executive,* or *monitor* is responsible for directing the computing system through whatever sequence of events is necessary to process the job, as illustrated in Figure 1-11.

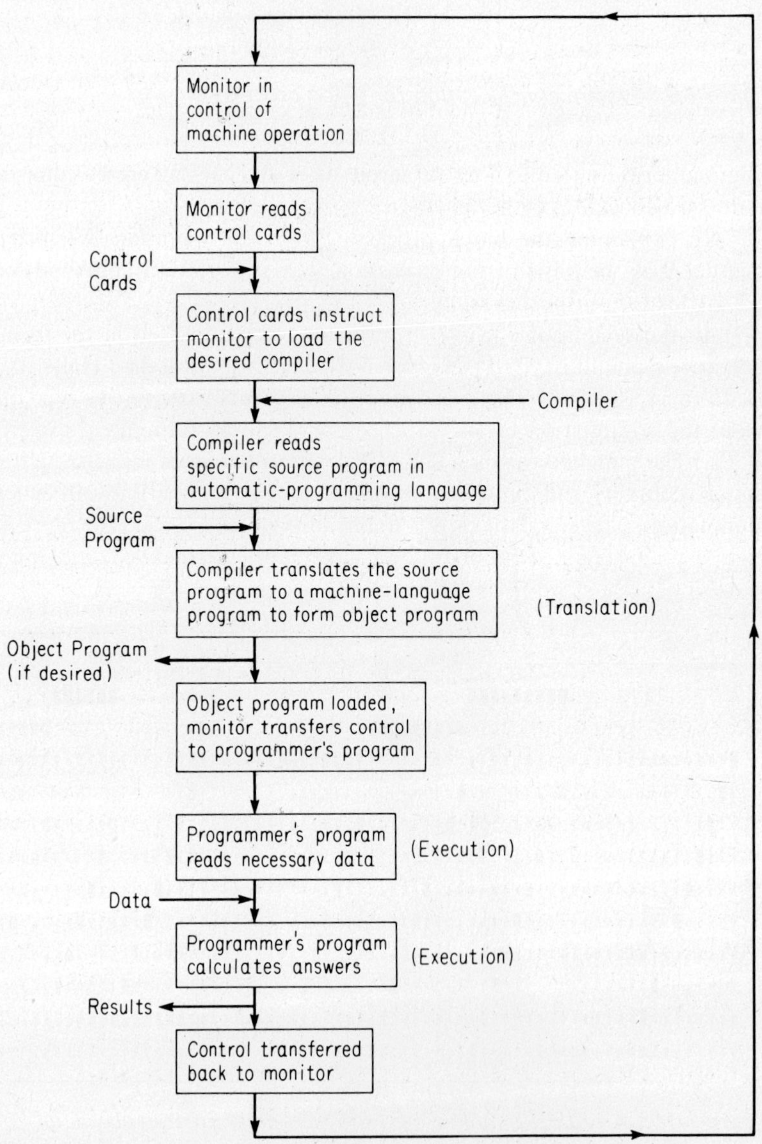

Figure 1-11. Role of the monitor

The programmer submits his program along with any necessary *control cards* with which he informs the operating system as to the nature of his program and what actions will be necessary to process it. Figure 1-12 illustrates a typical deck complete with control cards for processing a Fortran program. In computer terminology this complete deck is called a "job."

In the deck illustrated in Figure 1-12, each control card begins with the character $. The $JOB control card indicates the beginning of a new job. The programmer's name is given along with his identification number for bookkeeping purposes, an estimated maximum run time (1 minute), and an estimated maximum for pages of output (20 pages). Should this program run more than one minute or print more than 20 pages of output, the job will be "aborted," i.e., terminated, and the next job begun.

The next control card, $FORTRAN, indicates that the programmer is submitting a Fortran program. In response to this card, the operating system directs the CPU to copy into memory the Fortran compiler from an auxiliary storage device. Once this is completed, the statements comprising the Fortran program are processed. The LIST option on the $FORTRAN card instructs the compiler to list the source program as it is being compiled. If the compiler produces an object deck, it will be written into a preassigned area on the auxiliary storage unit.

Encountering the $LOAD card, the operating system copies into memory the loader from the auxiliary storage device. The loader in turn copies into memory the object deck from the auxiliary storage device. If a load-and-go compiler were used, this step would be unnecessary.

Upon processing the $EXECUTE card, the operating system directs the CPU to the first instruction in the program. If the Fortran program contains any READ statements, the actual READ operation does not occur until the program is executed. The program in Figure 1-12 is identical to the program in Figure 1-6 except that numerical values for D

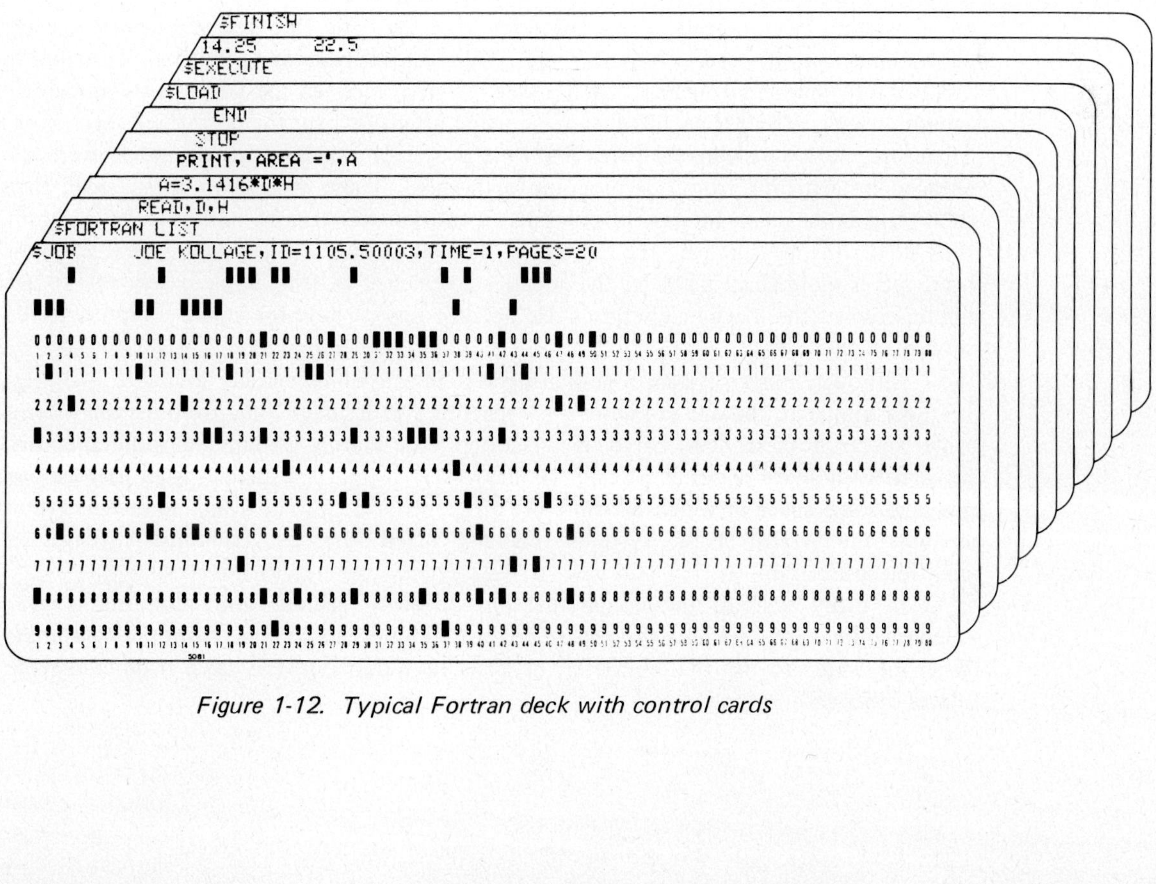

Figure 1-12. Typical Fortran deck with control cards

and H are entered via a READ statement. Therefore, one card containing the two numerical values is placed immediately after the $EXECUTE card.

Upon completion of the job, the operating system proceeds to the next control card to ascertain what other actions are needed. The $FINISH card informs the system that nothing else is to be done. Were another job waiting to be run, the $FINISH card could be removed and the next job immediately fed into the card reader.

While the batch processing system described in this section is fairly representative of one used on small- to medium-size computers, larger computers provide much more flexibility and capability in manipulating the processing of jobs to achieve maximum efficiency. However the basic process, at least as far as the programmer is concerned, is little different from that presented here.

One user might find this mode of operation very convenient, another might find it very inconvenient. Anyone who is running a large problem, or a problem that runs a long time, is generally content to leave his job for someone else to run when his turn comes. For the small user whose program is very short and runs quickly, the waiting time between job submission and return is, to say the least, inconvenient. Conversational time sharing is a more attractive alternative.

1-7. Conversational Time Sharing

The basic idea behind conversational time sharing is that several users have programs in progress simultaneously on the same computing system. In the simplest implementations, the only components needed in the computing system are the CPU, memory, some auxiliary storage, and a teletype for each of the users. Figure 1-13 illustrates the configuration of a conversational time-sharing system supporting four users simultaneously. The operating system occupies a region of memory, and the remainder is divided among the four users of the system.

In addition to receiving his proportionate share of the system's memory, each programmer gets his proportionate share of the central processing unit's time, which is divided into small increments called slices. A user receives the processor's undivided attention for one time slice, but then receives no attention over the next three time slices. Therefore, he is receiving 25 percent of the processor's time minus the small overhead entailed in switching from one program to the next. These time slices are so small that each programmer feels he has the computer's continuous services. Although his program runs slower (as measured by the "clock on the wall") than it would if he were the only user, this is more than offset by the added convenience of being immediately able to get his fraction of the machine's services. He needn't wait to have the entire computer at his service.

Although conversational time-sharing systems are commercially available in configurations similar to the one in Figure 1-13, machines with larger configurations can offer a wider spectrum of services. Large conversational time-sharing systems can simultaneously serve fifty or more users. If a large auxiliary storage unit is available, each user can be assigned some space in which he can store programs or data to be available the next time he uses the system. Large systems generally offer other programming languages in addition to Fortran.

In many systems the communication between terminal and computer is over telephone lines; this permits the user to be located hundreds of miles from the computer. When he wants to use the computer, he dials its number in the same manner that he places other calls.

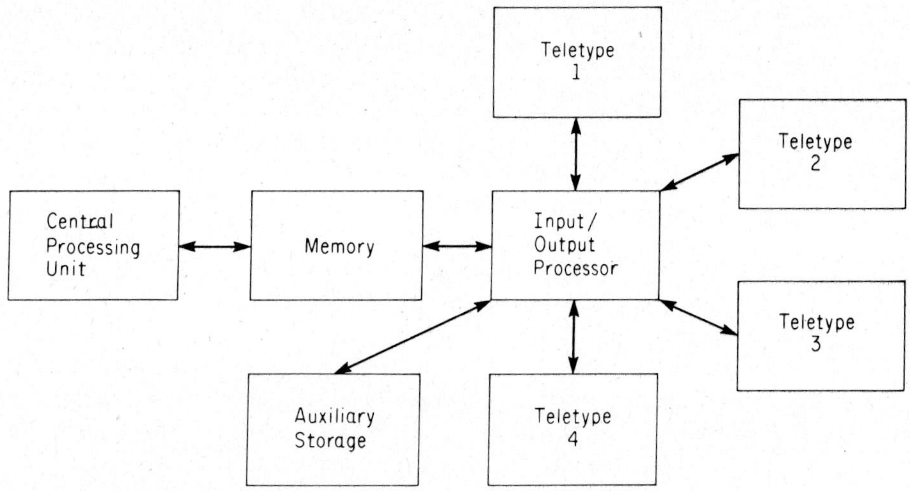

(a) Configuration

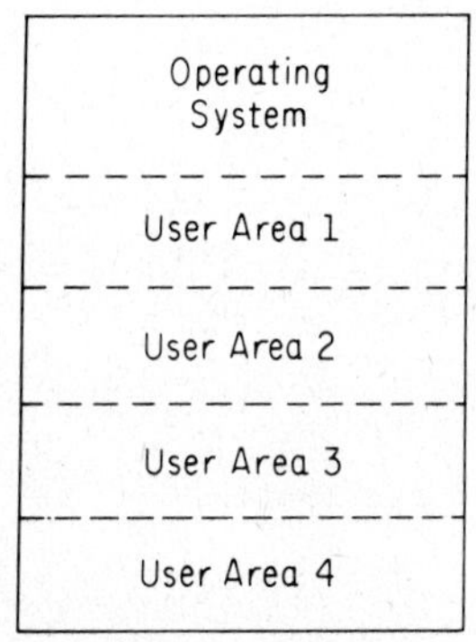

(b) Memory allocation

Figure 1-13. Small conversational time-sharing system for running Fortran

To illustrate the conversational nature of the dialogue between the user and the computer, a typical teletype printout is shown in Figure 1-14. All computer responses are underlined. In the left margin, numbers have been added to facilitate explanation of the printout.

1. After the call has been initiated, the computer responds with a message identifying the system along with other data of general interest such as the time of day and the number of other users.

2. The user must enter his identification number for bookkeeping purposes. To prevent the unauthorized use of this number by others, a password that is not printed on the teletype output must be entered. A proper identification number followed by an improper password will not be accepted as valid.

3. The user informs the computer that he wants to run a Fortran program.

4. By entering NEW, the user indicates that the program is to be created at the terminal.

5. The first file name, JOHN, that is entered is not accepted because the user

```
1  HILLBILLY TIME-SHARING SERVICE
   ON AT 10:27        TTY:   07

2  ENTER USER NO:   X547
   ENTER PASSWORD:

3  SYSTEM?   FORTRAN

4  OLD OR NEW?   NEW

5  NEW FILE NAME:   JOHN

   INVALID FILE NAME
   FILE NAME IN USE

   NEW FILE NAME:   MARY

   READY

6  10 ACCEPT,D,H
   20 A=3.1416*D*H
   30 PRINT,"AREA =",A
   40 STOP
   50 END
7  SAVE

   READY

8  RUN

   ?  14.25,22.5

   AREA =      1007.28

   READY

9  BYE

   OFF AT 10:51
```

Figure 1-14

already has a file by that name in the system. The name MARY is acceptable. Upon completion of the necessary housekeeping chores associated with creating a new file, the computer types READY to inform the user that he can proceed.

6. The Fortran program is entered from the terminal. Many systems scan the statements for syntax errors as they are entered, thus indicating errors immediately so that they can be corrected before proceeding.

7. By entering SAVE, the user instructs the computer to store a copy of the program on the auxiliary storage unit. Upon completion, the computer again types READY.

8. The command RUN instructs the computer to execute the program. The Fortran program in Figure 1-14 is identical to the one in Figure 1-6 except that the values of D and H are entered via an ACCEPT statement. Upon processing this statement during execution, the computer types the ? character, and then the programmer enters the appropriate numerical values. The answers are then typed by the computer as they are generated. Upon completion of the program execution, the computer again types READY.

9. When the user has completed his work at the terminal, he enters BYE and the computer changes his status from an active to an inactive user.

Most time-sharing systems provide the programmer with more features than are used in the example in Figure 1-14. Programmers can readily add to programs or make changes using editing features available at the terminal.

For the small or occasional computer user, the conversational time-sharing mode of operation is far more desirable than batch processing. For this reason the popularity of conversational time sharing has increased rapidly, and probably it will increase even more in the future. Batch processing is attractive only to the user with a very large program that requires virtually the entire machine in order to run it and to the user whose program runs so long that the wait at the terminal would approach the turnaround wait in the batch processing environment. The number of small users far exceeds the number of users in the later two situations.

1-8. Peripheral Devices

A peripheral unit serves one of two functions: as a programmer communication device or as an auxiliary storage unit. In this section we shall give a brief description of several peripheral devices and their use in computing systems.

In time-sharing systems the teletype or typewriter is a very popular unit. Although these units operate at the rather slow speed of 10 to 30 characters per second, they are so inexpensive that in some cases a single programmer can be provided with a terminal for his exclusive use. Although they are most popular with time-sharing systems, many batch processing systems permit programs to be submitted over these units. In these systems, editing features must be available at the terminal to permit the programmer to make corrections readily without having to reenter the entire program.

In many cases the main disadvantages of teletypes or typewriters are their low output speed and the noise levels associated with their operation; both of these can be eliminated by using a cathode-ray tube unit. In simplest terms, this device consists of a keyboard for entry of data and a screen similar to that of a TV except that only characters can be displayed. These units are competitive in price, but they do not produce *hard copy,* i.e., something that can be saved if desired.

In batch processing systems the most popular medium for the preparation of programs has been the punched card, as illustrated in Figure 1-10. Large computers are equipped with on-line card readers that can read cards at rates of 1000 cards per minute or higher and on-line card punches that can punch cards at about half this rate. Programmers punch cards off-line using a device called a keypunch machine. To eliminate the expense and bother of cards, some large centers are currently considering reusable cassette tapes as replacements for cards. To what extent this will prove successful is uncertain at this writing.

The most important method for getting information out of a computer is via *high-speed printers.* A photograph of a high-speed printer is shown in Figure 1-15. These printers are set up to print an entire line of information rather than a single character at a time as is common in most typewriters. Many of them are capable of printing rates up to 1200 lines a minute. The paper used in the high-speed printer may be of a special format for handling accounting information, statistical reports, warehouse data, etc., or it may be plain unruled paper in which the programmer is allowed to use his own individual format.

A second major means of communicating with a digital computer is via a roll of *magnetic tape* such as is illustrated in Figure 1-16. Magnetic tape has two major

Figure 1-15. High-speed printer capable of 800 lines/minute (Photo courtesy of J. R. Langley.)

advantages which make it highly desirable for use with digital computers. The first is that it can be read into the computer at extremely rapid rates. Some computers are capable of reading 120,000 characters per second from magnetic tape, which is approximately a hundred times faster than is possible from punched cards. The second major advantage is that a very small amount of tape can record huge amounts of information; e.g., a single 10 1/2-inch reel of tape can hold the contents of 250,000 punched cards. This magnetic tape is very similar to the type of tape used in home tape recorders. It is a plastic ribbon with an iron oxide coating that can be magnetized by external heads. A tiny area of the iron oxide coating can be magnetized to represent a "1" in the binary code, and if it is an unmagnetized area, it can be used to represent a "0." A pattern of symbols can be arranged in vertical columns on the tape in a manner very similar to that of the punched card. The magnetic tape symbols that are commonly used are "pure binary" and normally can be read directly by the computer. This allows magnetic tape to be used as a computer's external memory. The following analogy between magnetic tape and books is

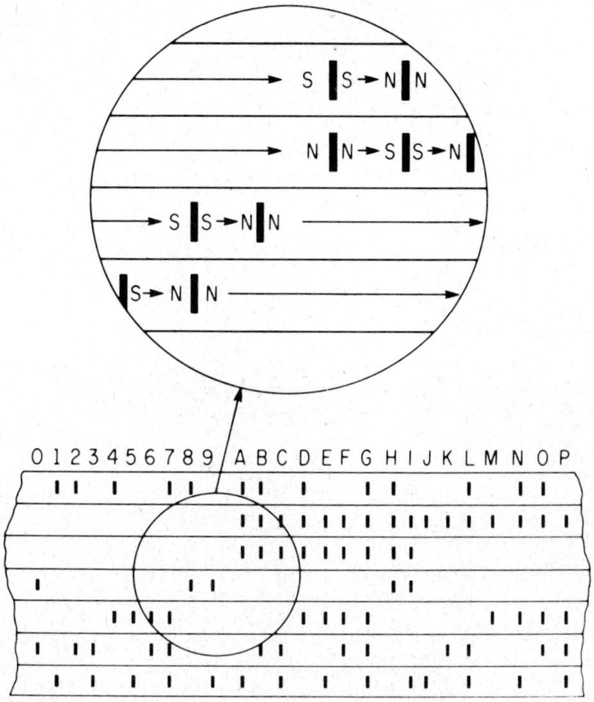

Figure 1-16. Magnetic recording of binary coded decimal information (Reprinted by permission from IBM Magnetic Tape Units, *Publication No. A22-6589-1, © by International Business Machines Corporation.)*

often used: the magnetic tape provides a sort of computer library, just as an individual's personal books provide a source of external memory for the individual. Magnetic tape is relatively inexpensive and it may be easily erased and reused.

One type of storage device used by the computer which might fall into the category of an input-output device to the central memory of the computer is the *magnetic disc.* These discs look like large phonograph records and have a surface that can be magnetized. Very large amounts of information may be stored on the magnetic surface of these discs, and they provide a type of external memory that is very similar to magnetic tape. The main advantage of the disc is that it transfers information into and out of the computer much more rapidly than is possible from magnetic tape. A *magnetic drum* offers similar advantages.

Another type of input-output device which has gained large usage in business work is *magnetic ink.* The most common example of magnetic ink is the coded personal check which many people have in their bank checking account, and this is illustrated in Figure 1-17. Magnetic ink can be "read" in much the same manner as magnetic tape, but it has the additional advantage that the magnetic ink can be read by people as well as by computers.

The *optical scanner* is another type of input device. The scanner is a device which can read typed or written numbers and words, not just those printed in magnetic ink. The primary advantage of such devices is that they eliminate the manual translation of information into special computer codes. Optical scanners are still in a rudimentary stage of their development; they work by allowing a photoelectric cell to scan material and convert characters into electronic pulses which are compared to patterns that are already

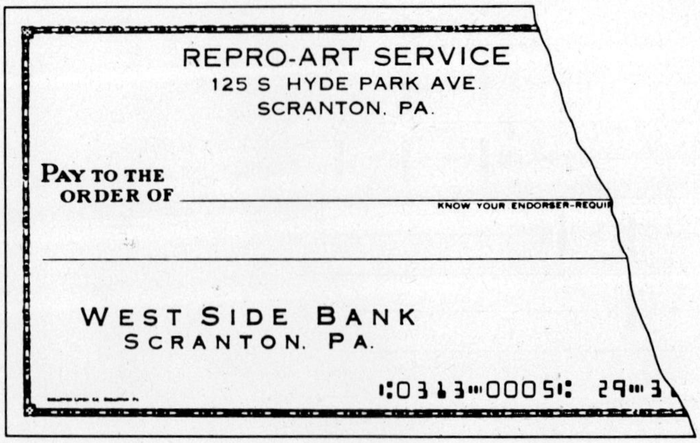

Figure 1-17. Magnetic-ink characters

stored in the computer's memory. As their development progresses, optical scanners will provide a very important adjunct to the use of the computer, and it will be much more feasible for individuals to communicate directly with the computer.

This section has by no means covered all types of peripheral units. For example, paper tape units were once very popular, but they have virtually disappeared except on very small systems. Incremental plotters enable the computer to prepare line drawings. In effect the list is almost endless, and it is steadily growing.

2

The Fortran Statement

The previous chapter introduced the role of automatic-programming languages. It will be the function of this chapter to illustrate the elementary programming concepts associated with Fortran. The main thrust of all the material presented in this chapter will be toward the development of skills related to the writing of simple arithmetic-type statements in Fortran. It is not the purpose of this chapter to try to develop skills in writing complete programs or even complete sections of programs; rather, the intention is to write statements to carry out simple, specific arithmetic calculations. In order to do this it will be necessary to gain a clear understanding of the use of constants, variables, operations, expressions, functions, and correct statement layout in Fortran.

While much of the material presented in this and subsequent chapters is applicable to all versions of Fortran, all of this material will be developed in terms of its application in Fortran IV. This is implied throughout the book unless stated to the contrary.

In studying the material in this chapter, it is strongly recommended that the student pay special attention to the distinction between integer and real. In fact, this distinction is so important that the final section of this chapter is dedicated to this topic.

2-1. Fortran Constants

In the working of everyday problems in science and engineering it is always necessary to make use of numerical constants. Upon a little reflection it becomes evident that there are inherently two types of constants involved in what we do: numerical constants related to the *counting* of quantities, and numerical constants related to the *measurement* of quantities. In our day-to-day usage of these two types of numbers we normally switch back and forth between them without really paying much attention to their inherently different nature. The digital computer in its operation, however, will make quite different usage of these types of numbers. They must be handled differently in the computer, and normally they are not interchangeable with one another. It is therefore necessary to have a good understanding of these two different types of numbers.

When we refer to counting numbers, we indicate implicitly that they have no fractional part. For example, we count the number of apples in a barrel, the number of paper clips in a box, the number of people in a room, etc., and we make no provision for fractional parts. It is understood that the decimal point in any such number is fixed. These numbers are always integer numbers, and the decimal point is implied to be immediately to the right of the last digit, although the decimal does not normally appear. In Fortran language these numbers which have been indicated as counting numbers are referred to as *integer numbers* which are a particular case of *fixed-point numbers.* Both of these terms are often used interchangeably. Fortran also recognizes double precision and complex constants, but these will be described only in Appendix A.

In Fortran, in order to distinguish integer numbers from other numbers, they are simply written without a decimal point, and it is not even allowable to have a decimal point associated with an integer number. It should also be noted that embedded commas within a number are not allowed. Arithmetic operations can be carried out using integer numbers, but the arithmetic is inherently integer in its nature; therefore, fractional parts cannot be shown and will be dropped by the computer. For example, in integer arithmetic if we divide 10 by 3 the answer is 3. Both positive and negative integer numbers are allowable, and the largest integer number that is permissible varies widely from one computer to the next. The appropriate limits are shown in Appendix B, but a typical value is that of the IBM System 360 which allows up to 2147483647, or $2^{31} - 1$. (This number is a result of the use of binary arithmetic in the operation of the computer.)

The following list is an example of some valid integer numbers:

```
     576
    -200
       0
       6
12345678
 -127982
```

The following integer numbers are incorrect:

76.2	(decimal present)
21.	(decimal present)
10000000000	(normally too large)
127,924	(embedded comma)

The second type of number encountered in Fortran is the type of number normally used for measuring. These numbers have the provision for expressing a fractional part. For example, if we want to measure the dimensions of a desk top it may be 27.2 inches, 26.9 inches, or 27.0 inches. These numbers for measuring quantities not only must express a fractional part, but it is also necessary that this part be preserved in any arithmetic calculations. For this reason these numbers are more useful for actual computational work in the computer. In Fortran these numbers are referred to as *real* or *floating-point* numbers. The decimal point does exist, and its location inside the number is not fixed but may have any location assigned to it by the programmer. The use of floating-point numbers is very common in scientific work where a number is often thought of as a fraction between 0.1 and 1.0 times a power to 10. In most systems the *magnitude* (sign not considered) of a floating-point number may be zero or somewhere between approximately 10^{-76} and 10^{76}. (See Appendix B for various actual limitations.) The terms *floating-point numbers* and *real numbers* are normally used interchangeably.

Fortran numbers can only contain a finite number of digits, and thus they must be rational numbers. Irrational numbers may only be approximated, i.e., represented by a finite number of digits.

Fortran real numbers may have an integer value or they may have a fractional part. Even if a real number has an integer value in Fortran, it must be written with a decimal point to indicate that it is a real number. In the calculations inherent in Fortran the computer will take care of all questions of "lining up" decimals before addition, subtraction, etc., and this is not something with which the programmer must be concerned. Embedded commas are not allowed in real numbers, and real numbers are considered to be positive if they are unsigned. It is permissible for them to be positive, zero, or negative.

The following are permissible floating-point numbers:

```
 96.7
-200.
 .00001
-999999.
```

The following are not acceptable real constants:

2,782.	(embedded comma not allowed)
+6	(no decimal present)

There is no restriction on the number of digits that may be written with a real constant, but no more than seven or eight significant figures will normally be retained by the computer; therefore, there is no need to write more than approximately eight significant figures on most systems.

It is also possible to have a real constant written in exponential format in which the real constant is followed by the letter E and a one- or two-digit number (some versions even allow a three-digit number) which may be positive or negative. This indicates an integer power of ten by which the number is multiplied. This facilitates writing very large or very small real numbers.

The following are acceptable real numbers in exponential form:

5.0E + 2	($5. \times 10^{2}$)
-50.E - 21	($-50. \times 10^{-21}$)
-.7E2	($-.7 \times 10^{2}$)
12.345E21	(12.345×10^{21})

The following are not permissible real numbers in exponential form:

E + 2	(exponent alone not permissible)
5E - 1	(no decimal–rejected by most Fortrans)
5.E76	(too large for most versions)
5.1E2.1	(exponent must be integer)

2-2. Fortran Variables

Variables are used in Fortran to denote a quantity that is to be referred to by name rather than by its appearance as a value. An arithmetic variable in Fortran refers to the memory address of a number. The number in the memory address is the value of the variable, and thus during the execution of a program this variable may take on many different values as different integer or real constants are stored in the address reserved for the variable. Note that a constant is restricted to a single value, but a variable may take on many different values.

Arithmetic variables in Fortran may denote the address of a number which may be either an integer constant or a real constant, and therefore arithmetic variables are said to have *type*, i.e., integer or real, depending on the kind of number which it names. (There are also the possibilities of double-precision, logical, and complex variables in addition to other types, but these are discussed in Appendix A.) There are two ways to denote the type of a variable. One is an implicit method and the other is an explicit method. The explicit method is based upon a *type declaration* (which is taken up in Chapter 5), and this is the only way to handle the specification of complex, logical, or double-precision variables. For integer or real variables the type declaration is normally not given explicitly, but it is implied by the nature of the name of the variable. An integer variable, of course, may take on any of the values permitted for an integer constant, and a real variable may take on the values permitted of real constants.

The name of an integer variable is composed of from one to six letters or digits. (The maximum allowable number of letters or digits may vary in some versions of Fortran.) The Fortran compiler places no "type" significance on the arrangement of the letters and digits beyond inspecting the first letter of the variable name. The first character of an integer variable must be a letter and must be either I, J, K, L, M, or N. Examples of acceptable integer variables are as follows:

JACK
NUTTY
LIT1
LIT200
JKL
KJL
LJK
I

Some examples of incorrect integer variables are as follows:

ANS	(does not begin with the correct letter)
I*JK	(contains a character other than a letter or digit)
M2.222	(contains a character other than a letter or digit)
NUTHOUSE	(contains more than six characters)
2I	(does not begin with a letter)

Real variables represent real constants inside the computer, i.e., as a fraction times a power of ten. The name of a real variable may be composed of from one to six letters or digits. The first character of the name of a real variable must be a letter, and it may be any letter except I, J, K, L, M, or N.‡ From this it becomes quite obvious that the Fortran compiler uses the first letter of the variable name in order to determine the type of variable being named. Therefore, by proper selection of the first letter of the variable name, there is an implicit declaration of variable type. Valid names for real variables are as follows:

ANS
ANSWER

‡In some Fortrans the character $ is considered to be alphabetic. It may be used in variable names, and a variable whose first character is $ is considered to be real.

X
X1
X2
ABC
CBA
BCA

Some examples of invalid names for real variables are as follows:

1ANS	(does not begin with a letter)
X - Y	(contains a character other than a letter or digit)
X123456	(contains too many characters)

It might be noted that the Fortran compiler will place no special meaning or significance on the letters and digits selected to form variable names (other than to make the implicit decision as to type specification). For example, when the computer sees A2 it does not consider this to be A squared, A "times" two, or A with a subscript two, i.e., a_2. It simply assumes this to be the name of a single real variable. This allows the programmer a great deal of freedom in the selection of variable names throughout his program, and it makes available a very large set of variable names. It also allows the programmer to make use of mnemonic names. For example, instead of calculating a variable which will be assumed by the programmer to mean answer, he may calculate a variable whose name is ANSWER.

One of the most common errors made by new programming students is the incorrect selection of the first letter of a variable name.

2-3. Operations

Fortran provides for five basic arithmetic operations. These are addition, subtraction, multiplication, division, and exponentiation, each represented by a separate and distinct symbol

Addition	+
Subtraction	-
Multiplication	*
Division	/
Exponentiation	**

These are the only mathematical operations that are allowed in Fortran, and all other mathematical operations must be built from these basic five. (The only apparent exception to this is the use of special mathematical "functions" that will be discussed in a subsequent section.)

Note that since the letter X is allowable as a variable name and since we do not use a lowercase "x," another character (the asterisk) must be used to indicate multiplication. The exponentiation combination ** is considered as two characters but as a single symbol, and it is never correct to write two consecutive mathematical operation symbols in a Fortran statement.

These arithmetic operations are useful in combining constants, variables, and functions (discussed later) into meaningful arithmetic *expressions.* The formulation of these expressions is the subject of the next section.

2-4. Expressions

Expressions are used in Fortran to specify the computation of a numerical value. An expression may consist of a single constant, a single variable, or a single function. In addition, it may specify a combination of two or more constants, two or more variables, a combination of constants and variables, or a combination of constants, variables, and functions (discussed later). Table 2-1 contains some examples of valid Fortran expressions.

By using parentheses with arithmetic operation symbols, it is possible to build up very complex Fortran expressions, and there are certain rules which the programmer must follow in order to calculate the exact numerical value intended. The following rules apply:

1. Parentheses may be used to indicate groupings just as in ordinary algebraic manipulations. Parentheses force the inner operation to be carried out first (just as in ordinary algebra), i.e., parentheses are cleared before other operations are performed. There is no penalty for the use of unnecessary parentheses; therefore, the student should not attempt to minimize the number of parentheses in an expression.

2. When the hierarchy of operations in an expression is not controlled by the use of parentheses, the computer follows the following hierarchy:
(a) Exponentiation
(b) Multiplication and Division
(c) Addition and Subtraction

That is, all exponentiations are performed first, then all multiplications and divisions, and finally all additions and subtractions. For example, the expression A + B * C is interpreted as A + (B * C). Similarly, A ** C * B is (A ** C) * B.

3. In some cases the hierarchy rules stated above are not sufficient to specify the order in which operations are performed. For example, the expression A/B/C could be interpreted as either (A/B)/C = A/(B * C) or A/(B/C) = (A * C)/B, completely consistent with the rules of hierarchy. This dilemma is resolved by adding the following rule: *Operations on the same level of the hierarchy are performed from left to right.* Therefore, A/B/C is interpreted as (A/B)/C = A/(B * C). The expression A/B * C is (A/B) * C = (A *C)/B. Also note the seventh entry in Table 2-2.

Table 2-1. Valid Fortran expressions

Fortran Expression	Its Meaning
J	The value of the integer variable J
54.40	The value of the real constant 54.40
X + 26.5	The sum of the value of X and 26.5
SAM - BILL	The difference in the values of SAM and BILL
X * Y	The product of the values of X and Y
GO/1.234	The quotient of the values of GO and 1.234
Z ** 2	The value of Z raised to the second power
(X + 1.)/(Y + Z)	The sum of the values of X and 1. divided by the sum of the values of Y and Z
1./(X ** 2)	The reciprocal of X^2

Table 2-2. Invalid Fortran expressions

Conventional Mathematical Notation	Incorrect Fortran Expression	Correct Fortran Expression
$x \cdot y$	XY	X * Y
$x \cdot (-y)$	X * - Y	X * (- Y) or - X * Y
$-(x + y)$	- X + Y	- (X + Y) or - X - Y
x^{i+1}	X ** I + 1	X ** (I + 1)
$x^{y+1} \cdot z$	X ** Y + 1. * Z	X ** (Y + 1.) * Z
$\frac{x \cdot y}{z \cdot s}$	X * Y/Z * S	X*Y/(Z * S) or X/Z * Y/S
$\left[\frac{x+y}{z}\right]^{3.14}$	(X + Y)/Z ** 3.14	((X + Y)/Z) ** 3.14
$x[r + y(r + z)]$	X(R + Y(R + Z))	X * (R + Y * (R + Z))
$\frac{x}{1 + \frac{y}{16.2 + z}}$	X/(1.0 + Y/16.2 + Z)	X/(1.0 + Y/(16.2 + Z))
x^{y^z}	X ** Y ** Z	X ** (Y ** Z) or (X ** Y) ** Z whichever is intended

4. In early computers, expressions were restricted to containing either all integer variables *or* all real variables. Mixing integers and real variables in an expression resulted in *mixed mode arithmetic* which was not allowed. Most current systems have removed this restriction, but there are some pitfalls for the beginning programmer as discussed in the last section of this chapter.

5. One exception to the above definition of mixed mode arithmetic is that raising a real variable to an integer exponent is not mixed mode arithmetic. Although real variables can be raised to real exponents, only positive real numbers can be raised to real exponents. For computational purposes, an expression such as $1.4^{2.6}$ would be evaluated using logarithms, i.e.,

$$1.4^{2.6} = \exp(2.6 \cdot \ln 1.4)$$

The problem with negative numbers is that their logarithm does not exist. When numbers are raised to integer exponents, results are effectively computed by successive multiplication, thus avoiding logarithms. Therefore A ** J is computable for negative A but A ** B is not. Even though B may not have a fractional part, it is a real variable, and the operation will be performed with logarithms as indicated above.

As mentioned earlier, operation symbols may never appear next to one another. Parentheses indicate grouping, and they do not specify or imply multiplication. Some mathematical operations must have a number of parentheses in order to achieve the desired numerical result. Table 2-2 gives examples of invalid Fortran expressions.

The value of an arithmetic expression will be a number, and the mode of that number will either be integer or real, depending on the mode of the expression itself. When all of the variables and constants in an expression are of the same mode, the mode of the expression will be the mode of the numerical quantity calculated as the value of the expression. For mixed mode expressions, the mode of the result will be real, a point we shall examine in more detail in the last section of this chapter.

It is very important that the programmer develop a good "feel" for the specific rules for the formulation of arithmetic expressions, because there are numerous specific problems that can be created by an inadequate understanding of arithmetic expressions. Some examples of these are appropriate.

The programmer should appreciate the difference between *accuracy* and *precision.* As indicated in earlier sections, most digital computers work with approximately eight digits of precision. This does not imply that every answer will be accurate to eight digits. As an example, 0.12345678 minus 0.12345670 would give an answer of 0.00000008, a result that has eight digits of precision but only one digit of accuracy.

Arithmetic operations, because of the way in which they are carried out, do not obey all of the normal rules of arithmetic. For example, the expression .5 + 12345678. − 12345670. would yield 8.0 if evaluated from left to right and 8.5 if evaluated from right to left. The use of parentheses here would have an obvious advantage in forcing the evaluation of the expression from right to left.

Another type of problem that might be encountered in a Fortran statement would be the situation in which it would not be possible to get any answer whatsoever from an arithmetic expression. For example, consider the expression X * Y/Z in which X, Y, and Z have values of the order of magnitude of 10^{50}. Without any parentheses the operation could be performed by multiplying X times Y and the intermediate answer would be of the order of magnitude of 10^{100}. On many machines the multiplication would cause an *overflow*. Overflow occurs when the resultant magnitude (that is, the exponent) of an arithmetic operation exceeds the upper limit of numbers that can be accommodated by the computer. It often occurs when the programmer attempts to divide by a variable which may take on the value of zero. In the particular situation just noted, overflow could be corrected by writing the expression as X * (Y/Z). It might also be noted that the reverse of overflow is *underflow*, which occurs when a number is too small for the computer. It is up to the programmer to avoid both overflow and underflow by properly structuring his program.

There are some very special problems that arise in the course of performing arithmetic in the integer mode. Division is the most common source of error in this type of expression. In integer division a quotient having a fractional part will be *truncated*, that is, dropped. For example, 10/3 is 3, 8/5 is 1, and −7/3 is −2.

The equivalent of the above situation can also occur in real arithmetic, where, for example, the sum (1.0/3.0 + 1.0/3.0 + 1.0/3.0) yields the result of 0.99999999 instead of 1.00000000. This is caused by each of the individual parts of the expression being evaluated as 0.33333333.

All of the above problems are nothing more than inconveniences, and in every case they can be overcome by proper programming. The most important problem is to appreciate and anticipate such difficulties.

2-5. Functions

There are many operations normally encountered in programming that involve rather common mathematical functions. Examples of these are square roots, logarithms, trigonometric functions, absolute values, and exponentials. Each of these represents a mathematical function that can be evaluated by the programmer through proper use and structure of the five basic mathematical operations. But since these are so commonly encountered, the Fortran system has special "subprograms" or equivalent machine language instructions which are useful for evaluating them. The exact list of functions available in any version of Fortran will vary, but there are some functions that are common to virtually all computers and compilers using Fortran. Some examples of these are illustrated in Table 2-3, and a complete list is given in Appendix C.

The use of a Fortran function in an expression is very simple. The Fortran function's name is written, and it is followed by an expression enclosed in parentheses. The compiler interprets this to mean that the expression contained in parentheses will be computed according to the function. As an example, suppose it is necessary to compute the natural logarithm of a variable X. This could be written as ALOG (X).

It is possible that the argument of a function may be an expression involving other mathematical operations and/or functions. In most cases (and in all the functions except IABS shown in Table 2-3) it is necessary that the expression which comprises the argument of the function be a real expression, and the functional value computed will appear in real form.

There are restrictions associated with the arguments of most Fortran functions, and these restrictions depend on the compiler and the specific computer installation. Typical of these kinds of restrictions is the fact that the argument of the square-root function may not be negative. When these restrictions on function usage are violated, the results are unpredictable. In some cases erroneous values will be computed and used in the program, and in other cases an error message may be generated and the program stopped.

It might be noted that some Fortran functions are not available in the form of subprograms but are translated into machine-language instructions. A simple example is the absolute-value function. The distinction between these types of functions is of no importance to the programmer.

Table 2-3. Some common Fortran real functions

Description	Fortran IV	Fortran II	Comments/Restrictions
Exponential: e^x	EXP(X)	EXPF(X)	
Natural logarithm	ALOG(X)	LOGF(X)	Argument must be larger than zero.
Logarithm to base 10	ALOG10(X)	LOG10F(X) (not available on all compilers)	Argument must be larger than zero.
Square root	SQRT(X)	SQRTF(X)	Argument must be positive.
Trigonometric sine	SIN(X)	SINF(X)	Argument in radians.
Trigonometric cosine	COS(X)	COSF(X)	Argument in radians.
Trigonometric arctangent	ATAN(X)	ATANF(X)	Result in radians in first or fourth quadrant.
Trigonometric arctangent of (Y/X)	ATAN2(Y,X)	not available	Result in radians in correct quadrant.
Absolute value	ABS(X) IABS(J)	ABSF(X) IABSF(J)	Real function Integer function

Note: X and Y stand for any real expression.

2-6. Fortran Statements

The general statements that comprise a program in Fortran may be classified in the following four categories:

1. Arithmetic assignment statements
2. Input-output statements
3. Branch or transfer statements
4. Informational statements

The statement that will be discussed in most detail in this section is the arithmetic assignment statement with which a new value of a variable may be computed. In general it is of the form A = B, in which A is a variable name written without a sign, and B is any expression as discussed in Section 2-4. The arithmetic assignment statement is interpreted by the Fortran compiler as meaning: evaluate the expression on the right-hand side of the equals sign and store the numerical value computed in the memory cell reserved for the variable indicated on the left-hand side of the equals sign.

From the above statement it is quite obvious that the equals sign in an arithmetic assignment statement is not equivalent to the equals sign normally used in conventional arithmetic and algebra. It is perfectly permissible, for example, to write a statement N = N + 1, which means to take the old value of N, add 1 to it, and store it in the storage location reserved for the variable N. This is quite obviously not true from an algebraic viewpoint, but it is perfectly permissible to use such a statement in Fortran.

Since the computer will interpret an arithmetic assignment statement as an operation in which the expression on the right will be evaluated and stored in the variable location indicated on the left of the equals sign, it is therefore illegitimate to try and do any kind of arithmetic operation on the left-hand side of the equals sign. For example, X − Y = A + B would be an incorrect arithmetic assignment statement.

The variables involved in the expression on the right-hand side of an arithmetic assignment statement will be read from memory and will not be destroyed, i.e., they are still available for subsequent calculations. The numerical value of the expression evaluated will be stored in the single-variable address associated with the variable on the left-hand side of the expression, and consequently the old value of the variable on the left-hand side of the arithmetic assignment statement is destroyed and is not available for subsequent computations. It is also very important to note that all of the variables named in the expression on the right-hand side of the statement must be available at the time the arithmetic assignment statement is executed, i.e., all of the variables must have numerical values available in their storage addresses. If not, an "undefined variable" error will occur and be detected by some computers but not detected by others.

As pointed out earlier, some computers do not permit mixing of the modes of arithmetic that occur in an expression. It is always permissible, however, to "mix modes" of arithmetic across an equals sign in an arithmetic assignment statement. For example, an integer expression on the right-hand side may be set equal to a real variable on the left-hand side of an arithmetic assignment statement. The reverse is also allowable. When such a statement is encountered, the computer will evaluate the expression on the right-hand side in the appropriate mode of arithmetic and then convert it to the other mode of arithmetic before it is stored. One comment might be made about the conversion of the results of real expressions to integer values. If an arithmetic assignment statement is written to compute a real number which is to be converted to integer form before storage, the real number always will be truncated past the decimal point. In order to obtain rounding, a statement such as I = A + 0.5 is sufficient to round the real number A to the integer number I if A is positive.

Table 2-4. Some valid arithmetic assignment statements

Meaning	Statement
$v = 16$	V = 16.
$\alpha = -\frac{3}{x^2} + \frac{a}{2x}$	ALPHA = - 3./X ** 2 + A/(2. * X)
$a = q_c \frac{m_1 m_2}{m_1 + m_2}$	A = QC * XM1 * XM2/(XM1 + XM2)
$g = \frac{x(x^2 + y^2)}{x^2 - y^2 + 2}$	G = X * (X ** 2 + Y ** 2)/(X ** 2 - Y ** 2 + 2.)
$x = (3 \cdot 10^{-12} + 2x^4)^{1/3}$	X = (3.E - 12 + 2. * X ** 4) ** (1./3.)
$z = \cos x + y \sin y$	Z = COS(X) + Y * SIN(Y)
$y = (\tan x)^{.2}$	Y = (SIN(X)/COS(X)) ** .2
$i_{new} = i_{old} + 1$	I = I + 1
$x_{new} = x_{old} + .1e$	X = X + .1 * E

Table 2-4 shows examples of arithmetic assignment statements, and Table 2-5 shows some errors which are commonly made in arithmetic assignment statements. A very careful review of these two tables is important to the reader.

The other types of Fortran statements discussed at the beginning of this section will be discussed in much greater detail during subsequent chapters of this book.

2-7. Statement Format

A Fortran program is a series of individual instructions or statements arranged in the order in which they are to be encountered and executed by the computer. For batch processing systems the arrangement of the statement on the card has become highly standardized. Therefore, we shall consider these systems first, followed by time-sharing systems.

Table 2-5. Some invalid arithmetic assignment statements

Statement	Error
X = 3.Y + 2.	* missing
2.14 = PI = 1.	Left side must be a variable; only one equals sign permitted
Z = ((X + Y) ** 2	Unequal number of right and left parentheses
- J = I ** (- 2)	Integer quantites raised to negative powers always give a zero result; variable on left must not be written with a sign.
X = 1./- 2. * Y	Two operation symbols side-by-side are not permitted, even though the minus sign here is not intended to indicate subtraction.
A = N * X ** (N - 1)	Mixed modes in multiplication; not accepted by some compilers
A * X = Y	Left side must be a single variable.
SQRT(X) = X ** 0.5	The left side must be a variable name.

Batch Processing Systems. Normally there is one statement prepared for each individual input card, i.e., there is a punched card (or its equivalent) for each statement that is to be fed to the Fortran compiler. It is necessary for the programmer to write on a Fortran *coding form* the instructions that are to be punched on the cards by a *keypunch operator.* There are some general guidelines that must be observed in preparing these Fortran coding forms for interpretation by the keypunch operator. A typical Fortran coding form is shown in Figure 2-1. Each line or row on the programming form corresponds to one card that will be punched by the keypunch operator. The two arithmetic assignment statements shown in Figure 2-1 are assumed to be part of a much greater program that will be run by the computer. The first statement calculates an individual's pay as being equal to his rate of pay times the time that he has worked, and then the net pay that the individual will receive will be equal to his gross pay minus whatever taxes he must pay and whatever other deductions he might have in his payroll computation.

These two arithmetic assignment statements will each appear later as an individual punched card. Their layout on the Fortran coding form is sufficient to illustrate the usage of the various columns on the coding form, but a few general statements about the program coding form are appropriate. Note that each row is marked off into a series of individual spaces. On the coding form shown there are 72 such spaces in each row. Only one symbol may be written in each space, and each symbol must be written separately in its own individual space. It does not make any difference if the symbol is a letter, a digit, a comma, a period, a parenthesis, or an arithmetic operation sign, etc. Each individual symbol must have its own individual space. The reason for this is obvious when it is

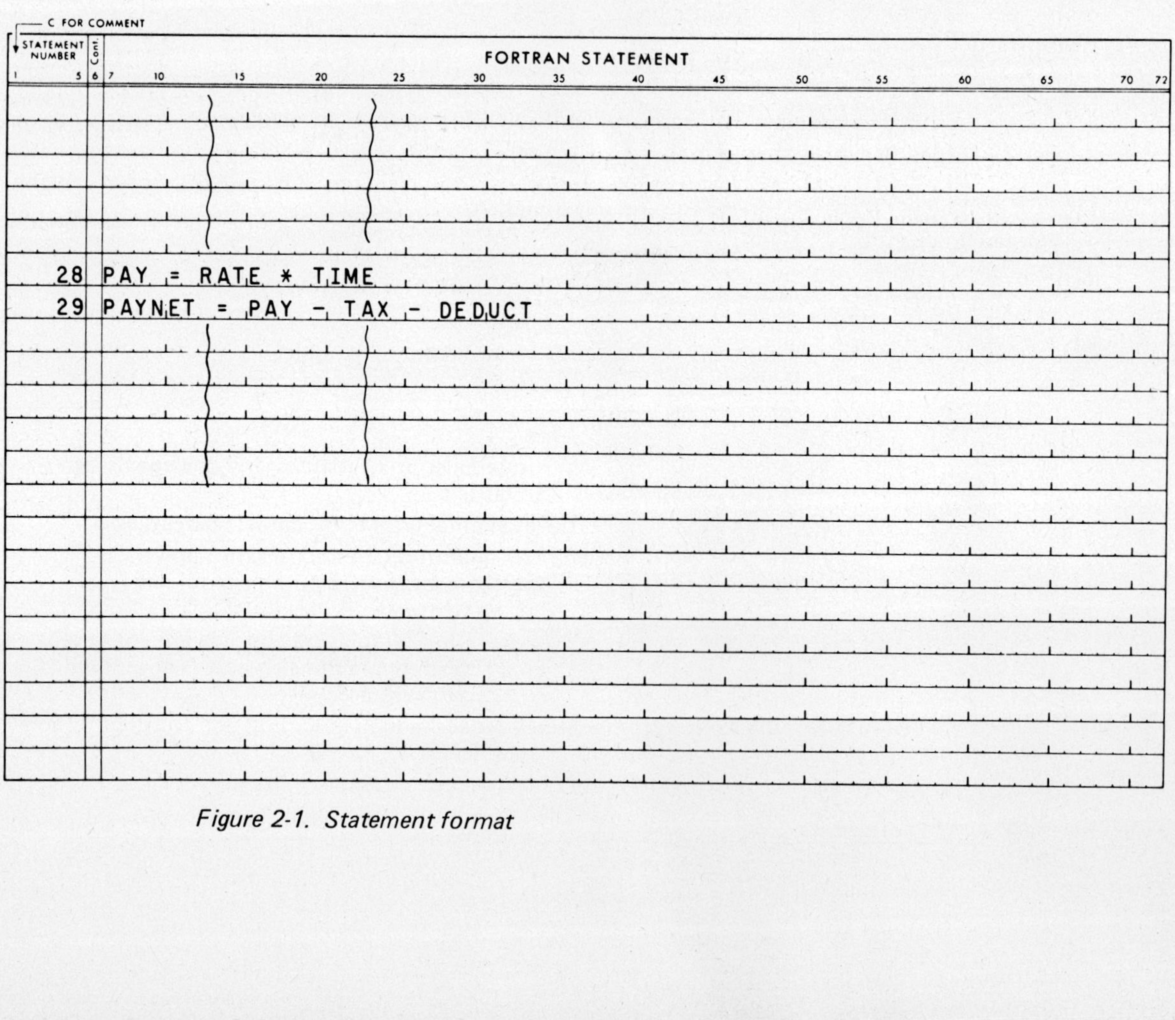

Figure 2-1. Statement format

recalled that each line on the coding form will correspond to a punched card at a later time in the development of the program, and consequently each individual space will correspond to a punch on a card. It might also be noted in the statements shown in Figure 2-1 that a number of blank spaces are present in the arithmetic assignment statements. These blanks are ignored by Fortran (except in the Hollerith format specification discussed later).

Columns 1-5 of the typical Fortran statement are reserved for a statement number which identifies an individual statement. It is not necessary that all statements have a statement number nor is it necessary that these statement numbers follow any distinct order or sequence. There are additional uses for column 1, but these will be discussed subsequently. The actual Fortran statement itself begins in column 7 and continues to the right but may not go past column 72. If it requires more characters to form the Fortran statement than can be placed in columns 7-72, then it is possible to continue a Fortran statement on the next line, i.e., the next card. Column 6 of the Fortran coding form is provided for this purpose. If there is any character punched in Column 6 (except a 0 or blank), it will serve as a "flag" to the Fortran compiler that this card is a *continuation card* for the statement above.

It might be recalled from Chapter 1 that punched cards normally have 80 columns on them. In Fortran programming, columns 73-80 of punched cards are not used. They *may* be used to punch identifying characters and/or sequence numbers into the cards for a direct indication of the numbered sequence of the cards. The Fortran compiler will ignore any information punched in columns 73-80, and for this reason many coding forms do not even show these columns on the coding form itself.

In general, Fortran programs will consist of a series of statements in the following typical structure. First, an input section; second, a series of calculations performed on the data read into the computer via the input section (these calculations may involve flow of control statements and arithmetic assignment statements); and third, an output section in which the results of the calculations will be obtained from the computer. All of these sections may contain informational statements. Most of the statements involved in the sections of the Fortran program will use the general format shown in Figure 2-1 (with a few possible exceptions which will be discussed as they are encountered).

It is very important for the beginning programmer to get a firm understanding of the typical card format for Fortran programming. It is equally important in the preparation of his Fortran coding form that he be very particular and neat in the preparation and writing of the symbols in the individual spaces on the form. For example, it is very common to confuse a 1 with an *i*, a 1 with a /, a 5 with an S, a 2 with a Z, or a "zero" with an "oh." Many computer installations require that the O be written with a slash through it to avoid confusion, but the reader is cautioned that the opposite convention is used at some sites, i.e., the zero is written with a slash. In computer listings in this text the letter O appears without a slash; the reader should become familiar with both styles. These individual details require the undivided attention of the beginning programmer because any one of the above mentioned errors or violations of the programming rules will be sufficient to reject the execution of an entire program.

Figure 2-2 illustrates a complete card deck for a simple Fortran program. Note the appearance of statement numbers, comment cards, and continuation cards.

Time-Sharing Systems. In batch processing systems, the program is in the form of a card deck. In order to add, delete, or change statements in the program, the programmer simply locates the proper cards and makes the desired changes. In time-sharing systems, no card deck as such exists, but the programmer must still be able to make program modifications in a convenient manner, a process often referred to as program editing.

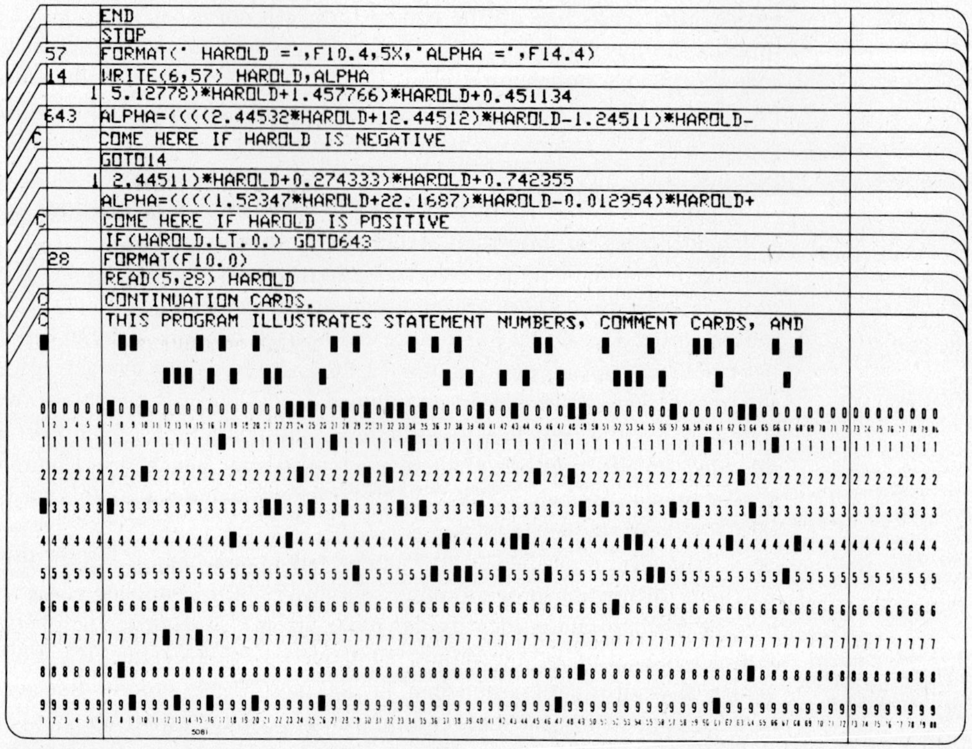

Figure 2-2. Card deck for Fortran program

To facilitate this process, each statement in the Fortran program for time-sharing systems is given a *line number* (not to be confused with or equated to a *statement number*). The line number is generally restricted to a five digit number and always appears prior to the Fortran statement. In essence the line number is not part of the Fortran statement, and it is present only to facilitate program editing.

Although some time-sharing systems adhere strictly to the statement format presented earlier in this section for batch processing systems, many systems use a freer statement format. As illustrated in Figure 2-3, the rules are as follows:

> A comment line is designated by a C immediately following the line number.
>
> A continuation line is designated by an ampersand (&) immediately following the line number.
>
> A blank column normally separates the statement from the line number.
>
> A blank column separates the statement number and the line number, and another blank column separates the statement number from the remainder of the statement.

Unfortunately, these rules are by no means universal, so the reader should not be surprised if his specific system does not follow them. Since these rules are not standardized, we shall in this manual always use the previously presented rules for punched cards.

In effect, the system maintains a program file that may be modified from the terminal by the programmer. To facilitate editing a program, the line numbers are generally entered in increments of 10, as shown in Figure 2-3. Editing is accomplished as follows:

```
10C THIS PROGRAM ILLUSTRATES STATEMENT NUMBERS, COMMENT LINES,
20C AND CONTINUATION LINES.
30 ACCEPT,HAROLD
40 IF(HAROLD.LT.0.) GOTO643
50C COME HERE IF HAROLD IS POSITIVE
60 ALPHA=((((1.52347*HAROLD+22.1687)*HAROLD-0.012954)*HAROLD+
70& 2.44511)*HAROLD+0.274333)*HAROLD+0.742355
80 GOTO14
90C COME HERE IF HAROLD IS NEGATIVE
100 643 ALPHA=((((2.44532*HAROLD+12.44512)*HAROLD-1.24511)*HAROLD-
110& 5.12778)*HAROLD+1.457766)*HAROLD+0.451134
120 14 PRINT57,HAROLD,ALPHA
130 57 FORMAT("HAROLD =",F10.4,5X,"ALPHA =",F14.4)
140 STOP
150 END
```

Figure 2-3. Fortran program for time-sharing system

To add a statement, simply give it a line number appropriate to its intended position in the program and type it in. The system will always maintain the program file with the statements in ascending order according to the line numbers.

To delete a statement, simply type its line number and depress RETURN.

To change a statement, simply reenter it. In essence, only the last statement entered with a given line number is retained.

Most systems provide special editing commands that permit listing the entire program or parts thereof, resequencing the line numbers, linking one program file with another, etc. For these, a manual for the specific system being used is required.

2-8. Integer versus Real

Before discussing the pitfalls for beginning (and experienced) programmers that stem from the existence of integer and real variables in Fortran, some explanation as to their origin may be enlightening. The tendency of Fortran to conform to the computing hardware is the primary reason for the two modes of variables. For scientific computations, numerical values can be represented in one of two ways (integer versus real) in storage. In integer form the number is stored directly, but fractional parts are not permitted. In real form the number is expressed as a fraction and an exponent, and the storage location is partitioned so that both the fraction and the exponent are stored in the same storage location.

Virtually all modern scientific computers use the binary number system as the basis for performing numerical operations. We shall, however, discuss only the three characteristics of the binary number system that are pertinent to our present subject.

A decimal number without fraction can be precisely represented in integer format in the binary number system. Arithmetic operations involving integer numbers can be performed precisely if we recognize the fact that any fractional parts resulting from divisions are lost. The equation

$$2 + 2 = 4$$

is true for integer variables but, as we shall see in the next paragraph, it is not quite true for real variables.

To store a numerical value in real format, the decimal number is converted to binary, the decimal point (or binary point, to be precise) is "floated" to obtain a fraction and an exponent, and the result is stored. Unfortunately, very few decimal numbers with fractional parts can be accurately represented in the binary number system. For example, if the decimal number 0.1 is converted to binary, the result stored in real format, and the value in storage converted back to decimal, we would obtain the number 0.0999999930295··· from one specific commercial computer. While the result is close to 0.1, it is not *exactly* 0.1. If we add 0.1 (as stored) to itself ten times and then have the computer check to see if the result is 1.0, the answer is *no*. Similarly, using real arithmetic, the equation

$$0.2 + 0.2 = 0.4$$

is not quite true. The error is typically in the seventh or eighth decimal place, which is negligible in most calculations *except* for counting purposes. In counting, if we add 1 to itself ten times, the result had better be *exactly* 10, not *almost* 10. Since counting numbers never have a fractional part, and since integer arithmetic is exact, integer variables and constants should always be used for counting. Integers should be used whenever fractional parts will not be encountered.

For many constants in Fortran, the integer and real expressions have nearly the same appearance, but results can often be significantly different. Consider the following two examples:

```
A ** 2          A ** 2.
```

Although these two expressions are quite similar, the difference between them is very significant. The exponent in the expression on the left is written without a decimal point, which defines it to be integer. The exponent in the expression on the right is written with a decimal point, which defines it to be real. We ask the question "What if A is negative?" to see that this difference is significant. The expression on the left is a real number raised to an integer exponent, i.e., A ** J, which is computable for all values of A, positive or negative. However, the expression on the right is a real number raised to a real exponent, i.e., A ** B, which is computable only for positive A. The fact that the real exponent does not have a decimal fraction is immaterial since the computer performs all arithmetic operations in the binary number system without making such a test. If the exponent is real, the evaluation is made according to the procedure for computing A ** B even though B may in fact not have a fractional part. Therefore, in exponentiations, integer exponents should be used in *all* cases where the exponent does not have a fractional part. A ** 2 is preferred over A ** 2. in all cases.

The prohibition on mixed mode arithmetic stems from the computing hardware. Arithmetic units in computers do not generally perform operations on mixed variables. Hardware logic is available to add an integer number to an integer number, to add a real number to a real number, but *not* to add a real number to an integer number or vice versa. A similar situation exists with respect to subtraction, multiplication, and division. Exponentiation is usually performed by routines similar to library functions; therefore, a real variable can be raised to either an integer or real exponent.

In view of this situation, most early Fortran compilers simply did not allow mixed mode arithmetic. If the product of variables A and N had to be computed and the result stored in B, two statements such as the following were typically used:

```
X = N
B =A * X
```

The numerical value stored in variable N is converted to real and stored in variable X by the first statement (the content of variable N is not changed). The second statement computes the desired product.

Mixed mode arithmetic applies only to an expression. It is always permissible to set an integer variable equal to a real expression or a real variable equal to an integer expression.

While most programmers follow the practice illustrated above, using two statements to avoid mixed mode arithmetic, an alternate approach is to use the two library functions INT and FLOAT, described below:

INT(X)	Computes the integer equivalent of the real variable or expression used as the argument
FLOAT(J)	Computes the real equivalent of the integer variable or expression used as the argument

In effect, the statement

```
X = N
```

in the above example is in essence

```
X = FLOAT (N)
```

with the function FLOAT inserted by the compiler.

Mixed mode arithmetic can be avoided in this example by using the following statement:

```
B = A*FLOAT(N)
```

If the result must be integer, a statement such as the following can be used:

```
J = INT(A)*N
```

The INT and FLOAT functions are available in all versions of Fortran, and can be used whenever the need arises.

As Fortran compilers continued to be developed, they steadily became "smarter." It was easy to insert a FLOAT or INT function and continue, instead of printing an error message on encountering mixed mode arithmetic. However, instead of attempting to decide which function would be more appropriate, most compilers simply insert the FLOAT function, changing *all* mixed mode arithmetic to real arithmetic. The statement

```
B = A*N
```

became perfectly acceptable, being computed as follows:

```
B = A*FLOAT(N)
```

which is quite appropriate.

Unfortunately, the unilateral insertion of the FLOAT function does not always lead to the most appropriate result. For example, the statement

```
J = A*N
```

is computed as

```
J = INT(A*FLOAT(N))
```

That is, variable N is floated, the result multiplied by A using real arithmetic, and the result (in real) converted to integer. An alternative approach would be to compute the statement

```
J = A*N
```

as follows:

```
J = INT(A)*N
```

In this case the value stored in variable A is converted to integer, the result multiplied by N, and the result stored in J. How do the two statements

```
J = INT(A*FLOAT (N))
J = INT(A)*N
```

compare? The latter statement does not require a conversion from integer to real, and is therefore computationally more efficient. However, the important difference is that these two statements do *not* always produce the same answer. Suppose A equals 2.5 and N equals 3. The statement

```
J = INT(A*FLOAT(N))
```

computes a value of 2.5 X 3 = 7.5 = 7 (integer) for J, whereas the statement

```
J = INT(A)*N
```

computes a value of 2 X 3 = 6 for J. Which is correct? That depends upon the problem, and it is therefore the responsibility of the programmer. If the value 7 is correct, the mixed mode statement

```
J = A*N
```

is appropriate, but the second statement must be used when the value 6 is correct.

Another problem with the use of mixed mode arithmetic is that the insertion of the FLOAT function is not consistent from compiler to compiler. In compilers that use real arithmetic for all computations in a mixed mode expression, the statement

```
A = J/N*100.
```

would be computed as follows:

```
A = FLOAT(J)/FLOAT(N)*100.
```

Other compilers perform the computations as dictated by the hierarchy and left-to-right rules discussed in Section 2-4, and they insert the FLOAT function only when a mixed mode operation is encountered. For the statement

```
A = J/N*100.
```

the sequence of operations would be to divide J by N and multiply the result by 100. Since J and N are both integer, their division does not involve mixed mode arithmetic. Therefore the FLOAT function is needed only when their result is multiplied by 100. Therefore, some compilers would treat the statement

A = J/N*100.

as

A = FLOAT(J/N)*100.

Is the statement above equivalent to the statement below?

A = FLOAT(J)/FLOAT(N)*100.

Suppose J equals 2 and N equals 5. The first statement computes a result of 0.0 for A (dividing 2 by 5 in integer gives a result of 0). The second statement computes a result of 40.0 for A. Which is correct? That depends upon the problem and is therefore the responsibility of the programmer.

To summarize this discussion, mixed mode arithmetic is a convenient feature, but it is not without its pitfalls. Many experienced programmers avoid its use, partly out of habit, since it was forbidden on earlier systems, and partly because of the pitfalls discussed above. The beginning programmer must be cautious.

One final note: the fact that the fractional part is always truncated when a real number is converted to integer in Fortran seems unnatural to many students, primarily because rounding is emphasized in many mathematics courses. In reality, there is a large number of problems in which truncation, as opposed to rounding, is required. Consider the following problem:

> A boy takes $1.00 into a department store to purchase as many baseballs as his money will buy. He discovers that baseballs cost 35¢ each. How many can he buy?

To solve this simple problem, we divide 100 by 35, obtaining 2 30/35 or 2 5/6. Do we round (obtaining 3) or truncate (obtaining 2) for the answer? Truncation is appropriate for this problem.

2-9. In Summary

This chapter has introduced Fortran statements in general and has presented a general discussion of the arithmetic assignment type of Fortran statement. Fortran constants, variables, operations, expressions, and functions have all been discussed along with many of the individual rules that must be followed in using these Fortran elements. Some of the numerous idiosyncrasies that may be present in many compilers have been mentioned. Various compilers have been written by different people at different times for different machines and with some variation in objectives. Specific limitations, rules, and regulations for individual compilers are always available in the form of individual programming manuals for compilers on specific machines. It is not necessary (or desirable) to get involved in individual idiosyncrasies at this point.

After this chapter has been carefully read, the student should be thoroughly familiar with the techniques and the rules governing the writing of arithmetic assignment statements. The next chapter will make these arithmetic assignment statements the basis of Fortran calculations and couple them with the necessary input-output statements to write simple programs for a Fortran compiler.

EXERCISES‡

2-1. Write the following as Fortran integer constants:

-2,486 4×10^2 -16.† 86,487.0†

2-2. Write the following as Fortran integer constants:

27.0 -2,726 5.86×10^2 -16,262.0

2-3. Write the following as Fortran real constants (using either decimal or exponential format):

10^{21} 0.0000082† -10^2 26,286.3

2-4. Write the following as Fortran real constants (using either decimal or exponential format):

-27,281† 10^{-17} 0.298612 27.83×10^4

2-5. Why are the following unacceptable as Fortran integer constants?

-121.8 5,241 27E21† 29342641893

2-6. Why are the following unacceptable as Fortran integer constants?

27E-03 16.8 27,243† 10^{14}

2-7. Why are the following unacceptable as Fortran real constants?

-2,871. 27.8E + 92† +21 6EO2

2-8. Why are the following unacceptable as Fortran real constants?

9.12-E01 281E3.2 -18,342† 16,221.3

2-9. From the following list of variable names you are to select those that are integer variable names, those that are real variable names, and those that are unacceptable as variable names.

(a) 2EASY	(g) IDIOT
†(b) TWO	(h) UNCLE
(c) IKE	†(i) ROOT
(d) ANSWER	(j) A - B
†(e) ANSWER1	(k) (LAST)
(f) TO.JO	(l) I

2-10. From the following list of variable names you are to select those that are integer variable names, those that are real variable names, and those that are unacceptable as variable names.

(a) ADDITION	(g) MUST
†(b) 23SKEEDO	(h) GAMMA
(c) T	(i) COBOL

‡Solutions to Exercises marked with a dagger † are given in Appendix E.

(d) TEE
†(e) A * B
(f) (X)
†(j) JERK
(k) DIRTY
(l) GO-GO

2-11. Write Fortran expressions to accomplish the following:

†(a) $\dfrac{a+b}{c+d}$

(b) x^3

(c) $a+\dfrac{b}{c+d}$

†(d) $\dfrac{a \cdot b}{c+10}$

(e) $\dfrac{x+2}{y+4}$

(f) $\dfrac{i+j}{k+3}$

2-12. Write Fortran expressions to accomplish the following:

(a) $\dfrac{i+j}{k+n}+m$

†(b) $\dfrac{a+b}{c+\dfrac{d}{e}}$

(c) $1+x+\dfrac{x^2}{2!}+\dfrac{x^3}{3!}$ (3! is 3 factorial)

(d) $\dfrac{3+y+y^2+4y^3}{x+4}$

†(e) $\dfrac{a}{b}+\dfrac{c \cdot d}{e \cdot f \cdot g}$

(f) $\dfrac{1}{x^2}\left(\dfrac{y}{10}\right)^z$

2-13. Write Fortran expressions to accomplish the following:

(a) $2\pi r^2$

(b) $a+x[b+x(c+dx)]$

(c) $\left(\dfrac{a}{b}\right)^{.86c+1}$

†(d) $\left[p\left(\dfrac{r}{s}\right)\right]^{t-1}$

(e) $k^3+\left(\dfrac{m \cdot n}{2i}\right)^{2k}$

(f) $\left(-\frac{-x + y + 27}{z^2}\right)^4$

2-14. State the numerical value of J that will be transferred to memory by the following arithmetic assignment statements:

†(a) J = 5 * 5/7
(b) J = 5 * (5/7)
(c) J = 2/3 + 2/3
(d) J = 2./3. + 2./3.
†(e) J = 2000 * (1999/2000)
(f) J = (2000 * 1999)/2000

2-15. State the numerical value of X that will be transferred to memory by the following arithmetic assignment statements:

(a) X = 5 * 5/7
†(b) X = 5/7 * 5
(c) X = 5. * 5./7.
(d) X = 4 ** (3 ** 2)
(e) X = (4 ** 3) ** 2
†(f) X = 5./3. + 3./3. + 5./3.

2-16. Write arithmetic assignment statements to compute the following:

(a) $x = -\frac{1}{2a} + \sin(a/2)$

†(b) $x = \cos(y) + x \cdot \sin(z)$

(c) $x = -\sin^3 y$

(d) $x = \cos^{i+2}(y)$

(e) $x = \sqrt{y^3 + 2z^2/6}$

†(f) $x = y \cdot \sin(\pi/z)$

2-17. Write arithmetic assignment statements to compute the following (log denotes $\log_{10}$ and ln denotes $\log_e$):

(a) $x = \frac{1 + \cos y}{1 - \cos y}$

†(b) $x = \left|\frac{1 + \cos y}{1 - \cos y}\right|$

(c) $x = \log\left|\frac{1 + \cos y}{1 - \cos y}\right|$

(d) $x = \pi \cdot \sin^2(y) \cdot \cos^{i+2}(z)$

†(e) $x = \log|\tan y|$

(f) $x = y \cdot \log|\arctan(z/3)|$

2-18. Write arithmetic assignment statements to compute the following:

(a) $x = \left(\frac{10}{\pi y z}\right)^{1/2} \cos y$

†(b) $x = (y)^{1/2}\,(z)^{i+1}\,(e)^{-y}$

(c) $x = e^{-\sqrt{y/13}}$

(d) $x = \cos\,(e^{-\sin x})$

(e) $x = \dfrac{1}{\sqrt{\sin y}} + \left|\dfrac{1}{\sqrt{\cos y}}\right|$

†(f) $x = \log\left|\dfrac{1}{\sqrt{\cos y}}\right| \cdot \log\left|e^{-x}\right|$

2-19. Identify the error(s), if any, in each of the following arithmetic assignment statements:

(a) X = I ** Y .
(b) X - 3 = Y * Z + 6
†(c) X = Y * - Z + 6.
(d) X = I + 3 = J + 4
(e) X = 27Z
†(f) X = (Y + 3) ** 2

2-20. Identify the error(s), if any, in each of the following arithmetic assignment statements:

(a) II = X - Y
(b) -X = (Y + Z) * 12.
†(c) X * Y = I ** 2
(d) X = 2,763 * A
(e) 3X + I ** 3
†(f) X = (Y + 4) ** 2
(g) X = (-3.5 * ABS(D + G)) ** B

3

Simple Fortran Programs

The previous two chapters have introduced the concept of automatic programming languages and developed the basic tools that are necessary to formulate some of the simpler individual statements of Fortran. The last chapter gave attention to the development of the arithmetic assignment statement, and it is the purpose of this chapter to carry this development forward and to explain some of the other types of Fortran statements. Based on this, some simple Fortran programs will be written. In this chapter statements will be introduced that are sufficient to write only a very elementary type of Fortran program.

It might be reemphasized that the procedures, formats, and rules given are those that are peculiar to Fortran IV.

3-1. Format-Free Input Statements

If a problem is to be done only one time, all of the necessary data associated with the problem can be entered into the Fortran program directly in the form of constants in the individual statements. This is not normally done, however, since a digital computer is best suited for doing repetitive-type calculations, and most problems encountered in the application of digital computers are those in which the program is to be executed a number of separate times on different data. This is usually handled by having the program read the data associated with an individual problem from cards (or their equivalent) at the time the program is to be executed. Constants are used in the program only for those quantities that are in fact constant, i.e., they are not dependent upon the input data. If the program is set up in this general format, the same program can be used for many different sets of input data. This means that the Fortran program must handle the input of data into the computer. This becomes a significant portion of the programmer's task and it will now receive our attention.

The primary thing to appreciate in considering input statements is the fact that the input data for the program may be entered into the machine from any number of different input units, e.g., from card reader units, from magnetic tape units, from paper-tape units, or perhaps even from a console typewriter. Furthermore, the individual numbers which comprise the input data for the program may appear in different layouts, i.e., formats.

In general there are two approaches to handling input and output statements: the format-free approach and the format approach. Both will be presented briefly. It is important to note that either one may be used in any given problem‡; the choice is up to the programmer. The format-free approach is simpler and easier to use, and the format approach is more general and more powerful.

First, the format-free approach. An input statement can take the form

READ, K,X,Y

where K, X, and Y comprise a *list* of variables whose value is to be read into the computer. By implication K is an integer variable and X and Y are real variables. The execution of this statement will cause the standard input unit for the computer, usually a card reader, to read in a card and to scan this card for the numerical values to assign to these variables. If the computer finds all three numerical values, then it will execute the next statement in the program. If it does not find all three, it will read in additional data cards until it has found three numerical values. These numerical values will be assigned in order to K, X, and Y. The first numerical value should be, therefore, integer, and the second and third numerical values should be real. The numerical values on the input card(s) may be punched anywhere, but successive values should be separated from each other by blanks or commas.

Several comments apply to this format-free approach

There is no need for the first numerical value to start in column 1.

A numerical value may not be continued across two cards.

Successive cards will be read until enough items have been found to satisfy the requirements of the list part of the READ statement.

Any numerical values remaining on the last data card read for a particular READ statement will be ignored.

The type (real or integer) of a data item should match the type of variable to which it is being assigned.

For integer values either signed or unsigned integer constants are acceptable.

For real values either exponential or floating-point constants are acceptable.

Format and format-free input-output statements may be mixed within the same computer program.

The general form of the format-free input statement is

READ, *variable list*

As indicated earlier, the value of the format-free statement is based on its simplicity and the ease with which it may be used.

For input via the teletype, many time-sharing systems use the ACCEPT statement.

‡This assumes that the Fortran IV compiler in use by your computer center has available on it both of these capabilities.

For example, to enter values for variables X, J, and C, the appropriate statement is

```
ACCEPT, X,J,C
```

Upon processing this statement the computer waits for the programmer to enter numerical values for X, J, and C. Most terminals have a light or other mechanism by which the user is aware that the system is ready to accept input. Many programmers precede the ACCEPT statement with a PRINT statement to tell them which variables appear in the ACCEPT statement.

The rules regarding entry of values for the ACCEPT statement are essentially the same as for the format-free READ statement. That is, the numerical values are separated by a comma or one or more blank spaces. Only integer constants may be entered for integer variables, but either exponential or floating-point constants may be entered for real variables. After all values have been entered and the RETURN key depressed, the computer continues processing the statements in the program.

3-2. Formatted Input Statements

Perhaps the easiest way to illustrate the nature of the standard formatted input statement is by way of example:

```
    READ (5,297)K,X,Y
297 FORMAT (I10,F10.2,E20.7)
```

These two statements are interpreted in the following manner. The READ indicates to the computer that data is to be entered into the computer memory from one of the many possible input units and in one of the many possible data formats that might exist on the typical input card (or its equivalent). The number 5 is a number whose value specifies the particular input unit to be used. This is an assignment that is made in a more or less arbitrary fashion with regard to specific machine configurations.

The 297 refers to the statement number of an associated FORMAT statement for the input READ statement. This FORMAT statement is not a statement that is executed by the computer; it is a statement which provides information to the computer telling it the arrangement of the various items of data on the input card (or its equivalent). The three variables in the list following the parentheses in the READ statement have the names K, X, and Y. These variables are assigned values from the data card when the READ statement is executed.

In statement 297 (the FORMAT statement) there are *field specifications* for the variables in the READ statement.

The FORMAT statement dictates the layout of data on the input card (or its equivalent), and there must be a format field specification for *each* of the variables in the input READ list. In the list shown, the variable K is an integer variable, and the field specification associated with the variable K is given as I10. The I10 indicates that the first variable in the list is an integer variable, and it will be found in the first 10 columns of the input data card.

The variable X is a floating-point variable, and the F10.2 is the field specification associated with the data layout for the value of X to be read into the computer. The F indicates that X is floating-point, and therefore the field specification is for a real number. The 10 indicates that the value of X will be found in the next 10 columns on the data card, i.e., columns 11-20, and the .2 indicates that when the number is processed, the decimal point will be assumed between the numbers in columns 18 and 19, i.e., two places will be found to the right of the decimal. It is better programming practice to actually write the decimal in the number on the data card rather than to rely on its assumed location. If the decimal is explicitly written, it would normally appear in column 18, but if it is placed in any other column, its actual column location will *override* the format specification given in statement 297. This freedom is, of course, limited by the fact that the entire numerical value of X, including the decimal point, must be completely contained within columns 11-20.

The variable Y is also a real variable, and it could have been given in the floating-point or F-type of field specification. For sake of illustration, the variable Y is shown here in an alternate type of real-number field specification—the exponential or E-type of field specification. The E-type of field specification calls for a numerical value plus an exponent raised to a power of 10. The 20 specifies a total of twenty columns for the field, and the .7 indicates that seven places will be assumed to the right of the decimal in the input number. The number must also contain an exponent giving the power of 10 by which the fractional part of the number is to be multiplied. As before, it is better programming practice to actually write the decimal in the numerical value of Y on the data card. The input information for this particular number might appear as .526E01 which would indicate the real number 5.26. Note in this instance that the number of decimal places indicated in the input number is less than that indicated in the field specification. This is perfectly permissible and the actual location will override the field specification given in statement 297. Also note that the input number proposed did not occupy the full 20 columns allowed, i.e., columns 21-40. This is permissible and perhaps even desirable because it allows the programmer to leave blank spaces (within limits) between his input data on the cards, and thus make the data easier for people to read. Since blanks on the input data card will be read by the computer as zeros, all numbers on the input card should be placed in the columns at the right of the field provided and all blank columns should be at the left of the field provided, i.e., the input should be *right justified.*

Summarizing, the individual input statements shown in the previous example would direct the computer to go to input unit number five and read in a single card which will contain the integer variable K and the real variables X and Y. They will be contained on a single card (or its equivalent) whose format is laid out in the arrangement shown in statement 297 of the program. The integer variable K will be contained in columns 1-10, the real variable X will be shown in normal decimal notation in columns 11-20, and the real variable Y will be shown in exponential notation in columns 21-40.

There are many modifications to the nature of input READ statements depending

Table 3-1. Formatted input statements

Input Unit	Standard Form	Alternate Form
Card reader, on-line		READ n, list
Magnetic tape (cards off-line)		READ INPUT TAPE j, n, list
	READ (j,n) list	
Paper tape		ACCEPT TAPE n, list
Console typewriter		ACCEPT n, list

Note: j stands for an integer whose value specifies the input unit, *n* stands for the statement number of the FORMAT statement, and *list* stands for the input variables.

on the individual compiler. More recent Fortran compilers have arrived at a single standard statement for use as a formated input statement, and that is the preferred form. Older Fortran compilers use different statements to identify different input units, and in general, different computer laboratories have preferred input units for standard jobs. A listing of possibilities is shown in Table 3-1. If the standard form of the READ statement shown in Table 3-1 is available, then its use is preferred.

3-3. Format-Free Output Statements

The general procedures associated with output statements are much the same as those presented in the previous sections on input statements. Again, there is a format-free and a format approach.

Suppose that the three variables K, X, and Y are read into the computer as indicated in the previous section, and an answer to a simple problem is calculated. It is then desired to obtain from the computer both the value of this answer and the values of K, X, and Y which were used to produce this answer. The format-free output statement would be

```
PRINT, K,X,Y,ANS
```

The numerical values of these four variables in the output list will then be printed across a page on the printer. Each value will be printed to full precision with blank spaces inserted between values for clarity. Eight values are typically printed across an output page, but this varies from one installation to another. Real numbers are normally printed in exponential format with seven significant figures. Typical output for the above statement might be

```
12     0.1623000 E 01     0.1000000 E - 01     0.4210000 E 02
```

When the PRINT statement has more output variables than may be printed on a single line, output is continued on the following line.

The general form of the PRINT statement is

PRINT, *variable list*

There is also an output PUNCH statement which produces output on cards and has the general form

PUNCH, *variable list*

It is also possible to produce explanatory messages in format-free output by inserting the material within single quotation marks in the output variable list. For example:

```
PRINT, 'THE ANSWER IS', ANS
```

would produce

```
THE ANSWER IS 0.4210000 E 02
```

This will be illustrated further.

3-4. Formatted Output Statements

Using the earlier example, the formatted output approach would use the following two statements:

```
   WRITE (6,28)K,X,Y,ANS
28 FORMAT (1X,I10,F10.2,E20.7,E20.5)
```

The WRITE statement is very similar to the READ statement. The WRITE statement directs the computer to write the variables using unit number 6. The layout of the variables will be given by FORMAT statement number 28, and the individual variables to be written are K, X, Y, and ANS.

For line printer output, the output FORMAT statement has one slight difference from the input FORMAT statement. The first column of an output list is used as a *carriage control indicator,* and the carriage of the output printer (which will ultimately produce a printed list of these variables) will be controlled by the character found in column 1. Here an X-type format specification indicates that the first column is blank. The X-type field specification is a convenient way to indicate blank spaces in the output list. The width of the field specification for an X-type format is given in front of the X specification, and a 1X field specification makes the first column in the output list a blank. Having column 1 blank will produce an output list that is single spaced. It might also be noted that the X-type format is not associated with any of the variables in the output variable list shown in the WRITE statement.

The carriage control indicator does not apply to teletypes such as those used in time-sharing systems, nor does it apply to card punches, magnetic tapes, etc.

The next field specification in the FORMAT list is the I10 specification associated with the integer variable K, and the F10.2 field specification is for the real variable X. The E20.7 is the exponential format specification associated with the real variable Y, and the E20.5 field specification is for the output variable ANS. Since it is possible that the size of the numerical value of the variable ANS is unknown, it is desirable to have it come out in an exponential format to take care of extremely small or extremely large numbers. The field specification E20.5 takes care of this and allows twenty columns with five significant figures.

Summarizing these output statements, they indicate to the machine that it should use output unit number 6 to list the four variables K, X, Y, and ANS according to the output format given by statement 28. Statement 28 indicates that in the output record the first column should be blank, columns 2-11 should contain the integer variable K, columns 12-21 should contain the floating-point variable X with two places to the right of the decimal, columns 22-41 should contain the real variable Y in exponential notation with seven places to the right of the decimal and with the fraction to vary between 0.1 and 1.0, and columns 42-61 should contain the variable ANS in exponential format with five places to the right of the decimal and with the fraction to vary between 0.1 and 1.0.

There are many alternate possibilities for output statements just as there are many alternate forms for input statements, and alternate forms are shown in Table 3-2.

One additional comment about input and output listings might be appropriate. As indicated earlier, there are more columns specified in many of the field specifications than are necessary to contain the variable. For example, in the sample output listing it is possible that the output variable X will require only four columns to contain the value of the variable. If the variable X took on the value 8.10, then it could be held in four columns and there would be six columns left over in the output field specification. In all cases such as this the computer will *right justify* the output. This means that the computer will take the output number and push it as far to the right as it can in the

Table 3-2. Formatted output statements

Output Unit	Standard Form	Alternate Form
Card punch, on-line		PUNCH n,list
Printer, on-line		PRINT n,list
Magnetic tape (for off-line printing and punching)	WRITE (j,n)list	WRITE OUTPUT TAPE j,n,list
Paper tape		PUNCH TAPE n,list
Console typewriter		TYPE n,list

Note: j stands for an integer whose value specifies the output unit, *n* stands for the statement number of the FORMAT statement, and *list* stands for the output variables.

output field specification, i.e., all of the output blanks will be on the left-hand side of the field. For the value of X above, columns 2-7 would be blank.

On input statements the computer does not control whether the data are right justified or left justified; this is up to the programmer. He may use any spacing within his given field width that he desires for his real variables. In the input READ statement the X could be placed either extremely to the left, i.e., *left justified,* or it could be right justified within the columns allotted. If the number of places to the right of the decimal in the actual value of X given is different from that called for in the field specification, then the format of the input variable itself will override the number of decimal places called for in the FORMAT statement field specification.

In the case of integer variables and real variables using exponential format the problem is more complicated, however, because the computer will recognize blank spaces as zeros. For this reason it is necessary that all integer variables and all real variables using exponential form must always be right-justified for input, or otherwise the computer will inadvertently enter an input constant that is orders-of-magnitude larger than intended. The basic format specifications discussed in this and the previous section are summarized in Table 3-3.

Table 3-3. Format field specifications

General form of the FORMAT statement for numerical data is

$$n \text{ FORMAT } (S_1, S_2 \dots S_k)$$

where n stands for a statement number, and each S_i is a format specification.

The following format specifications are available for single line input and output of real and integer data and to skip a field on the input and output record.

Format Code	External Representation	Internal Representation	Suggested Minimum Output Field Width
Iw	Integer, ±xxxx	Fixed-point number	Number of significant digits + 1
Fw.d	Real number without exponent, ±x.xxxx	Floating-point number	Depends on number size, at least $d + 3$
Ew.d	Real number with exponent, ±x.xxxE±xx	Floating-point number	$d + 7$ for most computers
wX	Skip field	None	Any

In the above, *w* stands for an unsigned integer constant which specifies the field width, *d* stands for an unsigned integer constant which specifies the number of digits in the fractional part of the number, and *x* stands for any decimal digit or a blank character which is interpreted as a zero.

3-5. PAUSE, STOP, and END Statements

There are several statements available for program termination and/or interruption. This termination and/or interruption may come during the compilation or during the execution of a program, and there are different statements available for these different purposes. As described in Chapter 1, the first phase of running a Fortran program will be the compilation of the program to produce an object program. There must be some way for the Fortran compiler to recognize the end of the program that it is compiling. This is true since a number of different programs may be stacked together and put into an input unit for compilation. Unless there is some way for the compiler to recognize the end of one program, it might try to compile all of these individual programs together as one large program. The compiler recognizes the end of a program by an END statement. This statement is not executable and does not itself produce any machine-language instructions. The END statement is the last statement in the list of the Fortran source program. This does not imply that it is the last statement to be executed, but it does indicate that there are no further statements in this particular program list. Saying this another way, there must be only one END statement in a program, and it must be the very last statement in the program listing (disregarding the fact that there may be data cards following the program itself).

Once the Fortran program has been compiled and the object program is ready for execution, there also must be a means to terminate and/or interrupt the execution of the program. The PAUSE and STOP statements are provided for these purposes. One of the most logical applications of a STOP statement is at the termination of the executable statements in the program. This says that the execution of a particular program is complete, and all of the instructions for this individual program have been executed, i.e., the machine has completed running the program. A STOP statement is sufficient for this purpose. Normally the computer cannot be made to continue within the given program after a STOP statement has been executed. In computers using a monitor the STOP statement normally shifts control back to the monitor to start a new program job. Note that the STOP statement is such that it stops the execution of the object program and can only take effect while the object program is being executed. The STOP statement does not cause termination of compilation.

It might be noted that in some Fortran compilers the END statement automatically causes the Fortran compiler to generate a STOP statement at the end of the object deck.

There are many additional useful applications of the STOP statement. For example, in many cases a program will direct the computer to read a set of input data and check all of these data for consistency. If some of the data are inconsistent, then the programmer might direct the computer to go to a STOP statement and not try to process the data. In such an application a STOP statement would be contained within the body of the program, and if it were ever executed, it would actually stop the running of the program before it had completed the entire sequence of calculations called for by the program. Note that this implies that the STOP statement will be compiled and will generate machine-language instructions that will appear in the object deck.

One of the difficulties with the STOP statement, as indicated earlier, is that the computer cannot conveniently be made to continue within the same program after the STOP statement has been executed. The PAUSE statement allows the operator to overcome this inconvenience and to restart the program. The PAUSE statement does, in fact, stop the computer, but it does allow restarting possibilities. This is usually done by pressing a button on the computer console, and when this is done, the computer will resume the execution of the object program beginning with the statement just after the

PAUSE statement. The PAUSE statement might be used to interrupt a program temporarily in order to check intermediate results, to mount a new magnetic tape, or to take other action.

There are many differences in computer centers as to their choice between the use of STOP and PAUSE statements. Many large computer centers will try to avoid the wasted (expensive) computer time that is consumed by encountering a STOP or PAUSE statement, and they may actually modify the basic Fortran compilers so that these statements are not acceptable. Large computer centers often have computers which are run under the control of a monitor program as discussed in Chapter 1. The monitor program normally does not provide for a STOP when a program reaches the normal completion of its execution; it is more desirable for the computer to return control to the monitor program. This is better than stopping execution completely. A convenient way to provide for return of control from the individual program to the monitor's control is through the use of the CALL EXIT statement. The CALL EXIT statement has the effect of simply returning the control of the computer to the monitor. Many compilers are set up so that a STOP statement has the same effect as a CALL EXIT statement, and the machine does not stop its operation. This point should be checked with any local computer center before use is made of the STOP statement.

Summarizing, the END statement must be the last statement in the source program. There may only be one END statement, and it is a signal to the compiler that it is the end of the program being compiled into an object program. It is not a statement that is executed during the running of the object program, and it does not generate any machine-language instructions in the object program. The PAUSE and STOP statements are statements that appear within the body of the program. There may be more than one of them within any individual program; they do generate machine-language instructions for the object program; and they may be executed during the course of running the object program.

3-6. An Example Program

It is possible to write a sample Fortran program with the statements discussed so far. We might want to evaluate the simple algebraic expression $X^2 + |Y| + 267K + 146$ as being the numerical value of a desired answer. The program should read in the values of K, X, and Y and calculate a numerical answer as indicated. If only one set of data were ever to be executed, it would be possible to write the program with the values of K, X, and Y appearing as constants within the program. Assuming it is desired to make this calculation quite often, the program will be written to read in values of K, X, and Y. For sake of illustration in this section, we will only read in one set of values of K, X, and Y and, based on these, calculate one numerical answer. To take care of many additional sets of input data, one or two additional statements will have to be added to our program at a later time.

In order to write the program one additional statement might be discussed. This is the *comment card* or *comment line*. This is an informational type of statement in a Fortran program as discussed in an earlier chapter. The comment card or comment line has a C in column 1 of the statement. When the Fortran compiler encounters a card which has a C in column 1, it does not process the information contained on the card. In other words, it is not treated as an executable statement or a statement to be compiled, but if the computer provides a "listing" of the program (a printed version of the program which may be produced during the compilation phase), then the comment cards will appear in the listing. The comment card makes the program more easily understandable by the programmer; it does not provide information for the computer. Liberal use of comment cards will make the program more easily understandable by the original programmer if he should return to the program some period of time after its original conception, and it also will make it easier for someone other than the original programmer to interpret the program. Comment cards are not necessary in short programs, but they become almost mandatory in large and complex programs. In order to help the reader get into the habit of using them, this entire book will make liberal use of comment cards. Comment cards must not appear in input data.

The sample program is shown in Figure 3-1. Both format and format-free I/O statements are shown. Note that comment cards have been used to indicate the name of the program, the input statements, the calculation statements, the output statements, and the terminal statements. The input statements for the program are exactly as discussed in Sections 3-1 and 3-2, the output statements are exactly as discussed in Sections 3-3 and 3-4, and the terminal statements are as discussed in Section 3-5. The calculation statements are indicated and the calculation itself is broken up into three statements for clarity. Both X and Y are real variables, while K is an integer variable; if they were all

```
C FOR COMMENT
STATEMENT NUMBER | Cont. | FORTRAN STATEMENT
C    EXAMPLE PRØGRAM FØR SECTIØN 3.6
C
C     INPUT STATEMENTS
C
      READ(5,297)K,X,Y                    } OR { READ,K,X,Y
  297 FØRMAT(I10,F10.2,E20.7)             }
C
C     CALCULATIØN STATEMENTS
C
      ANS1= X**2 + ABS(Y)
      ANS2= K * 267. + 146      <---  Mixed mode
      ANS = ANS1 + ANS2
C
C     ØUTPUT STATEMENTS
C
      WRITE(6,28)K,X,Y,ANS                     } OR { PRINT,K,X,Y,ANS
   28 FØRMAT(1X,I10,F10.2,E20.7,E20.5)         }
C
C     TERMINAL STATEMENTS
C
      STØP
      END
       526       16.8                .681E04   <---  Data card (layout
                                                     is given by
                                                     format statement 297)
                                                     if format approach used
```

Figure 3-1. Coding form for sample program in Sec. 3-6 showing both format and format-free I/O statements

three contained within a given expression, a "mixed mode" would be present and the program would not be executed on some compilers. In order to overcome this the calculation is done in three steps. An intermediate quantity, ANS1, is calculated using the real variables X and Y and taking advantage of the absolute value function. Another intermediate value, ANS2, is calculated by incorporating the integer constant 146 and the integer variable K into a single expression. Note that the expression in the calculation of ANS2 is carried out in integer arithmetic, and that when the number is stored, it is converted to a real number. Both ANS1 and ANS2 are real variables, and they may be combined to produce the numerical quantity ANS which is the purpose of the program. The Fortran coding form is written for a keypunch operator to produce all of the cards for the entire computer program, and a typical data card is added at the end of the form. Once this complete set of cards has been prepared by a keypunch operator, the program is ready for insertion into the computer for its actual compilation and execution.

To illustrate the point of mixed modes further the program listing shown in Figure 3-1 contains an intentional mixed mode in the expression for the calculation of ANS2. The variable K is an integer variable, and the 267. is a real constant. Multiplying an integer variable by a real constant will produce a mixed mode error in some compilers.‡ Removal of this mixed mode can be accomplished by removing the decimal after 267. When the program is run, the data shown will give the results (layout is for formated output)

```
526        16.80              0.6810000E 04        0.14768E 06
```

The format-free output would appear as follows:

```
526        0.1680000 E 02     0.6810000 E 04       0.1476800 E 06
```

EXAMPLE 3-1

A small box of width w, height h, and depth d contains a number n of identical spheres of radius r. It is desired to calculate the volume of the spheres themselves, the volume of empty space left in the box when it contains the spheres, and the surface area of the spheres. Set up a computer program to achieve these purposes. Consider that the width, height, and depth are all contained on one data card in F10.2 formats and assume that the number of spheres and the radius of these spheres are given on a second data card. The number of spheres is an integer variable in I5 format and the radius of the spheres is given in F10.4 format. The volume of the spheres, the volume of empty space, and the surface area of the spheres should be printed out in E20.7 format.

The program for making these calculations is given in detail in Figure 3-2. Note in this program that each of the READ statements in the input section will cause an individual card (or its equivalent) to be read into the computer. The first READ statement will introduce the width, height, and depth variables, and the second READ statement will read a second card containing the number and radius of the spheres. Note that it will be disastrous if these data cards are reversed inadvertently by the person running the program on the computer.

Note in the calculation of the variable VOLM1 that the set of parentheses in this arithmetic assignment is not absolutely necessary. Also note in this statement that the value of π must be specified by the programmer, i.e., the computer does not know the

‡In many present-day compilers this mixed mode is acceptable, but often it is wasteful of machine time. In most current compilers the presence of the real constant in the expression will signal the compiler to evaluate the entire expression in real arithmetic, i.e., convert all constants and variables to real quantities and then perform the arithmetic operations. This mixed mode is inserted and illustrated here to point out a potential programming problem for some compilers.

```
C FOR COMMENT
STATEMENT NUMBER | FORTRAN STATEMENT
C     EXAMPLE PRØGRAM FØR CALCULATING SPHERE AREA AND VØLUMES IN A BØX
C
C     READ IN BØX DIMENSIØNS, NUMBER AND RADIUS ØF SPHERES
C
      READ(5,10)W,H,D
   10 FØRMAT(F10.2,F10.2,F10.2)     OR       READ,W,H,D
      READ(5,11)N,R                          READ,N,R
   11 FØRMAT(I5,F10.4)
C
C     CALCULATIØN ØF VOLUME ØF ØNE SPHERE
C
      VØLM1 = (4./3.) * 3.1416 * R**3
C
C     CALCULATIØN ØF TOTAL SPHERE VØLUME
C
      XN = N          <---- This is one way to avoid mixed mode
      TØTVØL = VØL1 * XN      computations in a statement.
C
C     CALCULATIØN ØF EMPTY VØLUME
C
      BØXVØL = W * H * D
      EMPVØL = BØXVØL - TØTVØL
C
C     CALCULATIØN ØF SURFACE AREA ØF SPHERES
C
      SUR = 3.1416 * (2.* R) **2 * XN
C
C     ØUTPUT ØF ANSWER
C
      WRITE(6,100)TØTVØL,EMPVØL,SUR      OR     PRINT,TØTVØL,EMPVØL,SUR
  100 FØRMAT(1X, 3E20.7)
      STØP
      END
         6.        6.        6.
    5     .348
```

Figure 3-2. Coding form for Example 3-1

value of π. The program also illustrates that raising a real variable to an integer constant power is permissible. Also, to avoid a possible mixed mode problem in the calculation of the total valume of the spheres, the number of spheres is converted to a real variable before it is used in the arithmetic assignment statement for TOTVOL. An alternate way to circumvent the problem of mixed modes in this calculation is to read in the number of spheres as a real variable.

In the output FORMAT statement number 100 a new concept is introduced to save programming time. As indicated in the statement of the problem, it is intended that all three of the output variables be given in E20.7 format. Rather than write E20.7 three separate times, it is possible to use a *repetition number* in front of the E. This indicates the use of the field specification E20.7 three times.

In the ouput FORMAT statement number 100 the first column is left blank to prevent any undesired spacing of the carriage on the output printer for the computing system. In general, as indicated earlier, the contents of column 1 in an output line will control the printer's operation. The printer uses column 1 for carriage control, and thus the contents of this column do not appear on the printed sheet. Generally speaking the following printer actions are appropriate:

Contents of Column 1	*Action of Printer*
Blank	Single space before printing
Zero	Double space before printing
1	Skip to the top of a new page before printing

The usage of these symbols to control carriage spacing on the output printer will be illustrated further.

For the sample program the results are given below for input data in which the width, depth, and height of the box are all given as 6 inches. It is further assumed that there are five spheres, each of radius 0.348 inch. The results, reading from left to right, are the total volume of all the spheres, the empty volume remaining in the box, and the total surface area of all the spheres.

```
0.8826679E 00          0.2151173E 03          0.7609206E 01
```

EXAMPLE 3-2

A student goes into a laboratory and uses a refractometer to measure the refractive index of a liquid solution. The refractometer has a scale which reads an arbitrary scale factor instead of the refractive index. The manufacturer gives the following fourth-order polynomial to convert the scale reading to refractive index:

$$1.276239 \times 10^{-9} \times (\text{scale})^4 - 2.812322 \times 10^{-7} \times (\text{scale})^3$$
$$-2.0922072 \times 10^{-5} \times (\text{scale})^2 + 6.7203912 \times 10^{-3} \times (\text{scale}) + 1.2034111$$

In addition to this, the student knows that the refractive index for this solution can be used to indicate the composition of the solution, and he knows that the weight percent content of volatile component of the mixture is also given by the following fourth-order polynomial which expresses weight percent as a function of scale reading:

$$-1.0148081 \times 10^{-6} \times (\text{scale})^4 + 3.9809369 \times 10^{-4} \times (\text{scale})^3$$
$$-2.1381599 \times 10^{-2} \times (\text{scale})^2 - 2.7003377 \times (\text{scale}) + 1.7767899 \times 10^2$$

It is desired to write a computer program to read in the refractometer scale reading and convert it to the refractive index. It is further planned for the programmer to take the scale reading and calculate the weight percent of the volatile component present in the mixture. The scale reading can be read in F20.5 format, and the output variables should be in F20.5 format.

The computer program necessary to carry out the indicated calculations is shown in Figure 3-3 which uses comment cards (some of which are blank) to indicate the different portions of the program and make it easier to follow the contents of the Fortran

C FOR COMMENT | STATEMENT NUMBER | Cont. | FORTRAN STATEMENT

```
C   EXAMPLE PRØGRAM TØ CØNVERT REFRACTØMETER SCALE READING
C
C   INPUT ØF SCALE READING
C
      READ(5,1000)SCALE              } OR { READ,SCALE
 1000 FØRMAT(F20.5)
C
C   CALCULATIØN ØF REFRACTIVE INDEX
C
      REFIND = (((1.276239E-09*SCALE-2.812322E-07) * SCALE-2.0922072E-05
     1) * SCALE+6.7203912E-03) * SCALE + 1.2034111E-00
C
C   CALCULATIØN ØF WEIGHT PERCENT ØF VØLATILE CØMPØNENT
C
      PCT = (((-1.0148081E-06 * SCALE + 3.9809369E-04) * SCALE - 2.13815
     199E-02) * SCALE - 2.7003377E-00) * SCALE + 1.7767899E+02
C
C   ØUTPUT ØF RESULTS
C
      WRITE (6,2000)SCALE,REFIND,PCT   } OR { PRINT,SCALE,REFIND,PCT
 2000 FØRMAT(1X,3F20.5)
      STØP
      END
   32.370
```

Figure 3-3. Coding form for Example 3-2

statements themselves. Note the use of continuation cards in the arithmetic assignment statements associated with the calculation of the refractive index and the weight percentage. In both cases the arithmetic assignment statements would have run past column 72 on the Fortran coding form, and continuation statements were necessary. It is good programming practice to use a number in column 6 to indicate the number of the continuation line rather than some arbitrary symbol. This is, however, a matter of convenience and personal preference, since any symbol could have been used in column 6 to indicate that the card is a continuation card. In the output portion of the program a repetition number in the output format statement is again employed.

The results of running this program for a refractometer scale reading of 32.370 are shown below (for formated case):

```
32.37000        1.39089         80.25336
```

For format-free output:

```
0.3237000 E 02      0.1390890 E 01      0.8025336 E 02
```

3-7. Handling Program Decks

The physical arrangement of programs and data is dependent on the computer and monitor employed in a given center. The equipment associated with the computer and individual preference of the local computer center are also important. Because of this it is very difficult to generalize about the actual physical arrangement of programs and data, but several example situations will be discussed. As an an example of how the operation might be handled, consider a case in which a digital computer is used with an off-line printer, i.e., a printer that is not physically connected to the computer. Also assume that the installation is one in which all input to the computer is done primarily via punched cards and output also is obtained primarily via punched cards. In such an installation the compilation and execution of programs such as those illustrated in Examples 3-1 and 3-2 will be as follows. The coding form would be used to prepare a source program deck, and the source program deck would be fed through the computer along with the compiler program (and assembler program, if necessary) in order to produce an object program deck and, if appropriate, information on errors made in the language of the source program. This is illustrated in Figure 3-4. If source program language errors are encountered in the compilation of the program, the object program deck will not be one that is suitable for execution. The error information is taken to a printer to produce a listing or a hard copy of the information. As the object deck itself is in binary, it is not listed. (If too

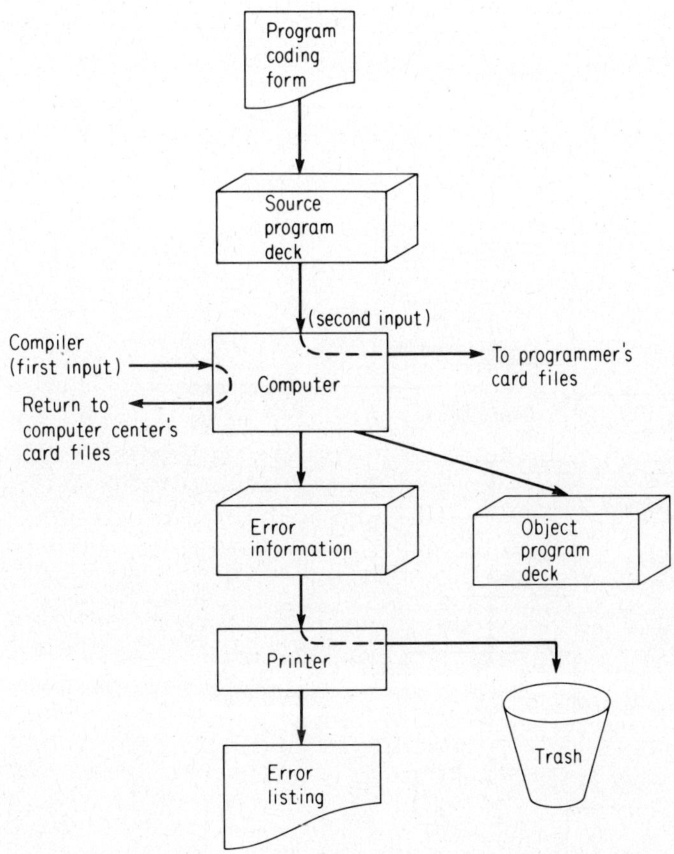

Figure 3-4. Example of compilation (A one-pass compiler illustrated)

many errors are present, an object deck may not be produced.) The common thing to do at this stage if errors are present is to go back and make changes to individual cards in the source program deck and recompile the source program deck. It is possible to go into the object program deck and make corrections in it, but it requires a deep understanding of absolute machine language on the part of the programmer. Consequently, except in the rarest cases, the source deck is modified and recompiled to eliminate any source program language errors, or *bugs*, that might have been encountered in the original compilation. Once this phase of *debugging* is complete, the program is ready for execution.

In order to be executed, a program similar to those discussed in the previous sections will require data cards in addition to the program itself. The data are prepared on coding forms much like the Fortran program itself but with no restrictions on the use of the various columns. These forms are converted into data cards by the keypunch operator. The object program and the data cards are then fed into the computer. The object deck will be introduced first, followed by the data cards. The results of the object program's execution on the specific data provided will produce answers in the form of an answer deck which may be taken to an off-line printer to produce a printed list or hard copy of the results obtained. This is shown schematically in Figure 3-5. In the execution of the program it is possible that execution errors will be encountered and further source program debugging will be necessary. (This is discussed further in Section 3-8.)

In Chapter 1 it was indicated that it may be desirable to have a load-and-go compiler in which no output object deck is produced. An example of a load-and-go compiler's operation on a card-input and card-output computer system is shown in Figure 3-6. Note in Figure 3-6 that the compiler is entered first, followed by the source program

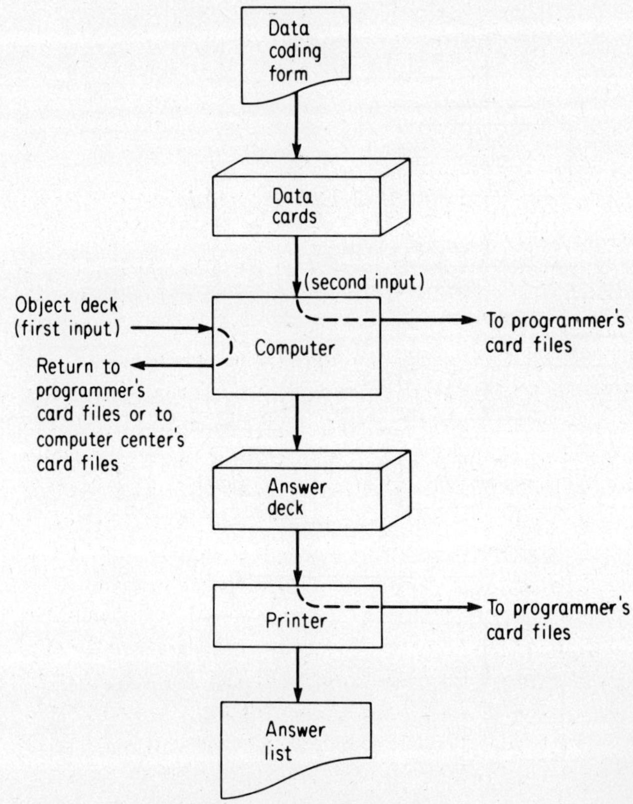

Figure 3-5. Example of execution

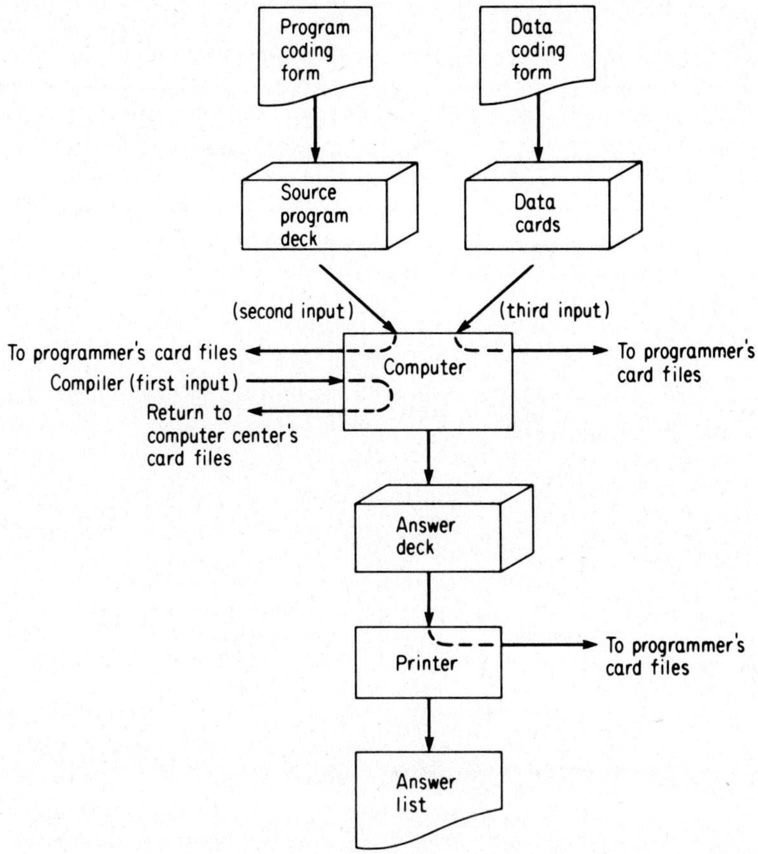

Figure 3-6. Load-and-go compiler

and then by the data cards. There is no object deck produced; there are no intermediate results produced; the answer cards are produced directly (assuming no program errors). These answers are taken to an off-line printer for preparation of an answer list or hard copy. The load-and-go compiler has the advantage of not requiring the time necessary to punch out an object deck, although the object program is internally prepared and stored in memory. The load-and-go compiler is simpler in operation and requires fewer steps in handling information external to the computer's memory. It has the obvious disadvantage that the program must be recompiled every time it is to be executed, and the compilation phase requires machine running time. If a program is to be used over and over again, then the load-and-go compiler is not very efficient. Load-and-go compilers are very useful in student programming laboratories where programs are normally run only once and where there are very large numbers of relatively simple programs to be handled. Also, a student may have several runs on the same program before it is bug-free.

Large computers operating under the control of a monitor system are more complex than the previous examples. Typically these larger machines have magnetic tape input and output because of the slow speed of the card-handling equipment. Programs and data must have *control cards* associated with them to make certain that the monitor understands when the program is to be compiled, when it is to be executed, and which input unit contains data for a program. It is not desirable to discuss control cards further because their use varies so widely from one computer to another. These control cards typically carry the name of the programmer or the number of the job, the maximum amount of time the program is expected to run, and other types of similar information. They also contain an indication as to the specific compiler that is necessary for the program, which input units and output units are assigned for the program, etc. In some installations some portion of this information is assigned by the monitor, and in other cases they are dictated by the control cards directly.

3-8. Debugging the Source Program

It can happen to the best of us! The original program as prepared, punched, and compiled on the computer is not properly written and errors exist in the program. These errors must be removed or the computer will not provide an object deck that is acceptable for actual execution. The purpose of this section is to give some insight into these errors.‡

There are three different types of errors that might be present in a computer program. There are source program language errors that prevent the compilation of the program, and these must be removed before compilation can be successfully completed. There are execution errors which will not be encountered until the actual execution of the program. For example, some of the most common execution errors are due to the programmer's use of inadequate field specifications in FORMAT statements. All of these execution errors must be removed before the computer will produce any complete answers. Finally, there are errors in the logic and formulation of the program or of individual statements by the programmer. These latter errors are the insidious ones that appear when a programmer writes a program that is perfectly acceptable to the computer and is a good program—except that it causes a computation to be made which is different from the one intended by the programmer.§ The only way that these errors of intent can be corrected is for the programmer to make a thorough check for consistency and reasonableness in the answers that are produced by the computer. There may be some kinds of internal checks in the program which the programmer may provide, but in general, there must be a final and thorough review of some typical answers of the program to see if the program is actually doing what the programmer intends.

Most compilers provide "error scans" in order to detect compilation and execution errors, and they give an indication to the programmer as to the nature of the error and its location in the program. In Section 3-6 the program given in Figure 3-1 contained a mixed mode. In the actual running of this program by some compilers an error will be detected and the actual execution of the program deleted. The compiler would indicate an error of "mixed mode" in statement 297 + 2 (which refers to the second line past statement number 297, not including comment cards). In many cases the compiler also will assign a *line number* to every statement in the Fortran program and provide an output listing of the source program with the associated line numbers and error messages (referenced to the appropriate line). The completeness of an error scan on any given computer depends on both the desires and operating procedures of the computer center, the nature of the compiler, and the nature of the computer. It might be recognized that the larger the error scan, the more memory its programming will require in the computer.

‡Debugging can be greatly assisted if a Fortran compiler such as the WATFOR or WATFIV compiler is used. (See Appendix F.)

§The statement has been made that the ultimate computer is one that does what we want it to do, not necessarily what we tell it to do.

Also, the larger the error scan, the more time it will take to check for errors. Generally speaking, error scans are very complete in load-and-go type compilers such as WATFOR or WATFIV which are usually used in student installations.

Sometimes an error made during compilation in one statement will produce a whole series of apparent errors in subsequent statements. For example, the potential error indicated in the example program of Section 3-6 was a mixed mode that could prevent some compilers from calculating the variable ANS2. Subsequently to this, ANS2 appears on the right-hand side of the statement which calculates ANS. Since the compiler has no record of ANS2 being defined (calculated), the compiler finds an error in the arithmetic assignment statement for the calculation of ANS because ANS2 is not defined, and therefore it is an *undefined variable.* This means that the compiler has no record of ANS being defined, and therefore, in the WRITE statement at the end of the program, ANS is not available for output. Thus an undefined variable is encountered in the output list. The simple correction of the mixed mode in the calculation of ANS2 will remove all three of these error indications.

For the exact error code for an individual computer, it will be necessary to contact the computer center itself. (In some cases, manufacturer's programming manuals contain error codes.) These codes are normally prepared in the form of handouts for all users.

A number of general conclusions are possible concerning the debugging of computer programs and the accompanying usage of error messages. These rules are as follows:

1. Never assume that a program is completely correct even though it may be accepted by the computer, completely compiled, and numerical results are achieved. It is possible that logical errors are present.

2. The checking or debugging of a computer program is made much simpler if values of intermediate variables are available. This means that quite often in the writing of a computer program there are extra WRITE statements to make these values available for debugging. Once the program is satisfactorily running, these extra WRITE statements can be removed and the program recompiled for routine use.

3. The tendency is to write a program on a "once-through" basis and present it immediately for keypunching and running on the computer. The programmer should resist this temptation and spend some time in making a careful check of his programs before they are punched and run.

4. When attempting to debug a computer program, there is a big temptation to assume that all aspects of a program are correct because it gives correct answers for an individual set of data. Make certain when choosing data for trial runs of your program that you select data which will execute every portion of your program.

5. When you are in the process of debugging a program, correct every error encountered before you attempt to return it to the machine to have the program recompiled. There is a temptation to make a single (or at least minimum) correction before recompiling. Avoid this temptation and try to approach the computer with as perfect a program as possible.

6. In writing your program make liberal use of comment cards, and for more complex programs be certain that you have the flowchart complete before you attempt to write any portion of the program. (Flowcharts will be discussed in more detail in Section 4-1.) In other words, make every possible effort to make your program as easy to interpret as possible, both for yourself and for others who may attempt to work with the program. This time is well spent and will make it much simpler for the individual to debug the program; it will result in a saving of both programmer and machine time.

3-9. In Summary

This chapter has proposed to introduce simple input and output statements and the termination and/or interruption statements that are necessary in the compilation and execution of a program. All of these have been combined into some simple sample programs. Finally, the arrangement of individual programs for execution has been discussed briefly along with some error messages that may be encountered. Unfortunately, many of the items discussed in this chapter are dependent on the individual computer center and will vary from one installation to the next.

It is hoped that the reader has gained an insight into the structure of Fortran programming. Rather than go on to more complex programs or get involved in the complexities of large programs, it is to the advantage of the student programmer to write many small programs rather than a few very large ones. The exercises associated with this chapter are structured with this in mind.

EXERCISES‡

Where you use formatted I/O in these exercises you are to assume that all input real variables are in F10.2 format, all input and output integer variables are in I10 format, and all output real variables are to be E20.7 format.

3-1. Write the Fortran format-free and formatted input statements necessary to read in the following:

(a) A, B, CAT, DO
(b) I, J, KID
†(c) X, J, YES
(d) A, SIMPLE, GO, I

3-2. Write the Fortran format-free and formatted input statements necessary to read in the following:

(a) IN, OUT, UP, DOWN
(b) R, S, TEE, J
(c) X, Y, ZEE, ALPHA
†(d) CONST, OUKID, A, J

3-3. Prepare the Fortran format-free and formatted output statements necessary to write out the variable lists of Exercise 3-1 plus a new variable ANS in each set. Assume the variables given are input and ANS is the result of calculations performed on the input variables.

3-4. Prepare the Fortran format-free and formatted output statements necessary to write out the variable lists of Exercise 3-2 plus a new variable ANS in each set. Assume the variables given are input and ANS is the result of calculations performed on the input variables.

†**3-5.** Repeat Exercise 3-3, except provide an additional three blank spaces between each output variable written. Do for formatted output only.

3-6. Repeat Exercise 3-4, except provide an additional three blank spaces between each output variable written. Do for formatted output only.

‡Solutions to Exercises marked with a dagger † are given in Appendix E.

Note: For the following exercises you are to read in the given variables, perform the desired calculations, and write out the results as directed. Write complete Fortran programs including a trial data card. Watch for inadvertent cases of mixed modes, and where necessary change variable names inside the program to avoid mixed mode errors. Your instructor will indicate whether to take a format-free or a formatted approach in each case.

3-7. Read: x, y, z

Calculate: $\text{RESULT} = \dfrac{2x^2 + 16y}{z}$

Write: x, y, z, RESULT

†3-8. Read: a, b, c, s

Calculate: $t = a \cdot \cos(s) + b \cdot \sin(s) + c \cdot \tan(s)$

Write: a, b, c, s, t

3-9. Read: x, y, z

Calculate: $\text{SOLN} = x^{17} + e^y + \log z$

$\text{BEST} = (\text{SOLN})^{0.5}$

Write: x, y, z, SOLN, BEST

3-10. Read: TOP, XMID, BOT

Calculate: $\text{TM} = (\text{TOP})^2 + \dfrac{1000.}{\text{XMID}} + \text{BOT}$

$\text{LM} = \text{TOP} + \dfrac{1000.}{\text{XMID}} + (\text{BOT})^2$

Write: TOP, XMID, BOT, TM, LM

3-11. Read: x, y, z

Calculate: $a = \sqrt{x^2 - 6}$

$b = |y^2 + 112.8| + e^z$

Write: x, y, z, a, b

†3-12. Read: a, b, c

Calculate: $\text{A1} = \dfrac{1}{1 - \dfrac{1 + abc}{1 + \left(\dfrac{a^2}{bc}\right)^{1/3}}}$

$\text{A2} = \tan(\text{A1}) + \log|\text{A1}|$

Write: a, b, c, A1, A2

3-13. Read: x, y, i

Calculate: $\text{GO} = x^2 + y + (i)^{1/2}$

$\text{STOP} = i^2 + y + (x)^{1/2}$

Write: x, y, i, GO, STOP

3-14. Read: h, i

Calculate: $g = (h)^{.16} + (i)^2 + hi$

$j = i \cdot \cos(h) + hi + \sqrt{hi}$

Write: h, i, g, j

†3-15. Read: x, y, z

Calculate: $\text{A1} = x^3 + x^2 + x + 1$

$\text{A2} = y^3 + y^2 + y + 1 + \text{A1}$

$\text{A3} = z^3 + z^2 + z + 1 + \text{A2}$

Write: (Line 1) x, y, z
(Line 2) A1, A2, A3

3-16. Read: r, s, t, u, v

Calculate: $HE = r + \frac{st}{u - v}$

$SHE = \cos(r) + \frac{(tu)^4}{1 - v}$

$DEL = HE - SHE$

Write: (Line 1) r, s, t, u, v
(Line 2) HE, SHE
(Line 3) DEL

3-17. Read: (Card 1) x, y
(Card 2) a, b
(Card 3) i
Calculate: $SOLN = ax + by + i$
Write: (Line 1) x, y, a, b
(Line 2) i, SOLN

†**3-18.** Read: (Card 1) r, s
(Card 2) t, u
(Card 3) x, y
Calculate: $UP = (r - s) + (t - u) + (x - y)$
$DOWN = (r + s) + (t + u) + (x + y)$
$FIRST = r + t + x$
$SEC = s + u + y$
$FINAL = e^{UP} + \sqrt{DOWN} + \cos(FIRST)$
Write: (Line 1) r, s, t, u, x, y
(Line 2) UP, DOWN, FIRST
(Line 3) SEC, skip thirty blank spaces, FINAL

3-19. Read: (Card 1) a, skip ten blank spaces, b
(Card 2) x, skip ten blank spaces, z
Calculate: $ANS = ax + bz$
$DIF = a - b$
$SUM = x + a$
Write: (Line 1) a, b, skip twenty-five blank spaces, x, z
(Line 2) SUM, skip twenty-five blank spaces, DIF
(Line 3) skip twenty-two blank spaces, ANS

3-20. Read: (Card 1) a (Card 4) d
(Card 2) b (Card 5) e
(Card 3) c (Card 6) f
Calculate: $SUM = abcdef + abcde + abcd$
$SUMTAN = \tan(a) + \tan(b) + \tan(c)$
$SUMCOS = \cos(d) + \cos(e) + \cos(f)$
$MINOR = abc + ab + a$
Write: (Line 1) SUM
(Line 2) skip twenty blank spaces, SUMTAN
(Line 3) skip forty blank spaces, SUMCOS
(Line 4) skip sixty blank spaces, MINOR

4

Transfer of Control

In the preceding chapter some simple Fortran programs were illustrated and developed, and each of these has one aspect in common. Each operates on a more or less "once-through" basis, and there are no loops or branches in the structure of the program's logic. Programs such as these are encountered, but usually programs take advantage of logical decision-making possibilities in the computer itself. At times the programmer would like to skip certain statements in the program under one set of conditions, or execute those statements under another set of conditions. At times the programmer might go back to the beginning of the program and read in new sets of data, transfer to the end of the program and terminate its operation, or go to some intermediate point in the program and begin a new series of calculations. The situations described above give rise to the need for *transfer of control* statements, and the purpose of this chapter is to introduce this type of statement and show its usage in Fortran programming. Before tackling this problem, however, it is desirable to introduce the subject of flowcharts.

4-1. Flowcharts

With possibilities for branches and loops within the logical structure of a computer program, it is increasingly difficult for the programmer to mentally account for all possible loops and branches. The programs that have been illustrated previously in this book have been simple, but with the introduction of transfer of control statements they can be made so complex that it is impossible for the programmer to visualize all of the logical decision loops with a purely mental memory process. Flowcharts provide an answer to this problem.

The flowchart is a type of schematic diagram or road map which allows the programmer to chart on paper the logical structure of his computer program. He may indicate all the branches and loops and their interrelationships with one another. The flowchart or block diagram provides a visual representation that not only is helpful to the individual programmer, but also is a valuable part of the documentation of his program that will allow someone else to interpret and use the program with a minimum of difficulty.

Flowcharts indicate the flow of control between the various executable statements that comprise the program. The flowchart is normally made up of a set of boxes or shapes which are coded to indicate the nature of the operations involved.

Appendix D gives a complete list of the American Standard flowchart symbols, but for the purposes of this chapter the following list is sufficient.

A rectangle is used to indicate a processing symbol (typically arithmetic operations).

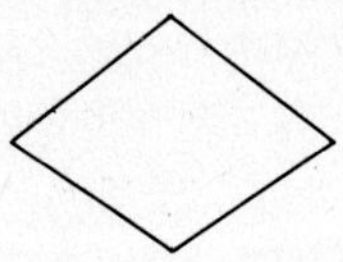

A diamond is used to indicate a decision, and the lines leaving the corners of the diamond are labeled with the decision results that are associated with each path.

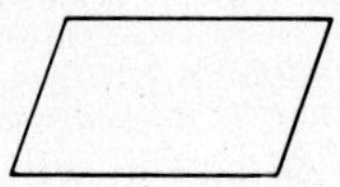

The parallelogram is used to indicate any basic input or output symbol. There are, in addition, many special symbols for input-output operations.

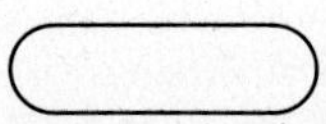

An oval is used to indicate either the beginning or the end of a program, i.e., a START or terminal STOP.

A small circle is used to indicate a connection between two points in a flowchart in situations where a connecting line between them would clutter the basic flowchart.

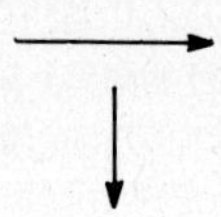

Arrows are used to indicate the direction of flow through the flowchart. Every line should have an arrow on it; the length of the arrow is not important.

Any text or notes may be placed beside or in these symbols. It is especially helpful to indicate numbers beside appropriate processing symbols to indicate the statement number that will be associated with that particular operation in the Fortran program.

Throughout the remainder of this book, examples of flowcharts will illustrate their usage.

It cannot be overemphasized to the beginning programmer that the flowchart represents the first step in the formulation of the program. Many beginning students participate in the foolish habit of first trying to write their program and *subsequently* constructing a flowchart to illustrate the logic of the program. This is exactly the opposite of the recommended route. It should be noted that beginning programmers cannot anticipate everything. Hence it is not until they have drawn a flowchart and tried to write the Fortran statements that they begin to find flaws in the flowchart.

4-2. Unconditional GO TO

The primary purpose of the unconditional GO TO statement (and every other transfer of control statement) is to allow the programmer to shift the execution of the program to some statement other than the one that would normally be executed in sequence. As has been pointed out in earlier chapters, a digital computer will execute each statement in sequence according to the list encountered. The general form of the unconditional GO TO statement is

GO TO *n*

where *n* is the number of an executable statement somewhere else in the program, either before or after the GO TO statement. When the GO TO statement is encountered, it transfers the program to statement number *n*, and statement number *n* will be the next statement executed in the program. After statement *n* has been executed, the statement immediately following statement *n* will be executed unless statement *n* is a transfer of control statement.

Every statement in Fortran programming may be classified as either executable or nonexecutable, and statement *n* must be an executable statement. No transfer of control statement may direct transfer to a nonexecutable statement. Nonexecutable statements include some definition statements, certain specification statements, and the FORMAT statement.

The statement number *n* illustrates quite vividly the only purpose which statement numbers serve in a Fortran program. Statement numbers, as pointed out earlier, are positive integer numbers of five digits or less, written in columns 1-5 of the Fortran coding form, and punched in columns 1-5 of the input card or its equivalent. The maximum value of the statement number varies, with some versions of Fortran allowing up to 99999. The statement numbers in Fortran programs provide a *cross reference*, allowing statements to refer to one another within the program. As indicated in earlier examples, there is no necessary numerical sequence in Fortran statement numbers, and it is not necessary that every statement be numbered. It is not permissible, however, for any two statements to have the same number.

The main use of the unconditional GO TO statement is to allow the programmer to return execution from logical branches in which he has been operating to the main body of the program. There might be several such side branches in the program, and each of these normally will be terminated either by a STOP statement or by an unconditional GO TO statement.

EXAMPLE 4-1

To illustrate the use of the unconditional GO TO statement, consider the problem in which a rocket is fired from the earth, and telemetering equipment is used to send back to the earth a large amount of data giving the horizontal and vertical velocity components, v_x and v_y, of the rocket's speed as a function of t, the time of flight. Consider these data to be in units of seconds for time and meters per second for velocity components. A large amount of these data would be received, and the velocity components could be used to calculate the speed of v of the rocket at any moment t as

$$v = \sqrt{v_x^2 + v_y^2}$$

Write a computer program to read in a number of data cards containing the time of measurement t and the horizontal and vertical velocity components, v_x and v_y. Calculate the rocket speed v. The output of the computer program should be the time-versus-speed data for each of the sets of input data. Consider for the moment that there will be an undertermined number of such sets of input data.

The flowchart for such a calculation might appear as shown in Figure 4-1 and the program as given in Figure 4-2. The program is relatively straightforward except that in

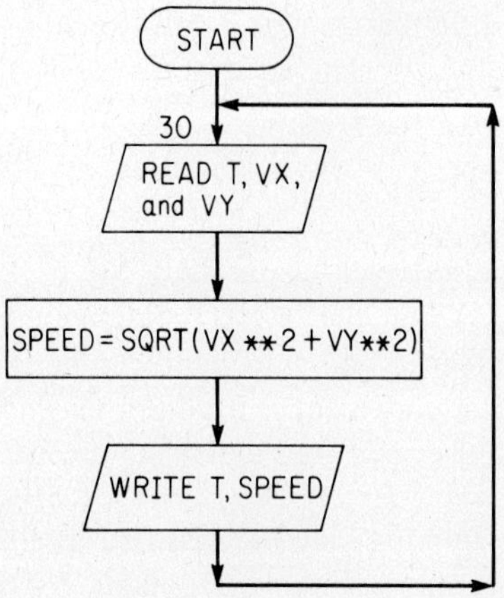

Figure 4-1. Flowchart for Example 4-1 (calculation of rocket speed)

C FOR COMMENT

STATEMENT NUMBER | CONT. | FORTRAN STATEMENT

```
C     EXAMPLE PRØGRAM TØ CALCULATE RØCKET VELØCITY
C
C     INPUT ØF VERTICAL AND HØRIZØNTAL VELØCITY VS. TIME DATA
C
   30 READ(5,10)T,VX,VY
   10 FØRMAT(3F10.2)
C
C     CALCULATIØN ØF THE RØCKET SPEED
C
   40 SPEED = SQRT(VX **2 + VY **2)
C
C     ØUTPUT ØF SPEED VS TIME DATA
C
   50 WRITE (6,20)T,SPEED
   20 FØRMAT(1X,F10.2,10X,F10.2)
C
C     UNCØNDITIØNAL TRANSFER ØF CØNTRØL
C
   60 GØ TØ 30
      END
         .1         .0         .01
       1.0        1.41       10.8
      10.0        4.56      147.8
```

Figure 4-2. Coding form for Example 4-1

output FORMAT statement 20 there is the provision to leave column 1 blank, to write the time of the rocket speed data in F10.2 format, and then to provide for ten blank spaces in the output line before writing the rocket's speed in F10.2 format. After the final output statement the program has an unconditional transfer of control statement, GO TO 30, in which the execution of the program is referred back to statement number 30 and a new card is read into the machine, i.e., a new set of data introduced. This program will continue to operate indefinitely as long as data cards are available.

When the last of the data cards has been read, the Fortran compiler will give an execution error indicating that there is a last-card error (or something equivalent). This execution error indicates that the computer has transferred control back to the READ statement, the READ statement has tried to bring in a new set of data, and an input data card is not available. From the viewpoint of the programmer this error is trivial, though it is not pleasing from an esthetic viewpoint. There are many ways to circumvent this type of error, and these will be discussed in detail in subsequent sections.

In order to illustrate the use of this program, some sample data are given and the program is run to calculate representative speeds at times of .1, 1.0, and 10.0 seconds. In an actual problem there would be much more data than these, but these values will be sufficient to illustrate the results of using this program. Results for the running of these data are shown below.

```
     0.10        0.01
     1.00       10.89
    10.00      147.87
     ERROR      (STATEMENT      30+      0 LINES)
```

The thing to note about this program is the permanent loop which has been formed by the program: the computer continues to iterate through identical calculations because of the transfer of control statement which appears as the last executable statement in the source program. This program will continue to run indefinitely as long as data cards are available for processing. Note that if the GO TO statement had inadvertently been GO TO 40, a permanent loop would have been formed from which there is no exit. There would have been an unending execution of statements 40, 50, and 60, and on each pass through this loop there would have been resultant output (unchanging) associated with statement 50.

4-3. Computed GO TO

The unconditional GO TO statement causes a transfer of control to some other statement in order to break the normal sequential execution of the program. A logical extension of the unconditional GO TO is to allow transfer of control to multiple branches within the program depending upon the value of an integer variable. The computed GO TO statement extends the capability of Fortran by providing the possibilities of entering multiple branches. The general form of the computed GO TO statement is

$$\text{GO TO } (n_1, n_2, \ldots, n_k), i$$

where n_1, $n_2, \ldots,$ n_k (integer numbers, not variables) stand for statement numbers of executable statements elsewhere in the program. The i stands for a simple integer variable which is written without a sign and must be in the range of values of 1 to k where k indicates the number of statement numbers that are enclosed within parentheses.

The operation of the computed GO TO statement is as follows. When the computed GO TO statement is executed, the value of the variable i may have any integer value within the range indicated earlier. If the value of the variable i is j, then the next statement to be executed in the Fortran program will be statement number n_j. The statement next in line for execution will be the statement following n_j in the Fortran statement list unless n_j is a transfer of control statement.

As an example of the use of the computed GO TO statement, consider the statement

```
GO TO (7, 127, 68, 41), LEAP
```

If the value of the integer variable LEAP is 2 when the computed GO TO statement is executed, the next statement to be executed will be 127; if the value of the integer variable is 4, the next statement to be executed will be statement number 41; etc. If the value of the integer variable LEAP is greater than 4, i.e., if it is above the number of statement numbers contained within the parentheses in the computed GO TO statement, the result is unpredictable. (Some compilers execute the statement immediately following the computed GO TO statement, and some cause termination of execution.)

EXAMPLE 4-2

As an example of the use of the computed GO TO, consider the problem in which a number of college students are given identical tests and raw scores from these tests are recorded in order to calculate percentile scores for comparing one student against another. It is necessary to weigh the raw scores depending on whether the individual student tested is a freshman, sophomore, junior, or senior. Assume that information on a particular student, his college level and his test scores, are input data.

The flowchart for the computer program might appear as shown in Figure 4-3. The Fortran program for this calculation is indicated in Figure 4-4. The variable LEVEL is fed into the program along with other information. LEVEL is used as the integer variable to determine which one of four possible branches might be used in the overall structure of the program. If the value of LEVEL is 1 (indicating a freshman), the program transfers

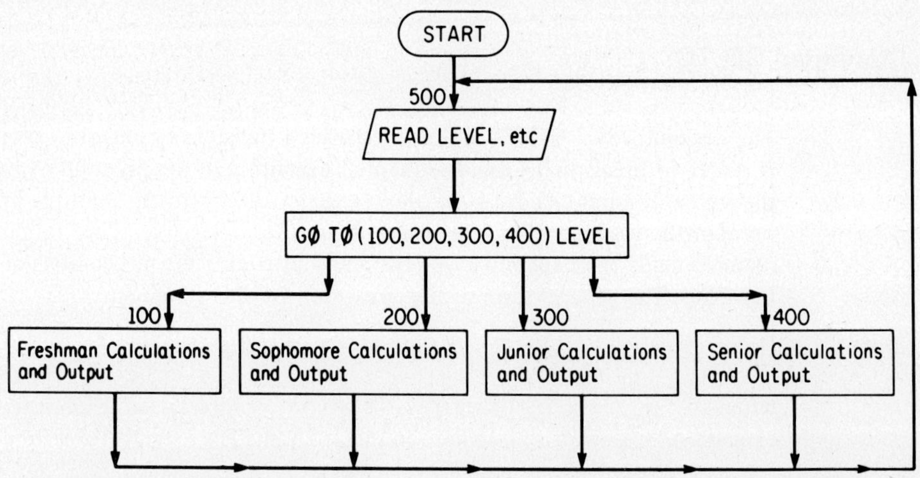

Figure 4-3. Flowchart for Example 4-2 (college test score evaluation)

```
C FOR COMMENT
STATEMENT NUMBER | FORTRAN STATEMENT
C     EXAMPLE PRØGRAM TØ SHØW USE ØF CØMPUTED GØ TØ IN SELECTING PRØGRAM
C          BRANCHES FØR CØLLEGE TEST SCØRE EVALUATIØN
C
C     INPUT ØF "LEVEL" PLUS ØTHER DATA INCLUDING SCØRES
C
  500 READ(5,1)LEVEL, plus other variables
    1 FØRMAT(I5, plus other field specifications
C
C     CØMPUTED GØ TØ FØR BRANCH SELECTIØN
C
      GØ TØ (100,200,300,400),LEVEL
C
C     BRANCHES
C
  100  Calculations for freshmen and output of results
      GØ TØ 500
  200  Calculations for sophomores and output of results
      GØ TØ 500
  300  Calculations for juniors and output of results
      GØ TØ 500
  400  Calculations for seniors and output of results
      GØ TØ 500
      END
```

Figure 4-4. Coding form for Example 4-2

control to statement number 100 where all the necessary calculations are made on the raw scores of the freshman student. Once these calculations have been completed and the appropriate results have been printed out by the computer, control is transferred back to the initial READ statement for a new set of data. The overall function of the program is the same for sophomores, juniors, and seniors, and the particular branch involved depends only on the value of LEVEL. There is a terminal END statement at the end of the Fortran program list. It might also be noted that this program will suffer the same error noted in Example 4-1 in which the compiler indicates an execution error when no more data cards are available for processing.

4-4. Arithmetic IF

The unconditional GO TO statement discussed in Section 4-2 provides a means for returning from a branch of the logical structure of a Fortran program while the computed GO TO statement of Section 4-3 provides a means of entering one of many possible branches in the logical structure. This section will discuss the arithmetic IF statement, which is similar to the computed GO TO statement in that it provides a means of branching to one of three possible branches. The IF statement and the computed GO TO statement appear quite different, but their operation and usage are often closely related.

The IF statement provides a means of branching to one of three statement numbers by means of examining an arithmetic expression called the *argument* of the IF statement. It causes transfer to one of the possible branches depending on whether the expression evaluated is less than zero, equal to zero, or greater than zero.

The arithmetic IF statement is of the following general form:

$$\mathrm{IF}(e)n_1, n_2, n_3$$

where e stands for any expression and n_1, n_2 and n_3 are numbers (not variables) of executable statements in the Fortran listing that may appear either before or after the IF statement. If the value of the expression within the parentheses is negative, the next statement to be executed will be n_1; if the value of the expression within the parentheses is zero, the next statement to be executed is n_2; and if the value of the expression in the parentheses is positive, the next statement to be executed is n_3.

It is possible for any two of the statement numbers in the arithmetic IF statement to be the same. (It is also possible for all three to be identical, but in such a case the result would be the same as an unconditional GO TO statement.) It is necessary that every statement number in the IF statement be the number of an executable statement in the Fortran listing. It is possible in some situations that one branch of the IF statement will never actually occur in execution with consistent data, but in any event it is still necessary to provide a statement number for this possibility, even though it does not exist from a practical viewpoint. Mixed modes of arithmetic are not normally allowed in the expressions found as the argument of an arithmetic IF statement. Either real or integer expressions are allowed, however. Complex expressions (to be discussed later) may not be used in arithmetic IF statements, and if a complex expression is inadvertently placed in an IF statement, the real part is tested.

One problem that may arise in the use of the arithmetic IF statement results from the computer requirement that the arithmetic expression which comprises the argument of the IF statement be *identically* zero before the second statement in the list of statements is executed. There may be some problems created in this situation because of the inherent manner in which the transition from binary to decimal arithmetic is accomplished. Problems also may be created by truncation and round-off errors in the representation of numbers (such as 1./3.). These do not present any difficulties when the IF statement is applied to integer expressions, since fixed-point representation of integers is inherently exact. When the argument of the IF statement is a real expression, however, problems may be present due to the fact that the computer may not have the argument *exactly* 0, and it may be to the advantage of the programmer to place some checks to avoid inadvertent errors caused by the inherent operation of the arithmetic calculations in the computer.

EXAMPLE 4-3

A convenient problem to illustrate the arithmetic IF statement is that encountered in the use of the familiar quadratic formula which determines the roots of a quadratic equation $ax^2 + bx + c = 0$. The formula is

$$x_{1,2} = \frac{-b \pm \sqrt{b^2 - 4ac}}{2a}$$

The use of the formula is very straightforward, but the quantity under the radical sign may be negative and introduce complex numbers. At this stage of the development of our programming skill we have not had any formal usage of complex Fortran arithmetic, so we will take a direct approach to this problem to illustrate the arithmetic IF statement.

A flowchart for the proposed program for this example is illustrated in Figure 4-5, and the program is given in Figure 4-6. In the program the three coefficients of the quadratic equation, A, B, and C, are READ into the computer, and the quantity under the radical sign, RAD, is calculated as B ** 2 - 4. * A * C. Depending on the value of this quantity under the radical sign, control then goes to one of three branches in the program. If the quantity under the radical sign is negative it is necessary to calculate two complex roots which are conjugates of one another, i.e., their real parts are equal and the complex parts are equal in magnitude. In this particular branch the output uses FORMAT statement 11 in which provision is made for A, B, and C to be recorded in the same format as that in which they were read. The real and imaginary parts of roots 1 and 2 are also recorded with five blank spaces between each of them and five blank spaces between the roots and the coefficients A, B, and C. After the completion of the output section, control is returned to statement 1 (the initial READ statement) to introduce a new set of coefficients.

If the quantity under the radical sign is zero, the two roots of the quadratic equation are both real and equal to one another. The appropriate output statement for this uses FORMAT statement 21, and the logic of this branch is much as before. When the quantity under the radical sign is positive, the roots of the quadratic equation are both real but unequal, and the calculations are made as shown in the third branch. In the output section of the third branch the same FORMAT statement is used as that in the second branch, i.e., statement 21. This is permissible. FORMAT statements are not executable, and they may appear at any point in the Fortran program list. They may even

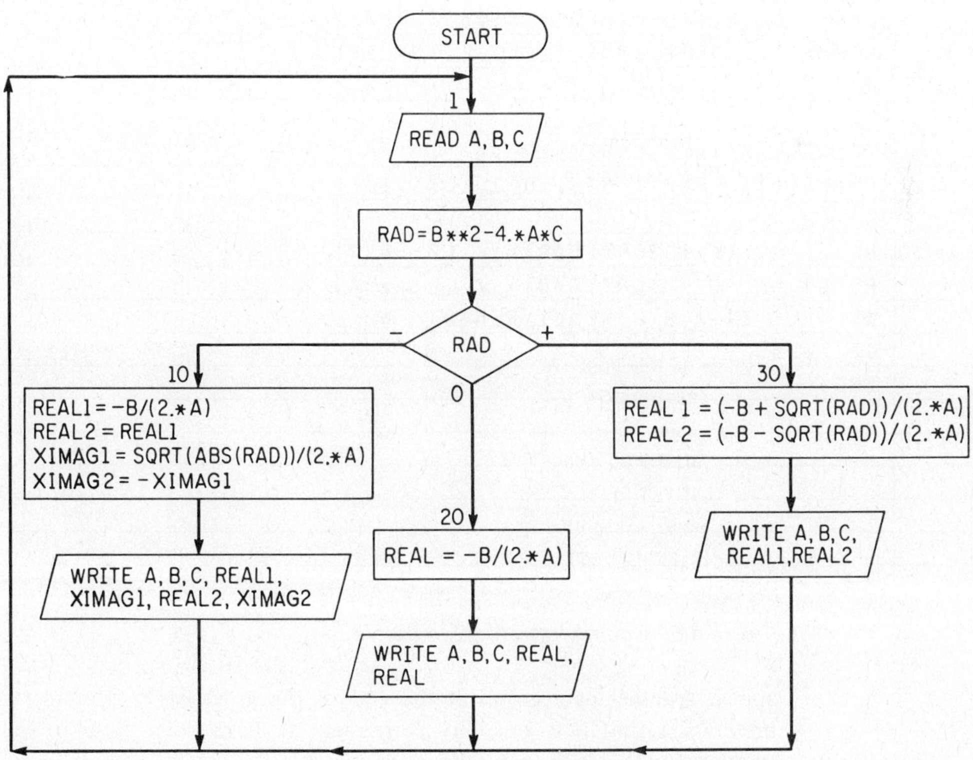

Figure 4-5. Flowchart for Example 4-3 (roots of a quadratic equation)

```
C     EXAMPLE PROGRAM TØ CALCULATE RØØTS ØF A QUADRATIC USING AN
C              ARITHMETIC IF STATEMENT
C
C     INPUT ØF CØEFFICIENTS
C
    1 READ(5,100)A,B,C
  100 FØRMAT(3F10.1)
C
C     CALCULATE RADICAL
C
      RAD = B **2 - 4. * A * C
C
C     CHECK VALUE ØF RADICAL
C
      IF(RAD)10,20,30
C
C     THREE BRANCHES
C
   10 REAL1 = -B / (2. * A)
      REAL2 = REAL1
      XIMAG1 = SQRT(ABS(RAD))/ (2. * A)
      XIMAG2 = - XIMAG1
      WRITE(6,11)A,B,C,REAL1,XIMAG1,REAL2,XIMAG2
   11 FØRMAT(1X,3F10.1, 5X, 2F10.2,10X,2F10.2)
      GØ TØ 1
   20 REAL = -B / (2. * A)
      WRITE(6,21)A,B,C,REAL,REAL
   21 FØRMAT(1X,3F10.1,5X,F10.2,10X,F10.2)
      GØ TØ 1
   30 REAL1 = (-B + SQRT(RAD)) / (2. * A)
      REAL2 = (-B - SQRT(RAD)) / (2. * A)
      WRITE(6,21)A,B,C,REAL1,REAL2
      GØ TØ 1
      END
         1.        7.        6.
         1.       12.       37.
         1.        2.        1.
```

Figure 4-6. Coding form for Example 4-3

appear together as a group at the end of the program. Programmers exhibit individual preferences, but it is generally convenient to have them close to the input or output statement with which they are associated.

This program also suffers from the last-card execution error shown in Examples 4-1 and 4-2.

In order to illustrate this program, some typical data are shown, and for these three sets of data the output results are shown.

```
1.0     7.0     6.0    -1.00           -6.00
1.0    12.0    37.0    -6.00    1.00                  -6.00     -1.00
1.0     2.0     1.0    -1.00           -1.00
 ERROR    (STATEMENT      1+     0 LINES)
```

4-5. Logical IF

The logical IF statement‡ is the last statement for transfer of control that is considered in this chapter. The logical IF statement has the general form

IF(*e*)S

where *e* is a Boolean (logical) expression with the value of true or false, and S is any statement except another logical IF statement, an arithmetic IF statement (allowable in some versions), or a DO statement. (The DO statement is considered in a subsequent chapter.) If the expression which comprises the argument of the logical IF statement is true, statement S is executed next, and then the next statement following the logical IF statement is executed unless the S statement itself is an arithmetic IF (if allowed) or a GO TO statement which would modify the normal sequence of execution. If *e* is false, the statement immediately following the logical IF statement is executed next. The Boolean expression *e* is a *logical expression* and these logical expressions are normally formed by the use of *relational operators* in order to write *relational expressions.* Typical questions are, for example, "is *x* greater than or equal to 3.14?" or "is *i* equal to *j*?" In order to form such logical expressions the following relational operators are available:

Relational Operator	*Meaning*
.LT.	Less than
.LE.	Less than or equal to
.EQ.	Equal to
.NE.	Not equal to
.GT.	Greater than
.GE.	Greater than or equal to

These relational operators may be used for both real and integer variables, but a change of mode is not normally permitted across a relational operator.

The periods in these relational operators are essential and are inserted to differentiate relational operators from identical variable names which may inadvertently have been chosen by the programmer.

The logical IF statement's usefulness is extended by the combination of *logical operators* such as .AND., .OR., and .NOT. with relational operators. These logical operators are used as follows: suppose that we desire to go to statement number 267 if X is greater than Y and if X is also greater than or equal to Z. If both of these conditions are not met, then the next statement to be executed should be the statement following the logical IF statement. This situation can be programmed into a single logical IF statement

```
IF (X.GT.Y.AND.X.GE.Z)GO TO 267
```

‡Some smaller Fortran compilers do not provide logical IF statement capabilities.

If *both* conditions are met, statement 267 will be executed; and if *either* of the conditions are not met, the next statement to be executed will be the one immediately following the logical IF statement.

Although it is not normally possible to mix arithmetic modes in logical expressions, it is normally allowable to have logical expressions of different arithmetic modes connected by a logical operator, e.g., the following example is correct:

IF (X.GT.Y.AND.I.GE.J)GO TO 267

In a similar fashion the .OR. operator is satisfied if *either* or *both* of the logical expressions it connects are true, and the .NOT. operator reverses the truth value of the expression it modifies. As an example of the use of the .NOT. operator, the expression

IF (.NOT.(X.LT.Y))X = Z

has exactly the same value as the logical IF statement

IF (X.GE.Y)X = Z

since "not less than" means the same as "greater than or equal to."

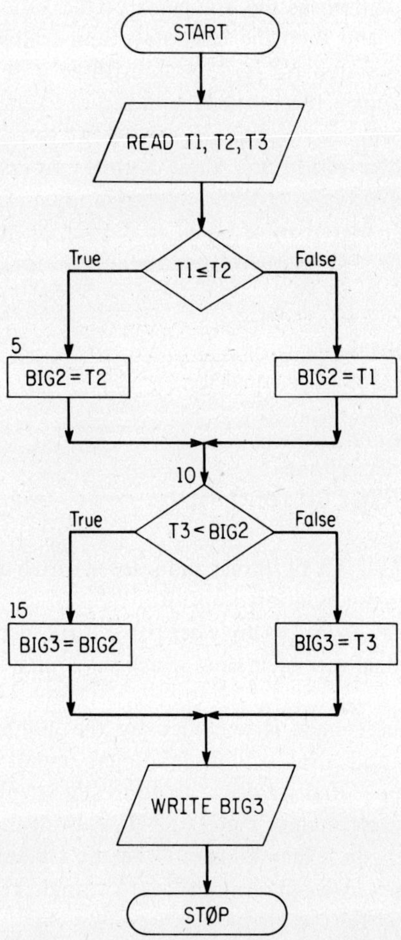

Figure 4-7. Flowchart for Example 4-4 (selecting the largest of three temperatures)

```
C EXAMPLE PRØBLEM TØ SELECT THE LARGEST ØF THREE TEMPERATURES
C
C READ IN THE THREE TEMPERATURES
C
      READ(5,1)T1,T2,T3
    1 FØRMAT(3F10.2)
C
C SELECT THE LARGER OF TWØ
C
      IF(T1.LE.T2)GØ TØ 5
      BIG2 = T1
      GØ TØ 10
    5 BIG2 = T2
C
C CØMPARE THE LARGER ØF TWØ WITH THE THIRD
C
   10 IF(T3.LT.BIG2) GØ TØ 15
      BIG3 = T3
      GØ TØ 20
   15 BIG3 = BIG2
C
C ØUTPUT ØF RESULTS
C
   20 WRITE(6,2) BIG3
    2 FØRMAT(F20.2)
      STØP
      END
72.46     81.27     74.21
```

(Lines from "C SELECT THE LARGER OF TWØ" through "15 BIG3 = BIG2" bracketed) OR:

```
      BIG3=T1
      IF(T2.GT.BIG3)BIG3=T2
      IF(T3.GT.BIG3)BIG3=T3
```

Figure 4-8. Coding form for Example 4-4

Logical IF statements are useful tools available to the user of Fortran IV (they are not available in earlier versions of Fortran), and the student should become familiar with them. Questions relative to the hierarchy of relational expressions and logical operators are covered in Appendix A.

EXAMPLE 4-4

As an example of the logical IF statement, consider the problem in which we intend to make three readings of air temperature during a six-hour period and use the computer to select the largest (highest) of these three temperatures. The computer will do nothing more than select the largest of the temperatures and write it out as an answer. The three input temperatures are in F10.2 format, and the output answer is to be in F20.2 format. The flowchart is shown in Figure 4-7, and the computer program is shown in Figure 4-8.

The structure of the computer program is based on using a logical IF statement to compare two of the temperatures and select the larger of these two. The larger of these two temperatures is then compared to the third temperature in order to select the highest temperature for the six-hour period. To select the larger of two temperatures a logical IF statement is used with the .LE. operator. Based on the use of this operator an intermediate variable BIG2 is calculated. A second logical IF statement is used to compare BIG2 with T3 in order to select BIG3, the highest of the three temperatures. In the second logical IF statement the .LT. operator is used although the .LE. operator also could have been used. Note from the alternative in Figure 4-8 that the manner in which the programming is done has a significant effect on the number of statements required.

In the output format statement the single temperature that was selected as being the highest is written out as BIG3 in F20.2 format. Since this variable, of necessity, is one of the original three temperatures read into the computer, it cannot possibly occupy twenty spaces since there were only ten spaces in the input field. The output answer will be right justified in the space available, and there will be at least ten blank spaces to the left of the output field. Since this is guaranteed, there is no need to provide a blank space in column 1 of the FORMAT statement of the output record. Unpredictable carriage control is prevented since this column will always be blank. The output result for the example set of data on this problem is, of course, 81.27.

This example illustrates the nature of the logical IF statement and its usage in a simple program. It may be pointed out that the problem proposed is a rather trivial one in terms of justification for the usage of the computer, but it does illustrate the programming concepts.

4-6. Simple Counters

One of the principal applications of integers in Fortran programming is in counting the repeated execution of a set of instructions, i.e., the counting of *iterations* of a program. In Example 4-1 the use of a loop in the program caused the computer to repeat the calculations over and over. When the last data card was read, the computer gave an execution error indicating a last-card error which was unavoidable with the programming knowledge available at that time. This problem can be avoided by the use of simple counters.

Suppose it is planned in advance to read in 100 sets of input data to the program of Example 4-1. A counter can be incorporated into the program for this problem, and the program can check at the end of each set of calculations to see if it has, in fact, run 100 data sets. Before reading in the first data set a counter variable, defined as I, could be set equal to zero, and on each execution of the READ statement the value of this integer counter I could be incremented by one. At the end of the program's calculation statements an arithmetic IF statement can be inserted to check on the arithmetic expression (I – 100). If this quantity is negative, control can be transferred back to the beginning of the program; if it is zero or positive, control can be transferred to a STOP statement at the end of the program. This action will prevent a last-card execution error, and it illustrates how counters may be used in programming.

Another example of a counter is in keeping track of the number of times that a computer program iterates through some trial-and-error calculation before an answer is achieved. The value of the counter can be printed out at the end of the calculations to give the programmer an indication of the quality of convergence which he has achieved in his program. Another typical use of the counter is to set an upper limit on the number of trials which may be run in a trial-and-error computation. For example, it may be desirable to use a trial-and-error method to find the roots of a polynomial by some typical root solving technique. Since it is entirely possible that these techniques converge very slowly, the programmer may desire to set an upper limit on the number of trials, 200, for example. It may be desirable to punch out the values of the roots at this stage of the trial-and-error calculation regardless of whether exact convergence has been achieved or not. These types of applications of the counter are typical and in no way limit their overall usage. Counters are extremely powerful tools for the programmer.

EXAMPLE 4-5

A single example will be sufficient to illustrate two different uses of the counter. Assume there are three separate data cards, each containing a single angle expressed in radians. Assume further that the value of these angles, all of which are positive, can vary quite widely. The purpose of the program is to read in each of these angles, one at a time, and subtract 2π radians (360°) from each one a sufficient number of times to reduce it to

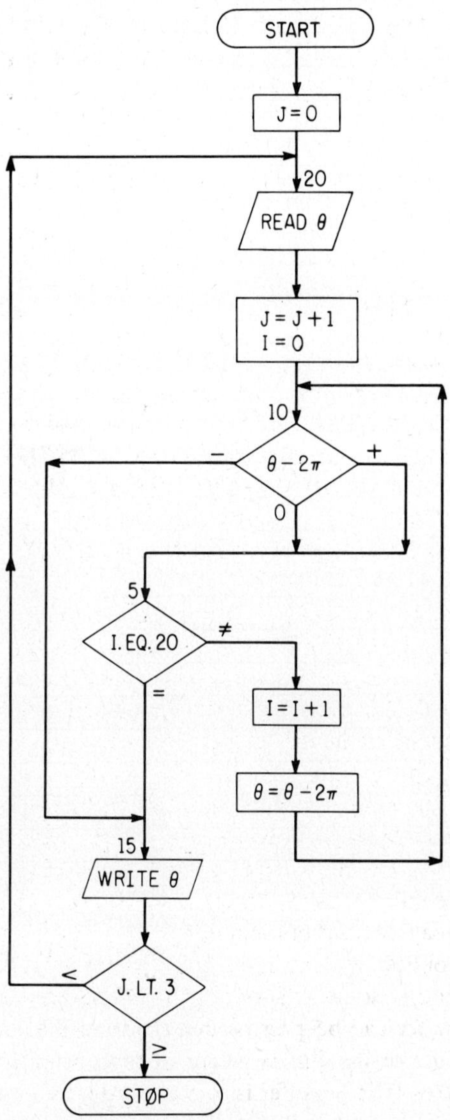

Figure 4-9. Flowchart for Example 4-5 (angle reduction)

```
C    EXAMPLE PRØBLEM TØ REDUCE ANGLES
C
C    INITIALIZE CØUNTER FØR RECØRDING NUMBER ØF DATA CARDS READ
C
      J = 0
C
C    INPUT ØF ØNE CARD
C
   20 READ(5,100)THETA
  100 FØRMAT(F20.5)
C
C    INCREMENT CARD CØUNTER AND SET ITERATIØN CØUNTER FØR THIS CARD
C
      J = J + 1
      I = 0
C
C    REDUCE THE ANGLE AS NECESSARY
C
   10 IF(THETA - 2. * 3.14159)15,5,5
    5 IF(I.EQ.20) GØ TØ 15
      I = I + 1
      THETA = THETA - 2. * 3.14159
      GØ TØ 10
C
C    ØUTPUT ØF ANGLE
C
   15 WRITE(6,200)THETA
  200 FØRMAT(1X,F20.5)
C
C    CHECK TØ SEE IF THERE ARE MØRE DATA CARDS
C
      IF(J.LT.3) GØ TØ 20
      STØP
      END
              3.4
          398.2
          100.00
```

Figure 4-10. Coding form for Example 4-5

an angle less than 2π radians. A counter will be used to instruct the computer to READ the three data cards, one at a time, before it completely stops its calculations.

It was previously stated that it is possible to use a counter as a means of setting an upper limit on the number of trial iterations that might be carried out in a particular loop of a program. The usage of counters also can be illustrated in this particular example by subtracting 2π radians from the angle no more than twenty times. After having made this reduction of the angle (call it θ) by 2π radians twenty times, if θ is still greater than 2π radians the reduced value of θ will be written on an output record.

The problem requires two counters as defined: one to handle the count of the number of data cards that have been read into the machine, and a second to keep track of the number of iterations made on any single data card. The flowchart for the program is given in Figure 4-9, and the computer program necessary to make these calculations is shown in Figure 4-10. It is first necessary to initialize the counter for reading data cards. Once this has been done it is possible to READ a card and set the values of both counters for that particular data card. The reductions of θ are then made, and on each reduction of the angle the counter I (used to keep track of the number of iterations) is incremented by one. In each iteration through the computation a check is made on the value of θ to see if it is less than 2π radians, and a separate check is made on the value of the iteration counter I. Once θ falls within its prescribed limits or the necessary number of iterations have been made, control is transferred to the output section of the program where the current value of θ is written on an output record. After θ has been written, a check is made to see if there are more data cards to be processed by using an IF statement on the data card counter J. If more data cards are to be processed, the flow of control is transferred back to the READ statement; if not, transfer is made to the STOP statement.

For the typical values of input data shown, the results are

```
  3.40000
272.53589
  5.75220
```

4-7. In Summary

This chapter has been devoted to some of the powerful statements that are available in Fortran programming, and the usage of these transfer of control statements unlocks the powerful tools of the computer. The GO TO statements and the IF statements have been discussed in some detail, and it is now assumed that the student has them at his command. As the student becomes more familiar with these powerful transfer of control statements, the logical structure of his program becomes more complex and the usage of flowcharts to illustrate the structure of his program becomes increasingly important.

It is recommended that the student carefully study the example problems worked out in this chapter. As stated at the end of an earlier chapter, it is important that the student make a number of separate, although simple, uses of the types of statements introduced in order to gain complete confidence in his ability to use them.

EXERCISES‡

4-1. Most of the exercises at the end of Chapter 3 were presented as cases in which only one set of input data was available. Assume that there are many sets of input data available for these exercises. You are to indicate how the computer programs would have to be written in order to process these multiple data sets using an unconditional GO TO statement for

‡Solutions to Exercises marked with a dagger † are given in Appendix E.

(a) 3-9
(b) 3-13
†(c) 3-15
(d) 3-17
(e) 3-20

4.2. A computer program is set up to calculate insurance premiums for various employees in a plant. The necessary calculations are dependent on the number of children which an employee has, i.e., 0, 1, 2, 3, or "more than 3." Set up the general outline of this program much as is done in Figures 4-3 and 4-4, using a computed GO TO statement.

†**4-3.** The age of a person is one of the principal factors in determining caloric intake requirements. Assume that a person's age is one part of input data to a program to make this type of calculation. Depending on whether the person is 0-10, 11-20, . . . , or 91-100, there will be an appropriate set of calculations. Use a computed GO TO to select the appropriate branch, and outline the program as in Figures 4-3 and 4-4.

Note: For all the following exercises you are to read in the given variables, perform the desired calculations, and write out the results as directed. Write complete Fortran programs including a trial data card(s).

4-4. Read in x and y. If $x > y$, set $z = 1$; if $x < y$, set $z = 2$; and if $x = y$, set $z = 3$. Write out x, y, and z. Assume there are many data cards, each containing a value of x and y. Use an arithmetic IF statement(s) to make the necessary decision(s). Be certain to draw a flowchart.

4-5. Repeat Exercise 4-4 using a logical IF statement(s).

†**4-6.** A number of data cards are available, each containing three adjacent values of the ordinates on a curve. Use an arithmetic IF statement(s) to check each set to see if a local maximum is present, i.e., if $y_2 > y_1$ and $y_2 > y_3$. If a local maximum is present in the input data set, write out the three ordinates. If no local maximum is present, do not write out anything and go to a new data set. Be certain to draw a flowchart.

4-7. Repeat Exercise 4-6 using a logical IF statement(s).

4-8. A number of data cards are available, each containing a value of the variable x. Use a logical IF containing two relational operators with the logical operator .AND. to see if $1 \leqslant x \leqslant 99$. If x is within this range, add the value of x to a running sum of all of the values of x contained on the input data cards, write out the current value of the sum, and read in a new data card. If x is outside the specified range, subtract 99 from x, add the reduced value of x to the running sum, write out the value of the sum, and read in a new data card. Be certain to draw a flowchart.

4-9. Repeat Exercise 4-8 using only one test in the logical IF in conjunction with the absolute value function.

4-10. Read in the real part (a) and imaginary part (b) of a complex number which are both contained on the same data card. The number is assumed to be in rectangular notation $(a + ib)$ and is to be converted to trigonometric notation $(re^{i\alpha})$ by

$$\alpha = \tan^{-1} b/a$$
$$r = \sqrt{a^2 + b^2}$$

where the equivalence of $(a + ib)$ and $(re^{i\alpha})$ notation is implied. Write out a, b, α, r, and K for the number, where

$K = 1$ if $\alpha < 90°$ and $r < 1$
$K = 2$ if $\alpha < 90°$ and $r \geqslant 1$
$K = 3$ if $90 \leqslant \alpha < 180°$ and $r < 1$
$K = 4$ if $90° \leqslant \alpha < 180°$ and $r \geqslant 1$
$K = 5$ if $180° \leqslant \alpha < 270°$ and $r < 1$
$K = 6$ if $180° \leqslant \alpha < 270°$ and $r \geqslant 1$
$K = 7$ if $270° \leqslant \alpha < 360°$ and $r < 1$
$K = 8$ if $270° \leqslant \alpha < 360°$ and $r \geqslant 1$

Use only arithmetic IF statements. Assume there are many input data cards, each containing a value of a and a value of b. Be certain to draw a flowchart.

4-11. Repeat Exercise 4-10, using logical IF statements.

†**4-12.** Read in a data card containing an initial value of x, a final value of x, and an increment on x. Write out these three values of x and then calculate y as a function of x:

$$y = 1 + x + \frac{x^2}{2!} + \frac{x^3}{3!} + \sin(x)$$

where x's first value is x initial. Keep calculating y for values of x (in each case adding the increment on x to the old value of x) until x exceeds the final value of x. In each calculation write out y and the value of x used to calculate y. When x exceeds the final value of x, read in a new data card and start over. Be certain to draw a flowchart.

4-13. Repeat Exercise 4-12, except that you are directed to stop calculating y whenever y exceeds 100 *or* when x final has been exceeded, whichever occurs first.

4-14. Set up a counter on Exercise 4-4 to handle four input data cards.

†**4-15.** Set up a counter on Exercise 4-6 to handle seven input data cards.

4-16. Set up a counter on Exercise 4-8 to handle five input data cards.

4-17. Set up a counter on Exercise 4-10 to handle six input data cards.

4-18. Set up a counter on Exercise 4-12 to handle three input data cards. Also add an iteration counter to stop calculations on a given set of input data if y is calculated as a function of x more than fifty times.

†**4-19.** An alternate way to determine when a particular input data card is the last card is to define a new input variable, e.g., N. Use a value of N as zero as a basis for reading in a new data card and a value of N as 1 as a basis for stopping the program. N will have to be included on each input card but since a zero value indicates further processing, N will only have to be punched on the last input data card. Do this for Exercise 4-6.

4-20. Repeat Exercise 4-19 for Exercise 4-8.

5

Introduction to DO Loops and to Subscripted Variables

Many technical problems require identical or very similar calculations to be repeated several times. Examples include searches for solutions of nonlinear equations, numerical solutions of differential equations, matrix multiplication, or simply solving the same problem for different values of the input data or parameters. As such repetitive operations are very common, a special feature, the DO loop, should be mastered at an early stage in programming. Actually, counters constructed around the IF statement as discussed in the previous chapter will accomplish the same tasks as the DO loop, but the latter is much more convenient. In addition to the DO loop, this chapter will introduce subscripted variables, a powerful and convenient way to handle large quantities of data.

5-1. Definition of DO Loops

Suppose the sum of all whole numbers from 1 to 100

$$\sum_{i=1}^{100} i$$

is to be calculated and stored in NSUM. Using the counters previously described, this can be programmed as a counter. (See Figure 5-1.) Note that five statements are required, three of which are necessary to form the counter.

This example illustrates that the DO statement is very convenient. Using the DO, this problem can be programmed as in Figure 5-1. Now only three statements are required.

The analogy between the counter and the DO can give insight into the operation of the DO, and it is used for that purpose in the ensuing explanation. The general form of the DO statement is as follows:

$$\text{DO } m\ i = n_1,\ n_2,\ n_3$$

In this statement m is the statement number of the *last statement* under control of the DO. In the example of the last paragraph m corresponds to 23. It is necessary that m be a statement number; it *cannot* be a variable. The *index* i of the DO is a *nonsubscripted integer variable.* The index of the DO in the above example is I, which is also used to form the counter. The value of the index upon initiation of the DO is given by n_1, which must be a *nonsubscripted integer variable* or a *positive integer constant.* In the previous example the index I is initiated at one, which corresponds to the statement I = 1 in forming the counter. The final value of the index is given by n_2, which also must be either a *nonsubscripted integer variable* or a *positive integer constant.* In the above example n_2 is 100. In the counter the final value is dictated by the statement IF (I.LE.100) GO TO 23. Finally, n_3 is the amount by which the index is incremented between iterations. In the above example n_3 is one, which is specified for the counter by the statement I = I + 1. If n_3 is not specified in the DO statement, it is assumed to be one. Thus the DO statement for the above example can be

$$\text{DO 23 I} = 1{,}100$$

Nothing else may be omitted. *Note carefully the location of commas.* No comma appears between the statement number and the index of the DO, but the indexing parameters (n_1, n_2 and n_3) must be separated by commas.

The DO statement DO 23 I = 1,100,1 can be read as follows: DO through statement 23 beginning with I equal to one and repeat from the DO statement, incrementing I by one, until I equals 100. The first time the DO is executed, I equals one; on the final execution I equals 100.

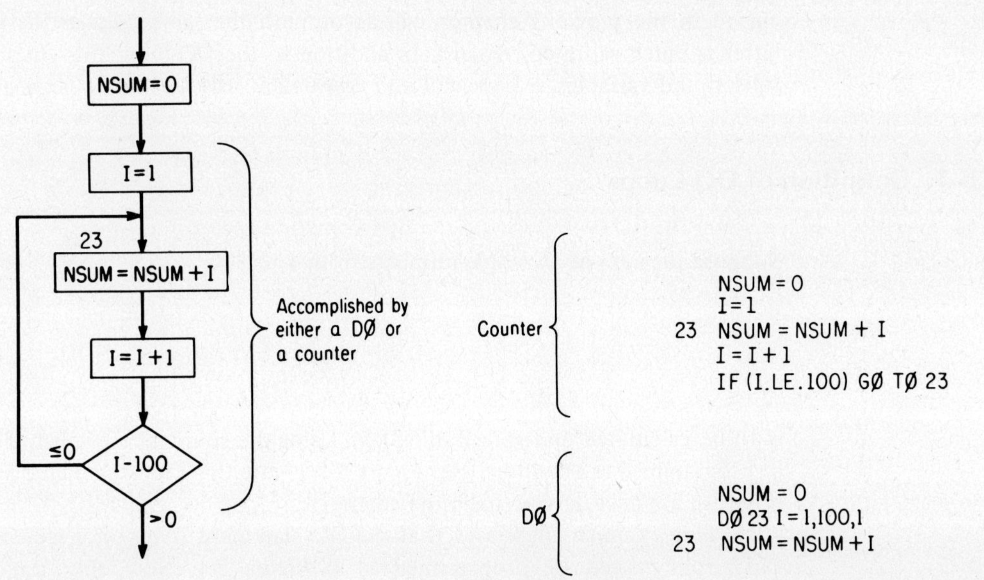

(a) Flowchart *(b) Equivalent parts of the counter and the DO*

Figure 5-1. Analogy between the DO and the counter

5-2. Complete Examples

Before continuing with other details of the DO, a complete program requiring a DO statement should clarify a few points. Consider the simple case in which five real variables are read (each from a separate card), their sum and average computed, and the average printed. The flowchart, the complete program, and possible data cards are shown in Figure 5-2. In this example two statements are in the *range* of the DO. The range begins with the first statement following the DO and ends with the one whose statement number is specified by the DO. The term *DO loop* denotes all statements in the range of the DO plus the DO statement itself. Note that upon completion of the DO, execution proceeds with the first executable statement following the DO loop.

As another example, consider the computation of the consumption of a quantity such as electric power. The data are the customer number, the reading of his meter at the

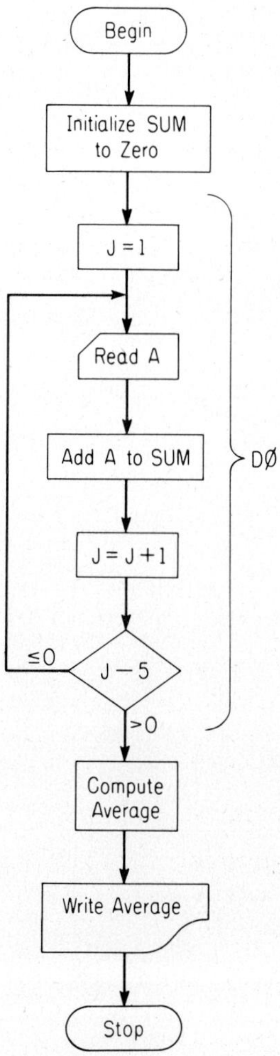

(a) Flowchart

```
C      FIGURE 5-2 CALCULATION OF AVERAGE
C
C      INITIALIZE SUM TO ZERO
C
       SUM=0.
C
C      CONSTRUCT DO LOOP TO READ THE VALUE FOR
C      A AND ADD TO SUM
C
       DO2J=1,5
       READ(5,3)A
     2 SUM=SUM+A
C
C      COMPUTE AVERAGE AND WRITE
C
       AVG=SUM/5.
       WRITE(6,4)AVG
       STOP
C
C      FORMAT STATEMENTS
C
     3 FORMAT(F5.0)
     4 FORMAT(1X,F12.4)
       END
```

(b) Complete program

```
1.
5.
12.2
-3.
.161
```

(c) Input data

```
3.0722
```

(d) Output

Figure 5-2. Calculation of average

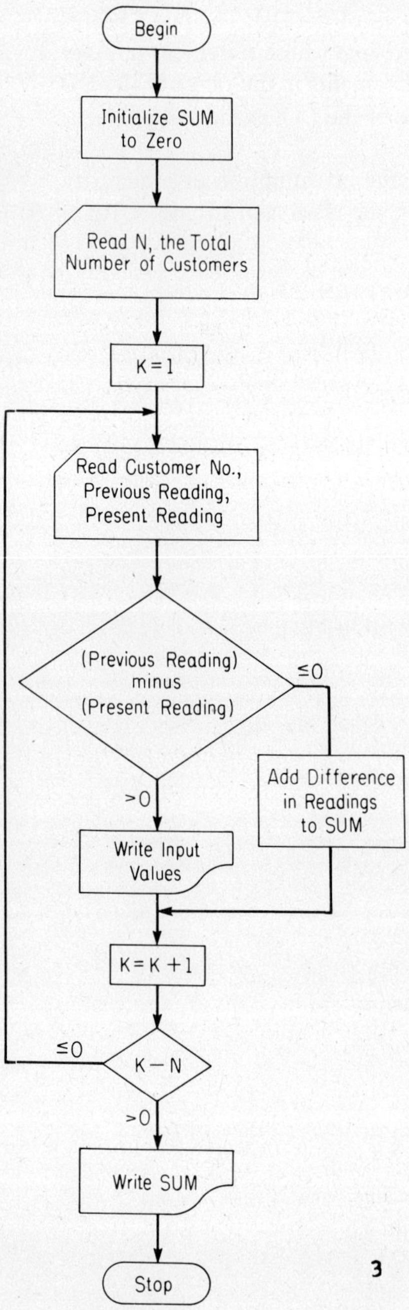

(a) Flowchart

```
C        FIGURE 5-3
C        ELECTRIC CONSUMPTION
C
C        INITIALIZE SUM TO ZERO AND READ N,THE
C        NUMBER OF CUSTOMERS
C
         SUM=0.
         READ(5,1)N
C
C        DO LOOP FOR READING INPUT FOR EACH
C        CUSTOMER AND PROCESSING APPROPRIATELY
C
         DO2K=1,N
         READ(5,12)J,PREV,PRES
C
C        CHECK IF PREVIOUS READING IS GREATER
C        THAN PRESENT
C
         IF(PREV-PRES)7,7,8
C
C        COME HERE IF READING IS VALID. SUM IS
C        INCREMENTED.
C
      7  SUM=SUM+(PRES-PREV)
         GOTO2
C
C        COME HERE IF READING IS INVALID. PRINT
C        THE INPUT VALUES.
C
      8  WRITE(6,3)J,PREV,PRES
C
C        DUMMY STATEMENT TO END DO LOOP
C
      2  CONTINUE
C
C        OUTPUT
C
         WRITE(6,4)SUM
         STOP
C
C        FORMAT STATEMENTS
C
      1  FORMAT(I5)
      3  FORMAT(1X,I5,2F12.4)
      4  FORMAT(1X,F15.4)
     12  FORMAT(I5,2F10.0)
         END
```

(b) Complete program

```
4
1      12.1      30.7
2      14.6      26.1
3      27.7      20.1
4      20.0      22.3
```

(c) Input data

```
    3      27.7000      20.1000
        32.4000
```

(d) Output

Figure 5-3. Electric consumption

beginning of the month, and the reading of his meter at the end of the month. To calculate the kilowatt-hours consumed by each customer, the previous reading is subtracted from the present and the difference is added to the running sum. (See Figure 5-3a for flowchart.) Since a case in which the previous reading is higher than the present indicates an erroneous condition, the computer upon detecting such a case should print the customer number and the reading. (Note the branch within the DO loop in the flowchart in Figure 5-3a.) Furthermore, this entry should be ignored in calculating the total power consumption. Upon completion, the computer prints the total power used by all the customers.

The specific program and a few sample data cards, the first giving the number of customers, are given in Figure 5-3b. First the program reads the number of customers (the value of parameter n_2 in the DO statement) and then enters the DO loop. Upon each iteration, the program reads the customer number, the previous reading, and the present reading. If the previous reading is less than the present reading, the difference is added to the sum, and the loop is repeated. If not, the customer and reading are printed, and the loop is repeated.

Note the use of the CONTINUE statement as a dummy statement to end the range of the DO. Use of the CONTINUE (or another dummy statement) to terminate the range of the DO loop as in the above example is frequently necessary. After the execution of either alternative of the DO, control must be transferred to the end of the range of the DO. Since the two alternatives have nothing in common, a dummy statement such as CONTINUE is required.‡ The CONTINUE statement is considered to be executable, but no machine language instructions are generated from this statement.

5-3. Further Clarification§

The following points regarding DO loops are worthy of special note:

1. The requirement that the initial, final, and incrementing values (n_1, n_2, n_3) specified by the DO statement be nonsubscripted integer variables or positive integer constants eliminates the following possibilities:

(a) DO 7 J = 1, N(I). The subscript is not allowed, but the same result can be obtained with the following two statements:

```
M = N(I)
DO 7 J = 1,M
```

(b) DO 7 J = 1, N + 2. A general rule to remember is that *no numerical calculations may be performed in the* DO *statement itself.* The desired result can be obtained by

```
M = N + 2
DO 7 J = 1,M
```

2. Consider the statement DO 1 I = 1,4,2. On the first pass, I = 1; on the second

‡Many compilers permit free use of the CONTINUE statement, while others, the IBM 360, for example, require that the CONTINUE statement have a statement number.

§In this section the idiosyncrasies of various Fortran IV compilers lead to some double-talk. Fortran IV compilers are available for many different computers, and the differences of opinion of the individuals who wrote the compilers are reflected by certain minor points of the DO being treated differently by different compilers. In a general manual such as this, the more common or safe variations are given.

pass, I = 3; on the third pass, I = 5. Consequently, I never equals four, the value for which the DO is satisfied. Will the DO be terminated after I equals three, after I equals five, or will it be terminated at all? The answer is clear after considering the *effective manner* in which the computer executes the DO. The behavior will be the same as when executing a counter of the following type:

```
    I = 1
  1 {range
     of
     DO}
    I = I + 2
    IF (I.LE.4) GO TO 1
```

From the above counter, it is apparent that I equals three on the last execution of the statements in the range of the DO, although the value of I is five when leaving the counter.

What will result from the following DO statement?

```
DO 7 I = 4,4
```

The statements within the range of the DO will be executed only once. However, the DO statement DO 7 I = 4,3 will generate an error and will not be executed by many Fortrans (note that a machine executing it according to the counter described in the previous paragraph would execute it once). These situations are sometimes encountered when variables are used as the indexing parameters n_1 and n_2.

3. The index of the DO may not be altered within the range of the DO. For example, consider the hypothetical case in which the ten elements in a one-dimensional array A are to be summed, except that the third element is to be omitted from the sum. The following statements are proposed:

```
    SUM = 0.
    DO 7 I = 1,10
    IF (I.EQ.3) I = I + 1
  7 SUM = SUM + A(I)
```

However, this series of statements will not be accepted by the compiler, as the IF statement attempts to change the index. Instead, the following procedure is appropriate:

```
    SUM = 0.
    DO 7 I = 1,10
    IF(I.EQ.3)GO TO 7
    SUM = SUM + A (I)
  7 CONTINUE
```

This accomplishes the same result, but does not tamper with the DO index. *The DO index is available for calculations within the range of the DO, but must not be altered by arithmetic statements or by reading a new value of the index within the range of the DO.* This same rule applies to the indexing parameters n_1, n_2, and n_3.

4. Control may be transferred outside the range of a DO by two methods. First, when the execution of the statements in the range of the DO as specified by the indexing parameters (n_1, n_2 and n_3) is accomplished, the DO is said to be satisfied and a *normal exit* is achieved. Control is simply transferred to the first executable statement following the DO loop. All examples cited previously involved normal exits.

However, it is possible to transfer control from within the range of the DO to a statement outside the range of the DO. Consider the following statements:

```
       DO 100 I = 1,20
       X = function(I,other variables)
       IF (X.GT.XLIMIT)GO TO 200
       WRITE (6,10)I,X
 10    FORMAT (1X,I10,E20.6)
100    CONTINUE
200    X = XLIMIT
```

If X never exceeds XLIMIT as I varies from one to twenty, a normal exit is made from the DO loop. If, however, X exceeds XLIMIT as I varies from one to twenty, control is transferred to statement 200.

In most Fortrans the index is not available after a normal exit, whereas the index is available after all other exits. This problem can be readily circumvented by setting another variable as equal to the index of the DO loop, for example N = I. The variable N will be retained outside the loop no matter what type of exit is made.

5. Control can be transferred to the statements within the range of a DO *only* by the DO statement. That is, the following sequence is not acceptable in most versions of Fortran IV:

```
      I = 5
      GO TO 7
      .
      .
      .
      DO 5 I = 1,12
7     (some valid statement)
      .
      .
      .
5     (Some valid statement)
```

It is, however, possible to re-enter a DO after an exit other than a normal exit, but no rules governing the DO may be violated between exit and re-entry.

6. The last statement in the range of the DO must be executable. The main mistake is the use of a FORMAT statement to terminate the DO loop.

7. The last statement in the range of the DO must *not* be a GO TO, an arithmetic IF, a STOP, or another DO statement. However, these may be used freely elsewhere within the range of the DO.

The use of a logical IF statement as the last statement in the range of the DO is permissible. Consider the following case:

```
      DO 7 I = 1,5
7     IF (t)s
```

where *t* is a logical expression that is either true or false and *s* is an executable statement. If the logical expression *t* is false, the DO index is incremented without executing *s*. If the logical statement is true, statement *s* is executed and the DO index incremented. However, if *s* were a transfer statement and *t* were true, the transfer is executed.‡

‡A few Fortrans will not accept transfer statements in a logical IF statement when it terminates the range of a DO. Even this uncertainty can be surmounted as follows:

```
      DO 7 I = 1,5
      IF(t)s
7     CONTINUE
```

8. The statement *s* used in a logical IF of the type

IF (t)s

may *not* be a DO statement.

EXAMPLE 5-1

Least-Squares Fit. In many applications a straight-line approximation to experimental data is considered, and the least-squares technique statistically ascertains the best fit. The observations consist of a value Y_i for the dependent variable corresponding to the value X_i for the independent variable. The total number of observations is N.

The procedure is as follows:

Average value of X

$$\overline{X} = \left[\sum_{i=1}^{N} X_i \right] \Big/ N$$

Average value of Y

$$\overline{Y} = \left[\sum_{i=1}^{N} Y_i \right] \Big/ N$$

Corrected sum of squares

$$\sum_{i=1}^{N} x_i^2 = \sum_{i=1}^{N} X_i^2 - \frac{\left(\sum_{i=1}^{N} X_i \right)^2}{N}$$

Corrected sum of cross product

$$\sum_{i=1}^{N} x_i y_i = \sum_{i=1}^{N} X_i Y_i - \frac{\left(\sum_{i=1}^{N} X_i \right) \left(\sum_{i=1}^{N} Y_i \right)}{N}$$

Slope

$$b = \frac{\sum_{i=1}^{N} x_i y_i}{\sum_{i=1}^{N} x_i^2}$$

Intercept

$$a = \overline{Y} - b\overline{X}$$

where a and b are coefficients for the linear approximating equation $Y = a + bX$.

A program is to be prepared that reads N from the first card, followed by the N observations (i.e., X and corresponding Y entered one observation per card.) The flowchart and the detailed program are shown in Figure 5-4.

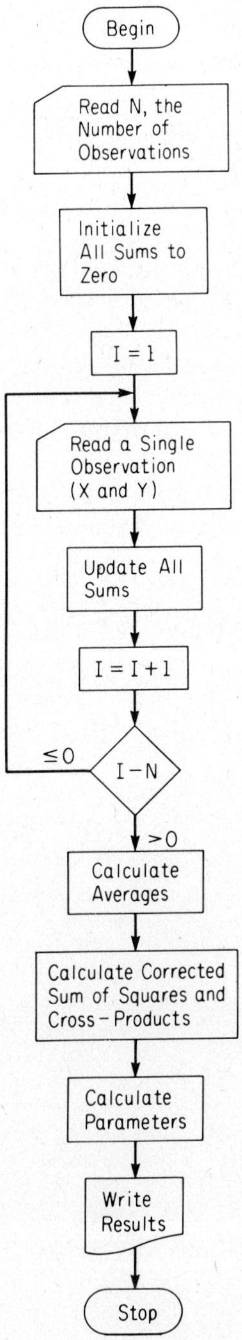

(a) Flowchart

```
C        READ NUMBER OF DATA POINTS,N
C
         READ(5,1)N
C
C        DEFINE FLOATING POINT VARIABLE AN EQUAL
C        TO N
C
         AN=N
C
C        INITIALIZE ALL SUMS TO ZERO
C
         SUMX=0.
         SUMY=0.
         SUMXY=0.
         SUMXX=0.
C
C        THE FOLLOWING DO LOOP READS THE INPUT
C        VALUES AND CALCULATES THE SUMS
C
         DO2I=1,N
         READ(5,3)X,Y
         SUMX=SUMX+X
         SUMY=SUMY+Y
         SUMXY=SUMXY+X*Y
       2 SUMXX=SUMXX+X**2
C
C        COMPUTE AVERAGES
C
         XAV=SUMX/AN
         YAV=SUMY/AN
C
C        COMPUTE CORRECTED SUMS AND CROSS PRODUCTS
C
         CSCP=SUMXY-SUMX*SUMY/AN
         CSS=SUMXX-SUMX**2/AN
C
C        CALCULATE FIT PARAMETERS AND PRINT
C
         B=CSCP/CSS
         A=YAV-B*XAV
         WRITE(6,4)A,B
         STOP
C
C        FORMAT STATEMENTS
C
       1 FORMAT(I3)
       3 FORMAT(2F10.0)
       4 FORMAT(1X,2E20.8)
         END
```

(b) Complete program

```
  5
1.          2.1
2.          3.9
4.          7.7
6.          13.
9.          18.
```

(c) Input data

```
-0.33009171E-01        0.20393263E 01
```

(d) Output data

Figure 5-4. Least-squares analysis

As subsequent calculations are in floating point, a floating-point variable AN is defined equal to the fixed-point variable N immediately following the READ statement. The sums are all initialized at zero, and the sums are calculated as the data is entered.

5-4. Usefulness of Subscripted Variables

One of the most powerful features of Fortran IV is the capability of using subscripted variables. Use of subscripted variables gives the programmer an easy and flexible means to handle complex tasks involving large amounts of data with a minimum of programming effort. The ability to feel at ease in the use of subscripted variables is an absolute necessity for a Fortran programmer.

The need for subscripted variables and the motiviation for their use may be understood best by means of an example. Consider the rather elementary problem shown in Figure 5-5 in which it is desired to find the area under the curve $y = f(x)$ when y is an irregular curve. This is typically done by numerical integration, and the procedure involved is breaking the area under the curve into a large number of small, thin regular elements.

Often the small elements are considered to be rectangles, but one of the more popular methods considers the individual elements to be trapezoids. In the case of a trapezoid the area of an individual element can be considered to be $0.5\,(y_i + y_{i+1})h$. Summing all the individual intervals between the limits a and b on the curve, the area is then given as

$$\text{Area} = \int_a^b f(x)dx = \frac{h}{2} \sum_{i=1}^{n} (y_i + y_{i+1}) = \frac{b-a}{2n} \sum_{i=1}^{n} (y_i + y_{i+1})$$

The computation outlined by the formula for the area under the curve is relatively straightforward and is one that is extremely well suited for a computer. It is necessary to read in all the appropriate y values and the width of the elements h (or a, b, and n).

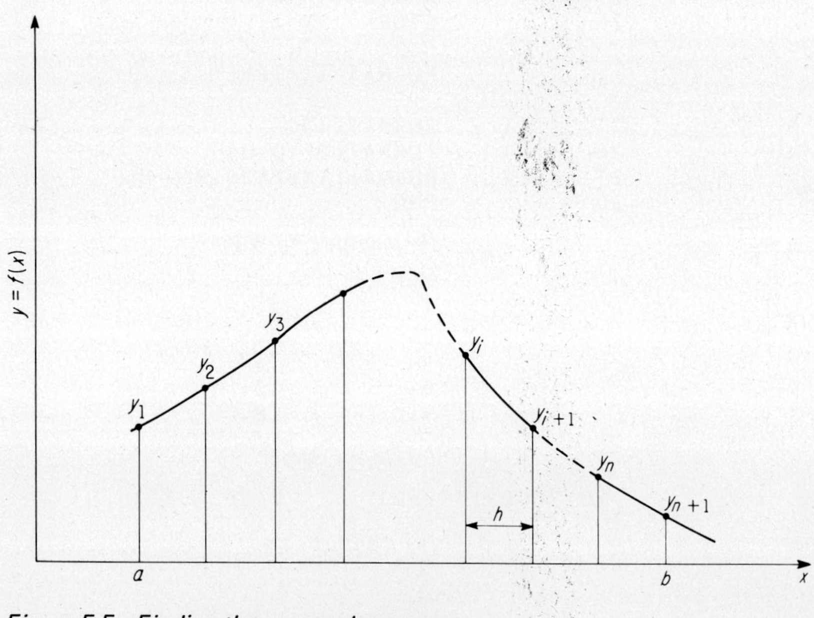

Figure 5-5. Finding the area under a curve

In carrying out this numerical integration, assume that there are forty values of y available as points on the curve. The numerical integration of these points can be accomplished using the tools that were developed in earlier chapters. The points can be named Y1, Y2, Y3, . . . , Y40, and these forty individual and distinct variables can be read into the computer separately. Once in the computer they are summed using the formula for the area. In such an approach the area can be computed by an arithmetic assignment statement, but it might be noted that this arithmetic assignment statement is quite long, since it would involve terms for each of the forty values of y. Such an arithmetic assignment statement can be written (using continuation statements), but this approach to the problem represents a strong-arm approach to a simple problem. An alternate way to program this calculation using tools already introduced is to read one value of y at a time, add it to the sum, and then read the next value of y. In this manner only one value of y is in memory at one time.

The type of problem illustrated above can be handled easily and with facility by the use of subscripted variables, and this will be the solution approach employed. Subscripted variables are not new to scientists and engineers because they are accustomed to working with large *arrays* of data in which the individual *elements* of the arrays are indicated by subscripts. It is done in this manner to simplify cumbersome problems in notation. We have done this in the integration problem mentioned earlier by referring to the values as $y_1, y_2, \ldots, y_i, \ldots, y_{40}$. Fortran provides the same possibility for handling subscripted variables with minor changes in notation. Instead of writing the values of y as indicated above (conventional mathmematical notation), Fortran subscript notation can be used to write Y(1), Y(2), Y(3), . . . , Y(I), . . . , Y(40). We take values of y and indicate them as being elements of a one-dimensional array with forty elements. The subscript of the

```
      AREA = 0.
      XN = N
      PREFIX = (B-A)/(2. * XN)
      I = 1                                       DØ 200 I = 1,N,1
  200 AREA = PREFIX * (Y(I) + Y(I + 1)) + AREA    200 AREA = PREFIX* .....
      I = I + 1
      IF(I.LE.N) GØ TØ 200
```

Figure 5-6. Statements to calculate the area under a curve

individual element of the array is enclosed in parentheses immediately following the name of the array, and this subscript is illustrated as an integer constant and as an integer variable. Using subscripted variables, the summation indicated by the area formula can be accomplished by the series of statements shown in Figure 5-6.

As indicated in subsequent sections of this chapter, the problems associated with the input and output of the array of information used in Figure 5-6 can be simplified. Referring to Figure 5-6 and noting the ease with which the area of the thirty-nine individual trapezoids created by the forty points has been summed should help in gaining an insight to the use of subscripted variables. The advantage gained if there are a thousand (or more) data points is obvious since the complexity of the subscripted variable program is not increased.

5-5. Definitions and Subscript Arguments

Many quantities may be represented with one variable name through the use of subscripts as indicated in the previous section. Only one-dimensional arrays are considered in this chapter, with two- and higher-dimensional arrays reserved for the next chapter. For convenience in orienting the individual's thinking, the one-dimensional array can be considered (in a geometric sense) as representing points along a line. Alternatively, it may be viewed as a column or a row of numbers, elements of which can be referenced by their position within the column or row.

A one-dimensional array will be referenced in a Fortran program by entries of the following form:

Name (Subscript)

The name of a subscripted variable follows the same rules as those for nonsubscripted variables. Furthermore, the variable name must not be identical to that of a Fortran function: SQRT, ABS, etc. It is important to note that all the elements of any given array must be of the same type. A subscripted variable may be integer or real, the type being specified by the first letter in the array name according to the rules for nonsubscripted variables.

Most Fortran systems allow only integer subscripts, but these may be integer constants, integer variables, or limited forms of integer arithmetic expressions. (Some advanced systems permit unlimited integer expressions and real subscripts.) The allowable forms of subscript arguments are restricted on most machines to the following, where I is used to indicate a nonsubscripted integer variable, and L and L′ are used to indicate unsigned integer constants.

General Form	*Example*
I	K2
L	6
I ± L	J + 6
L * I	6 * K
L * I ± L′	6 * K - 2

The value of the subscripted variable normally may not be less than one, nor may it be greater than the value dictated at the beginning of the program through the use of the DIMENSION statement (discussed in the next section). Fortran IV does not normally allow the variable in the subscript expression to be subscripted, but some advanced forms of automatic programming languages do allow this freedom.

Some examples of invalid subscripts are as follows:

GOGO (A - 2)	A is not an integer variable.
LSD (2 + I)	The variable must normally precede the constant, i.e., I + 2.
TD (-I)	The variable may not be signed.
VAR (I(J))	Subscripted subscript is not normally allowed.
VAR (I + J)	Variable plus variable addition is not normally allowed.

The operation of the Fortran compiler is such that each element in the array is associated with a unique memory address, and these addresses set aside these memory address locations and maintain a simple system for reference to any individual element of an array. For this reason it is necessary that the Fortran compiler know how many locations to allocate for an individual array, and this leads to the use of the DIMENSION statement which will be discussed in the next section.

For example, consider the following statements in a Fortran program:

```
.
.
Y(J) = C
.
.
.
A = Y(K)
.
.
```

The entries Y(J) and Y(K) refer to the same array, namely Y. Before the statement Y(J) = C can be executed, the integer variable J must have been defined previously in the program. Thus, the value of C is stored in the position in array Y corresponding to the numerical value of J when this statement is executed. Similarly, the variable K must be defined when the statement A = Y(K) is executed.

EXAMPLE 5-2

One crude indication of the expected value of a person's blood pressure is to add the age in years of the person to 100. Assume that we record the age and blood pressure of 200 men and arrange them in two arrays named PRESS and AGE. Use them to calculate a third array DIF, i.e., the difference between the man's actual blood pressure and the blood pressure given by the crude rule above. The ith element in DIF is given as

DIF(I) = PRESS(I) - (AGE(I) + 100.)

A portion of the computer program necessary to carry out this calculation is shown in Figure 5-7.

EXAMPLE 5-3

In geometry the distance between two points in a plane (a two-dimensional space) is given as

$$D = \sqrt{(x_1 - x_2)^2 + (y_1 - y_2)^2}$$

This may be generalized to a multidimensional space.

Two one-dimensional arrays named X and Y each contain fifty elements. Consider these to be coordinates of two points in a fifty-dimensional space. It is desired to

```
      I = 1
    5 DIF(I)+PRESS(I)-(AGE(I)+100.)
      I = I + 1
      IF(I.LE.200) GØ TØ 5
```

```
      DO 5 I=1,200
    5 DIF(1)=PRESS(I)-(AGE(I)+100.)
```

Figure 5-7. Statements for Example 5-2

calculate the following quantity, which might be referred to as a "distance function in 50-space":

$$D = \left[\sum_{i=1}^{50} (x_i - y_i)^2 \right]^{1/2}$$

where the x's are used to denote the coordinates of one point and the y's are used to denote the coordinates of the other point. A portion of the computer program necessary to carry out this calculation is shown in Figure 5-8.

5-6. The DIMENSION Statement

The use of subscripted variables in a Fortran program necessitates supplying information about the individual subscripted variables to the Fortran compiler. This information includes

1. The names of the variables to be subscripted
2. The number of subscripts to be used for each subscripted variable
3. The maximum value of each individual subscript for each individual subscripted variable

```
      I = 1
      D2= 0.
    5 D2= D2+ (X(I) - Y(I)) ** 2
      I = I + 1
      IF(I.LE.50) GØ TØ 5
      D = SQRT(D2)
```

Figure 5-8. Statements for Example 5-3

Providing this information to the Fortran compiler is done by DIMENSION statements which normally appear at the beginning of the Fortran program. The DIMENSION statements must include every variable that is to be subscripted in the program, and the inclusion of the subscripted variable in a DIMENSION statement must take place prior to the first occurrence of the subscripted variable anywhere in the program. The DIMENSION statement may mention any number of subscripted variables. It is not necessary, however, that they all have the same number of subscripts. The DIMENSION statement is a nonexecutable statement and normally takes the following form for one-dimensional arrays:

$$\text{DIMENSION } name_1\,(d_1),\ name_2\,(d_2), \ldots$$

In the above, $name_1$ and $name_2$ stand for array names of subscripted variables appearing in the program, and the *d*'s stand for the dimension of an individual subscript. *The individual d's must be unsigned, nonzero integer constants.* As an example of a DIMENSION statement, consider the following:

```
DIMENSION I(2),X(15),Y(8)
```

This DIMENSION statement would cause the Fortran compiler to assign a total of two storage locations to the I array for storage of the two integer constants which comprise the elements of the array. The compiler will also reserve fifteen storage locations for the real constants which comprise the X array, and eight storage locations for the real elements of the Y array. The order of listing arrays in the DIMENSION statement is not important, and more than one DIMENSION statement may be used.

It is usually not permissible to use zero or negative subscripts. (They are allowed in relatively few Fortran compilers.) Neither is it permissible for the program to have any subscript in an executable statement that is larger than the maximum size previously specified in the DIMENSION statement. Although subscript values less than one or larger than the maximum size indicated in the DIMENSION statement are invalid subscripted variable references, many computers do not check subscripts for validity. The result is that programs incorporating this error may be executed, and erroneous results are obtained.

Even though the DIMENSION statement indicates the probable maximum size of subscripted variable requirements, it is not necessary that the programmer use all the element address locations that are reserved, i.e., it is permissible to overdimension arrays in the DIMENSION statement. It must be pointed out, however, that overdimensioning of arrays can be expensive in terms of computer running time and memory requirements. Since most computers only have a limited amount of high-speed access or fast memory, the use of unreasonably large arrays may necessitate the inclusion of a large amount of slow-speed memory in the array address locations that are reserved. For each individual array the compiler will reserve storage for the number of elements indicated by the subscripts specified in the DIMENSION statement.

As some examples of the use of DIMENSION statements, the following are appropriate. For the distance function program discussed in Example 5-3, it would be necessary to have a DIMENSION statement of the form

```
DIMENSION X(50), Y(50)
```

For the calculation of the blood pressure difference of Example 5-2, it would be necessary to have a DIMENSION statement of the form

```
DIMENSION AGE(200),PRESS(200),DIF(200)
```

When referring to an array in a DIMENSION statement, as opposed to an arithmetic assignment statement, there is an implied difference between the two notations used. In a DIMENSION statement the reference to the array is not to one individual element, but it refers to the maximum size of the subscript. In a statement such as an arithmetic assignment statement, a reference such as A(2) would refer to a specific element in the array.

A common mistake of beginning programmers is to attempt to use the following DIMENSION statement for the blood pressure example cited above:

```
N = 200
DIMENSION AGE(N),PRESS(N),DIFF(N)
```

This is unacceptable because the information in the DIMENSION statement is used during compilation, whereas N is not actually assigned the value of 200 until the statement is encountered during execution of the program.

There is a case in which the DIMENSION statement is not needed directly. Chapter 2 introduced the convention of denoting an integer variable by beginning the name with one of the letters I, J, K, L, M, or N and a real variable by beginning the name with any other letter. Electrical engineers use L for inductance, chemical engineers use μ (mu) for viscosity, and similar conventions occur in other disciplines. Thus in some cases it is desirable for a real variable to begin with one of the letters I, J, K, L, M, or N, and vice versa for an integer variable. A *type* statement is used to accomplish this, as illustrated by the following examples:

```
REAL L, MU
INTEGER A, B
REAL C, I(50), G(2,3)
INTEGER J(10), F(2,7), K
```

In the first example the TYPE statement causes L and MU to be treated as real variables throughout the program. Similarly, the second example causes variables A and B to be treated as integer variables. In the third and fourth examples the variables C and K could have been omitted, but there is no harm in including them. These examples also illustrate the use of the TYPE statement to dimension the real variables I, G, J, and F. When variables are dimensioned in a TYPE statement, a separate DIMENSION statement is not necessary. However, the TYPE statement and DIMENSION statement may be used jointly in some Fortrans as follows:

```
REAL C, I
DIMENSION I(50), G(2,3)
```

Their order makes no difference,‡ but simultaneous dimensioning in both statements is not allowed.

Although most programmers place all their TYPE statements early in the program, the only restriction is that the TYPE statement must appear prior to the first use of the variable concerned.

Array names may appear in certain nonexecutable specification statements, in references to subprograms, and in input-output statements without any of the subscripts being mentioned, for example:

```
READ (5,10)A
```

Since such reference to an array without any mention of subscripts is permissible, it is obvious that no other variable in the program may have the same name as the array itself. In all cases other than those mentioned above, only array elements may be used. This is particularly important in arithmetic expressions.

EXAMPLE 5-4

One current use of a computer is in maintaining an up-to-date account of items in inventory. Suppose an inventory at the beginning of the month is punched on cards, the stock number in the first five columns and the quantity in stock in the next five columns. To keep the number of cards reasonable, suppose we write our program to handle only six items in stock. The first section of the program in Figure 5-9 reads cards specifying the initial inventory.

Suppose further that each time a shipment is received, cards are punched for each item giving the stock number in the first five columns and the quantity received in the second five. These cards will be in random order, and depending upon the number of shipments received, there may be zero, one, or several cards for any one item. To alleviate the necessity of counting the cards, a blank card will be the last card in this group. When

‡Some compilers require that type statements appear prior to the first executable statement *and* in the following order:

Type statements (REAL, INTEGER, etc.)
EXTERNAL (see Section 8-11)
DIMENSION
COMMON (see Section 8-7)
EQUIVALENCE (see Section 8-8)

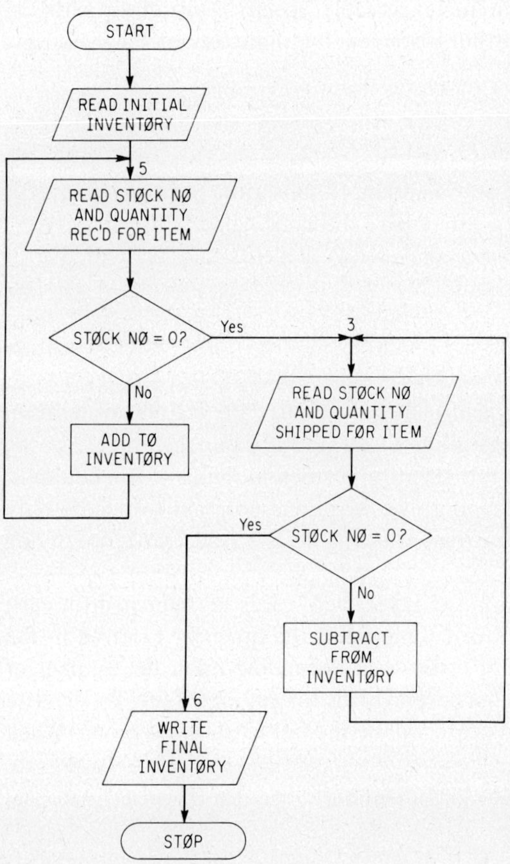

(a) Flowchart

```
C      INVENTØRY PRØGRAM
C
       DIMENSIØN ISTK(6),IQUAN(6)
C
C      READ INITIAL INVENTØRY
C
       DØ1I=1,6
  1    READ(5,2) ISTK(I),IQUAN(I)
  2    FØRMAT(2I5)
C
C      UPDATE INVENTØRY FØR STØCK RECEIVED
C
  5    READ(5,2) NSTK,NQUAN
C
C      CHECK FØR ZERØ STØCK NUMBER
C
       IF(NSTK.EQ.0)GØTØ3
C
C      ADD TØ INVENTØRY
C
       DØ4I=1,6
  4    IF(NSTK.EQ.ISTK(I))IQUAN(I)=IQUAN(I)+NQUAN
       GØTØ5
C
C      UPDATE INVENTØRY FØR STØCK SHIPPED
C
  3    READ(5,2)NSTK,NQUAN
C
C      CHECK FØR ZERØ STØCK NUMBER
       IF(NSTK.EQ.0)GØTØ6
C
C      SUBTRACT FRØM INVENTØRY
C
       DØ7I=1,6
  7    IF(NSTK.EQ.ISTK(I))IQUAN(I)=IQUAN(I)-NQUAN
       GØTØ3
C
C      WRITE FINAL INVENTØRY
C
  6    DØ8I=1,6
  8    WRITE(6,9)ISTK(I),IQUAN(I)
  9    FØRMAT(1X,2I5)
       STØP
       END
```

(b) Program

```
1207   12  ┐
1049    1  │
0907    5  │ Old Inventory
0412    0  │
1222    7  │
0015    2  ┘
0412    5  ┐
0015    3  │
1049    7  │ Received
1222    5  │
0412    5  │
0015    2  ┘

1207    2  ┐
1049    3  │
1222   10  │ Shipped
0015    4  │
0412    7  ┘
```

(c) Input

```
1207   10
1049    5
 907    5
 412    3
1222    2
  15    3
```

(d) Output

Figure 5-9. Inventory program

read, the stock number will be zero, which indicates the end of this set of cards. The second section of the program in Figure 5-9 reads these cards and updates the inventory.

Cards analogous to the above are punched for shipments of items. The third section of the program in Figure 5-9 processes these cards. The final section prints the new inventory.

In practice, the old inventory is stored on a more convenient medium than cards, probably a disc or magnetic tape. The program reads the old inventory from the appropriate source, updates it, writes the new inventory back on this medium, and prints it.

5-7. Input and Output

One straightforward means of providing input and output statements for the elements of an array is listing explicitly every individual element of the array in the input or output statement. As an example, the information for the input of a four-element array A and a two-element array B may be done by a READ statement as follows:

```
      READ (5,100)A(1),A(2),A(3),A(4),B(1),B(2)
100   FORMAT (6F10.2)
```

The four elements of the A array and the two elements of the B array can be written in the READ statement in any sequence whatsoever. The only restriction, of course, is that the information on the data card has to be in the corresponding order.

One of the advantages of subscripted variables is that it is possible to deal with all of the elements of an entire array without having to list them explicitly. As an example, an input or output statement may contain only the name of the array without any reference whatsoever to any subscript, and the entire array will be completely read or written. When this is done it is absolutely necessary to have a complete understanding of the implicit convention regarding the sequence in which the elements appear on the input or output record. For one-dimensional arrays the elements are taken in an increasing sequence, i.e., first the element with subscript 1, then the element with subscript 2, etc., up to the largest subscript in the DIMENSION statement (which must have appeared earlier).

This means that the previous READ statement can be written as

```
      READ (5,100)A,B
100   FORMAT (6F10.2)
```

In such a case the elements on the data card *must* be punched in the following sequence:

A(1),A(2),A(3),A(4),B(1),B(2)

This implied sequence will always exist.

When an array is called for without explicit reference to subscripts, the entire array will be assumed to exist in the size given in the DIMENSION statement, and any overdimensioning of array sizes will present problems because the computer will attempt to read all of the elements of the array whether they exist or not.

FORMAT statements have an important effect on the handling of information associated with arrays. One format field specification is necessary for each individual element in the array. As the elements of the array are read or written, the FORMAT statement is scanned from left to right. When the last right parenthesis of the FORMAT statement is reached, the FORMAT statement is exhausted and the computer will return to the first left parenthesis and go to a new record, a new line or card, for example, and repeat (scan again) the FORMAT statement from left to right. Assume we have a one-dimensional array with ten elements called the A array. If we write the statements

```
      DIMENSION A(10)
      READ (5,100)A
100   FORMAT (F10.2)
```

the computer reads the ten values of the ten elements of A from ten successive cards or records. This means that element A(1) is assumed to appear in the first ten columns in F10.2 format on the first card or input record; the second element, i.e., A(2), is expected to appear in the first ten columns of the second input record or card in F10.2 format, etc, and the tenth element, i.e., A(10), is expected to appear in the first ten columns of the tenth record or card in F10.2 format.

As another example, if all five values of an array referred to as the one-dimensional X array were to be found on a single data card, we could read all of these by the following statements:

```
      DIMENSION X(5)
      READ (5,20)X
20    FORMAT (5F10.4)
```

This statement causes the computer to look for X(1) in columns 1-10, X(2) in columns 11-20, etc. through X(5) in columns 41-50.

The individual elements in an array must all be of the same mode, i.e., real or integer, but it is not necessary that they all be read or written in the same format code. As an example, some of the elements in an integer array may be written in 15, some in 17, and some in I15 format.

Sometimes it is desirable to transfer only part of the values into or out of an array with a READ or WRITE statement, and on other occasions it is desirable to have the subscripts in an array vary in some manner other than the sequence normally assumed by the compiler. In such situations it is possible to have as a part of the input or output statement an expression which will dictate the exact order in which the subscripts will

$$\cdots(v(i),\ i=m_1,\ m_2,\ m_3)\cdots$$

where		
	v	is an array name.
	i	is an integer variable used as an indexed (controlled) subscript.
	m_1	is either an unsigned integer constant or an unsigned integer variable whose value is used as the initial value of i
	m_2	is either an unsigned integer constant or an unsigned integer variable whose value is compared with the current value of i at the completion of reading, or writing, each array element. When the current value of i becomes greater than the value of m_2, the reading or writing operation is terminated.
	m_3	is either an unsigned integer constant or an unsigned integer variable whose value is added to the current value of i after each array element is read or written, but before the comparison between i and m_2 is made. It can be omitted if 1 is to be added to i as the increment.
	m_1, m_2, and m_3	must be greater than zero.

Figure 5-10. General form of an indexed or controlled subscripted variable

vary.‡ The general form of this portion, called an implied DO, of an input or output statement is indicated in Figure 5-10. As an example, it may be desirable to read only elements six to ten of a one-dimensional array. The statements for this would be

```
      READ (5,10)(V(I),I = 6,10)
10    FORMAT (5F10.2)
```

The statement shown in Figure 5-10 can be extended to handle more than one array. For example, we might have statements

```
      READ (5,10)(A(I),B(I),I = 1,3)
10    FORMAT (F10.2)
```

These statements would read two arrays in the following fashion:

A(1)
B(1)
A(2)
B(2)
A(3)
B(3)

The use of input and output statements for arrays and the associated effect of FORMAT statements on their execution will be shown in examples that follow and in solved examples at the end of this chapter.

5-8. A Final Example

EXAMPLE 5-5

Sum of squares example. As an example of the use of subscripted variables, assume that a student makes thirty measurements of a quantity. These thirty measurements which he makes will comprise the elements of a one-dimensional array whose name is DATA. The student also can calculate a value for each of his measurements, and he will therefore have thirty calculated or expected values of these data points. These thirty values comprise a second one-dimensional array named CALC. Assume that these two arrays are read into the computer, and their differences are calculated and squared for each point

As an example, assume that each of the input elements of DATA will appear on a separate card in F10.2 format in the first ten columns of the card. Further assume that the values of CALC will be found on five additional input cards, six values to a card in 6F10.2 format. For the output of this program it is desired to have the record appear with the values of DATA in a vertical column; just to the right of DATA the corresponding values of CALC should appear in a vertical column; and just to the right of CALC the square of the value of the difference between the DATA element and the CALC element should appear. These thirty individual point values of the difference squared will be named PTSUM. Below these three vertical columns of DATA, CALC, and PTSUM it is desired to write out the value of the total sum of the squares for all thirty data points, and this should be written in E20.7 format. The flowchart for a program necessary to make the calculations is shown in Figure 5-11, and the program itself is shown in Figure 5-12.

‡This is completely covered in Section 7-5. Depending on the desires of the individual instructor, it is possible to defer study of this type of statement until that point.

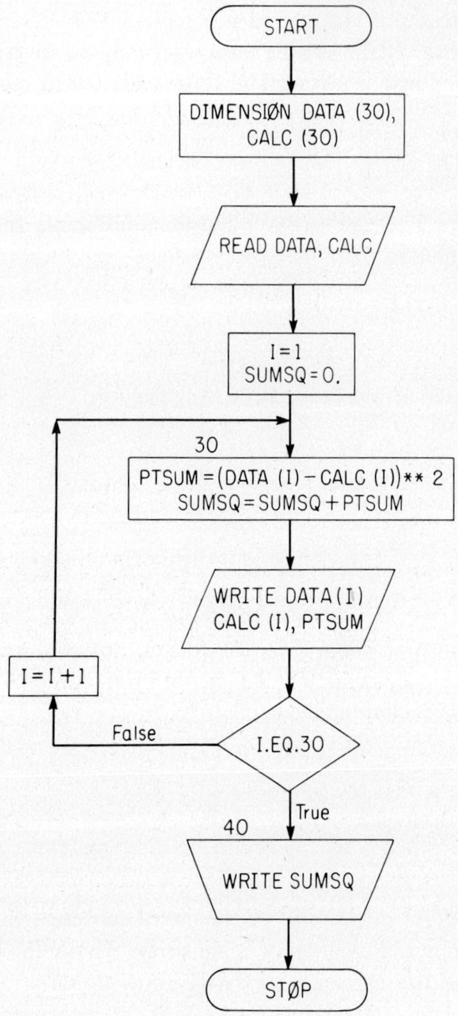

Figure 5-11. Flowchart for Example 5-5 (sum of squares calculation)

In the input of the two one-dimensional arrays into the computer, the READ statements contain implicit assumptions about the sequence which the individual elements of the arrays have on the data cards. Since the values of DATA are each in F10.2 format on a separate card, the input cards must be arranged so that the subscripts on DATA vary from one to thirty. Since FORMAT statement number 10 has a single field specification, the computer will read in one input card, look for a single element on that card in F10.2 format, and then go to a new card or new record to look for the next element of the DATA array, etc. In the case of CALC the computer will see that FORMAT statement 20 has a repetition number of six associated with the field specification. The computer will expect the first six values of the CALC array to be found on the first CALC input card, and then proceed to a new input card or record for elements 7-12, to a third card for elements 13-18, etc., until five cards have been read for the CALC array. The computer knows there are thirty elements in both DATA and CALC because of the DIMENSION statement.

In the calculation of the sum of the squares a loop is used to calculate all of the individual differences between DATA and CALC, and in each case the difference at a point is squared. The sum of all of these squares is retained in the computer, but the

```
C FOR COMMENT
STATEMENT NUMBER | Cont | FORTRAN STATEMENT
C    EXAMPLE CALCULATIØN ØF SUM ØF SQUARES
C
C    DATA INPUT SECTIØN
C
      DIMENSIØN DATA(30),CALC(30)
      READ(5,10)DATA
   10 FØRMAT(F10.2)
      READ(5,20)CALC
   20 FØRMAT(6F10.2)
C
C    CALCULATIØN ØF SUM ØF SQUARES AND ARRAY ØUTPUT
C
      I = 1
      SUMSQ = 0.
   30 PTSUM = (DATA(I) - CALC(I)) **2
      SUMSQ = SUMSQ + PTSUM
      WRITE(6,50)DATA(I),CALC(I), PTSUM
   50 FØRMAT (1X,3F10.2)
      IF(I.EQ.30) GØ TØ 40
      I = I + 1
      GØ TØ 30
C
C    SUM ØF SQUARES ØUTPUT
C
   40 WRITE(6,60)SUMSQ
   60 FØRMAT(1X,E20.7)
      STØP
      END
     18.62
     17.79
     17.42
     17.01
     16.89
     16.62
     16.31
     16.09
     15.82
     15.04
     15.11
     14.87
     14.47
     14.26
     14.00
     13.75
     13.53
     13.27
```

Figure 5-12. Program for Example 5-5

```
13.00
12.79
12.56
12.34
12.17
12.03
11.88
11.66
11.47
11.21
11.03
10.69
18.07     17.62     17.43     17.21     17.00     16.78
16.45     16.28     15.87     15.61     15.21     15.05
14.96     14.81     14.62     14.46     14.11     13.75
14.62     13.42     13.02     12.71     12.46     12.25
11.98     11.78     11.51     11.36     11.12     11.01
```

Figure 5-12. (Continued)

point value, PTSUM, is written out as soon as it is calculated. Since PTSUM is not retained, it is not subscripted, it is not stored, and it is not available for future processing.

The output FORMAT statement has a 1X to keep the carriage-control column blank on the output record, and a repetition number of three is used in the output field specification. A blank, the first element of DATA, the first element of CALC, and PTSUM for the first elements will be written on one output record; and on the second output record the first column also will be blank, followed by the second element of DATA, the second element of CALC, and PTSUM for the second elements (all in F10.2 format). This will continue through the thirty sets of values for the arrays. After all the output arrays have been written, the computer then encounters a new WRITE statement which records the sum of the squares.

For input data appearing in the example the output of the program will appear as

```
18.62    18.07    0.30
17.79    17.62    0.03
17.42    17.43    0.00
17.01    17.21    0.04
16.89    17.00    0.01
16.62    16.78    0.03
16.31    16.45    0.02
16.09    16.28    0.04
15.82    15.87    0.00
15.04    15.61    0.32
15.11    15.21    0.01
14.87    15.05    0.03
14.47    14.96    0.24
14.26    14.81    0.30
14.00    14.62    0.38
```

13.75	14.46	0.50
13.53	14.11	0.34
13.27	13.75	0.23
13.00	14.62	2.62
12.79	13.42	0.40
12.56	13.02	0.21
12.34	12.71	0.14
12.17	12.46	0.08
12.03	12.25	0.05
11.88	11.98	0.01
11.66	11.78	0.01
11.47	11.51	0.00
11.21	11.36	0.02
11.03	11.12	0.01
10.69	11.01	0.10

0.6493900E 01

5-9. In Summary

The combined use of the subscripted variables and DO loops provides one of the most powerful tools available to the Fortran programmer. They allow him to handle large amounts of data with a minimum of programming effort. Tedious calculations and laborious input and output instructions also can be handled through the use of the subscripted variable notation. The programmer should make every effort to gain facility in the use of subscripted variables and DO loops. The extension to multidimensional arrays and nested DO loops (one within another) is treated in the next chapter.

For the above reasons, the student should make every effort to work a large number of the problems at the end of this chapter to make certain he is familiar with the use of subscripted variables and DO loops.

EXERCISES‡

Note: For all the following exercises you are to read in the given variables, perform the desired calculations, and write out the results as directed. Write complete Fortran programs including trial data card(s). The following exercises are designed to focus the student's attention on understanding and using the DO statement. Problems of a scientific, engineering, and business nature are included. Exercises 5-1 through 5-23 do not require knowledge of subscripted variables.

5-1. Write a program to condense statistics on students in a class. One data card is provided for each student; it contains (1) his or her age in columns 1 and 2; (2) the student's sex in column 5, the code being 1-male, 2-female; and (3) the student's standing in column 7, the code being 1-freshman, 2-sophomore, 3-junior, 4-senior. The output should be the average age of the students, the percent males, and the percent freshmen, sophomores, juniors, and seniors. The cards are not counted, so use a blank card to indicate last card as in the inventory program in Example 5-4. Use the following data:

‡Solutions to Exercises marked with a dagger † are given in Appendix E.

21	1	3
23	2	2
19	1	1
24	1	4
20	2	2
21	1	2
18	2	1
27	1	4
20	1	2
21	2	3
21	2	2
20	1	2

†**5-2.** A plant whose production rate is P lbs/year produces a product whose value is V \$/lbs. The product costs C \$/lb to produce. The gross profit is then $P \cdot (V - C)$. The total tax rate is 52%, so the profit after taxes is .48 times the gross profit. If the plant costs B \$ to build, the pay-out time in years is B divided by the profit after taxes.

Suppose the values of C, B, and P are known to be \$1.50/lb, \$900,000, and 200,000 lbs/yr, respectively. Write a program to calculate the pay-out time for values of V from \$2.75/lb to \$3.25/lb in increments of \$0.05/lb. The listing should be in columnar fashion, with a value of V and a corresponding value of the pay-out time.

5-3. A man invests \$600 per year at 8% interest. How much will he have after ten years? Write a Fortran program to calculate this using a DO loop. Read the amount invested annually, the interest rate, and the number of years for which the value of his investment is to be calculated.

5.4. At an interest rate of 6%, how much must you deposit at the first of each year so that at the end of five years you will have \$8,000? Write a program to calculate this. Assume \$1.00 is deposited each year and calculate the amount available at the end of five years as in the previous program. The amount to be deposited is \$8,000 divided by this value. Read the interest rate, how much is to be accrued, and the number of years in which deposits will be made.

5-5. A calculation encountered in financial analysis is the computation of depreciation. One popular technique for doing this is the sum-of-the-years'-digits method. Suppose \$15,000 is to be depreciated over a five-year period. The sum-of-the-years'-digits is $1 + 2 + 3 + 4 + 5 = 15$. According to this method, 5/15 of \$15,000 is depreciated the first year, 4/15 the second, 3/15 the third, etc. Write a program that reads the amount to be depreciated and the number of years over which the depreciation is made. The output should be tabulated as follows for the above case:

1	5000.00
2	4000.00
3	3000.00
4	2000.00
5	1000.00

Run this program to calculate the annual depreciation if \$50,000 is to be depreciated over ten years.

5-6. Prepare a program to read N and calculate N!. N is always a nonnegative number, but may be zero (0! = 1). The output should be N and N! (N! = 1 X 2 X . . . X (N - 1) X N). N! is pronounced "N factorial."

†**5-7.** In business applications, a quantity known as the capital-recovery factor is defined as follows:

$$\text{capital-recovery factor} = \frac{i(1+i)^n}{(1+i)^n - 1}$$

where i is the interest rate and n is the number of years. Write a program to print a tabulated set of values for $n = 1$ through $n = 25$ for $i = 8\%$. The output should appear as follows:

```
1     1.08000
2     0.56077
3     0.38804
     etc.
```

5-8. A man borrows \$100.00 at an interest rate of 1 1/2% per month. If he pays \$10.00 at the end of each month, how much does he owe at the end of ten months? Write a program to solve this problem. Read the amount he borrows and the amount he pays each month. Note that the interest for the first month is 0.015 X \$100 = \$1.50. Since he pays \$10 at the end of the month, he owes \$100.00 + \$1.50 - \$10.00 = \$91.50. Use a DO loop to iterate these calculations for each month.

5-9. For the situation given in the previous problem, suppose he wants to know how long it takes to pay off his debt. Determine (1) how many months he must pay \$10.00, and (2) his payment for the last month required to leave a balance of exactly zero. Run the program for the case in which he borrows \$250 instead of \$100.

†**5-10.** Write a program to calculate the geometric average and the arithmetic average of the following data:

12.2
7.9
20.2
13.5
49.4
2.1
5.8

As output, write only the two averages. The program should read the number of data points from the first card, followed by the data, one value per card. For n data points, the geometric average is the nth root of the product of all the values.

5-11. Evaluate the series

$$\sum_{n=0}^{20} \frac{1}{a+nb} = \frac{1}{a} + \frac{1}{a+b} + \frac{1}{a+2b} + \frac{1}{a+3b} + \cdots + \frac{1}{a+20b}$$

for $a = 2$ and $b = 0.5$. Read a and b from a data card, and write only the value of the sum.

5-12. On the interval $0 < X \leqslant 2$, log (X) can be represented by the following infinite series:

$$\log(X) = \frac{\left[(X-1) - \frac{(X-1)^2}{2} + \frac{(X-1)^3}{3} - \cdots\right]}{2.303} = \frac{\sum_{n=1}^{\infty} \frac{(-1)^{n-1}(X-1)^n}{n}}{2.303}$$

Prepare a program that reads a value for X and sums the series, printing the answer after 3, 5, 10, 50, and 100 terms. Also print the answer using ALOG 10 for comparison. Run the program for $X = 1.8$. In programming, assume X will always be in the above interval.

5-13. The function $\sin^2 X$ can be represented by the following series:

$$\sin^2 X = X^2 - \frac{2^3 X^4}{4!} + \frac{2^5 X^6}{6!} - \cdots = \sum_{n=1}^{\infty} \frac{(-1)^{n+1} 2^{2n-1} X^{2n}}{(2n)!}$$

Prepare a program to evaluate this series for $X = 2.0$, printing the results after 5, 10, 50, and 100 terms and comparing to the true solution. The program should read the value of X. Note that the term for $n = 1$ is X^2, and that all consecutive terms can be obtained by multiplying the previous term by $\frac{-(2X)^2}{2n(2n-1)}$

†**5-14.** The following definite integral:

$$\int_0^2 (1 + X^2)dX = \int_0^2 f(X)dX$$

can be evaluated analytically to be 4.6667. However, not all integrals can be evaluated analytically. The purpose of this and the next few problems is to illustrate some of the features of numerical integration techniques.

Perhaps the simplest of all numerical techniques is the rectangular approximation. The interval of integration is divided into smaller intervals, and the value of the function over the entire interval is assumed to be the value at either end. This is shown in the illustration, using the value at the left end. The smooth curve is the plot of $1 + X^2$ versus X, and the shaded area is the result of the numerical integration. The accuracy of the result increases as the number of intervals increases (width decreases).‡ The approximate value of the integral is

$$\int_0^2 (1 + X^2)dX \doteq \Delta X\,[f(0) + f(\Delta X) + f(2\Delta X) + \cdots]$$

Prepare a program to perform the following functions:

(a) Read in the number of increments (fixed point).
(b) Evaluate the integral numerically.
(c) Print the number of increments and the numerical result.
(d) Return to Step (a) and repeat.

To illustrate the effect of increment size, run the program using increments of 4, 10, 20, 50, 100, and 1000.

‡This is true up to a point. For very small intervals the round-off error may be serious.

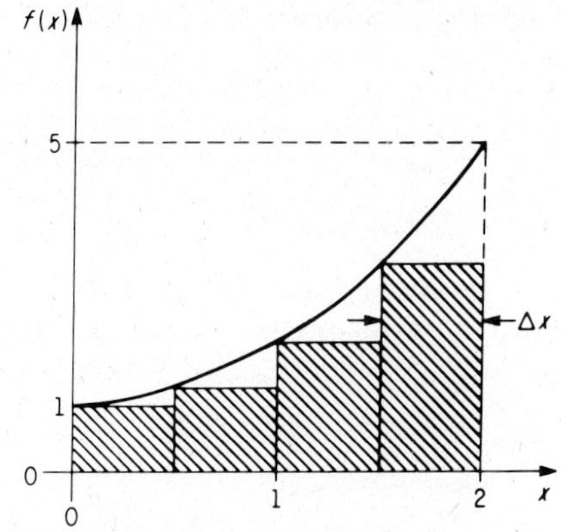

Exercise 5-14. Rectangular integration

5-15. From an inspection of the accompanying figure, some improvement can be seen by evaluating the function at the midpoint of the increment. The result, as shown in the illustration, is given by

$$\int_0^2 (1 + X^2)\,dX \doteq \Delta X \left[f\left(\frac{\Delta X}{2}\right) + f\left(\frac{3\Delta X}{2}\right) + f\left(\frac{5\Delta X}{2}\right) + \cdots \right]$$

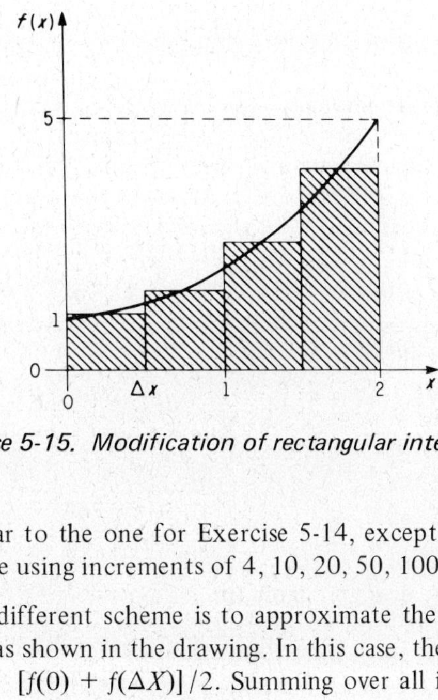

Exercise 5-15. Modification of rectangular integration

Prepare a program similar to the one for Exercise 5-14, except use the above integration technique. Again evaluate using increments of 4, 10, 20, 50, 100 and 1000.

5-16. A slightly different scheme is to approximate the function by straight lines over a given increment, as shown in the drawing. In this case, the integral over the first increment would be $\Delta X \cdot [f(0) + f(\Delta X)]/2$. Summing over all increments yields the following equation, known as the trapezoid rule:

$$\int_0^2 (1 + X^2)\,dX \doteq \Delta X \left[\frac{f(0)}{2} + f(\Delta X) + f(2\Delta X) + \cdots + f(2 - \Delta X) + \frac{f(2)}{2} \right]$$

Prepare a program similar to the one for Exercise 5-14, except use this integration technique. Again, evaluate using increments of 4, 10, 20, 50, 100, and 1000.

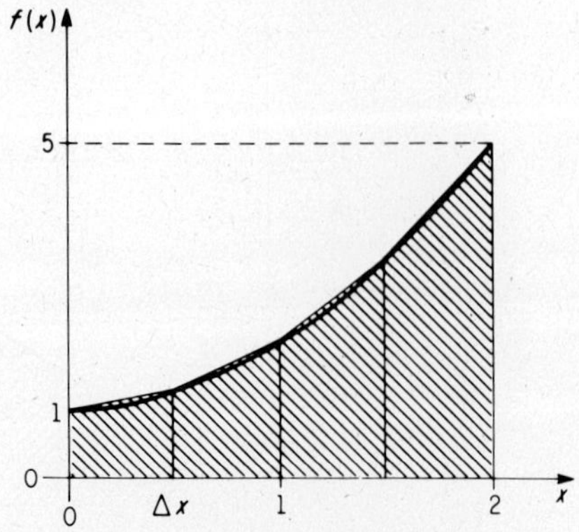

Exercise 5-16. Trapezoidal rule

5-17. The method known as bisection or interval halving is a simple, effective, and easy-to-program technique for finding roots of many polynomials. The method proceeds as follows:

Consider a function $f(x)$ similar to the function in the accompanying figure. The main feature is that the function has one and only one root on the interval (a,b). The root in this case can be found by the following technique:

(a) Evaluate $f(x)$ at the midpoint of the interval, say $x = c = (a + b)/2$.
(b) If $f(c)$ is zero, the root is found. However, this is an extremely unlikely outcome.
(c) If $f(c)$ is positive, note that the root must now lie on the interval (a,c). If $f(c)$ is negative, the root must lie on the interval (c,b). In either case, the interval on which the root is known to lie is cut in half.
(d) The procedure is repeated for the new interval. As the interval is halved on each iteration, after twenty iterations the size of the interval is $1/2^{20}$, or negligibly small. After twenty iterations, the midpoint of the final interval is assumed to be the value of the root.

The function of $f(x) = x^3 - x^2 - x - 1.9$ is very similar to the function shown in the accompanying sketch. Assuming a root lies between 0.0 and 5.0, use the method described above to locate the root.

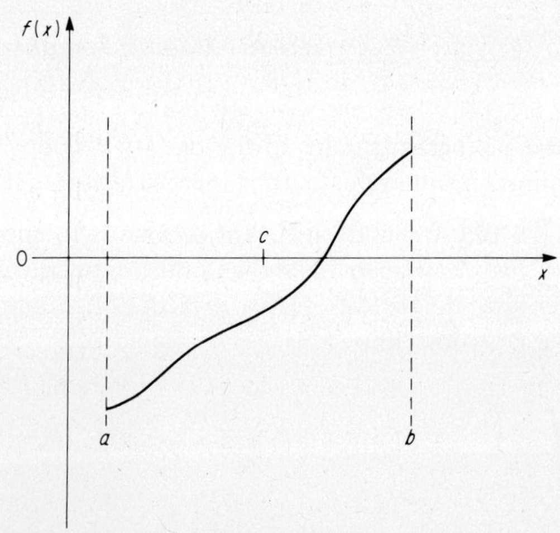

Exercise 5-17. Function suitable for bisection

5-18. Another technique for solving for roots of an equation is known as Newton's method. This technique proceeds as follows:

(a) Assume a value, say $x = a$, for the root.
(b) Evaluate $f(a)$. If $|f(a)| \leqslant \epsilon$, the root is found.
(c) If not, evaluate $df(a)/dx = f'(a)$, the slope of the line tangent to $f(x)$ at $x = a$. This line is shown in the figure.
(d) Determine the point b at which this tangent line intercepts the x-axis. This point is given by

$$b = a - f(a)/f'(a)$$

(e) The procedure is repeated from Step 1 by assuming b as the new value for the root.

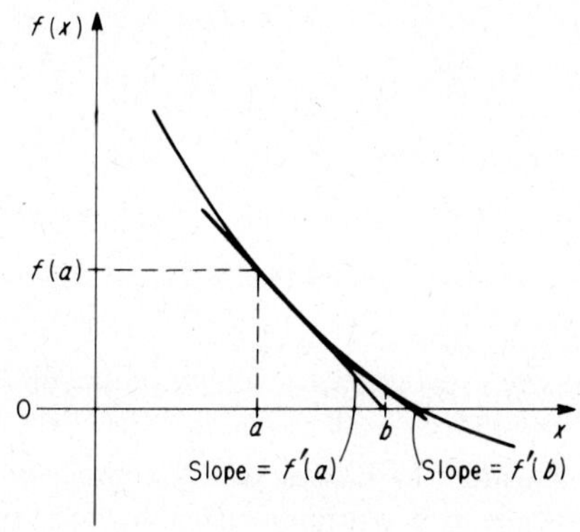

Exercise 5-18. Illustration of Newton's method

Prepare a program to perform these calculations for $f(x) = x^3 - x^2 - x - 1.9$. The input is to be a value for a and ϵ, and the output should be the root. Furthermore, the search will be terminated after twenty iterations with no output if the root has not been found. Let $a = 1.5$ and $\epsilon = 0.001$.

Although this method will work for $f(x)$ given above, it is not difficult to find functions for which this iterative procedure diverges.

†**5-19.** Suppose the following equations are to be solved for x and y:

$$y = 1 - e^{-x}$$
$$y = x\,|\,x\,|$$

As we have two equations and two unknowns, they can be solved for x and y. Graphically, this is the problem of determining the intersection of the two curves in the illustration. One could equate the two equations to obtain one equation in one unknown, but the result would be nonlinear. Suppose the following procedure is implemented:

(a) Let $y_1 = 1 - e^{-x}$ and $y_2 = x\,|\,x\,|$
(b) Let $\delta = y_1 - y_2$
(c) Assume a value for x, say b.
(d) Compute y_1, y_2, and δ.
(e) If $|\,\delta\,| \leqslant \epsilon$, the solution is found.

(f) If not, note that when b is less than x_0 (the true solution), δ is positive. Now suppose b is increased by an amount proportional to δ, that is,

$$b = b + k\delta$$

(where k is a proportionality constant), and the procedure repeated from Step (d). The value for b should progressively approach x_0. Note also that this same equation can be applied when $b > x_0$, as the negative value of δ will cause a decrease in b.

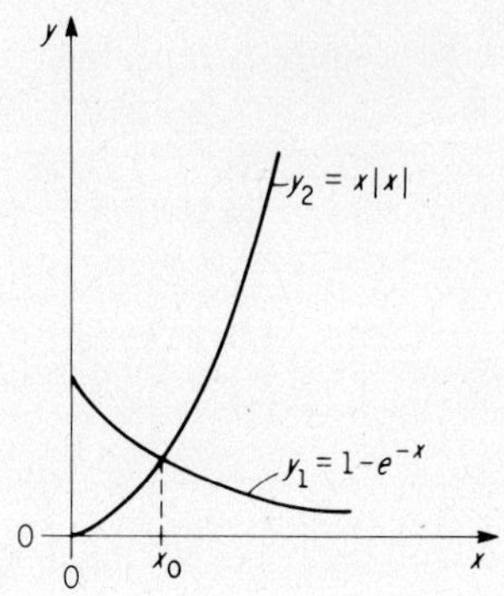

Exercise 5-19. Solution of nonlinear equations

Prepare a program to read a value for b, ϵ, and k, and print the value of b, ϵ, and k (use F-format) followed by values of b, y_1, y_2, and δ (use E-format) for each iteration. Let $b = 1.$, $\epsilon = 0.001$, and run the program for values of k of 0.1, 0.5, 1., and 2. If convergence is not obtained after twenty iterations, abandon the search. Note that the difficulty with this technique is selecting the appropriate value for k: a small value requires too many iterations and a large value produces an unstable situation.

†**5-20.** The digital computer is often called upon to solve differential equations numerically. Consider the following equation:

$$\frac{dc(t)}{dt} + c(t) = 1$$

$$c(0) = 0$$

This equation with specified initial condition is known to have the solution $c(t) = 1 - e^{-t}$, which can be used to compare with a numerical solution.

Consider the following scheme, known as the Euler technique:

(a) Solve the differential equation for the first derivative, yielding

$$\frac{dc(t)}{dt} = 1 - c(t)$$

(b) Select a time increment for the numerical integration.
(c) As $c(0)$ is known, $dc(0)/dt$, the initial slope, can be calculated.
(d) The point at the end of the first time increment is determined by assuming the derivative (or slope) is constant over the first time increment, as illustrated.
(e) This procedure is repeated for consecutive time increments, and is known as the Euler technique for solving ordinary differential equations.

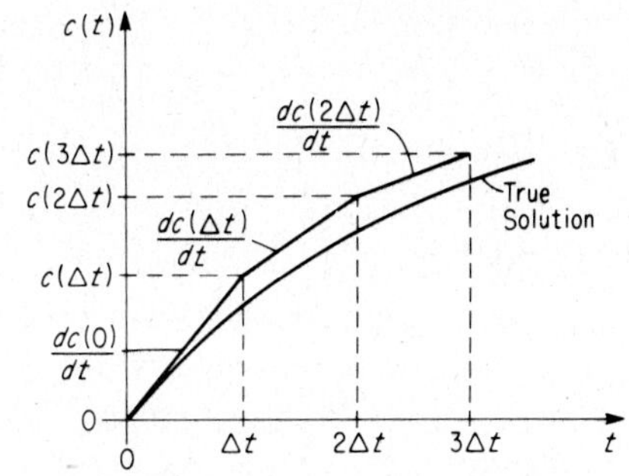

Exercise 5-20. Euler technique

Another way to obtain the same formulation is to approximate $dc(t)/dt$ by a forward difference, yielding

$$\frac{dc(t)}{dt} \doteq \frac{c(t+\Delta t) - c(t)}{\Delta t} = 1 - c(t)$$

Solving for $c(t + \Delta t)$ yields

$$c(t + \Delta t) = c(t) + [1 - c(t)]\,\Delta t$$

This recursive relationship is identical to the Euler technique.

Prepare a program to use the above procedure to calculate the solution of the differential equation at $t = 1$. The program should read the number of increments to be used, and write as output the number of increments, the numerical solution, and the true solution. Determine these for increments of 4, 10, 20, 50, 100, and 1000.

5-21. The Euler technique can be modified slightly to obtain some improvement. The procedure is as follows:

(a) Evaluate the derivative at the beginning of the increment, i.e., $c'(t)$.
(b) Using this slope, determine a first estimate of $c(t + \Delta t)$, say $g(t + \Delta t)$. Note that $g(t + \Delta t) = c(t) + (\Delta t)\,c'(t)$.
(c) Now evaluate the slope at the end of the increment, i.e., $g'(t + \Delta t)$, using the original differential equation with g substituted for c.
(d) Average the slopes determined in Steps (a) and (c), and use this value to determine $c(t + \Delta t)$ by the equation

$$c(t + \Delta t) = c(t) + (\Delta t)\,[c'(t) + g'(t + \Delta t)]/2$$

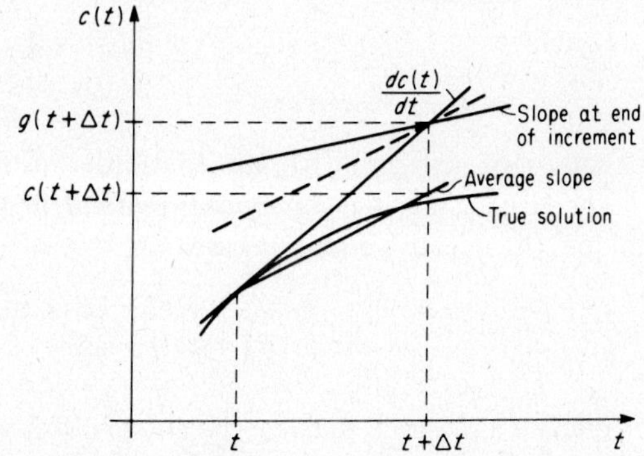

Exercise 5-21. Modified Euler technique

This technique, illustrated above, is know as the modified Euler technique.

Repeat Exercise 5-20 using this technique.

5-22. Probably the most popular high-order integration technique is a fourth-order Runge-Kutta. Let the differential equation be of the form $dc(t)/dt = f[t,c(t)]$, where $c(t)$ is the dependent variable and t is the independent variable. Then the point $c(t + \Delta t)$ at a small increment Δt from a known point $c(t)$ is given by

$$c(t + \Delta t) = c(t) + (\Delta t)(K_1 + 2K_2 + 2K_3 + K_4)/6$$
$$K_1 = f[t,c(t)]$$
$$K_2 = f\left[t + \frac{\Delta t}{2}, c(t) + \frac{K_1 \Delta t}{2}\right]$$
$$K_3 = f\left[t + \frac{\Delta t}{2}, c(t) + \frac{K_2 \Delta t}{2}\right]$$
$$K_4 = f[t + \Delta t, c(t) + K_3 \Delta t]$$

Use this procedure to solve the differential equation in Exercise 5-20.

†**5-23.** The above methods for numerically solving first-order differential equations can be readily extended to higher-order differential equations. For example, consider the following equation:

$$\frac{d^2c(t)}{dt^2} + \frac{dc(t)}{dt} + c(t) = 1$$
$$c(0) = 0$$
$$\frac{dc(0)}{dt} = 0$$

Define a new variable $z(t)$, as follows:

$$\frac{dc(t)}{dt} = z(t) \quad \text{(a)}$$

Now the original equation becomes

$$\frac{dz(t)}{dt} + z(t) + c(t) = 1 \quad \text{(b)}$$

The boundary conditions are

$$c(0) = 0$$
$$z(0) = 0$$

Now equations (a) and (b) are first-order differential equations and can be solved simultaneously using the concepts presented in the previous exercises. Using the Euler technique, the iterative equations are

$$c(t + \Delta t) = c(t) + (\Delta t)\ [z(t)]$$
$$z(t + \Delta t) = z(t) + (\Delta t)\ [1 - z(t) - c(t)]$$

Prepare a program to solve the above differential equation for $c(4)$. Let the input be the number of increments, and solve for increments of 4, 10, 20, 50, 100, and 1000.

Note: The following examples are all designed to use subscripted variable concepts.

5-24. Identify the errors, if any, in each of the following subscripts [array A dimensioned A(5)]:

(a) A(B)
(b) A(1 + J)
(c) A(10)
(d) A(J/2)
(e) A(J * 2 + 1)
(f) A(- J)

5-25. A data card contains a list of six numbers, each in F10.2 format, which we shall consider as a one-dimensional array A. Read in the six numbers, find their sum, and find what fraction each of these numbers is of their sum. The fractions shall be considered as a second one-dimensional array F. Write out A in a single vertical column alongside of which is located the corresponding F elements. Use F10.4 format for the elements in F.

5-26. Twenty students take an exam on which the marks are from 0 to 100. Write a program to determine how many students make a mark higher than the average. For input data assume one mark per card in F10.1 format. Write out the array of marks and the number (in I10 format) earning a mark higher than the average. Make up some trial data.

5-27. The accounting procedure at the typical computer center consists of assigning to each user a charge number, which he must submit with each job. At the end of each job, the computer punches a card containing the user's charge number in columns 1-5 and the number of minutes run in F format in columns 6-15.

Write a program that reads these cards and calculates the total amount of time used by each user on all jobs he ran. The output should be in columnar fashion with user number, total time used, and percent of total. Use a blank card to indicate last card. Input data are shown below:

```
40709   1.27
80001   2.34
50200   2.11
40709   4.02
40201   3.11
70207   2.06
50200   3.09
80001   1.02
40709   0.79
70207   3.04
```

5-28. As a conscientious student in basket weaving, Joe Kollage has performed some bursting tests on his products. Since higher mathematics still baffle him, he decides to use the computer.

The experiment consisted of placing weights in each basket until it ruptured. Joe used three different weights—weight one weighing five pounds, weight two, ten pounds, and weight three, twenty-five pounds. He performed this experiment on four baskets, and he has the number of weights of each type in the basket when it ruptured. The data for each test are entered on a separate card as follows:

	Number of Weight 1	*Number of Weight 2*	*Number of Weight 3*
Test 1	12	1	0
Test 2	6	2	1
Test 3	8	1	1
Test 4	0	2	2

Joe is confident he can keep the cards in order, so only the number of weights of each type for each test is entered according to FORMAT (3I3). The program should proceed as follows:

(a) Read input.
(b) Calculate total weight in basket at rupture. This value should be stored in an array.
(c) Calculate average weight at rupture.
(d) Calculate the difference between individual test value and average test value.
(e) Print test number, total weight at rupture, and difference from average for each test.
(f) Print average weight at rupture.

5-29. Revise the inventory program in Example 5-4 to print the final inventory in ascending order of the stock numbers.

†**5-30.** Read in a one-dimensional array A containing eight elements in F5.1 format on a single data card. Sort the elements into ascending order based on their absolute value. Write out the results on a single data card in F5.1 format.

5-31. Redo Exercise 5-30 for descending order.

†**5-32.** Given two one-dimensional arrays, A and B, each containing ten elements in F20.4 format. Data card one contains a_1 and b_{10}, data card two contains a_2 and b_9, etc. for ten data cards. Read in the arrays and calculate the norm as

$$\text{ABNORM} = \sqrt{\sum_{i=1}^{10} a_i b_i}$$

Write out the norm in E20.7 format.

5-33. Joe Bleaux needs to borrow \$1500 for a period of three years. After consulting three loan departments, he has the following possibilities:

(a) 8% per year, compounded monthly
(b) 8½% per year, compounded annually
(c) 8¼% per year, compounded quarterly

Which one is the most attractive?

Write a Fortran program to calculate this. Read i, the annual interest rate, and m, the number of compounding periods annually. The final amount owed is $\$1500 \cdot (1 + i/m)^{3m}$. The output should be the annual interest rate, the number of compounding periods annually, and the amount owed after three years. The output should be ordered so that the most attractive appears first and the least attractive last. Assume that the data cards are *not* read in this order.

5-34. Suppose we have the coordinates of five points in the x,y plane, and would like to find the distance between the two points that lie the farthest apart. The five points are read from five cards punched as follows:

x	y
-0.94	-3.22
-4.02	8.17
7.07	-9.11
5.49	8.76
0.20	4.45

The distance between the first two points is $\sqrt{(x_1 - x_2)^2 + (y_1 - y_2)^2}$; between the first and third is $\sqrt{(x_1 - x_3)^2 + (y_1 - y_3)^2}$; etc. Only the value of the farthest distance is to be printed. Be sure to check all possibilities (a total of ten).

†**5-35.** Prepare a program to calculate telephone bills. Our booming company has ten customers, whose identification numbers and base charges are punched on data cards, one card per customer. In addition, we have several cards containing charges for each long distance call made along with the customer number of the calling party. Of course, a given customer may make no calls or several calls. The cards for long distance are neither counted nor ordered. Write a program to compute and print the total charges for each customer. Don't forget to add 10 percent federal excise tax for long distance calls, but base charges are not taxable. Place the ten cards with base charges first in the input data, and make up your own data.

5-36. Suppose the sales slips on merchandise sold in a given department contain the amount of the sale and the salesperson's identification number. At the end of the day, these are punched onto cards with the salesperson's identification number in columns 1-3 and the amount of the sale in F format in columns 4-13. We would like to prepare a program to (a) calculate the total sales of each salesperson, (b) calculate the percent of the total, and (c) calculate his or her commission for the day (3 percent of the sales above \$50). These cards are neither counted nor ordered in any way. The program's output should be in columns containing the salesperson's identification number, the total amount of his or her sales for the day, the percent of the total, and his or her commission. Make up your own data cards.

5-37. An array of data consists of n experimental measurements of the variable x. They are in F5.1 format on the minimum number of data cards. Read them in and calculate their mean value and standard deviation:

$$\text{Mean value} = \frac{1}{n} \sum_{i=1}^{n} x_i = \bar{x}$$

$$\text{Standard deviation} = \sqrt{\frac{1}{n-1} \sum_{i=1}^{n} (x_i - \bar{x})^2}$$

Write out the mean value, the standard deviation, and n.

5-38. Redo Exercise 5-37, except you are also to write out the value of x which is most different from the mean value of x.

5-39. A one-dimensional array X contains twenty elements which represent experimental measurements. These may be smoothed by calculating

$$sX_i = \frac{X_{i-1} + X_i + X_{i+1}}{3}$$

for all but the first and twentieth elements. Read in X, calculate SX, and write out the two arrays, one above the other.

5-40. Read in a one-dimensional array X containing sixteen elements in F10.2 format on two input data cards. Calculate the first, second, and third differences

DELX1(I) = X(I + 1) - X(I) for I = 1, . . . , 15
DELX2(I) = DELX1(I + 1) - DELX1(I) for I = 1, . . . , 14
DELX3(I) = DELX2(I + 1) - DELX2(I) for I = 1, . . . , 13

Write out X, DELX1, DELX2, and DELX3 in four vertical columns which are side by side.

5-41. Let $f(x) = a_n x^n + a_{n-1} x^{n-1} + \cdots + a_1 x + a_0$. A program is to be prepared to read n, read the coefficients of $f(x)$, read b, and evaluate $f(b)$. The first card contains the value of n, the next $n + 1$ cards contain the values of the coefficients (beginning with a_0), and the last card contains the value of b. Store the coefficients of $f(x)$ in a one-dimensional array, storing a_0 in A(1), a_1 in A(2), etc. Assume n will always be less than fifty. Print b and $f(b)$.

As input, let $f(x) = -0.8x^5 - 0.06x^4 + 1.7x^3 - 3.2x^2 + 7x + 1$ and evaluate at $x = 0.75$. Although not the easiest to program, the most efficient manner for evaluating this polynomial is as follows:

$$((((-0.8x - 0.06)x + 1.7)x - 3.2)x + 7)x + 1$$

†**5-42.** Let $f(x) = a_n x^n + a_{n-1} x^{n-1} + \cdots + a_1 x + a_0$, let $g(x) = cx + d$, and let $h(x) = f(x)g(x) = b_{n+1} x^{n+1} + b_n x^n + \cdots + b_1 x + b_0$. Prepare a program to read from the first card the values of n, c, and d, read the coefficients of $f(x)$ from the next $n + 1$ cards (beginning with a_0), calculate the coefficients of $h(x)$, and print the results. Use array A to store the coefficients of $f(x)$, storing a_0 in A(1), and similarly for the coefficients of $h(x)$. The maximum value of n is thirty. in Appendix E.

As input, let $g(x) = 1.7x + 2.1$ and let $f(x) = x^5 + 1.6x^4 - 0.7x^3 + 0.2x^2 + 6.1x + 0.8$.

5-43. Prepare a program to multiply polynomials $f(x)$ of order n and $g(x)$ of order m to obtain $h(x)$. This is a generalization of the previous program. The maximum value for n and m is thirty, and $n \geqslant m$. Use input similar to above, reading n and m, then the coefficients of $f(x)$, and finally the coefficients of $g(x)$.

As input, let $f(x) = x^4 + 1.7x^3 - 2x^2 + 0.71x + 1.1$ and $g(x) = x^2 + 2.1x + 1.8$.

5-44. The three coordinates of a point in space (X_1, X_2, X_3) are to be considered as elements in a one-dimensional array. The direction cosines associated with this point also may be considered as a one-dimensional array and are given as

$$c_1 = \frac{X_1}{\sqrt{X_1^2 + X_2^2 + X_3^2}}$$

$$c_2 = \frac{X_2}{\sqrt{X_1^2 + X_2^2 + X_3^2}}$$

$$c_3 = \frac{X_3}{\sqrt{X_1^2 + X_2^2 + X_3^2}}$$

Assume you have five points and for each point you desire to calculate the direction cosines. Structure the program to read in the coordinates of a point, calculate the direction cosine array, write out the X and C arrays, and go to a new data card. For each point processed, an identifying output number also should be written to identify the point as the first, second, third, fourth, or fifth point. (A counter handles this last requirement nicely.) Use F10.2 or I5 for all input and output format field specifications.

†**5-45.** Given a one-dimensional array A containing sixteen elements in F10.2 format. Calculate a new array B whose elements are given as

$$b_i = i \cdot a_i$$

Write out all the A elements in a single vertical column alongside of which is located the corresponding B elements. Use F10.2 format for all output.

5-46. Read in a one-dimensional array A which contains twelve elements in F20.2 format. Calculate a new array B whose elements are given as

$$b_i = (-1)^i (a_i)^{i+1}$$

Write out the A array in F20.2 format on three output records. This should then be followed by the B array in E20.7 format on the next three output records.

5-47. Read in the one-dimensional array A which contains twenty elements in F20.5 format. Calculate two sums, x and y, given as

$$x = \Sigma a_i \text{ for } i \text{ odd, i.e., } x = a_1 + a_3 + \cdots + a_{19}$$
$$y = \Sigma a_i \text{ for } i \text{ even, i.e., } y = a_2 + a_4 + \cdots + a_{20}$$

Write out the A array in two vertical columns. The left-hand column should contain all the odd elements and the right-hand column should contain all the even elements. Use F20.5 format. Now write out x and y in E20.5 format so that they appear below the appropriate columns.

5-48. Read in the one-dimensional array A containing ten elements in F10.2 format. Calculate the following:

SUMNEG = sum of all the negative elements
SUMPOS = sum of all the positive elements
NNEG = number of negative elements
NPOS = number of positive elements

Write out these results in E20.2 or I10 format, as appropriate.

†**5-49.** Read in two one-dimensional arrays, A and B, containing five elements each. Assume each input data card contains a single element of A and the single corresponding element of B. Calculate a new array C where

$$c_i = a_i + b_i \text{ if } b_i \geq a_i$$
$$c_i = a_i - b_i \text{ if } b_i < a_i$$

Write out A, B, and C, in three vertical columns. Use F10.2 format on all input and output.

5-50. Read in two one-dimensional arrays, A and B, containing ten elements each.

Assume the A array is contained on two data cards in F10.2 format and the B array is contained on the next three data cards in E20.7 format. Calculate a new array C where

$$c_i = (a_i + b_i)^2 \text{ if } a_i > b_i$$
$$c_i = (a_i - b_i)^2 \text{ if } a_i \leqslant b_i$$

Write out the C array in E20.7 format on three data cards.

†**5-51.** Consider the following problem in vapor-liquid equilibria: A liquid containing n components is in equilibrium with its vapor at total pressure P_i . Let the mole fraction of component i in the liquid be X_i, its vapor pressure be P_i, and its relative volatility be R_i. For component i, its vapor pressure P_i can be calculated from temperature T by

$$\log_{10}P_i = \frac{-0.05223\, A_i}{T} + B_i$$

where A_i and B_i are experimentally determined constants for component i.

The problem is, given P_t and the mole fraction of each component, to calculate the temperature T at the bubble point. The input is as follows:

The first card contains values for n, P_t, and an initial estimate of T using FORMAT (12, 2F 10.0).

This card is followed by n cards, each containing the values of X_i, A_i, and B_i for component i, using FORMAT (3F10.0).

The calculations proceed as follows:

(a) Assume T. Initially this is the value read from the first data card.
(b) For each of the n components, calculate P_i from T, A_i and B_i using the equation above.
(c) For each of the n components, calculate R_i from $R_i = P_i/P_1$. Of course, $R_1 = 1$.
(d) Calculate $\sum_{i=1}^{n} R_i X_i$.
(e) Calculate P_a by: $P_a = P_t \Big/ \sum_{i=1}^{n} R_i X_i$.
(f) Calculate T_a, the new estimate of T, by: $T_a = \dfrac{0.05223\, A_1}{B_1 - \log_{10}P_a}$.
(g) Compare T_a with T. If $|T_a - T|/T_a < 0.001$, the solution is found. Write T_a. If not, set $T = T_a$ and repeat from Step (b).

The maximum value for n is ten. Use the following inputs:

$n = 2,\quad P_t = 2000.,\quad T = 273.$

i	X_i	A_i	B_i
1	.5	23450.	7.395
2	.5	27691.	7.558

5-52. Let **a** be an n-dimensional vector (an $n \times 1$ matrix) defined as follows:

$$\mathbf{a} = \begin{bmatrix} a_1 \\ a_2 \\ a_3 \\ \cdot \\ \cdot \\ \cdot \\ a_n \end{bmatrix}$$

Norm $|\mathbf{a}|$ of a vector is defined as follows:

$$|\mathbf{a}| = (a_1^2 + a_2^2 + \cdots + a_n^2)^{1/2}$$

Prepare a program to read n followed by $a_1, a_2, \ldots, a_n$ (each on a separate card), compute the norm of **a** and print the result. The maximum value for n will be fifty. For data, let

$$\mathbf{a} = \begin{bmatrix} 2 \\ 1 \\ 0 \\ 3 \end{bmatrix}$$

†**5-53.** A normalized vector is one whose norm is unity. Any given vector can be normalized by dividing each of its elements by the norm. Prepare a program to read the elements of a vector as in the previous problem, compute the normalized vector, and print the results (the elements of the normalized vector, one to a line). Use same input as in previous problem.

5-54. Let **a**, **b**, and **c** be vectors defined as in the previous exercises. If vector **c** is to be the sum of **a** and **b**, i.e., $\mathbf{c} = \mathbf{a} + \mathbf{b}$, then c_i, the ith element of **c**, is the sum of a_i and b_i, i.e., $c_i = a_i + b_i$. Prepare a program to

(a) Read n, the order of each of the vectors. The maximum value of n is fifty.
(b) Read the elements of **a**, one to a card.
(c) Read the elements of **b**, one to a card.
(d) Compute **c**.
(e) Print the elements of **c**, one to a line.

As input, let

$$\mathbf{a} = \begin{bmatrix} 4 \\ 0 \\ 7 \\ 2 \end{bmatrix} \qquad \mathbf{a} = \begin{bmatrix} -1 \\ 2 \\ 1 \\ -2 \end{bmatrix}$$

†**5-55.** The dot product of vectors **a** and **b** is a scalar whose value equals

$$\sum_{i=1}^{n} a_i b_i$$

Prepare a program to

(a) Read n, the order of each of the vectors. The maximum value of n is fifty.
(b) Read the elements of **a**, one to a card.
(c) Read the elements of **b**, one to a card.
(d) Compute the dot product and print the results.

As data, use the two vectors in Exercise 5-54.

5-56. Early in a course on vector algebra, the following theorem is proved:

$$|\mathbf{a} + \mathbf{b}|^2 = |\mathbf{a}|^2 + |\mathbf{b}|^2 + 2\mathbf{a} \cdot \mathbf{b}$$

Prepare a program to prove this for a specific case by evaluating each side of the relationship. The input is arranged in the same manner as in the previous two exercises, and the output is to be the value of both sides printed on the same line. For input use the vectors in Exercise 5-54.

5-57. Exercise 5-55 considered the dot product of two vectors. Let **a**, **b**, **c**, and **d** be vectors, where **d** is defined as follows:

$$\mathbf{d} = (\mathbf{a} \cdot \mathbf{b}) \cdot \mathbf{c}$$

Note the $(\mathbf{a} \cdot \mathbf{b})$ gives a scalar, which is then multiplied by **c**. Prepare a program to read vectors **a**, **b**, and **c** in a manner similar to Exercise 5-55, compute **d**, and print the results in columnar fashion. Use the following vectors as input:

$$\mathbf{a} = \begin{bmatrix} 1 \\ 0 \\ 4 \\ 2 \end{bmatrix} \qquad \mathbf{b} = \begin{bmatrix} 7 \\ -3 \\ 2 \\ 1 \end{bmatrix} \qquad \mathbf{c} = \begin{bmatrix} 2 \\ 2 \\ -2 \\ 7 \end{bmatrix}$$

Let the maximum dimension of the vectors be fifty.

6

Multidimensional Arrays and Nested DO Loops

The previous chapter treated single DO loops and one-dimensional arrays. The objective of this chapter will be to expand upon this material and thus extend the usefulness of subscripted variables and DO loops to the programmer.

6-1. Multidimensional Arrays

Many quantities may be represented with one variable name through the use of subscripts as indicated in the previous chapter. A subscripted variable in Fortran may have one, two, or three subscripts (separated by commas within the parentheses of the subscript), and these in turn represent one-, two-, or three-dimensional arrays. For convenience in orienting the individual's thinking, the one-dimensional array can be considered (in a geometric sense) as representing points along a line, the two-dimensional array as representing points in a plane, and the three-dimensional array as representing points in a three-dimensional space or points in a series of planes stacked one on top of the other.

An alternate way of viewing arrays is to consider the one-dimensional array as a column or a row of elements; to consider the two-dimensional array as a table of elements, i.e., made up of rows and columns; and to consider the three-dimensional array as a series of tables, i.e., a series of two-dimensional arrays.

The concept of one-, two-, and three-dimensional arrays refers to the number of subscripts for the element and not to the number of elements themselves. For example, a one-dimensional array can have many elements, and it would be possible for a three-dimensional array to have only one element. It might also be pointed out that some versions of Fortran allow more than three subscripts (some systems allow seven-dimensional arrays).

A two-dimensional array, in its geometric interpretation, may be thought of as being composed of horizontal rows and vertical columns. The first subscript of the variable refers to the row number in the array, and it will vary from one to the total number of rows. The second subscript refers to the vertical column number, and it will vary from one to the number of columns. As an example, two entrants in a beauty contest might have their conventional measurements stored in a 2 X 3 array which might be shown in mathematical notations as follows:

$$\begin{matrix} a_{1,1} & a_{1,2} & a_{1,3} \\ a_{2,1} & a_{2,2} & a_{2,3} \end{matrix}$$

These could be written in Fortran subscript notation as A(1,1), A(2,1), A(1,2), A(2,2), A(1,3), and A(2,3). Note that the subscripts are separated by commas.

In a more general sense an $n \times m$ array named A might be presented as follows:

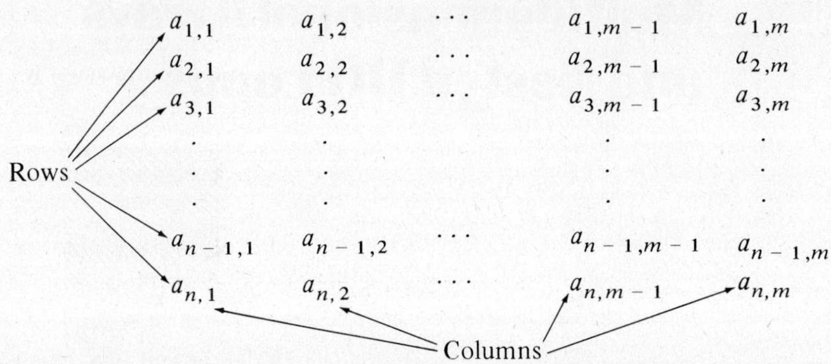

In general, $a_{i,j}$ would be the element in the ith row and the jth column.

In the DIMENSION statement, multidimensional arrays must be included in the same manner as one-dimensional arrays. For example, the statement

DIMENSION A(2,3), K(2,3,4)

would establish $2 \times 3 = 6$ storage locations for array A and $2 \times 3 \times 4 = 24$ storage locations for array K. As can be seen from Appendix B, most machines allow up to three-dimensional arrays, a few allow up to seven, and one or two permit even more.

The order in which higher dimensional arrays are stored in memory is important. The rule is that storage is arranged as if the first subscript were varied most rapidly and the last subscript varied least rapidly. That is, the storage for an array dimensioned A(2,3) would be in the following order:

A(1,1) A(2,1) A(1,2) A(2,2) A(1,3) A(2,3)

This is important in the reading of arrays. The read statement

READ (5,10) A

would read the elements of array A in the same order as they are stored. If a two-dimensional array is viewed as a table, as suggested previously, then the table is read by columns.

EXAMPLE 6-1

As an example of the use of subscript notation, consider the two-dimensional array associated with solving a set of simultaneous algebraic equations. A system of two equations and two unknowns is sufficient to illustrate the technique.

```
C FOR COMMENT
STATEMENT NUMBER | Cont. | FORTRAN STATEMENT

      DENØM = A(1,1) * A(2,2) - A(2,1) * A(1,2)
      X(1) = (B(1) * A(2,2) - B(2) * A(1,2)) / DENØM
      X(2) = (B(2) * A(1,1) - B(1) * A(2,1)) / DENØM
```

Figure 6-1. Statements for Example 6-1

$$A_{1,1}X_1 + A_{1,2}X_2 = B_1$$
$$A_{2,1}X_1 + A_{2,2}X_2 = B_2$$

By Cramer's rule, these may be solved by the following relationships:

$$X_1 = \frac{B_1 A_{2,2} - B_2 A_{1,2}}{A_{1,1}A_{2,2} - A_{2,1}A_{1,2}}$$

$$X_1 = \frac{B_2 A_{1,1} - B_1 A_{2,1}}{A_{1,1}A_{2,2} - A_{2,1}A_{1,2}}$$

In general, simultaneous equations are not solved by Cramer's rule, but it is used to illustrate the programming concepts rather than the numerical analysis concepts. The program to make these individual calculations is shown in Figure 6-1.

6-2. Nested DO's

Consider the table containing five rows and three columns as shown in Figure 6-2a. This table is stored in a two-dimensional array TABLE(I,J), where the first subscript denotes the row number and the second subscript denotes the column number. A program is to be prepared to calculate the sum of each column, storing the result in a one-dimensional array SUM.

1.31	−1.17	4.23	TABLE (I,J)
2.06	−0.11	0.45	
−1.17	2.10	1.97	
−2.01	5.09	0.88	
0.02	1.25	−1.78	
0.21	7.16	5.75	SUM (J)

(a) The table to be summed

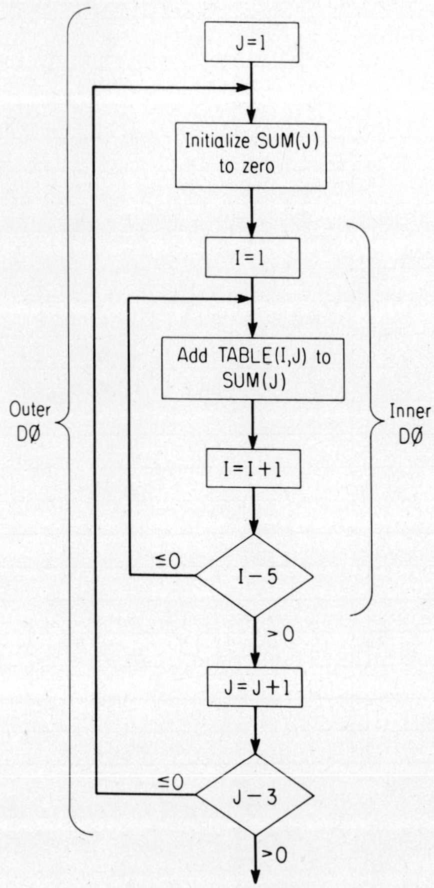

(b) Flowchart

Figure 6-2. Summing the columns of a table

Using a DO loop, the sum of the first column is calculated with the following statements:

```
      J = 1
      SUM(J) = 0.
      DO 3 I = 1,5
  3   SUM(J) = SUM(J) + TABLE(I,J)
```

This set of statements is reflected in the inner loop of the flowchart in Figure 6-2b. To calculate the sums for all the columns, these statements must be executed for J = 2 and J = 3. This is accomplished with a DO, and all the sums are calculated with the following statements:

```
      DO 4 J = 1,3
      SUM(J) = 0.
      DO 3 I = 1,5
  3   SUM(J) = SUM(J) + TABLE(I,J)
  4   CONTINUE
```

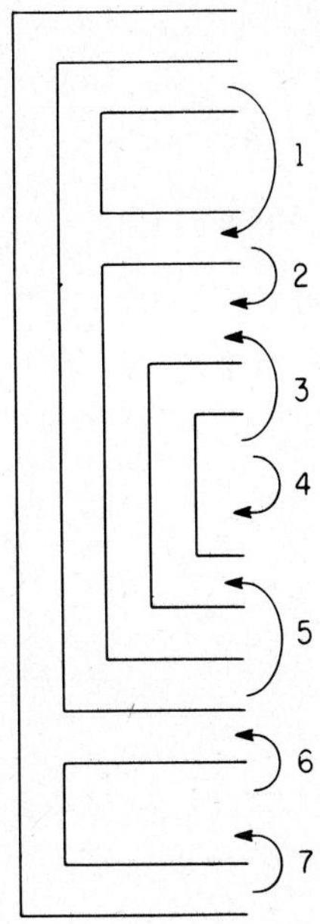

Figure 6-3. Examples of permissible and unpermissible transfers in nested DO loops: transfers 1,3,4 and 6 are permissible; transfers 2, 5, and 7 are not permissible

This series contains one DO (the *inner* DO) within the range of another DO (the *outer* DO). DO statements occurring in this fashion are called *nested* DO's.

The rules applying to DO's used in this manner are essentially the same as applicable to single DO's. The important features of such DO's are enumerated below:

1. As the index of a DO cannot be redefined within its range, the index of the inner DO must not be the same as the index of the outer DO.

2. The range of the inner DO must not extend beyond the range of the outer DO. However, this does not prohibit the ranges of nested DO's from terminating with the same statement. That is, the CONTINUE statement in the previous example could be eliminated as follows:

```
      DO 3 J = 1,3
      SUM(J) = 0.
      DO 3 I = 1,5
3     SUM(J) = SUM(J) + TABLE (I,J)
```

3. The rules applying to transfer are identical for nested and unnested DO loops. However, transfers within nested DO's can be somewhat intricate, and several permissible and unpermissible transfers are illustrated in Figure 6-3.

EXAMPLE 6-2

In the preceding paragraphs the DO loops for calculating the sums of each column in a table were presented. Now consider the preparation of a complete program as given in Figure 6-4 to read into memory the elements of TABLE in Figure 6-2, calculate the

```
      DIMENSION SUM(10),TABLE(10,10)
C
C     READ TABLE
C
      DO2I=1,5
 2    READ(5,3)TABLE(I,1),TABLE(I,2),TABLE(I,3)
C
C     DO LOOP FOR SUMMING EACH COLUMN
C
      DO5J=1,3
C
C     INITIALIZE SUM TO ZERO
C
      SUM(J)=0.
C
C     DO LOOP FOR ADDING EACH ELEMENT TO SUM
C
      DO4I=1,5
 4    SUM(J)=SUM(J)+TABLE(I,J)
C
C     WRITE STATEMENT
C
 5    WRITE(6,6)SUM(J)
      STOP
C
C     FORMAT STATEMENTS
C
 3    FORMAT(3F5.0)
 6    FORMAT(1X,F15.4)
      END
```

(a) Complete program

```
 1.31-1.17 4.23
 2.06-0.11 0.45
-1.17 2.10 1.97
-2.01 5.09 0.88
 0.02 1.25-1.78
```

(b) Input data

```
0.2100
7.1600
5.7500
```

(c) Output data

Figure 6-4. Summation of columns in a table

sum of each column, and write the results. First, a DO loop is used to read the table. The statements in the program in Figure 6-4 read each row of the table from a single card. Alternatively, the entries of the table can be arranged one per card, and two DO's can be used as follows:

```
      DO 2 I = 1,5
      DO 2 J = 1,3
 2    READ (5,3)TABLE(I,J)
 3    FORMAT (F5.0)
```

The data cards are arranged such that the elements appear in the order TABLE (1,1),

TABLE (1,2), TABLE (1,3), TABLE (2,1), TABLE (2,2), etc. Alternatively, the DO's can be reversed, yielding

```
   DO 2 J = 1,3
   DO 2 I = 1,5
2  READ (5,3)TABLE(I,J)
3  FORMAT (F5.0)
```

The data is now entered in the order TABLE (1,1), TABLE (2,1), TABLE (3,1), TABLE (4,1), TABLE (5,1), TABLE (1,2), etc.

The statements for calculating the sums are as discussed earlier, except that the write statement is incorporated into the outer DO loop.

EXAMPLE 6-3

In many instances it is preferable, or necessary, for the elements in an array to be in relative numerical (ascending or descending) order. An individual could do this with very little thought for small arrays, but how would you tell a machine to do it?

To define the problem more completely, let A be a one-dimensional array of N elements. The original values of the elements are stored in A, and it is desirable to obtain the rearranged array in A.

If a person were doing this, he would probably begin by finding the smallest element and placing it in A(1), placing the second smallest in A(2), etc. The computer could proceed in a similar manner by first finding the smallest element in the array and switching with the original A(1). The smallest element could be located by first assuming A(1) is smallest, and comparing with the remaining elements. When a smaller element is found, the assumption is updated. Letting M be the assumed position of the smallest element, it can be located as follows:

```
   M = 1
   DO 2 I = 2,N
2  IF(A(I).LT.A(M))M = I
```

See flowchart in Figure 6-5. Upon completion of the DO, it has been determined that element M is the smallest element in array A.

Now it is necessary to place A(M) in A(1) and A(1) in A(M). Using an intermediate storage position called TEMP, this may be achieved by

```
TEMP = A(1)
A(1)  = A(M)
A(M)  = TEMP
```

The elements are thus switched.

At this point the smallest element is found in A(1), but the remainder of the elements are unordered. In a similar manner, the elements 2 through N must be searched for their smallest value, which is stored in A(2). For this case the statements for locating the smallest element and switching with A(2) are

```
   M = 2
   DO 2 I = 3,N
2  IF (A(I).LT.A(M))M = I
   TEMP = A(2)
   A(2) = A(M)
   A(M) = TEMP
```

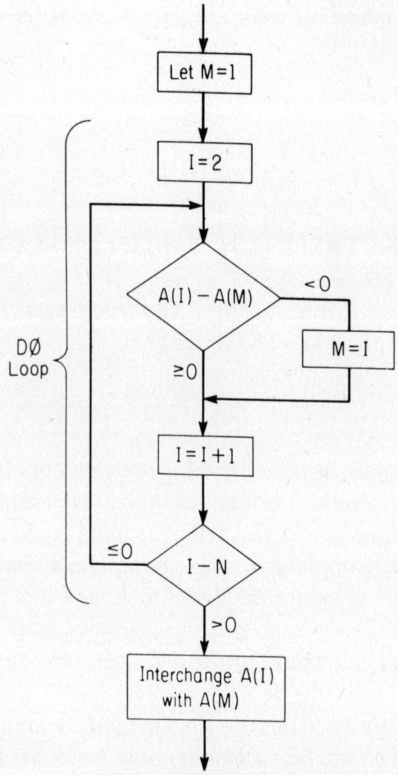

Figure 6-5. Flowchart for locating smallest element in an array and placing in first position

As this procedure must be repeated for A(3), A(4), . . . , A(N − 1), the logic of the flowchart in Figure 6-6 can be used. Coding with the use of DO loops produces the following statements:

```
      NA = N - 1
      DO 3 J = 1,NA
      M = J
      MA = J + 1
      DO 2 I = MA,N
    2 IF (A(I).LT.A(M))M = I
      TEMP = A(J)
      A(J) = A(M)
    3 A(M) = TEMP
```

For a specific case, let array A be 1.0, 2.0, 0.5, 4.0, 1.5. In the first iteration, elements 1 and 3 are interchanged, yielding 0.5, 2.0, 1.0, 4.0, 1.5. Elements 2 and 3 are switched on the second iteration, yielding 0.5, 1.0, 2.0, 4.0, 1.5. On the third iteration, elements 3 and 5 are switched to form 0.5, 1.0, 1.5, 4.0, 2.0. Switching elements 4 and 5 on the fourth iteration yields 0.5, 1.0, 1.5, 2.0, 4.0. Thus, the array is successfully ordered after four or N − 1 iterations.

Could the outer DO in this example be DO 3 J = 1,N? If so, what would be the

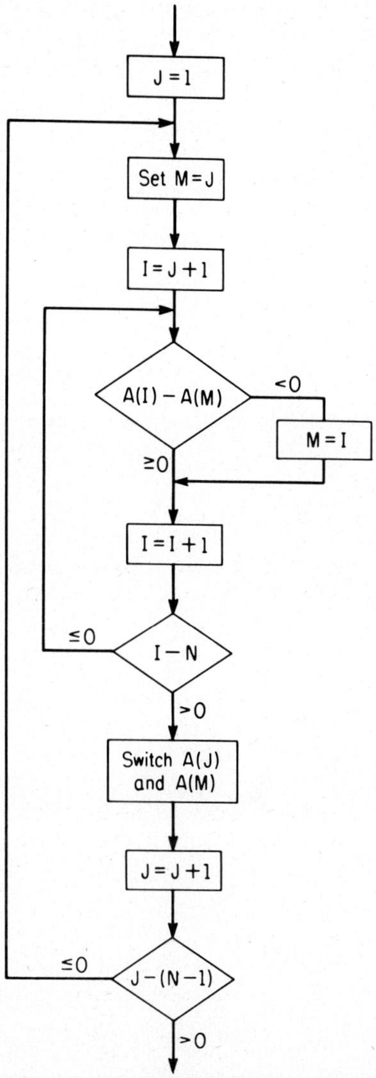

Figure 6-6. Flowchart for ordering elements in an array

value of MA when J = N? This means that the first index for the inner DO is larger than the second index, which does not seem reasonable (See Item 2, Section 5-3).

6-3. Implied DO

The implied DO described in Figure 5-10 can be extended to handle multidimensional arrays in a manner analogous to nested DO loops. For example, to read a two-dimensional array A, the following statement is appropriate:

```
      READ (5,10)((A(I,J),J = 1,4),I = 1,2)
10    FORMAT (8F10.0)
```

The data must appear in the following order:

A(1,1), A(1,2), A(1,3), A(1,4), A(2,1), A(2,2), A(2,3), A(2,4)

The following combination is also permissible:

```
      WRITE (6,12)(I,(B(I,J),J=1,3),I=1,3)
12    FORMAT (1X,I5,3F10.2)
```

The output would be as follows:

```
1    2.2    3.4    9.1
2    1.7    2.9    0.9
3    0.5    6.3    3.1
```

This form could *not* be used in a READ statement, since reading I would redefine the index of the implied DO.

EXAMPLE 6-4

Assume that two arrays are each 2 X 2. The two arrays are read into the computer, and a third two-dimensional array is calculated. Assume that the input arrays are named A and B and the third array to be calculated is named C. The elements of C are calculated by the following equations:

$$c_{11} = a_{11}b_{11} + a_{12}b_{21}$$
$$c_{12} = a_{11}b_{12} + a_{12}b_{22}$$
$$c_{21} = a_{21}b_{11} + a_{22}b_{21}$$
$$c_{22} = a_{21}b_{12} + a_{22}b_{22}$$

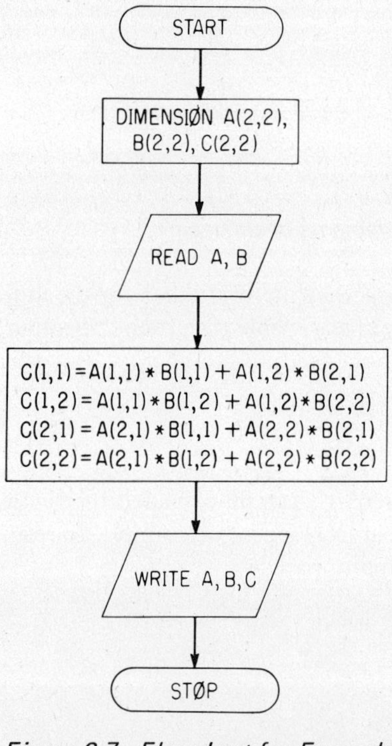

Figure 6-7. Flowchart for Example 6-4 (calculating a two-dimensional array)

```
C FOR COMMENT
STATEMENT NUMBER | CONT | FORTRAN STATEMENT
C   EXAMPLE IN CALCULATING A TWØ-DIMENSIØNAL ARRAY
C
C   INPUT SECTIØN
C
      DIMENSIØN A(2,2),B(2,2),C(2,2)
      READ(5,100)A
  100 FØRMAT(4F10.0)
      READ(5,100)B
C
C   CALCULATIØN ØF NEW ARRAY
C
      C(1,1) = A(1,1) * B(1,1) + A(1,2) * B(2,1)
      C(1,2) = A(1,1) * B(1,2) + A(1,2) * B(2,2)
      C(2,1) = A(2,1) * B(1,1) + A(2,2) * B(2,1)
      C(2,2) = A(2,1) * B(1,2) + A(2,2) * B(2,2)
C
C   ØUTPUT SECTIØN
C
      WRITE(6,200)A,B,C
  200 FØRMAT(1X,4F10.0)
      STØP
      END
        12.       -6.       27.       -2.
         0.       14.       16.       -2.
```

Figure 6-8. Program for Example 6-4

Those readers who are familiar with matrices will recognize the above relationship as indicating the multiplication of two 2 X 2 matrices. The flowchart for the program necessary for the indicated multiplication is shown in Figure 6-7 and the program itself is shown in Figure 6-8.

Note that in each case the various arrays involved will be written with the (1,1) element, (2,1) element, (1,2) element, and (2,2) element in this implied sequence. This must be the format of the A and B array on the input cards, and it is the output order of the A, B, and C arrays with the results as illustrated:

```
 12.     -6.     27.     -2.
  0.     14.     16.     -2.
378.    -28.    138.    -92.
```

6-4. In Summary

This chapter virtually completes the description of subscripted variables and DO loops. The utility of both of these cannot be emphasized too highly. The exercises following this chapter are designed to require that they be used.

EXERCISES‡

6-1. Identify the errors, if any, in each of the following subscripts:

(a) COPS(H,I,J)
(b) ROBBER(I - 2,J * 3 + 2)
(c) LSU(I + J,K + 2,L - 3)
(d) GOGO (I,I(2),NONO)
†(e) METWO(A(I),J,K * 3)
(f) HOHO(27,I,NO,YES)

6-2. Assume that you write a computer program which includes the following statements:

```
DIMENSION EXTRA (5000)
DIMENSION BIG (50)
DIMENSION BIGGER (4,4,4), SLIM (16)
A = 25.
BIGGER (1,1,1) = 5280
I = 4
J = 5
K = 3
```

If this is true, then all the following subscripts are invalid. Why?

(a) EXTRA(40,20)
†(b) BIG(B)
(c) EXTRA(BIGGER(1,1,1))
(d) B(I-2)
(e) SLIM(2 * J-12)
†(f) BIGGER(I,J,K)

†**6-3.** Five students take four examinations. Their marks are

	Exam 1	*Exam 2*	*Exam 3*	*Exam 4*
Student 1	48.6	30.	62.8	23.4
Student 2	40.1	40.	60.1	29.6
Student 3	63.4	50.	63.7	31.2
Student 4	56.2	60.	58.2	27.3
Student 5	71.0	70.	67.3	26.4

Read their marks as a table (a two-dimensional array) named DATA. Assume one row per input card in F10.1 format. Calculate the average on each test, the average for each student on all four tests, and the average for all students on all tests. Write out these three sets of results in F10.2 format on three data cards.

6-4. Three construction men work a week (five days) and put in the hours shown:

	Day 1	*Day 2*	*Day 3*	*Day 4*	*Day 5*
Worker 1	8.0	8.5	9.5	8.0	8.5
Worker 2	8.0	8.5	10.0	8.0	9.0
Worker 3	8.0	9.0	9.0	9.0	8.5

Read in their hours as a table (a two-dimensional array) named WORK. Assume one row

‡Solutions to Exercises marked with a dagger † are given in Appendix E.

per input card in F10.1 format. Calculate the total hours worked for each man, and the total hours worked by all men in the week. Write out these results in F10.2 format on a single data card.

6-5. Redo Exercise 6-4 except assume that there are two different projects to which each man can be assigned. In the three-dimensional array below assume the first number applies to Project Number 1 and the second number applies to Project Number 2.

	Day 1	*Day 2*	*Day 3*	*Day 4*	*Day 5*
Worker 1	5.0,3.0	5.0,3.5	4.5,5.0	5.0,3.0	4.5,5.0
Worker 2	5.5,2.5	5.5,3.0	5.0,5.0	4.5,5.5	5.0,4.0
Worker 3	6.0,2.0	4.5,4.5	4.0,4.5	4.0,5.0	6.0,2.5

Read in this three-dimensional array row by row with one worker's hours on a single input data card. Calculate the total hours worked on Project Number 1 and on Project Number 2. Write these results out in F10.1 format. Now calculate the average hours worked on each project on each day and write these results out in F10.1 format with a single day's totals on a single output card.

6-6. One useful item to a contractor on a constuction project is the number of men of each craft required each week. Suppose he will need carpenters, plumbers, and electricians, referred to as crafts 1, 2, and 3, respectively. The contractor usually divides his total effort into various jobs which he then schedules to start on a given week. For each job, he estimates how many weeks are required and how many of each craft are needed. Suppose he punches this information onto cards, the job number in columns 1-2, the starting week in columns 4-5, the weeks required in columns 7-8, and the number of workers in crafts 1, 2, and 3 in columns 11-12, 14-15, and 17-18, respectively.

Assuming the total duration of the contract is ten weeks, write a program that determines the number of workers in each craft needed each week. The output should be in columnar fashion, with the week number and the number of craftsmen needed in each craft. Use as input the following:

Job	*Start*	*Duration*	*Craft 1*	*Craft 2*	*Craft 3*
01	2	4	5	1	2
02	1	2	2	0	0
03	4	1	0	4	0
04	2	2	3	0	1
05	5	5	2	0	0
06	7	1	0	1	0
07	9	1	1	1	1

6-7. Multiply a matrix A (a two-dimensional array) times a five-element vector B (a one-dimensional array) to calculate their product C:

$$c_i = \sum_{j=1}^{5} A_{ij} b_j \quad i = 1, \ldots, 5$$

Read in A and b as

A					b
16.1	12.3	14.3	176.0	2.3	12.3
12.3	-8.4	-16.2	12.7	18.1	14.2
19.3	127.1	-6.	12.7	18.1	-8.1
27.1	-12.9	-8.2	121.	18.92	0.9
12.4	12.2	-6.3	-17.2	19.4	126.2

†**6-8.** A set of simultaneous equations is given as

$$\begin{aligned} a_{1,1}x_1 &= b_1 \\ a_{2,1}x_1 + a_{2,2}x_2 &= b_2 \\ a_{3,1}x_1 + a_{3,2}x_2 + a_{3,3}x_3 &= b_3 \\ &\vdots \\ a_{n,1}x_1 + a_{n,2}x_2 + \cdots + a_{n,n}x_n &= b_n \end{aligned}$$

Read in N, the A array, the B array, and calculate the X array.

6-9. Redo Exercise 6-8 if the set of equations is given as

$$\begin{aligned} a_{1,1}x_1 + \cdots + a_{1,n-1}x_{n-1} + a_{1,n}x_n &= b_1 \\ &\vdots \\ a_{n-2,n-2}x_{n-2} + a_{n-2,n-1}x_{n-1} + a_{n-2,n}x_n &= b_{n-2} \\ a_{n-2,n-1}x_{n-1} + a_{n-1,n}x_n &= b_{n-1} \\ a_{n,n}x_n &= b_n \end{aligned}$$

6-10. What integer number would be stored in each element of the array by the following program (what number would be stored in TEST(1,1), TEST(1,2), etc.)?

```
      DIMENSION TEST(3,3)
      K = 1
      DO 40 J = 1,3
      DO 40 N = 1,3
      TEST(N,J) = K
   40 K = K + 1
```

†**6-11.** What integer number would be stored in each element of the AGAIN array by the following program?

```
      DIMENSION AGAIN(2,2,3)
      K = 2
      DO 6 J = 1,2
      DO 6 L = 1,3
      DO 6 N = 1,2
      AGAIN(J,N,L) = K
    6 K = K + 2
```

6-12. Prepare a program to insert either zeros or ones into an array to give the following result for a 4 × 4 array:

$$\begin{bmatrix} 1 & 0 & 0 & 1 \\ 0 & 1 & 1 & 0 \\ 0 & 1 & 1 & 0 \\ 1 & 0 & 0 & 1 \end{bmatrix}$$

That is, place ones on both diagonals and zeros elsewhere. Read the size (⩽20) of the array from a data card, but do not read values for the elements. Print your final result.

6-13. Read in a two-dimensional array A. Calculate a new array B where

$$b_{i,j} = a_{j,i}$$

The A array is 3 X 3 and in F10.2 format. Use an implied variation in subscript in reading in the elements of A which are

10.1	16.8	-4.2
0	27.1	-3.4
21.26	-12.3	.01

Write out the B array in F10.2 format as

10.1	0	21.26
16.8	27.1	-12.3
-4.2	-3.4	.01

B is called the transpose of A.

†**6-14.** Redo Exercise 6-13 where A has three rows and five columns, and therefore B will have five rows and three columns. Make up trial data.

6-15. Redo Exercise 6-13 where i varies from one to n and j varies from one to m. Let the first input data card contain n and m and assume the following data cards will contain A.

6-16. Consider the following set of simultaneous equations:

$$\begin{aligned} a_{11}x_1 \quad &= b_1 \\ a_{21}x_1 + a_{22}x_2 &= b_2 \\ &\vdots \\ a_{n1}x_1 + a_{n2}x_2 + \cdots + a_{nn}x_n &= b_n \end{aligned}$$

Prepare a program to read the a's and b's and solve for the x's. The a's are to be stored in a two-dimensional array, but no zero elements are to be read. The input data are the value of n (always less than twenty), the a's (one to a card, beginning with a_{11}), and the b's (one to a card beginning with b_1). The output should be the x's. Solve the third set of equations given in the following problem.

†**6-17.** Consider the following set of simultaneous equations:

$$\begin{aligned} 3x_1 + 4x_2 + x_3 &= 4 \\ x_1 + 4x_2 - 2x_3 &= 0 \\ 2x_1 + x_2 + x_3 &= 1 \end{aligned}$$

Suppose the following two operations are performed: (1) multiply third equation by (-2.)/1. and subtract from second equation, and (2) multiply third equation by 1./1. and subtract from second equation. These operations yield

$$\begin{aligned} x_1 + 3x_2 \quad &= 3 \\ 5x_1 + 6x_2 \quad &= 2 \\ 2x_1 + x_2 + x_3 &= 1 \end{aligned}$$

Now multiply the second equation by 3./6., and subtract from first to obtain

$$\begin{aligned} -1.5x_1 \quad\quad\quad &= 2 \\ 5x_1 + 6x_2 \quad &= 2 \\ 2x_1 + x_2 + x_3 &= 1 \end{aligned}$$

This example is a variation of the procedure known as the Gauss reduction. Note that a set of equations of this type was solved in the previous problem.

Program this procedure for the general case. The input should be n, the coefficients of the original set of equations in the order a_{11}, a_{12},etc., and the b's. The output should be the coefficient, including the zero elements, of the reduced set of equations. The coefficients of the original equations are to be stored in a two-dimensional array A, and the coefficients of the reduced set should also appear in this array. The maximum value for n is twenty.

6-18. Now consolidate the above two programs into one program whose input is the input to Exercise 6-17 and whose output is that of Exercise 6-16.

6-19. Instead of the set of equations given in Exercise 6-16, suppose they had been as follows:

$$\begin{aligned} a_{11}x_1 + a_{12}x_2 + \cdots + a_{1n}x_n &= b_1 \\ a_{22}x_2 + \cdots + a_{2n}x_n &= b_2 \\ &\vdots \\ a_{nn}x_n &= b_n \end{aligned}$$

Again store the a's in a two-dimensional array, read the nonzero elements beginning with a_{11}, read the b's, and calculate and print the x's. Solve the same set of equations as before.

6-20. Program the Gauss reduction described in Exercise 6-17 in a manner such that the resulting reduced set of equations resembles those given in Exercise 6-19. Use the same input as in Exercise 6-17. The program for this Exercise and the program for Exercise 6-19 could be combined in a manner similar to that in Exercise 6-18.

6-21. Now for the program for the Gauss reduction. Using the two-dimensional array as in the previous exercises is inefficient with respect to storage, as almost half of array A contains zeros. In this exercise, prepare a program to solve the set of equations in Exercise 6-19 using a one-dimensional array for storing the coefficients. The next exercise treats the reduction step.

†**6-22.** If storage space is to be conserved throughout the program, it must be conserved in the reduction step also. This precludes reading the coefficients of all the equations and then performing the manipulations. This requires that the reduction be accomplished as the data is read. The procedure must proceed as follows:

(a) Read the coefficients and b for Equation 1. These remain unchanged; they are the first n elements in the one-dimensional array.
(b) Read the coefficients and b for Equation 2. Equation 1 is used to eliminate the first coefficient, and the resulting coefficients form the next $n - 1$ elements in the resulting array.
(c) Read the coefficients and b for Equation 3. Equatiqn 1 is used to eliminate the

first coefficient, Equation 2 is used to eliminate the second coefficient, and the results form the next $n - 2$ elements in the resulting array.

(d) This procedure is applied to each succeeding equation.

Program this technique and use it to reduce the equations in Exercise 6-17.

6-23. The following data are available for specific gravity of NaOH solutions as a function of temperature (*International Critical Tables,* Vol. III, McGraw-Hill, 1926-33, p. 79):

Percent NaOH \ Temp., °F	50	86	122	176	212
2	1.023	1.018	1.010	0.993	0.980
6	1.068	1.061	1.052	1.035	1.022
10	1.113	1.104	1.094	1.077	1.064
14	1.158	1.148	1.137	1.120	1.107
18	1.202	1.192	1.181	1.162	1.149
22	1.247	1.235	1.224	1.205	1.191

Prepare a program to do the following:

(a) Read the above table into a two-dimensional array.

(b) Read a value of temperature and concentration of NaOH for which the specific gravity is desired.

(c) Using linear interpolation, determine the specific gravity. Assume the input is always within the range of the table. First interpolate by rows, then by columns, or vice versa. Note that temperatures are not at equally spaced intervals.

(d) Write the temperature, concentration, and corresponding specific gravity.

(e) Go to Step (b) to read new values.

Determine the specific gravity at the following values:

Percent NaOH	*Temperature, °F*
5.876	130
21.77	210
15.20	58

6-24. Let A be an $n \times m$ matrix defined as follows:

$$A = \begin{bmatrix} a_{11} & a_{12} \cdots a_{1m} \\ a_{21} & a_{22} \cdots a_{2m} \\ \cdot & \cdot & \cdot \\ \cdot & \cdot & \cdot \\ \cdot & \cdot & \cdot \\ a_{n1} & a_{n2} & a_{nm} \end{bmatrix}$$

When n equals m, A is said to be a square matrix. The transpose of such matrices is obtained by interchanging the rows and columns. For example, the matrix

$$\begin{bmatrix} 1 & 2 & 0 & 5 \\ -1 & 3 & 7 & 1 \\ 0 & -5 & 1 & 4 \\ 8 & -9 & 0 & 0 \end{bmatrix}$$

has as its transpose

$$\begin{bmatrix} 1 & -1 & 0 & 8 \\ 2 & 3 & -5 & -9 \\ 0 & 7 & 1 & 0 \\ 5 & 1 & 4 & 0 \end{bmatrix}$$

Prepare a program to read matrix A, compute its transpose, and print the results. This program is easy when the transpose is stored in a different array than the original matrix, however, this is undesirable as it consumes storage. Prepare a program that produces the transpose of A in the same array as A with a minimum of storage.

In order to facilitate input-output, prepare this program specifically for 4 X 4 matrices. Each card on input contains the elements of a row of A, and the output (the transpose of A) is to be arranged similarly. Use the above example for data.

†**6-25.** Two matrices of equal order (i.e., equal number of rows and equal number of columns) can be added in a manner analogous to vector addition. For example, let A, B, and C be matrices of order $n \times m$. Then c_{ij}, the element on the ith row and jth column of C, equals a_{ij} plus b_{ij}. Prepare a program to read n (for simplicity on input-output, let $m = 4$), read the elements of A (one row per card), read the elements of B, compute C, and write the results (one row per line). As data use the following matrices for A and B:

$$\begin{bmatrix} 2 & 1 & -2 & 0 \\ 7 & 8 & -6 & 5 \\ 0 & 7 & 1 & -3 \end{bmatrix} \qquad \begin{bmatrix} -4 & 4 & 0 & 3 \\ 2 & 7 & -3 & 1 \\ 0 & 0 & 2 & 0 \end{bmatrix}$$

Let the maximum value for n be ten.

6-26. An $n \times m$ matrix and an mth-order vector can be multiplied to produce an nth-order vector. For example, consider the following product:

$$\begin{bmatrix} 2 & 0 & 1 & -3 \\ 3 & -1 & 2 & 5 \end{bmatrix} \begin{bmatrix} 1 \\ -1 \\ 3 \\ 0 \end{bmatrix} = \begin{bmatrix} 5 \\ 10 \end{bmatrix}$$

$$\mathrm{A} \cdot \mathrm{b} = \mathrm{c}$$

The ith element of c is given by the following expression:

$$c_i = \sum_{j=1}^{n} a_{ij} b_j$$

Prepare a program to read n (for simplicity on input-output, let $m = 4$), read A (one row per card), read b (all elements on one card), multiply, and write c (one element per line). The maximum value for n is ten. As input, use the above example.

6-27. The vector-matrix multiplication of the above exercise is really a special case of matrix-matrix multiplication. An $n \times m$ matrix A can be multiplied on the right by $m \times k$ matrix B to give an $n \times k$ matrix C, that is, $A \cdot B = C$. The element of C on the ith row and jth column, c_{ij}, is given by

$$c_{ij} = \sum_{k=1}^{m} a_{ik} b_{kj}$$

For example:

$$\begin{bmatrix} 1 & 0 & -2 & 4 \\ 2 & 1 & 7 & 3 \\ 5 & -2 & 0 & 0 \end{bmatrix} \begin{bmatrix} 1 & 2 \\ 2 & 0 \\ 0 & 7 \\ 3 & 6 \end{bmatrix} = \begin{bmatrix} 13 & 12 \\ 13 & 71 \\ 1 & 10 \end{bmatrix}$$

Prepare a program to solve the above specific example. Use any input-output procedure you desire.

†**6-28.** The Gauss reduction technique can also be used to evaluate a determinant. Recall that the multiplication of one row by a constant and adding to another does not alter the value of the determinant. For example, this procedure can be used to modify the determinant

$$\begin{vmatrix} 2 & 1 & 1 \\ 4 & -1 & 5 \\ 2 & -2 & 7 \end{vmatrix}$$

to

$$\begin{vmatrix} 2 & 1 & 1 \\ 0 & -3 & 3 \\ 0 & -3 & 6 \end{vmatrix}$$

and finally to

$$\begin{vmatrix} 2 & 1 & 1 \\ 0 & -3 & 3 \\ 0 & 0 & 3 \end{vmatrix}$$

The value of this determinant is simply the product of the diagonal elements, namely, -18. Prepare a program that utilizes this technique to evaluate the following determinant:

$$\begin{vmatrix} 5 & 0 & 1 & 7 \\ 2 & 3 & 0 & 5 \\ -1 & 2 & -9 & 1 \\ 7 & -4 & 0 & 2 \end{vmatrix}$$

The output should be the value of the determinant.

6-29. Unfortunately, life is not quite so simple as the previous problem infers. For example, consider the following case:

$$\begin{vmatrix} 2 & 1 & 1 \\ 4 & 2 & 3 \\ 2 & -2 & 7 \end{vmatrix} \longrightarrow \begin{vmatrix} 2 & 1 & 1 \\ 0 & 0 & 1 \\ 0 & -3 & 6 \end{vmatrix} \longrightarrow ?$$

Due to the zero on the diagonal, the third and final rearrangement cannot be made directly. If the program prepared in the previous exercise is used, a division by zero is encountered. To surmount this difficulty, the column, namely the second column in the above example, in which the zero causing the difficulty appears, is switched with a column without a zero in this location. Recall that this multiplies the value of the determinant by −1. If no column is found without a zero in this location, then the determinant has a zero row and its value is zero. Alternatively, rows could be switched.

In the above example, interchanging the last two columns yields

$$-\begin{vmatrix} 2 & 1 & 1 \\ 0 & 1 & 0 \\ 0 & 6 & -3 \end{vmatrix} \longrightarrow -\begin{vmatrix} 2 & 1 & 1 \\ 0 & 1 & 0 \\ 0 & 0 & -3 \end{vmatrix}$$

The value of the last determinant is 6.

Prepare a program to evaluate the following determinant:

$$\begin{vmatrix} 2 & 1 & 3 & 7 \\ 4 & 0 & 5 & 3 \\ 2 & -1 & 2 & 0 \\ 1 & 5 & -9 & 6 \end{vmatrix}$$

In preparing this program, switch columns if the value of the diagonal element is less than 10^{-5}.

You might note that this same difficulty plagues the Gauss reduction technique when used to solve sets of equations.

6-30. Another good exercise is to evaluate cofactors of a matrix. The cofactor A_{ij} of matrix A is $(-1)^{i+j}$ times the determinant formed by deleting row i and column j from the matrix. Prepare a program that performs the following:

(a) Reads matrix A.
(b) Reads i and j.
(c) Evaluates A_{ij}.
(d) Prints A_{ij}, i, and j.

Evaluate A_{13} for the following matrix:

$$\begin{bmatrix} 1 & 7 & 3 & 1 \\ 5 & -1 & 2 & 4 \\ -3 & 0 & -5 & 1 \\ 7 & 6 & 9 & -7 \end{bmatrix}$$

You may assume zeros never appear on the diagonal.

7

Input-Output Operations

In the previous chapters, input-output features were introduced only to the extent that enabled the input-output for the programs to be accomplished in a convenient manner. At this point it seems appropriate to devote an entire chapter to the subject of input-output in Fortran. Our previous discussion has been fairly complete with regard to most implementations of format-free input-output. We have by no means discussed all of the features of the FORMAT statement, and we will devote the first two sections of this chapter to this statement. Carriage control will also be described in more detail along with other forms of input-output statements.

Although Fortran was designed primarily for the processing of numerical data, the capabilities for processing character data are extensive. Although some other languages are superior to Fortran in this respect, the features available in Fortran permit some interesting problems involving character data to be undertaken. We shall devote an entire section to this subject, but the DATA statement in the previous section should be reviewed before undertaking this topic.

The final sections of the chapter describe features such as direct-access input-output and the NAMELIST statement that are powerful but not in widespread use.

7-1. FORMAT Field Specifications

Since I, E, and F fields were introduced in Chapter 3, the reader should be familiar with the concept of a field. However, some concepts will be repeated for completeness.

The *I field* is used in input-output operations involving fixed-point or integer variables. Important points are

1. The field specification is *rIw,* where *r* is the repetition number and *w* is the width of the field.

2. On input, any blanks within the I field are interpreted as zeros; hence, the input must be right justified. The computer automatically right justifies any output in the I field.

3. If no sign is provided on input, the number is assumed positive. On output a column must be provided for the sign if the number is negative. Positive numbers are written without a sign.

4. Any nonnumerical character other than the sign that appears in an I field on input is taken to be an indication of error.

5. When the field width on output is insufficient (for example, attempting to write -127 in field I2, a *format overflow* occurs. Some systems simply fill the specified field with asterisks (that is, the output is ** for the aforementioned case), while others write what they can starting from the right (that is, the output for this case is 27 with no indication of a format overflow. Asterisks or other mention that format overflow has occurred is the preferable and more common treatment.

As the I field has been used frequently in previous chapters, further discussion is unnecessary.

The *E field* is appropriate when a floating-point or real variable on either input or output is to appear with a numerical value accompanied by an exponent. The following points are pertinent:

1. The field specification is *rEw.d,* where *r* is the repetition number, *w* is the number of columns in the width of the field, and *d* is the number of digits following the decimal point.

2. The computer automatically right justifies the output in the E field. Normally, the value appears as $\pm 0.X_1X_2 \cdots X_dE \pm YY$ or minor variations thereof (e.g., $\pm X_0.X_1 \cdots X_dE \pm YY$, where $X_1X_2 \cdots X_d$ are the specified digits and YY is the exponent. Thus, if the value of 9727. is printed under E12.5, the result is b0.97270Eb04 (the b symbolizing a blank column). If the exponent is Eb00, these four characters are omitted by many computers.

3. On output, the minimum width of the E field can be readily obtained by accounting for each character:

Leading sign	1 column
Leading zero	1 column
Decimal point	1 column
d digits	*d* columns
Character E	1 column
Sign of the exponent	1 column
Exponent digits	2 columns
Total	$d + 7$

Thus the *minimum* value of *w* in *Ew.d* must be at least $d + 7$, or mathematically

$$w \geqslant d + 7$$

The E field is commonly used when the magnitude of the corresponding variable in the output list cannot be predicted with certainty. If the field width is insufficient, a format overflow occurs with results analogous to the results for the I field discussed previously. *Caution:* If the output specification is E7.0, the output is ±0.E ±YY. No significant digits are obtained, only the exponent.

4. Although the E field used for output is very regular in appearance, several variations can be conveniently used on input. Useful features include these:

(a) If a decimal point is provided, it overrides *d* in the field specification *Ew.d.* If the decimal is omitted, the *d* digits preceding the exponent in the field are placed to the right of the decimal. For example, if the value 13848 were entered as 13848E03 right justified in a field with specification E15.3, the number entered would be 13.848E03. If large amounts of data are to be keypunched, this feature saves time.

(b) If the exponent is E±00, the exponent can be omitted entirely. Furthermore, if the decimal point is provided, the E field need not be right justified. This applies only to this specific case. In all other cases, the entry in the E field must be right justified.

(c) If sufficient, only one digit of the exponent need be punched.

(d) Unsigned value or exponent is taken as positive.

(e) If the sign is present for both positive and negative exponents, the letter E may be omitted.

(f) A decimal point must not appear in the exponent.

As an illustration of these rules, the value 13848. may be entered in field E15.3 by any of the following entries:

```
+13848E+03
   13848E3
   13848+3
     13848.
 13.848E03
 1384.8E01
  13848+03
```

All except the entry 13848. must be right justified.

The *F field* is used whenever a floating-point or real variable without an exponent is to appear in the input or output. This field specification is *rFw.d,* where *r* is the repetition number, *w* columns are contained in the width of the field, and *d* digits appear after the decimal point.

On output, a decimal point is always provided (hence a space must be provided), and a space must be allowed for the sign if the number is negative. The F field must be used carefully on output. For example, the field specification F6.2 provides enough spaces only for numbers in the range −99.99 to 999.99. If the number is less than 1.0, a space must be provided for a zero before the decimal point. Furthermore, if the number 0.00127 is written under the specification F6.2, the output is 0.00 (two digits following decimal point). The F field is always right justified on cutput, and format overflows are treated in a manner analogous to their treatment for the I field.

On input the use of a decimal point overrides *d* and also removes the necessity of right justification. If no decimal point is provided, the last *d* digits in the F field are placed to the right of the decimal point. In this case, the entry must be right justified. For example, the entry 14276 read under F5.2 becomes 142.76 (two digits following decimal point).

A *scale factor* may be incorporated into the field specification whenever E or F fields are used. However, the scale factor does *not* act the same for F fields as for E fields, although the specification is *sPrFw.d* or *sPrEw.d* for the respective fields. In each case, *s* may be a positive or negative integer.

When used with the F field for either input or output, its effect is

$$\text{External value} = \text{internal value} \cdot 10^{s}$$

For example, if the fraction 0.278 is to be expressed as a percent, a field specification of 2PF10.1 gives the result 27.8. It can also be used on input and output if, for example, the values of certain variables are to be in kilograms on input and output but grams internally.

When the scale factor is used with the E field, the magnitude of the result is not altered. In fact, scale factors with E fields are ignored entirely on input. On output the fractional part is multiplied by 10^s and the exponent is reduced by s. Thus the magnitude is not affected, but the results are often more readable. For example, the field specification 1PE15.3 for listing 0.00137 yields 1.370E−03 instead of 0.137E−02. *Caution:* The rule $w \geq d + 7$ for E fields must be modified whenever a scale factor is used.

Another precaution is that a scale factor accompanying an E or F field is automatically applied to succeeding E *and* F fields until another scale factor is encountered. Thus if the scale factor is to affect only one field, the next E or F field must be accompanied by scale factor 0P.

The *G field* is a generalized format code that may be used for input-output of either integer or real data. The general form is *rGw.d*, where *r* is the repetition number, *w* is the width of the field, and *d* depends upon the type of the corresponding variable in the I/O list. If this variable is integer, the *.d* is ignored, and *rGw.d* is equivalent to *rIw*. On input of real variables, the data may appear with or without an exponent, and *d* is the number of digits to the right of the decimal point. On output, *d* is the number of significant digits to be transmitted. If the number is between .1 and 10***d*, the number is printed without an exponent. Otherwise, output is similar to that from the E field. The field width *w* should be sufficient to allow four spaces for the exponent if it is required.

The G field appears only in a few recent systems; therefore, programmers must check its availability before using it.

The *X field* is used to insert blanks into the output list or to ignore columns on input. The field specification *rX* on input causes *r* columns, which may or may not be blank, to be skipped. On output, *rX* causes *r* blank columns to be inserted. For example, the statements

```
      READ (5,5)A,B
    5 FORMAT (F6.0,6X,E7.0)
```

read the value of A from columns 1-6, skip columns 7-12, and read the value of B from columns 13-19. Columns 7-12 may or may not be blank. The use of the X field in the FORMAT statement is not reflected in the input or output variable listing, since no information transfer is associated with the X field.

On output, the X field can be used to provide additional spacing. To illustrate, the statements

```
      WRITE (6,7)A,B
    7 FORMAT (1X,F7.2,4X,E10.3)
```

yield the output (recall that the first character is used for carriage control, and does not appear in the output)

□□12.70□□□□□□0.170E□02

where □ designates a blank character.

The *T code* is a tab code used to specify the column with which the reading or writing for the following format code begins. The general form is *Tw*, where *w* is the column number. For example, consider the READ statement

```
READ (5,4)J,B
```

using the FORMAT statement

```
4   FORMAT (T4,I4,T27,F14.6)
```

The integer variable J is read from columns 4-7 and B is read from columns 27-40. Similarly, the statement

```
4   FORMAT (T4,I4,F14.6)
```

causes the input scan to begin with column 4.

The above manipulations could be obtained using the X field, but the T code is more powerful than this. For example, using the statement

```
4   FORMAT (T27,I4,T4,F14.6)
```

causes J to be read from columns 27-30 and B from columns 4-17. This specification can be used to read two variables from the same positions on the card. For example, using the statements

```
    READ (5,1)J,B
4   FORMAT (T4,I4,T4,F4.0)
```

causes the information in columns 4-7 to be stored in integer format in variable J and in real format in variable B.

The *Hollerith* or *H-field* is used in the format statement to insert characters into the output line. In the simplest version of this field specification, the desired characters to be output are simply enclosed in apostrophes.‡. For example, the statements

```
     A = 1.2
     WRITE (6,18) A
18   FORMAT (1X,'A□ =',F5.1)
```

generate the following output:

```
A□ = □□1.2
```

where □ designates the blank character. As a second example, the statements

```
    K = 12
    J = 1967
    WRITE (6,2)K,J
2   FORMAT (1X,'JUNE',I3,',',I5)
```

generate the following output:

```
JUNE□12,□1967
```

‡Although apostrophes are used in this text, many systems require quotation marks instead.

Special treatment must be given to apostrophes that occur naturally within the character data. For each apostrophe that appears in the message, an extra apostrophe must be inserted, giving consecutive apostrophes. On output, a single apostrophe is obtained. For example, the statements

```
   WRITE (6,30)
30 FORMAT (1X,'IT''S□TIME□TO□GO)
```

produce the output

```
IT'S□TIME□TO□GO
```

The use of apostrophes to designate a Hollerith field did not appear in early versions of Fortran, and it is not acceptable on a few current systems (generally small ones). These systems require that the field specification consist of the characters to be printed preceded by the letter H preceded by the number of characters in the message. Using this implementation, the FORMAT statements presented previously in this section appear as follows:

```
18 FORMAT (1X,3HA =,F5.1)
 2 FORMAT (1X,4HJUNE,I3,1H,,I5)
30 FORMAT (1X,15HIT'S TIME TO GO)
```

Apostrophes are not repeated in this version.

The main disadvantage of this version is that the programmer must count the characters in the message. However, this version is universally accepted, even on systems that also recognize the use of apostrophes.

The *A field* permits character data to be read and stored in variables. This field will not be discussed until a subsequent section devoted to character data in this chapter.

7-2. Carriage Control

The carriage on the high-speed printer can be controlled in much the same fashion as the carriage on a typewriter. Essentially all computing systems have adopted the convention of using the first character *in each line* of output for this purpose. This character is never printed, and it causes paper spacing as follows:

Character in Column 1	*Printer Action*	*Resulting Spacing*	*Field Specifications*
Blank	Advance carriage one line and then print	Single space	1X or '□' or 1H□
Zero	Advance carriage two lines and then print	Double space	'0' or 1H0
One	Advance carriage to top of page and then print	Skip to next next page	'1' or 1H1
Plus	Print without advancing carriage	Overprint	'+' or 1H+

As all output FORMAT statements considered in the previous sections began with 1X, single spacing was obtained.

The carriage control can be integrated with other field specifications. For example, the output from the statement

```
FORMAT (6X,F12.2)
```

is five blank columns followed by the floating-point number. The first blank from the X field causes the printer to single space. As a further illustration, consider the following statements:

```
    WRITE (6,2)
2   FORMAT ('1INPUTbPARAMETERS')
```

The words INPUT PARAMETERS are printed at the top of the next page, as dictated by the 1 in the first column.

Several characters besides the 0, the blank, the 1, or the + can be used to obtain carriage manipulations. These other options are used so infrequently that they will not be discussed here. However, the programmer should pay careful attention to carriage control, as some characters will cause the printer to continuously eject pages of blank paper. For a 600 line per minute printer, this is undesirable.

Another similar situation may arise when using a '1' or 1H1 field for carriage control (skip to a new page) in a statement to be executed repeatedly. Proper use is

```
    WRITE (6,10)
10  FORMAT ('1')
    DO 12 J = 1,N
    .
    .
    .
12  WRITE (6,11)ANSWER
11  FORMAT (1X,F20.6)
```

instead of placing the 1H1 within the DO loop as follows:

```
    DO 12 J = 1,N
    .
    .
    .
12  WRITE (6,11) ANSWER
11  FORMAT ('1',F20.6)
```

The first procedure places the first answer on a new page, subsequent answers appearing on the same page. The second procedure places each answer on a new page.

7-3. FORMAT Options

The repetition number used with an individual field can also be used with a group of fields by placing the group of fields within parentheses and placing the repetition number before the parentheses. Thus, the specification 2(F10.2,I6) is equivalent to F10.2,I6,F10.2,I6, but not to 2F10.2,2I6.

Another frequently used option is the slash (/) within the FORMAT statement, such as

```
      WRITE (6,1)N,A,B
    1 FORMAT (1X,I14/1X,2F14.4)
```

The slash causes one record line to be terminated and another to be begun. In the above case, N appears on the first line and A and B appear on the second line of the output. Note that carriage control is required for each line of output, and thus the 1X for carriage control follows the slash in the above example. Slashes on input are treated similarly.

Consecutive slashes simply cause consecutive record lines to be terminated. Although treated the same by the computer, slashes in the middle and at the end of the FORMAT statement appear to give slightly different results. Consider the statement

```
      READ (5,4)A,B
```

with the FORMAT statement

```
    4 FORMAT (/2F10.2)
```

Two cards in the input data are read, but the information on the first card is ignored entirely. On the other hand, if the FORMAT statement is

```
    4 FORMAT (F10.2/F10.2)
```

two cards are still read, but one value is read from each card. To read the value of A from the first card, skip the next card, and read the value of B from the third card, the appropriate FORMAT statement is

```
    4 FORMAT (F10.2//F10.2)
```

The first slash terminates the scan of the first card after reading a value for A. The second slash terminates the scan of the second card without reading any values, which in effect causes it to be skipped.

To generalize, $n + 1$ slashes at the beginning or end of the FORMAT statement cause $n + 1$ records to be skipped on input or $n + 1$ blank records to be written on output. However, $n + 1$ slashes in the middle of the FORMAT statement cause only n records to be skipped on input or n blank records to be written on output.

If the number of variables in an output list is less than the number of field specifications, output continues through Hollerith fields and slashes between the last used field specification and the next unused one (or the end of the FORMAT statement if the number of fields exactly equals the number of variables in the output list). That is, the output from

```
      WRITE (6,1)RES
    1 FORMAT (1X,F12.4'□OHMS'/)
```

appears as (RES = 1.7126)

```
□□□□□□1.7126□OHMS
```

followed by a blank line.

Parentheses within the FORMAT statement may be used in a manner other than with a repetition number. Consider the statements

```
      READ (5,2)N,A,B,C,D
    2 FORMAT (I5/(2F10.2))
```

Note that these parentheses are not preceded by a repetition number. The value of N is read from the first card, and the slash causes the input scan to proceed to the next card. The inner parentheses are ignored on the first pass through the FORMAT specifications, and variables A and B are read from the second card. Now the end of the FORMAT has been reached with two variables, C and D, remaining to be read. Control now reverts back to the *first preceding open parenthesis and the record line is terminated* (equivalent to a slash). Thus C and D are read from the third card according to 2F10.2. Such parentheses are treated analogously on output.

In order to ascertain how the Fortran compiler will treat parentheses in FORMAT statements, it is necessary to introduce the concept of *levels* for the parentheses. The pair of parentheses consisting of the open parenthesis following the word FORMAT and its associated close parenthesis are designated level 0 parentheses. The rule used to assign a level to a pair of parentheses is that their level is one higher than that of the pair of parentheses within which they are enclosed. This is illustrated by the following example:

```
19 FORMAT(1X,I5/2(5X,2F14,4)/3(4X,I5,2(I4, F8.4),3X),F10.1)
                                        level 2
                  level 1           level 1
                             level 0
```

When the format scan reaches the final close parenthesis (level 0), the rescan rule is that control reverts back to the repetition count of the rightmost level 1 sub-pair of parentheses. If there are no level 1 parentheses, then control reverts back to the first field in the FORMAT statement.

Although this book has generally followed the practice of using commas to separate all fields in a FORMAT statement, most compilers permit a comma to be omitted provided that the result would not be ambiguous. For example, the comma in 1X,3F10.5 can be omitted to give 1X3F10.5, which can only be interpreted as fields of 1X and 3F10.5. However, the comma in 3F10.5,12X cannot be omitted since 3F10.512X could be interpreted as either 3F10.5,12X or 3F10.51,2X. However, it is not incorrect to insert commas between all fields, and many programmers insert them for clarity. Furthermore, the compilers are not consistent with respect to the rules governing which commas may be omitted.

7-4. Other Input-Output Statements

In the previous cases the input or output statements have followed the form READ (5,*i*) or WRITE (6,*i*), where *i* specified the FORMAT statement. The more general forms are WRITE (*n*,*i*) or READ (*n*,*i*), where *n* denotes the *logical unit* involved. Although the statement number *i* must be an integer number, *n* may be either an integer variable or constant. The specific configuration of the logical units depends upon the particular installation, but the total number is usually about ten. Logical unit 5 is the card reader, logical unit 6 is the systems output tape which is subsequently printed, logical unit 7 is the card punch, and the use of the remaining logical units varies so much from one installation to the next that the specific computer center should be consulted for this information. Generally, these units are used for intermediate storage of large amounts of data, and the center can advise as to the best units to use.

When reading cards online, the logical unit may be omitted from the READ statement in some versions of Fortran IV to give

READ *i, list*

where *i* is the FORMAT statement number. Note that *i* is not enclosed in parentheses, but it is followed by a comma. Similarly, printing and punching online (as explained previously in Table 3-2) on some machines can be dictated by

PRINT *i,list*
PUNCH *i,list*

In other installations, the statement

PRINT *i, list*

is equivalent to

WRITE (6,*i*) *list*

in that all output is on logical unit 6, the system output tape.

When transferring large amounts of information to or from logical devices other than 5 or 6, the use of binary (the internal numbering system in the machine) can speed up the process by eliminating the conversion from binary to BCD (binary coded decimal), or vice versa. As this also eliminates the need for a FORMAT statement, the READ and WRITE statements become

READ (*n*)*list*
WRITE (*n*)*list*

To facilitate these intermediate input-output operations, the instructions END FILE *n*, REWIND *n*, and BACKSPACE *n* are used, respectively, to place a mark denoting that the last record has been encountered, to rewind the tape, or to backspace one record (the information corresponding to one card or printed line). Of course, these instructions are not permitted for logical units 5 (the card reader), 6 (the systems output unit), or 7 (the card punch).

Recent versions of Fortran IV also permit extension of the READ statement to include transfers upon encounter of an end-of-data and/or an error in the input data. For example, the statement

READ (5,7,END = 19,ERR = 8)A,I,D

would read information from logical unit 5 according to FORMAT statement 7. If an end-of-data is encountered, control is transferred to statement 19. If an error is encountered in the input control is transferred to statement 8.

To illustrate the use of the END = option, suppose we write a program to compute the arithmetic average of a set of numbers which are punched one per card in the first ten columns in F10.0 format. It is not known how many numbers are in the set, but we will assume there are too many to be conveniently counted. Using the END = option in the READ statement, the program in Figure 7-1 counts the cards, sums the numbers, and computes their average. The END = transfer is made upon encounter of a control card in the input data. The deck arrangement must therefore be such that a control card always follows the input data.

```
              N=0
              SUM=0.
      2       READ(5,1,END=4) A
      1       FORMAT(F10.0)
              SUM=SUM+A
              N=N+1
              GOTO2
      4       AVG=SUM/N
              WRITE(6,3)AVG
      3       FORMAT('  AVERAGE =',F10.3)
              STOP
              END
```

(a) Program

```
5.872
15.422
1.245
-2.111
12.55
6.222
```

(b) Input data

```
AVERAGE =        6.533
```

(c) Output

Figure 7-1. Example of the use of the END = option

Many systems that do not recognize the END = feature as described here provide an alternate mechanism to accomplish the same objective. For example, some systems recognize the following special form of the IF statement:

$$\text{IF (EOD)}n_1,n_2$$

which must appear immediately following the READ statement. Upon encounter of end-of-data (EOD), control is transferred to statement n_2; otherwise, control is transferred to statement n_1.

7-5. The DATA Statement

Up to this point, the value 2.7 could be stored in the variable A by either reading the information from a card or by equating with an arithmetic statement such as A = 2.7. If the value of A never changed from one run to the next, reading the value of A would be a nuisance when preparing the data cards. The use of the statement A = 2.7 suffers the disadvantages that, first it is an executable statement and requires time to execute, and second the storage of the associated instructions may consume critically needed storage for large programs. To alleviate these situations, the DATA statement is used to assign the desired values to such variables *before* execution of the program begins. Since this occurs before execution, the DATA statement is not executable.

The general form of the DATA statement is

$$\text{DATA } \mathit{list}/d_1,\ n_1 * d_2,\ \cdots,\ d_n/,\ \mathit{list}/d_1,\ d_2,\ \cdots\ d_m/,\ \cdots/$$

The rules governing the list are the same as in READ or WRITE statements. That is, implied DO's (only with numerical values for n_1 n_2 n_3), use of array names without subscripts, use of subscripted variables (subscript must be given a numerical value unless within an implied DO), and other options available in READ or WRITE lists are permissible.‡ The list is separated from the values by a slash, and the numerical values are separated by commas. The use of $n_1 * d_2$, where n_1 is an integer constant, denotes that d_2 is repeated n_1 times. The number of variables in the list should equal the number of constants supplied.

As an example, the nonsubscripted variables X,Y,J,B, and A may be assigned values with either of the following DATA statements:

```
DATA X,Y,J,B,A/12.1,1.7E-2,5,2 * 8./
DATA X,Y/12.1,1.7E-2/,J/5/,B,A/2 * 8./
```

Several other possibilities may be suggested. The implied DO can be used to set the first twelve elements of one-dimensional array C equal to 1.0 as follows:

```
DATA (C(J),J = 1,12)/12 * 1.0/
```

If C were dimensioned as containing only twelve elements, this could also be accomplished by

```
DATA C/12 * 1.0/
```

Recall that the DATA statement is not executable. Thus, these variables are assigned these values at the beginning of execution with the DATA statement. It is permissible to redefine these variables in any way desired, but the DATA statement may not be reexecuted to reassign to them their initial values.

Further examples of the use of the DATA statement will be given in the following section.

7-6. Character Data

In all examples presented up to this point, only numerical values were stored in variables. Although Fortran's main advantages lie in the realm of numerical computations, Fortran permits rather extensive character manipulation.

As an example of a program that involves the processing of character data, we shall write a program that reads a temperature from columns 1-10 in F10.0 format and reads the scale from column 11, an F representing Fahrenheit and C representing Centigrade. The program should print the temperature in both °F and °C. The appropriate conversions are

$$°F = 1.8 \times °C + 32$$
$$°C = (°F - 32)/1.8$$

In order to solve this problem, we must first discuss the FORMAT features as they apply to character data. The appropriate field specification is the A field whose general form is rAw, where r is the repetition number and w is the width of the field. For example, the statements

‡Not all machines will accept implied DO's or variables written with subscripts in DATA statements. However, all will accept nonsubscripted array names.

```
      READ (5,8)T,J
 8    FORMAT (F10.0,A1)
```

read a numerical value from the first ten columns and store it in variable T and read a character from column 11 and store it in variable J.

In Fortran, character data can be stored in either integer or real variables. That is, the above READ statement could be changed to

```
      READ (5,8)T,S
```

However, in some systems real arithmetic can cause strange things to happen, making the use of integer variables preferable. We shall return to this point later.

The number of characters that can be stored in a single variable depends upon the system, with values commonly ranging from two to ten. Since a number of current systems permit four characters to be stored in a single variable, we shall use four throughout this text. For example, suppose the characters COMPUTER are punched in the first eight columns of a card, and are to be read and stored in memory. Since the word COMPUTER consists of eight characters, two storage locations will be required. The following three examples will produce the desired results:

```
      READ (5,4)JA,JB
 4    FORMAT (2A4)
```

```
      DIMENSION J(2)
      READ (5,4)(J(K),K = 1,2)
 4    FORMAT (2A4)
```

```
      DIMENSION J(2)
      READ (5,4)J
 4    FORMAT (2A4)
```

The following example is not correct (K is a simple variable):

```
      READ (5,4)K
 4    FORMAT (A8)
```

These statements specify the entry of eight characters of data into a single storage location, which in our system can store only four characters. In these cases, the system will store only the four rightmost characters in the A8 field.

Similarly, the following example is incorrect:

```
      DIMENSION J(2)
      READ (5,4)(J(K),K = 1,2)
 4    FORMAT (A8)
```

The FORMAT statement specifies that each card contains one field eight columns in width. The READ statement calls for the entry of the values for two variables. Recall that the contents of each field in the FORMAT statement are entered into a single variable. Therefore these statements cause the characters in columns 5-8 of the first card to be stored in J(1) and the characters in columns 5-8 of the second card to be stored in J(2).

In the temperature problem described above, an appropriate READ statement is as follows:

```
      READ (5,4)T,J
 4    FORMAT (F10.0,A1)
```

How do we determine if J contains the character F or the character C? The logical IF may be used to determine equality or inequality, or the arithmetic IF may be used to determine if an expression is zero or nonzero.

A few systems permit the use of alphanumeric constants as in the following statements:

```
IF (J.EQ.'F')GO TO 8
IF (J - 'F')9,8,9
```

where control is transferred to statement 8 only if J contains the character 'F'. However, most systems do not recognize alphanumeric constants used in this fashion.

The only alternative is to read character data into variables or to initialize character data into variables by the DATA statement. For example, variables ICHF and ICHC could be initialized to the characters F and C, respectively, by the following DATA statement:

```
DATA ICHF,ICHC/'F','C'/
```

All systems will now recognize the following statements:

```
IF (J.EQ.ICHF)GO TO 8
IF (J - ICHF)9,8,9
```

These statements are examples that justify the previous suggestion that integer variables be used to store character data. If real variables are used, the problems mentioned in Chapter 4 regarding comparing real variables for equality apply. Comparing real variables for equality is always a questionable undertaking.

Another problem that may occur is illustrated by the following statements:

```
DATA CHC,ICHC/'C','C'/
IF (CHC.EQ.ICHC)GO TO 20
```

At first glance, it appears that we are comparing character C to character C, which are surely equal. However, Fortran evaluates such comparisons using arithmetic operations. The above IF statement calls for the comparison of an integer variable to a real variable. In such cases, the integer variable is converted to real before the comparison is made. If an integer variable containing the character C is converted to real, the result is not the character C. Therefore, the above statement would conclude that ICHC does not equal CHC.

The complete program for the temperature example posed earlier in this section is given in Figure 7-2. The character in column 11 is read into variable J, and it is then compared to the character F in ICHF and the character C in ICHC. If equality is found, the appropriate conversion is made. If no equality is found, an error message is printed.

To illustrate the flexibility of Fortran in character manipulations, suppose we write a program to prepare a plot on the printer. Specifically, we shall plot the following arrays:

x	y
1.2	52.7
4.6	8.1
1.8	40.2
0.2	75.6
3.2	23.5
2.5	31.6

We shall plot x on the horizontal axis (columns) and y on the vertical axis (lines). The plot shall be fifty columns in width and forty columns in height. The scales are 0 to 5 for x and 0 to 100 for y.

The flowchart, the program, and the resulting plot are given in Figure 7-3. The values of x and y are first read. In preparing the plot, the general approach is to use an

```
        DATA ICHC,ICHF/'C','F'/
    8   READ(5,4)T,J
    4   FORMAT(F10.0,A1)
        IF(J.EQ.ICHF)GOTO2
        IF(J.EQ.ICHC)GOTO3
        WRITE(6,6)J
    6   FORMAT(' INVALID SCALE ',A1)
        GOTO8
    2   TF=T
        TC=(T-32.)/1.8
    7   WRITE(6,5)TF,TC
    5   FORMAT(' TEMPERATURE IS',F8.2,' DEG F OR',F8.2,' DEG C')
        GOTO8
    3   TC=T
        TF=1.8*TC+32.
        GOTO7
        END
```

(a) Program

```
156.2      F
147.5      D
22.1       C
```

(b) Input data

```
TEMPERATURE IS   156.20 DEG F OR    69.00 DEG C
INVALID SCALE D
TEMPERATURE IS    71.78 DEG F OR    22.10 DEG C
```

(c) Output

Figure 7-2. Program for temperature conversions

array IP of fifty elements to store the fifty characters to be printed on each line of the plot. Since we start plotting at the top, the line index I is set equal to forty and decremented. Each line of the plot entails the following computations:

1. Each element of array IP is set equal to a blank character.
2. For each value of Y, the line IY on which the point should appear is computed.
3. If IY equals the current value of I, the column IX in which the point should appear is computed, and IP(IX) is set equal to the asterisk character.
4. The line is printed, with every tenth line bearing an annotation for the y-axis.

After printing the forty lines of the graph, the x-axis is printed.

Some increase in the efficiency of the program in Figure 7-3 could be obtained by precomputing the line indices for each value of Y and storing them in an array.

As a final example of the processing of character data, we shall prepare a program to code a message, a process known as *enciphering*. In our approach we begin with an original message (called the *clear*) such as the following:

HE HAD A BAD DAY

In performing the enciphering, we will use another message called the keyword. In our example, the keyword will be COMPUTER.

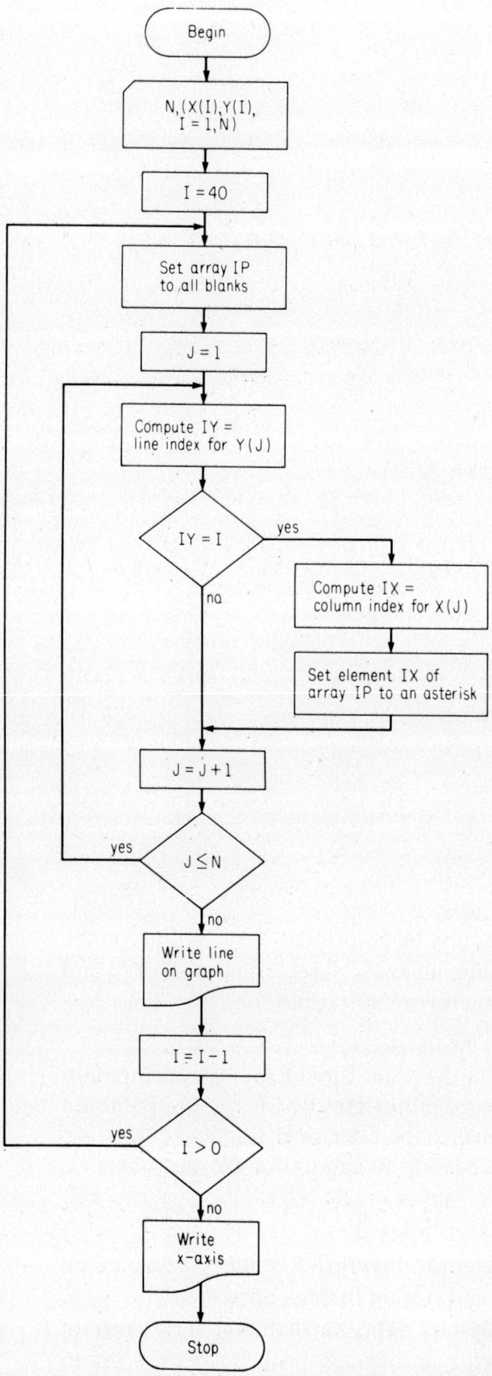

(a) Flowchart

```
      DIMENSION X(20),Y(20),IP(50)
      DATA IB,IA/' ','*'/
C-----READ DATA TO BE PLOTTED
      READ(5,1)N,(X(I),Y(I),I=1,N)
 1    FORMAT(I5/(2F10.0))
C-----ADVANCE TO NEW PAGE
      WRITE(6,10)
 10   FORMAT('1')
C-----START AT TOP LINE OF PLOT (I=40)
      I=40
C-----BLANK ENTIRE LINE
 5    DO2K=1,50
 2    IP(K)=IB
C-----EXAMINE DATA POINTS TO SEE IF ANY SHOULD
C             APPEAR ON THIS LINE
      DO3J=1,N
C-----COMPUTE LINE INDEX
      IY=Y(J)/2.5+.5
C-----IF LINE INDEX NOT EQUAL TO THIS LINE
C             PROCEED TO NEXT POINT
      IF(IY.NE.I)GOTO3
C-----COMPUTE COLUMN INDEX
      IX=X(J)*10.+.5
C-----PLACE * AT COLUMN INDEX
      IP(IX)=IA
 3    CONTINUE
C-----Y-AXIS ANNOTATION IS EVERY 10 LINES
      IF((I/10)*10.EQ.I)GOTO4
C-----WRITE WITHOUT Y-AXIS ANNOTATION
      WRITE(6,20)IP
 20   FORMAT(11X,'*',50A1)
      GOTO6
C-----WRITE WITH Y-AXIS ANNOTATION
 4    YP=2.5*I
      WRITE(6,21)YP,IP
 21   FORMAT(1X,F8.0,2X,'+',50A1)
C-----GO TO NEXT LINE
 6    I=I-1
C-----STOP AFTER 40 LINES (I=0)
      IF(I.GT.0)GOTO5
C-----WRITE X-AXIS
      YP=0.
      WRITE(6,22)YP
 22   FORMAT(1X,F8.0,2X,'+',5('*********+'))
C-----COMPUTE X-AXIS ANNOTATION
      DO9I=1,6
 9    X(I)=I-1
C-----WRITE X-AXIS ANNOTATION
      WRITE(6,12)(X(I),I=1,6)
 12   FORMAT(2X,6F10.1)
      STOP
      END
```

(b) Program

```
    6
1.2       52.7
4.6       8.1
1.8       40.2
0.2       75.6
3.2       23.5
2.5       31.6
```

(c) Input data

Figure 7-3. Plotting on the output printer

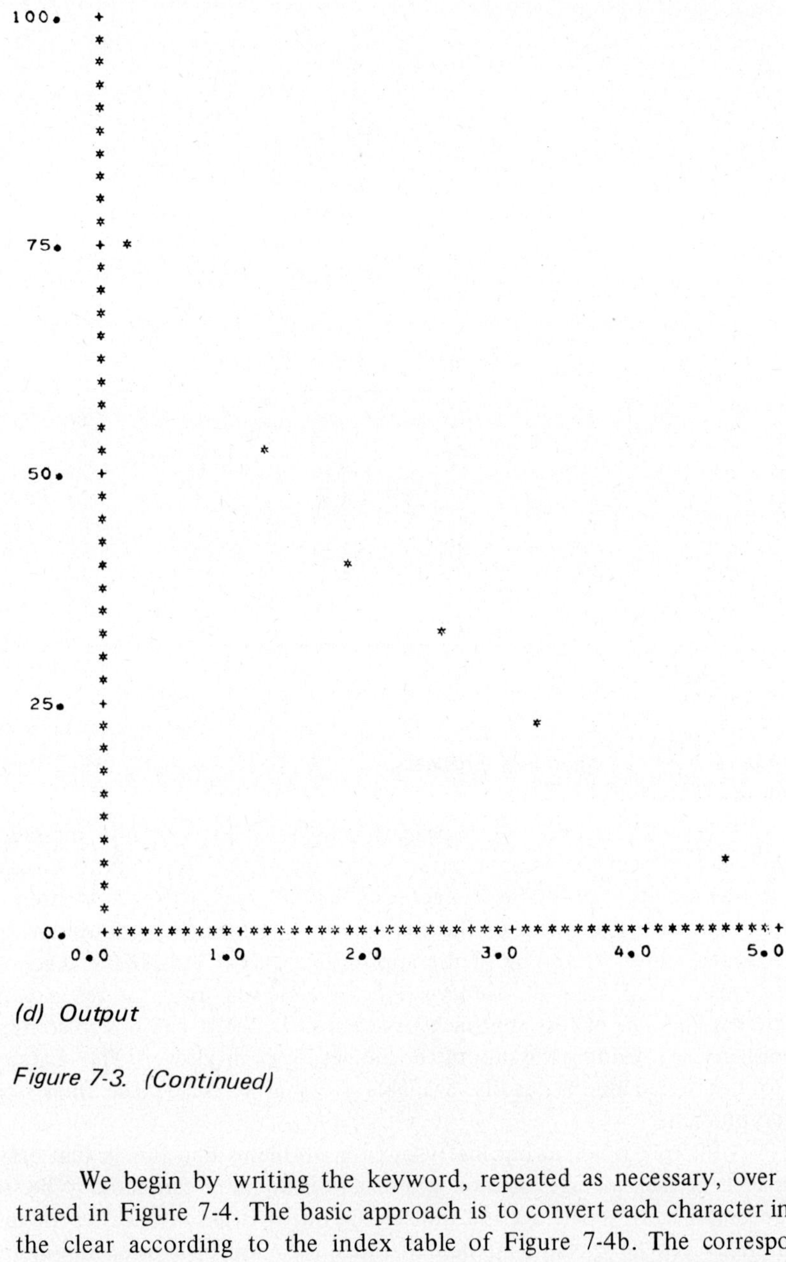

(d) Output

Figure 7-3. (Continued)

We begin by writing the keyword, repeated as necessary, over the clear, as illustrated in Figure 7-4. The basic approach is to convert each character in the keyword and the clear according to the index table of Figure 7-4b. The corresponding indices are added; the result is then increased by ten, and then twenty-seven is subtracted whenever necessary in order to obtain a result between zero and twenty-six. Looking up the corresponding character in the index table gives the coded message.

The flowchart and program for the enciphering process are given in Figure 7-5. The keyword and message are read into arrays KEY and MSG, storing one character per storage location. The next step is to convert each character of the keyword to its index, which is stored in array NKEY. To do this for a given character, it is compared to each element of array SYM (defined in the DATA statement) until an equality is located. The appropriate index is one less than the index of the element in SYM.

KEYWORD	C	O	M	P	U	T	E	R	C	O	M	P	U	T	E	R
CLEAR	H	E	□	H	A	D	□	A	□	B	A	D	□	D	A	Y
KEYWORD INDEX	3	15	13	16	21	20	5	18	3	15	13	16	21	20	5	18
CLEAR INDEX	8	5	0	8	1	4	0	1	0	2	1	4	0	4	1	25
SUM	11	20	13	24	22	24	5	19	3	17	14	20	21	24	6	43
ADD 10	21	30	23	34	32	34	15	29	13	27	24	30	31	34	16	53
SUBTRACT 27	21	3	23	7	5	7	15	2	13	0	24	3	4	7	16	26
CODED MESSAGE	U	C	W	G	E	G	O	B	M	□	X	C	D	G	P	Z

(a) Enciphering a message

Character	Index	Character	Index	Character	Index
□	0	I	9	R	18
A	1	J	10	S	19
B	2	K	11	T	20
C	3	L	12	U	21
D	4	M	13	V	22
E	5	N	14	W	23
F	6	O	15	X	24
G	7	P	16	Y	25
H	8	Q	17	Z	26

(b) Index table

Figure 7-4. The enciphering process

The next section then processes the characters in the message one at a time, converting them to the appropriate character in the cryptogram. Variable J serves as the pointer to the appropriate character in the keyword. It is incremented to eight, and then reset to one. The index of the character in the message is determined by the approach outlined above. The value of the appropriate element in NKEY is added, ten is added to the result, and units of twenty-seven are removed until the result is between zero and twenty-six. The easiest approach to accomplish the last step is to compute the remainder obtained by dividing the sum of the indices by twenty-seven. The character corresponding to this remainder is readily available from array SYM. The final step is to print the cryptogram.

Fortran is somewhat inefficient for problems like this in that only one character is stored in each storage location whereas four or more can actually be stored. This can be accomplished by packing and unpacking, but it is usually not worth the effort. Even so, Fortran can be used to introduce students to the processing of nonnumeric data, and several exercises on this topic are available at the end of this chapter.

7-7. Execution-Time FORMATs

Consider the case in which a general program has been prepared for use in several applications. Furthermore, assume that there is considerable input according to the read statement

```
READ (5,8) N,(A(J),B(J),J = 1,N)
```

Using only previously discussed features of Fortran, each user must prepare his data to be consistent with FORMAT statement number 8.

To surmount this disadvantage, the object-time FORMAT can be employed. In this case, the READ statement is modified to

```
READ (5,X) N,(A(J),B(J),J = 1,N)
```

where X is a one-dimensional array containing the FORMAT specifications. Specifically, consider the case in which the data are to be entered according to

```
FORMAT (I5/(F12.2,E17.3))
```

The pertinent parts of the program are

```
      DIMENSION X(10), A(200), B(200)
      READ (5,6) (X(J),J = 1,10)
    6 FORMAT (10A4)
      READ (5,X) N, (A(J), B(J), J = 1,N)
```

The data card containing the format would contain the following information anywhere in the first forty (dictated by 10A4) columns:

```
(I5/(F12.2,E17.3))
```

Note that the word FORMAT and the statement number are not punched.

The array X in the above example is dimensioned as ten for illustrative purposes only. It may be as large (or small) as necessary, and extremely long FORMATs may be read from more than one card as necessary. Of course, the field specification A4 varies from machine to machine as discussed in the previous section.

7-8. Direct Access Input-Output

Programs for problems requiring the storage of significant amounts of data on peripheral storage devices tend to require input-output capabilities beyond that normally required for most programs. All previous input-output statements involve the reading or writing of records in a sequential fashion. That is, there is no means by which an individual record can be retrieved directly. The direct access I/O statements can only be used with direct access storage devices such as a magnetic disc, but these statements allow individual records to be stored and retrieved directly from such devices.

The direct access statements permit the programmer to define files on the peripheral devices, and then under program control to locate a record in these files, to read the contents of this record, or to write new information in this record. The four statements are

DEFINE FILE *j*(*m*,*r*,*f*,*v*)
FIND (*i'u*)
READ (*i'u*,*n*) *list*
WRITE (*i'u*,*n*) *list*

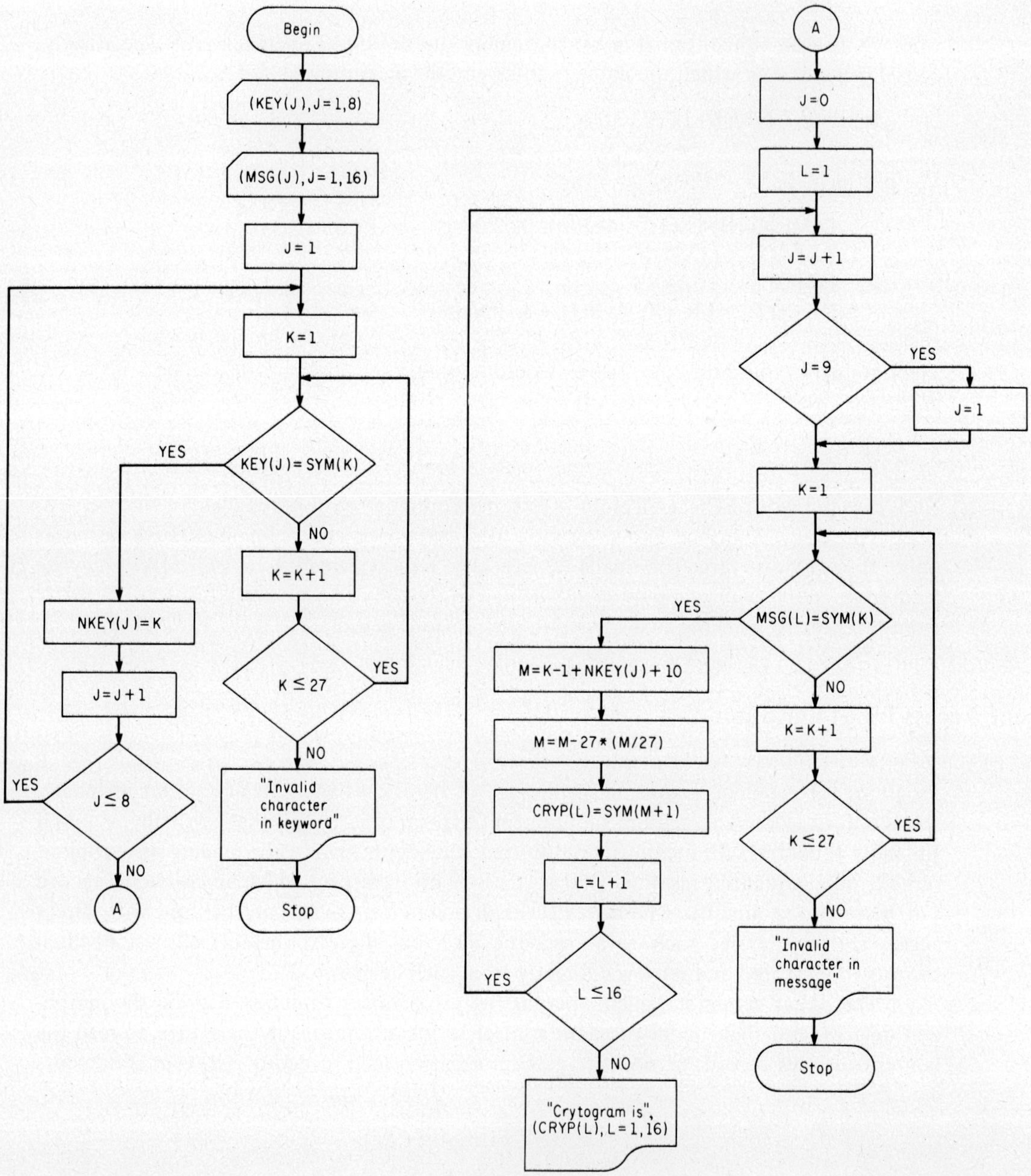

(a) Flowchart

Figure 7-5. Flowchart and program for the enciphering problem

```
      INTEGER KEY(8),MSG(16),SYM(27),NKEY(8),CRYP(16)
      DATA SYM/' ','A','B','C','D','E','F','G','H','I','J','K',
     1 'L','M','N','O','P','Q','R','S','T','U','V','W','X','Y','Z'/
      READ(5,1)KEY,MSG
    1 FORMAT(8A1/16A1)
      DO2J=1,8
      DO3K=1,27
      IF(KEY(J).EQ.SYM(K))GOTO2
    3 CONTINUE
      WRITE(6,4)
    4 FORMAT(' INVALID CHARACTER IS KEYWORD')
      STOP
    2 NKEY(J)=K-1
      J=0
      DO5L=1,16
      J=J+1
      IF(J.EQ.9)J=1
      DO6K=1,27
      IF(MSG(L),EQ.SYM(K))GOTO7
    6 CONTINUE
      WRITE(6,8)
    8 FORMAT(' INVALID CHARACTER IN MESSAGE')
    7 M=K+NKEY(J)+9
      M=M-27*(M/27)
    5 CRYP(L)=SYM(M+1)
      WRITE(6,9)CRYP
    9 FORMAT('0CRYPTOGRAM IS ',16A1)
      STOP
      END
```

(b) Program

```
$ENTRY
COMPUTER
HE HAD A BAD DAY
```

(c) Input data

```
CRYPTOGRAM IS UCWGEGOBM XCDGPZ
```

(d) Output

Figure 7-5. (Continued)

Typical examples of each are

DEFINE FILE 2(15,20,E,JFL)
FIND (2'JFL)
READ (2'JFL,7)A
WRITE (2'JFL,8) B

Each of these will be discussed in detail.

The DEFINE FILE is a specification statement used to establish the file on the peripheral device. The various items in the above statement are defined as follows:

- *j* is an unsigned integer number that designates a particular file.
- *m* is an unsigned integer number that specifies the number of records in a particular file.
- *v* is a nonsubscripted integer variable (called an associated variable) that after execution of a READ or WRITE statement contains the designation of the next record in the file.

f must be one of the following letters:

- E specifies that a FORMAT statement will be used in conjunction with the READ or WRITE statements. Information is thus stored in the form of characters.
- U specifies that a FORMAT statement will not be used. Information is thus stored in binary representation.
- L specifies that the READ or WRITE statements may be used with or without a FORMAT statement. Information is thus stored in either binary or character representation.

r is an unsigned integer number that specifies the size of each record in the file. Depending upon *f* (E,U, or L), *r* is one of the following:

f	*r*
E	characters
U	words
L	bytes

The *byte* probably deserves some explanation. On machines like the IBM 360, the fundamental storage unit is the byte, which contains eight bits. Thus, one word contains four bytes. Furthermore, one character may be stored in one byte. Thus, if *f* equals L and *r* is 400, then 400 characters or 100 words may be stored in one record on the file.

The WRITE and READ statements are quite similar to the more common statements of this type discussed earlier. The only difference is that the logical unit number is replaced by the file and record designation, *i'u*. The possibilities are

WRITE (*i'u,n*) *list*
READ (*i'u,n,* ERR = *d*) *list*

The individual items in these statements are defined as follows:

- *i* is an unsigned integer number *or variable* that designates the file to be used. Of course, the file must be specified in a DEFINE FILE statement.
- *u* is an integer variable *or expression* that designates the particular record in the file that is to be read or written. After execution of the READ or WRITE statement, the value of the associated variable (*v* in the DEFINE FILE statement) contains the designation of the next subsequent record in the file.
- *n* is a FORMAT statement number, if required.
- *list* is the same as in standard READ and WRITE statements, but it must not contain the associated variable.

The *i'u* appearing in the FIND statement is defined in the same manner as for the READ or WRITE statements.

Now for a few examples. Suppose two files are defined as follows:

```
DEFINE FILE 8(50,100,E,IFL8), 33(10,20,U,IFL33)
```

Thus file 8 contains fifty records of 100 characters each; file 33 contains ten records of twenty words each. A FORMAT statement must be used to read or write on file 8, but must not be used for file 33.

Suppose variables A and B are to be written into the fifth record on each file. The statements are

```
       WRITE (8'5,20)A,B
  20   FORMAT (2F10.4)
       WRITE (33'5)A,B
```

After execution of these statements, both IFL8 and IFL33 equal 6. Similarly, these READ statements may be used to retrieve this information

```
  K = 8
  IFL8 = 5
  READ (K'IFL8,20)A,B
  J = 3
  READ (33'J + 2)A,B
```

If A and B are to be written on successive records in file 8, a slash in the FORMAT statement or other equivalent measures can be used. For example, the statements

```
      WRITE (8'10,4)A,B
  4   FORMAT (F10.4/E20.7)
```

cause A to be stored in record ten and B in record eleven. After execution of this statement, IFL8 equals twelve.

The FIND statement is used to keep the computer's processing unit from being idle during the finite time required for the peripheral device to locate the record. For example, the statements

```
  FIND (8'7)
     .
     .
     .
  READ (8'7,20)A,B
```

allow the record to be located while the computer is also performing the calculations for the statements between the FIND and the READ. However, the FIND in consecutive statements such as

```
  FIND (8'4)
  READ (8'4,20)A,B
```

serves no useful purpose and should be omitted. After execution of a FIND statement, the associated variable contains the location of the record designated in the FIND.

7-9. NAMELIST

Many recent versions of Fortran IV permit input-output using the NAMELIST feature. A NAMELIST statement such as

```
  NAMELIST /XYZ1/I,J,P,X(2,3)
```

designates which variables are to be read or printed by input-output statements of the type

```
  READ (5,XYZ1)
  WRITE (6,XYZ1)
```

The NAMELIST statement has the general form

NAMELIST $/x/a,b, \cdots, c/z/d,e, \cdots, f$

where x and z are NAMELIST names and $a,b, \cdots, f$ are variable or array names. Note the use of slashes to enclose the NAMELIST names, and commas to separate the variable or array names.

Subsequent to the appearance of the NAMELIST statement, input-output statements of the form

```
READ (n,x)
WRITE (n,x)
```

may be used. The n denotes the logical unit to be used, and x is the appropriate NAMELIST name.

On input, the data must be in a special form in order to be read using the NAMELIST feature. For example, consider the statements

```
DIMENSION I(5)
NAMELIST /ME/A,B,I
READ (5,ME)
```

An appropriate input card could be (b symbolizes a blank column)

```
b&MEbI=7,3*0,14,A=1.76,B=-2.01,&END
```

The rules are

1. The first column *must* be blank.
2. The second column *must* contain the character &.
3. This character is immediately followed by the NAMELIST name, with no embedded blanks.
4. The NAMELIST name is followed by a blank.
5. The items in the list *must* be separated by commas.
6. The two types of permissible items are
   (a) *Variable name = constant,* where the variable name may be a subscripted array name.
   (b) *Array name = set of constants,* where the array name is *not* subscripted. The constants are separated by commas, and successive occurrences of the same constant are entered in the form *k* ∗ *constant* as for the DATA statement. The number of constants *must* be less than or equal to the number of elements in the array.
7. The order is insignificant, but all variable and array names *must* have appeared in the NAMELIST list.
8. The list of items is terminated with &END, which may or may not be separated from the last item by a comma (Note: WATFIV requires either a space or a comma). Successive cards are processed until &END is found, thus allowing several cards to be used for entering the data.

On execution of the READ statement, successive entries in the input data are examined until the entry with the appropriate NAMELIST name is located.

On output, the data written using the NAMELIST list is in a form that can be read using the NAMELIST list. The fields for all entries are appropriately selected such that all significant digits are retained. For example, using the statement

WRITE (6, ME)

with the NAMELIST given above gives the following output:

1st line	&ME
2nd line	A=1.76000000,B=-2.01000000,I=7,0,0,0,14
3rd line	&END

The constants in the list may be of any type, including literal (Note: WATFIV prints real constants in the exponential format, and places &END at the end of the list of constants instead of on a separate line.).

7-10. In Summary

Since the ability to communicate with the computer is an important part of programming, this chapter should be given due attention. Not all format features are treated in this chapter, but the ones treated are common to essentially all Fortrans. The following exercises should elucidate the use of the concepts presented in this chapter.

EXERCISES‡

The following exercises emphasize the input-output of information. An effort has been made to keep the numerical calculations to a minimum, or to use programs presented earlier. The figures associated with the exercises are intended to give the general form of the output, and it is not intended that the student count the exact number of blank spaces, indented spaces, etc. Pay careful attention to carriage control.

7-1. Prepare a program to evaluate the factorials of the numbers 1 through 12. The output should be in columnar fashion, the columns labeled NUMBER and FACTORIAL.

7-2. The binomial coefficients $\binom{n}{j}$ are given by the following expression:

$$\binom{n}{j} = \frac{n!}{j!\,(n-j)!}, \qquad j = 0, 1, \cdots, n$$

Prepare a program to read a value for n (use $n = 8$ for this case), compute the binomial

```
THE BINOMIAL COEFFICIENTS FOR N =        8

  N        J         COEFFICIENT
  8        0                   1
  8        1                   8
  8        2                  28
  8        3                  56
  8        4                  70
  8        5                  56
  8        6                  28
  8        7                   8
  8        8                   1
```

Exercise 7-2

‡Solutions to Exercises marked with a dagger † are given in Appendix E.

coefficients, and print the results as in the illustration. Assume n is always greater than 1. The cautious programmer will note that the first term is 1, and each succeeding term is simply $(n - j + 1)/j$, $j = 1,2, \ldots, n$, times the preceding term. Programming in this manner avoids overflows which may occur if the factorials are evaluated directly. (This is not the case for $n = 8$, and such programming may be used if desired.)

†**7-3.** Consider the following experiment:

(a) Fill a vessel of known size and weight with a porous medium, sand, for example, and weigh.
(b) Fill all voids with water, and weigh again.

The difference between the weights gives the weight of water, which can be divided by its density (62.4 lb/ft^3) to give the volume of water or void volume. The void fraction is the void volume divided by the total volume. The true density is the dry weight minus the weight of the container, all divided by the total volume minus the void volume.

The input to the program is the two weights (in pounds). The container is cylindrical, 0.333 ft in diameter and 0.75 ft in height, weighing 1.04 lb. Enter these and the density of water via a DATA statement. The output should appear as shown.

```
DIMENSIONS OF CONTAINER -
     DIAMETER            0.3330 FT
     HEIGHT            0.7500 FT
     WEIGHT            1.0400 LB


WEIGHT WITHOUT WATER              7.1200

WEIGHT WITH WATER              8.3000

VOID FRACTION            0.2895

DENSITY OF MATERIAL            131.0093 LB/CU FT
```

Exercise 7-3

7-4. In elementary physics courses, the following experiment is often run in the laboratory:

(a) An object is weighed in the atmosphere.
(b) The same object is weighed while suspended under water.

The objective is to calculate the specific gravity or density of the material in the object. Of course, this only works for objects whose specific gravity is greater than one.

The calculations are: first, subtract the weight in water from the weight in air to obtain weight of displaced water, then divide by the density of water (1.0 gm/cc) to obtain the volume of the object. The normal weight of the object divided by its volume is its density (gm/cc) or specific gravity.

Prepare a program to read the respective weights, perform the calculations, and print the results in a fashion similar to that shown.

```
DENSITY DETERMINATION

WEIGHT IN AIR          147.2000

WEIGHT SUBMERGED          134.7000

DENSITY          11.7760 GMS/CC
```

Exercise 7-4

†**7-5.** Prepare a program to calculate and print the function $f(t) = 1 - e^{-t}$ from $t = 0$ through $t = 4$ for increments of 0.2. The output should be t and $f(t)$ in columnar fashion, labeled TIME and RESPONSE, respectively.

7-6. Evaluate the following expressions for $\tau = 0.5$ and values of T from 0.5 to 1.0 in increments of 0.02:

$$K_1 = \frac{(1 + e^{-T/\tau}\, e^{-T})(\tau - 1)}{\tau e^{-T}(e^{-T/\tau} - 1) + e^{-T/\tau}(1 - e^{-T})}$$

$$K_2 = \frac{(1 + e^{-T/\tau} + e^{-T} + e^{-T/\tau}\, e^{-T})(\tau - 1)}{\tau(1 - e^{-T/\tau}) + (e^{-T} - 1) - \tau e^{-T}(e^{-T/\tau} - 1) - e^{-T/\tau}(1 - e^{-T})}$$

As input, read τ, the initial value of T, the final value of T, and the increment. The output should appear as shown.

```
EVALUATION OF CRITICAL GAINS FOR TAU =          0.5000

     T              K(1)            K(2)

   0.500       0.13026E 02     0.36075E 02
   0.520       0.12380E 02     0.32372E 02
   0.540       0.11807E 02     0.29187E 02
   0.560       0.11296E 02     0.26432E 02
   0.580       0.10840E 02     0.24036E 02
   0.600       0.10430E 02     0.21942E 02
   0.620       0.10063E 02     0.20102E 02
   0.640       0.97315E 01     0.18479E 02
   0.660       0.94328E 01     0.17042E 02
   0.680       0.91631E 01     0.15764E 02
   0.700       0.89192E 01     0.14623E 02
   0.720       0.86984E 01     0.13602E 02
   0.740       0.84985E 01     0.12684E 02
   0.760       0.83174E 01     0.11857E 02
   0.780       0.81535E 01     0.11109E 02
   0.800       0.80050E 01     0.10432E 02
   0.820       0.78708E 01     0.98159E 01
   0.840       0.77496E 01     0.92548E 01
   0.860       0.76402E 01     0.87424E 01
   0.880       0.75419E 01     0.82734E 01
   0.900       0.74537E 01     0.78431E 01
   0.920       0.73750E 01     0.74476E 01
   0.940       0.73049E 01     0.70833E 01
   0.960       0.72430E 01     0.67472E 01
   0.980       0.71888E 01     0.64364E 01
   1.000       0.71416E 01     0.61485E 01
```

Exercise 7-6

7-7. The roots of the equation $ax^2 + bx + c = 0$ are given by the quadratic formula

$$r_{1,2} = \frac{-b \pm \sqrt{b^2 - 4ac}}{2a}$$

Note that the roots may be real or complex.

Prepare a program that reads values of a, b, and c, determines if the roots are real or complex, and calculates their values. The program should accept as many data cards as provided, and the output for the two possible cases should be arranged as shown.

```
COEFFICIENTS
          A                2.00000
          B               -7.00000
          C                9.00000

     ROOTS ARE COMPLEX
          REAL PART                       1.7500
          IMAGINARY PART                  1.1990


COEFFICIENTS
          A                3.00000
          B                1.00000
          C                1.00000

     ROOTS ARE COMPLEX
          REAL PART                      -0.1667
          IMAGINARY PART                  0.5528


COEFFICIENTS
          A                2.00000
          B               -3.00000
          C               -7.00000

     ROOTS ARE REAL
          ROOT 1                    2.76556
          ROOT 2                   -1.26556


COEFFICIENTS
          A                3.00000
          B                1.50000
          C                0.40000

     ROOTS ARE COMPLEX
          REAL PART                      -0.2500
          IMAGINARY PART                  0.2661
```

Exercise 7-7

Determine the roots of the following equations:

$$2X^2 - 7X + 9 = 0$$
$$3X^2 + X + 1 = 0$$
$$2X^2 - 3X - 7 = 0$$
$$3X^2 + 1.5X + 0.4 = 0$$

7-8. The equation of a line in the x-y plane is

$$ax + by + c = 0$$

Given a point (x_0, y_0), find the equations of lines through this new point that are, respectively, parallel $[a(x - x_0) + b(y - y_0) = 0]$ and perpendicular $[a(x - x_0) - b(y - y_0) = 0]$ to the original line.

The input to the program should be *a, b, and c* on the first card followed by cards containing values of x_0 and y_0. The output should be arranged as shown.

```
EQUATION OF ORIGINAL LINE
              ( 3.0000E 00)*X + ( 2.0000E 00)*Y + (-8.0000E 00) = 0.

POINT                  2.0000E 00,-1.0000E 00

PARALLEL LINE
              ( 3.0000E 00)*X + ( 2.0000E 00)*Y + (-4.0000E 00) = 0.

PERPENDICULAR LINE
              ( 3.0000E 00)*X + (-2.0000E 00)*Y + (-8.0000E 00) = 0.



POINT                  4.0000E 00, 0.0000E-39

PARALLEL LINE
              ( 3.0000E 00)*X + ( 2.0000E 00)*Y + (-1.2000E 01) = 0.

PERPENDICULAR LINE
              ( 3.0000E 00)*X + (-2.0000E 00)*Y + (-1.2000E 01) = 0.



POINT                  2.0000E 00, 3.0000E 00

PARALLEL LINE
              ( 3.0000E 00)*X + ( 2.0000E 00)*Y + (-1.2000E 01) = 0.

PERPENDICULAR LINE
              ( 3.0000E 00)*X + (-2.0000E 00)*Y + ( 0.0000E-39) = 0.
```

Exercise 7-8

Run the program for the following input:

$3x + 2y - 8 = 0$
(2, - 1)
(4,0)
(2,3)

7-9. The derivative of a function $f(x)$ at $x = a$ can be approximated by the following expression:

$$f'(a) \cong \frac{f(a + h) - f(a)}{h}$$

The approximation is exact in the limit as h approaches zero. For $f(x) = x^2$ and $a = 1$, prepare a program to compute the approximate values of the derivative for the following values of h: 1.0, 0.5, 0.2, 0.1, 0.05, 0.02, 0.01, 0.001. Compare to the true derivative. The output should appear as shown.

```
APPROXIMATION OF DERIVATIVE OF F(X) = X**2 AT X = 1.

TRUE DERIVATIVE = 2*X = 2.

    H        APPROX. DER.
 1.0000        3.00000
 0.5000        2.50000
 0.2000        2.20000
 0.1000        2.10000
 0.0500        2.05000
 0.0200        2.02000
 0.0100        2.01000
 0.0010        2.00097
```

Exercise 7-9

7-10. A function $f(x,y)$ of two variables may be linearized about a point (x_0, y_0) as follows:

$$f(x,y) \cong f(x_0, y_0) + \left.\frac{\partial f(x,y)}{\partial x}\right|_{(x_0, y_0)} (x - x_0) + \left.\frac{\partial f(x,y)}{\partial y}\right|_{(x_0, y_0)} (y - y_0)$$

For the function $f(x,y) = xy$, linearize about the point (5,4). Evaluate the function and its linear approximation at (6,5), compute the percentage error of the approximation, and write the results in a manner similar to that shown. Use only one WRITE statement.

```
 LINEARIZATION OF F(X,Y) = X*Y AT (5,4)

EXACT AND APPROXIMATE RESULTS COMPARED AT (6,5)

   RESULT FROM LINEARIZATION -    29.000                    EXACT VALUE -    30.000
        PER CENT ERROR -    -3.333
```

Exercise 7-10

†**7-11.** The function $(x + a)^n$ is given by the following expression (n an integer):

$$(x + a)^n = \binom{n}{0} x^n a^0 + \binom{n}{1} x^{n-1} a^1 + \cdots + \binom{n}{n} x^0 a^n$$
$$= \sum_{j=0}^{n} \binom{n}{j} x^{n-j} a^j$$

The quantities $\binom{n}{j}$ are the binomial coefficients given by (see Exercise 7-2)

$$\binom{n}{j} = \frac{n!}{j!\,(n-j)!}$$

Prepare a program to calculate the $n + 1$ coefficients in the expansion of $(x + a)^n$. The program should read n and a. The output should appear as in the accompanying figure. Let $n = 10$ and $a = 1.2$.

```
COEFFICIENTS OF (X+A)**N
         N =      10
         A =      1.2000

POWER OF X        COEFFICIENT

        10             1.0000
         9            12.0000
         8            64.8000
         7           207.3600
         6           435.4560
         5           627.0566
         4           627.0566
         3           429.9817
         2           193.4918
         1            51.5978
         0             6.1917
```

Exercise 7-11

7-12. Prepare a program to read a date in the form XX/XX/XX and write in a fashion such as AUGUST 12, 1962. Use only one WRITE and FORMAT statement for this. Store names of months in an array with a DATA statement. Select and process one date from each month. If the month is greater than 12 or the day is greater than 31, print the words ERRONEOUS DATE XX/bXX/bXX.

If the DATA statement has not been studied, this can be accomplished either by reading the names of the months or by twelve WRITE statements and a computed GO TO statement.

7-13. Prepare a program to read the table presented in Exercise 6-23 in a similar fashion and print the table as in the figure. Use implied DO's for the input, and use only one WRITE statement.

```
                         TEMPERATURE, DEG F

                50        86        122       176       212

             *   *         *         *         *         *

        2    *  1.023     1.018     1.010     0.993     0.980

        6    *  1.068     1.061     1.052     1.035     1.022
PER
       10    *  1.113     1.104     1.094     1.077     1.064
CENT
       14    *  1.158     1.148     1.137     1.120     1.107
NAOH
       18    *  1.202     1.192     1.181     1.162     1.149

       22    *  1.247     1.235     1.224     1.205     1.191

            (SOURCE - INT. CRIT. TABLES, VOL. III,
             PAGE 79)
```

Exercise 7-13

†**7-14.** Same as the previous problem, except that the table is entered with a DATA statement.

7-15. In Figure 5-4 a program for fitting a set of data points to a straight line was presented. Modify this program such that its output appears as in the accompanying figure.

```
                         LEAST SQUARES FIT

           Y = ( 1.95724E 00)*X + (-2.23498E-01)

   OBS            X                  Y             PREDICTED

    1           1.716              3.021             3.135
    2           5.911             10.819            11.346
    3           3.726              7.502             7.069
    4           9.123             17.801            17.632
    5           4.022              7.688             7.649
```

Exercise 7-15

Run the program for the following data:

x	y
1.716	3.021
5.911	10.819
3.726	7.502
9.123	17.801
4.022	7.688

The input should be the same as in Figure 5-4, i.e., the number of observations is not fixed. Use only one WRITE statement.

7-16. Let A be an $n \times n$ matrix, n less than eight. Prepare a program to read n, followed by n^2 cards (not in order) containing the row number of the element in the first five columns, the column number in the second five, and the value of the element in the next ten columns. Use only one read statement. The output should appear as shown.

```
   *****   MATRIX A   *****

          COLUMN 1             2              3
   ROW
     1     -4.900           2.800          2.700
     2      1.700           3.500          1.200
     3      6.900          -7.800          7.000
```

Exercise 7-16

†**7-17.** Let $f(x)$ be defined by the following equation:

$$f(x) = x^2 \sin(\pi x)$$

Prepare a program to perform the following functions:

(a) Compute $f(x)$ for values of x of 0., .1, .2, . . . , 1.0.
(b) Locate the maximum of these values.
(c) Divide each of the above values by the maximum value to obtain normalized values.

(d) Print as shown in the figure.

F(X) = X**2 * SIN(3.1416*X)

X	F(X)	NOR F(X)
0.0000	0.0000	0.0000
0.1000	0.0031	0.0078
0.2000	0.0235	0.0593
0.3000	0.0728	0.1837
0.4000	0.1522	0.3839
0.5000	0.2500	0.6306
0.6000	0.3424	0.8637
0.7000	0.3964	1.0000
0.8000	0.3762	0.9489
0.9000	0.2503	0.6314
1.0000	-0.0000	-0.0000

Exercise 7-17

7-18. One frequent use of the computer is to generate tables of unusual functions. Suppose that someone needed a table of values of the function

$$\frac{\ln(x)}{(1 + |\sin x|)^2}$$

over the range 1 to 3 in steps of 0.02. Prepare a computer program to arrange the output as shown. This is similar to the common $\log_{10}$ tables.

X	*	0	2	4	6	8
1.0	*	0.00000	0.00584	0.01157	0.01718	0.02270
1.1	*	0.02665	0.03169	0.03663	0.04150	0.04628
1.2	*	0.04884	0.05327	0.05763	0.06191	0.06613
1.3	*	0.06805	0.07201	0.07591	0.07975	0.08354
1.4	*	0.08536	0.08895	0.09250	0.09600	0.09945
1.5	*	0.10162	0.10494	0.10822	0.11145	0.11464
1.6	*	0.11755	0.12066	0.12373	0.12676	0.12975
1.7	*	0.13377	0.13672	0.13963	0.14251	0.14536
1.8	*	0.15087	0.15370	0.15651	0.15928	0.16203
1.9	*	0.16944	0.17220	0.17494	0.17765	0.18033
2.0	*	0.19014	0.19287	0.19557	0.19825	0.20090
2.1	*	0.21372	0.21645	0.21915	0.22183	0.22449
2.2	*	0.24107	0.24384	0.24658	0.24930	0.25199
2.3	*	0.27331	0.27615	0.27897	0.28176	0.28453
2.4	*	0.31187	0.31482	0.31776	0.32066	0.32355
2.5	*	0.35861	0.36173	0.36482	0.36789	0.37094
2.6	*	0.41603	0.41936	0.42268	0.42596	0.42922
2.7	*	0.48751	0.49113	0.49472	0.49829	0.50184
2.8	*	0.57773	0.58172	0.58568	0.58962	0.59353
2.9	*	0.69329	0.69776	0.70221	0.70662	0.71101

Exercise 7-18

7-19. Prepare a program to read the four coefficients of the polynomial

$$1.217x^3 + 1.798x^2 - 4.102x + 9.17$$

and print in the following fashion (b symbolizes a blank space):

(bl.217)bX ** 3b + b(b1.798)bX ** 2b + b(-4.102)bXb + b(b9.171)

Use implied DO's in both the READ and WRITE statements. The input should be one coefficient per card, and should not have a decimal point punched.

†**7-20.** If the order of the polynomial is unknown beforehand, the arrangement in the above exercise is not convenient. Instead, the output could be more conveniently arranged as follows:

(b1.217)bX ** 3b+
(b1.798)bX ** 2b+
(-4.102)bXbbbb+
(b9.171)

Prepare a program to read the degree (maximum will be fifty) of the polynomial followed by the coefficients, one per card. Use only one READ statement.

The program should be able to read the data for one polynomial, print the results, and return to the READ statement for another polynomial. Each should be on a separate page.

Use this program to print the following polynomials:

$1.712x + 1.000$
$5.917x^4 + 1.722x^3 - 1.001x^2 + 0.022x + 1.00$
$1.000x^2 + 1.222x - 1.710$

7-21. The following timetable is given for train schedules:

Distance	*City*	*Time, P.M.*
0	Chicago	4:00
93	Niles	6:42
141	Kalamazoo	7:28
164	Battle Creek	7:53
210	Jackson	8:39
248	Ann Arbor	9:18
284	Detroit	10:00

Prepare a program to read the above information, calculate the remaining entries in the table shown in the figure, and print in a similar fashion.

TRAIN SCHEDULE

DISTANCE	CITY	TIME	TIME FROM LAST STOP	ELAPSED TIME
0	CHICAGO	4- 0 P. M.	0 MIN	0 MIN
93	NILES	6- 42	162	162
141	KALAMAZOO	7- 28	46	208
164	BATTLE CREEK	7- 53	25	233
210	JACKSON	8- 39	46	279
248	ANN ARBOR	9- 18	39	318
284	DETROIT	10- 0	42	360

Exercise 7-21

†**7-22.** A function $f(x)$ with continuous derivatives can be represented by a Taylor series expansion about some point x_0 as follows:

$$f(x) = f(x_0) + (x - x_0)f'(x_0) + \frac{(x - x_0)^2}{2} f''(x_0)$$

$$+ \cdots + \frac{(x - x_0)^n}{n!} f^{[n]}(x_0) + \cdots$$

For $f(x) = \sin 2x$ and $x_0 = 1.$, evaluate this series for $x = 1.1$, truncating after the first derivative, second derivative, etc., up to and including the tenth derivative. Print the output as in Exercise 7-9, comparing the results to the true value. For $f(x) = \sin 2x$, the derivatives are given by

$$f^{[n]}(x) = \begin{cases} 2^n(-1)^{(n-1)/2} \cos 2x, & n \text{ odd} \\ 2^n(-1)^{n/2} \sin 2x, & n \text{ even} \end{cases}$$

7-23. Let $f(x)$ be evaluated at equally spaced intervals of x. For convenience, denote $f(x_i)$ as f_i. The first forward difference Δf_i can be defined as follows:

FINITE DIFFERENCES

X	F(X)	DEL	DEL**2	DEL**3
1.00	4.0000			
		2.9696		
1.20	6.9696		1.3504	
		4.3200		0.3456
1.40	11.2896		1.6960	
		6.0160		0.3840
1.60	17.3056		2.0800	
		8.0960		0.4224
1.80	25.4016		2.5024	
		10.5984		0.4608
2.00	36.0000		2.9632	
		13.5616		0.4992
2.20	49.5616		3.4624	
		17.0240		0.5376
2.40	66.5856		4.0000	
		21.0240		0.5760
2.60	87.6096		4.5760	
		25.6000		0.6144
2.80	113.2096		5.1904	
		30.7904		0.6528
3.00	144.0000		5.8432	
		36.6336		0.6912
3.20	180.6336		6.5344	
		43.1680		0.7296
3.40	223.8016		7.2640	
		50.4320		0.7680
3.60	274.2336		8.0320	
		58.4640		0.8064
3.80	332.6975		8.8384	
		67.3024		0.8448
4.00	399.9999		9.6832	
		76.9856		0.8832
4.20	476.9855		10.5664	
		87.5520		0.9216
4.40	564.5375		11.4880	
		99.0400		0.9600
4.60	663.5775		12.4480	
		111.4880		
4.80	775.0655			

Exercise 7-23

$$\Delta f_i = \frac{f_{i+1} - f_i}{h}$$

where h is the difference between successive values of x. The second difference $\Delta^2 f_i$ is defined as

$$\Delta^2 f_i = \frac{\Delta f_{i+1} - \Delta f_i}{h}$$

Higher-order differences can be computed similarly

$$\Delta^{k+1} f_i = \frac{\Delta^k f_{i+1} - \Delta^k f_i}{h}$$

Let $f(x) = (x^3 + x^2)(x + 1)$. Let $h = 0.2$ and evaluate this function for twenty consecutive values of x, beginning with $x = 1.0$. Calculate the first, second, and third differences and print as shown. Use a 20 X 5 array to store x, f, and the differences.

7-24. Prepare a program to perform the following:

(a) Read the number of students in a class.
(b) Read one quiz score for each student along with his name.
(c) Arrange the scores in descending order.
(d) Compute the average score.
(e) Read a header card and reproduce as first line of output.
(f) Write average grade, the number of students making above average, and the number of students making below average.
(g) List the scores in descending order along with names. Write MEDIAN by median grade.

An example is shown in the accompanying illustration. The maximum number of students is fifty and allow twelve characters for each name.

```
              COOKIE CUTTING LABORATORY

      AVERAGE SCORE              78.2857

      NUMBER ABOVE AVERAGE                4

      NUMBER BELOW AVERAGE                3

         SCORE               NAME

         99.00          ROBERTS
         91.00          STEPHENS
         87.00          KILROY
         82.00          JONES                      MEDIAN
         71.00          LEVEQUE
         62.00          NO NAME
         56.00          JAMES
```

Exercise 7-24

Note: Machines storing six alphameric characters per word will require two words per name; machines storing five alphameric characters per word will require three words per name (field specification 2A5, A2 or 3A4); and similarly for other machines.

†**7-25.** Consider the following equations:

$$y = (x + 1)^{1.2}$$

$$z = \frac{x^2}{x + 2}$$

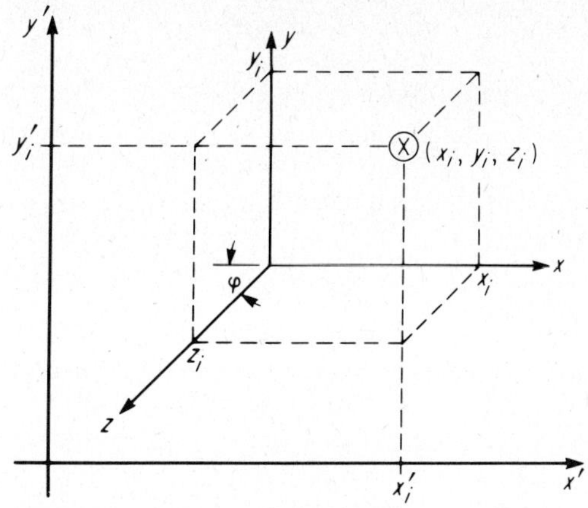

(a) Axes for oblique projection drawing

```
***** THREE-DIMENSIONAL PLOTTING *****

        PHI =     35.00 DEGREES

     EXTREMITIES OF AXES         XP          YP

                     X          4.000      -0.000
                     Y         -0.000       4.000
                     Z         -3.277      -2.294
```

X	Y	Z	XP	YP
0.00000	1.00000	0.00000	-0.00000	1.00000
0.10000	1.12117	0.00476	0.09610	1.11844
0.20000	1.24456	0.01818	0.18511	1.23414
0.30000	1.37004	0.03913	0.26795	1.34759
0.40000	1.49745	0.06667	0.34539	1.45922
0.50000	1.62671	0.10000	0.41808	1.56935
0.60000	1.75770	0.13846	0.48658	1.67828
0.70000	1.89033	0.18148	0.55133	1.78625
0.80000	2.02454	0.22857	0.61276	1.89345
0.90000	2.16025	0.27931	0.67120	2.00006
1.00000	2.29740	0.33333	0.72694	2.10622
1.10000	2.43592	0.39032	0.78026	2.21206
1.20000	2.57577	0.45000	0.83137	2.31768
1.30000	2.71690	0.51212	0.88048	2.42318
1.40000	2.85926	0.57647	0.92777	2.52863
1.50000	3.00281	0.64286	0.97339	2.63411
1.60000	3.14752	0.71111	1.01747	2.73967
1.70000	3.29334	0.78108	1.06016	2.84536
1.80000	3.44025	0.85263	1.10154	2.95123
1.90000	3.58821	0.92564	1.14174	3.05732
2.00000	3.73719	1.00000	1.18082	3.16365
2.10000	3.88717	1.07561	1.21888	3.27027
2.20000	4.03813	1.15238	1.25600	3.37719
2.30000	4.19003	1.23023	1.29222	3.48444
2.40000	4.34285	1.30909	1.32762	3.59203
2.50000	4.49657	1.38889	1.36225	3.69999
2.60000	4.65118	1.46957	1.39616	3.80832
2.70000	4.80664	1.55106	1.42940	3.91705
2.80000	4.96295	1.63333	1.46201	4.02617
2.90000	5.12009	1.71633	1.49402	4.13571
3.00000	5.27803	1.80000	1.52548	4.24566

(b) Output

Exercise 7-25

These equations are to be evaluated for values of x from 0.0 to 3.0 in increments of 0.1. As the resulting function is to be plotted in an oblique projection, consider the three-coordinate set of axes x, y, and z shown in the drawing. Although the axes are really perpendicular, the drawing must be made in two dimensions. Thus the z-axis is drawn at some angle φ to the x-axis. Given x_i, y_i, z_i, the coordinates of point i, an exact location is specified in respect to the x-, y-, and z-axes as illustrated. However, this cannot be plotted very conveniently.

The plot would be much easier to make indirectly. That is, the coordinates (x_i, y_i, z_i) are transformed into (x_i', y_i') for plotting on the two-dimensional coordinates superimposed in the drawing. The equations for these transformations are

$$y_i' = y_i - z_i \sin \varphi$$

$$x_i' = x_i - z_i \cos \varphi$$

Prepare a program to perform the following:

(a) Read the value of φ.
(b) Print φ and the (x_i', y_i') coordinates of points (4,0,0) (0,4,0), and (0,0,4) thus locating the extremities of the x-, y-, and z-axes.
(c) For the prescribed values of x, calculate y, z, x' and y'. The output should appear as shown. Let $\varphi = 35°$.

7-26. In Exercise 6-27 a specific case of matrix multiplication was considered. Now that further input-output techniques have been presented, this program can be generalized. Consider the multiplication of an $n \times k$ matrix A by a $k \times m$ matrix B, n, k, and m less than twenty-five. The program should be organized as follows:

(a) Read n, k, and m.
(b) Read a variable FORMAT to specify the input arrangement for matrix A.
(c) Read matrix A.
(d) Read another variable FORMAT for B, and read B.
(e) Compute the product.
(f) Read another variable FORMAT for output, and write results.

Run this program for the example in Exercise 6-27.

†**7-27.** Write a program that reads a sentence that contains a maximum of eighty characters (including the period at the end) and counts the total number of characters (excluding blanks and commas) in the sentence. The sentence should be punched on a single card, and the characters should be read into an array as one character per element. Only alphabetic characters, blanks, and commas will appear in the sentence. A comma is always followed by a blank.

7-28. Same as Exercise 7-27, except count the number of occurrences of the letter E in the sentence.

7-29. Same as Exercise 7-27, except count the number of occurrences of each letter of the alphabet within the sentence. The output should appear as in the accompanying figure.

7-30. Same as Exercise 7-27, except count the number of occurrences of words containing three letters or less.

```
ORIGINAL SENTENCE
     AN IMPORTANT CHARACTERISTIC OF DIGITAL COMPUTERS IS THEIR INCREDIBLE SPEED,

CHAR.        OCCURRENCES          CHAR,    OCCURRENCES
  A               5                 N           3
  B               1                 O           3
  C               5                 P           3
  D               3                 Q           .
  E               7                 R           6
  F               1                 S           4
  G               1                 T           7
  H               2                 U           1
  I               9                 V
  J               0                 W
  K               0                 X
  L               2                 Y
  M               2                 Z
```

Exercise 7-29

7-31. Same as Exercise 7-30, except compute the average length of the words in the sentence. Print the answer to two decimal places.

7-32. Instead of processing a single sentence, suppose we process a paragraph. The paragraph will be punched on a maximum of ten cards as illustrated in the accompanying figure. A blank character always follows the decimal point, and no hyphenated words will be used. For this exercise, the paragraph should be read into a single array of 800 elements, one character to each element. Compute the average number of words in the sentences in the paragraph and print the answer to two decimal places.

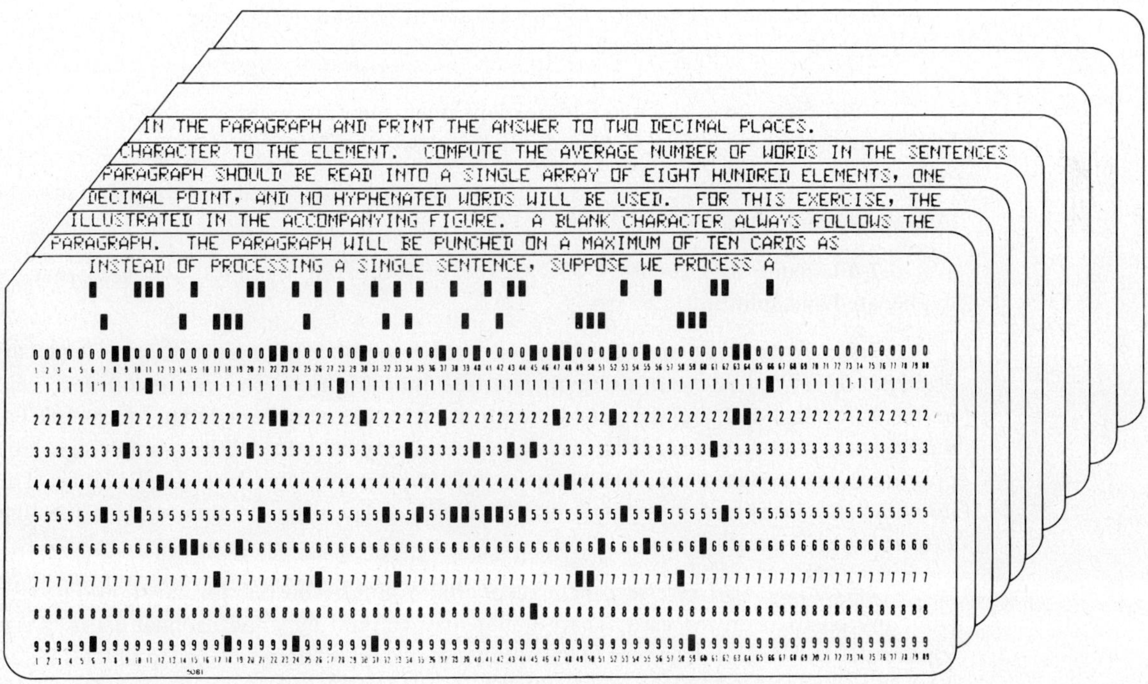

Exercise 7-32

7-33. Same as Exercise 7-32, except print the number of words in each sentence and the average number of characters per word for each sentence.

† **7-34.** Same as Exercise 7-32, except print the distribution of the number of characters in each word as shown in the accompanying figure. Words containing over twelve characters can be considered as containing twelve characters.

```
        WORD LENGTH DISTRIBUTION

CHS./WORD          OCCURRENCES
    1                   5
    2                  16
    3                  15
    4                   6
    5                   8
    6                   7
    7                  13
    8                   3
    9                   7
   10                   2
   11                   1
   12 OR MORE           1
```

Exercise 7-34

†**7-35.** Same as Exercise 7-32, except process the cards one at a time, That is, the array should be defined as containing only eighty characters. A card is read into this area, the computations performed, and then the next card is read into this same area.

7-36. Same as Exercise 7-33, but with the modification suggested in Exercise 7-35.

7-37. Same as Exercise 7-34, but with the modification suggested in Exercise 7-35.

7-38. Same as Exercise 7-35, except that the last word on the card may be hyphenated (using the minus sign) and split onto two cards.

7-39. Same as Exercise 7-36, except that the last word on the card may be hyphenated and split onto two cards.

7-40. Same as Exercise 7-37, except that the last word on the card may be hyphenated and split onto two cards.

†**7-41.** Write a Fortran program to read a number in integer format from any position on a card *without* using format-free input-output. The card should be read under A format, and the characters stored in an array, one character per element. The number may contain as many digits as desired, and may be preceded by a minus sign, by a plus sign, or no sign at all. The number will not contain any embedded blanks. This number is to be stored in a single integer variable. The program should print the final answer to verify correctness.

7-42. Same as Exercise 7-41, except that a number in real format should be read from any position on the card. The number may contain only the decimal digits, a sign (optional), and a decimal point. The following examples should be acceptable: 127.23, +12.72, -1200., +.02007, and .00030. The number should be stored in a real variable and printed.

7-43. Same as Exercise 7-41, except that the number should be read in exponential format. The number may contain only the decimal digits, an optional sign for the exponent, and a decimal point (in the fraction only). The number should be stored in a real variable and printed.

7-44. A simple approach to preparing cryptograms is to simply interchange the letters in the original message. The original message should contain less than eighty characters, and should end with a period. This sentence should be punched on a card and read into memory. Then a card should be read containing the two characters to be exchanged in the first two columns. For example, suppose these two characters were E and H. Each E in the original message should be replaced by an H, and each H should be replaced by an E. The program should accept multiple cards with letters to exchange, and a card with an asterisk indicating end-of-data. The output should appear as in the accompanying figure.

```
ORIGINAL MESSAGE
     AN IMPORTANT CHARACTERISTIC OF DIGITAL COMPUTERS IS THEIR INCREDIBLE SPEED.

CRYPTOGRAM AFTER EXCHANGING CHARACTERS I AND X
     AN XMPORTANT CHARACTERXSTXC OF DXGXTAL COMPUTERS XS THEXR XNCREDXBLE SPEED.

CRYPTOGRAM AFTER EXCHANGING CHARACTERS A AND N
     NA XMPORTNAT CHNRNCTERXSTXC OF DXGXTNL COMPUTERS XS THEXR XACREDXBLE SPEED.

CRYPTOGRAM AFTER EXCHANGING CHARACTERS G AND V
     NA XMPORTNAT CHNRNCTERXSTXC OF DXVXTNL COMPUTERS XS THEXR XACREDXBLE SPEED.

CRYPTOGRAM AFTER EXCHANGING CHARACTERS M AND K
     NA XKPORTNAT CHNRNCTERXSTXC OF DXVXTNL COKPUTERS XS THEXR XACREDXBLE SPEED.

CRYPTOGRAM AFTER EXCHANGING CHARACTERS C AND U
     NA XKPORTNAT UHNRNUTERXSTXU OF DXVXTNL UOKPCTERS XS THEXR XAUREDXBLE SPEED.

CRYPTOGRAM AFTER EXCHANGING CHARACTERS D AND P
     NA XKDORTNAT UHNRNUTERXSTXU OF PXVXTNL UOKDCTERS XS THEXR XAUREPXBLE SDEEP.

CRYPTOGRAM AFTER EXCHANGING CHARACTERS A AND G
     NG XKDORTNGT UHNRNUTERXSTXU OF PXVXTNL UOKDCTERS XS THEXR XGUREPXBLE SDEEP.
```

Exercise 7-44

7-45. Write a program to decode the cryptogram produced by the program in Figure 7-5 and obtain the original message.

8

Functions and Subroutines

In this chapter we will introduce those features of Fortran that are applicable only to functions and subroutines or are generally used only with functions and subroutines. We begin with a fairly general discussion of the concept of a subprogram and the use of arguments. This is followed by a detailed description of the Fortran features of statement function, function subprogram, and subroutine. The COMMON declaration is then introduced, followed by the EQUIVALENCE declaration. The chapter concludes with a discussion of less commonly used features, including adjustable dimensions, BLOCK DATA, EXTERNAL, and multiple ENTRY and RETURN.

8-1. Concept of a Function, a Subprogram, and a Subroutine

In Chapter 2, we introduced several functions (for example the square root function, SQRT) available in Fortran. In essence, these are pre-programmed or "canned" routines in the computing system available to anyone who writes a Fortran program. This frees the programmer from having to write his own routine, and functions such as SQRT are written for widespread use, are completely debugged, programmed in an extremely efficient manner, and always produce the correct answer.

The concept of a function is one of unambiguous designation. For any positive value of X, SQRT(X) designates another specific value which can be computed by the library routine. By a mechanism that we shall cover in more detail in a later section, the numerical value of X, the *argument*, is communicated to this library routine, and the value computed by this routine is communicated back, or *returned*, to the point in the program where SQRT appeared.

The use of the SQRT routine is analogous to the use of the "number-processing machine" illustrated in Figure 8-1. The number whose square root is to be taken is fed to the machine, which in turn produces the desired square root. As long as the user is

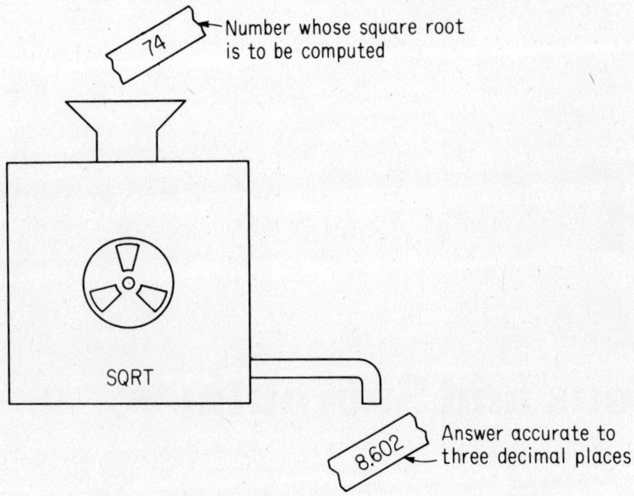

Figure 8-1. Number-processing machine

confident that the machine produces the correct answer in an efficient manner, there is little incentive short of plain curiosity to ascertain how the machine works.

In Fortran, a programmer may define his own functions in one of two ways. One is the statement function feature which, as we shall see shortly, has its limitations in that the entire function must be defined in a single statement. This statement is defined in, and is a part of, the program in which it appears.

The second approach to defining a function is to prepare a function subprogram. In Fortran, a subprogram is very similar to the programs, called main programs, that we have been preparing except that they are executed only when *called* by another program. Subprograms have their own structure, their own specification statements (DIMENSION, INTEGER, REAL, etc.) and their own END statement. The compiler treats the subprogram as a separate entity, and the subprogram is compiled separately from the main program and other subprograms.

Communication among the subprogram, the main program and other subprograms is restricted to that which the programmer specifies in terms of arguments (in a later section we shall see that COMMON can play a role). Suppose variable K is used in both the main program and in a subprogram. The compiler will always reserve a storage location for K in the main program. If K does not appear in the argument list of the subprogram, the compiler will also reserve a storage location for K in the subprogram. Since these two storage locations are not the same, there is absolutely no connection between variable K in the main program and variable K in the subprogram.

Being compiled separately from the main program, a transfer statement in the subprogram such as

```
GO TO 56
```

will always transfer control to statement 56 in the subprogram even though there may be a statement 56 in the main program. Similarly, suppose the following specification statement appears in the main program:

```
DIMENSION A(27)
```

This statement defines A as an array of twenty-seven elements in the main program but not in the subprogram. In the subprogram, A may be used as a simple variable or may be specified in any manner desired, for example,

```
INTEGER A(7,9)
```

Being compiled separately, all specification statements applicable to the subprogram must appear therein.

Fortran permits two types of subprograms: a function subprogram and a subroutine. The distinction is basically that the subroutine is called by a special statement (the CALL statement), whereas the function is called by its use within an expression. In addition, the function returns a value, the functional value, that is used in the expression in which the function call appears. For example, in the statement

```
Y = A + B * SQRT(G)
```

the functional value ($\sqrt{G}$) is used in computing the value to be assigned to Y. Since subroutines do not appear in expressions, there is no function value.

The programmer benefits from the use of functions and subroutines. Since function subprograms and subroutines are separate programs, they can be written, tested, and debugged separately from the remainder of the program. This enables the programmer to prepare several components of the total program, debug them simultaneously, and assemble them into the total program. Several programmers may be assigned portions of large programs to prepare and debug simultaneously.

Another use of functions or subroutines occurs when the same computation is required at different points in the same program. In this case a single routine can be made a function or subroutine, rather than coded at each point in the program where it is needed.

8-2. Introduction to Fortran Function and Subprogram Features

In this section, an example illustrates the features of statement function, function subprogram, and subroutine. In later sections, we shall examine each of these in detail and present more examples of their use.

The example used in this section consists of the conversion of civilian time to military time. We shall use the following variables:

JHOUR	Hour in civilian time
JMIN	Minutes in civilian time
JAMPM	Morning-afternoon designator for civilian time (0 = AM; 1 = PM)
MTIME	Military time

Military time is expressed on a twenty-four hour basis. For example, 8:45 AM in civilian time is 0845 military time; 4:27 PM is 1627. In preparing our programs, we shall make the convenient assumption that JHOUR will never equal 12.

The Fortran program in Figure 8-2 illustrates the use of a statement function to convert from civilian time to military time. The first statement in this program defines the statement function JTME. This function is then called from the fourth line. When the function is executed, the value of variable JHOUR is used for I in the function, JMIN for J, and JAMPM for K.

The use of a function subprogram to convert from ~~military~~ to ~~civilian~~ time is
civilian to military

```
      JTME(I,J,K)=I*100+J+1200*K
      READ(5,20) JHOUR,JMIN,JAMPM
 20   FORMAT(3I5)
      MTIME=JTME(JHOUR,JMIN,JAMPM)
      WRITE(6,30)MTIME
 30   FORMAT(' TIME IS',I5)
      STOP
      END
```

(a) Program

```
    4    27     1
```

(b) Input data

```
TIME IS 1627
```

(c) Output

Figure 8-2. Example of a statement function

illustrated in Figure 8-3. The first statement in the function subprogram is the FUNCTION statement (line 8), which should not be confused with the statement function feature described in the previous paragraph. The FUNCTION statement defines the name of the function and designates the arguments. This function is called in line 3 in the same manner as the statement function was called in Figure 8-2. In the function JTME in Figure 8-3, the values of JHOUR, JMIN, and JAMPM are communicated to the subprogram by the arguments. The value of military time assigned to variable MTIME in line 3 is the value of variable JTME in the subprogram at the time the RETURN statement is executed. The value returned to the calling program is the value of the variable in the subprogram whose name is identical to the name of the function. In all function subprograms, a value must be returned to the main program in this manner.

Figure 8-4 illustrates the use of a subroutine to convert from civilian to military time. The first statement in the subroutine is the SUBROUTINE statement which defines the name of the subroutine and designates the arguments. The subroutine is called by the CALL statement in line 3 of the main program. In this case, communication is entirely via the arguments. Values used for variables I, J, and K in the subroutine are the values of variables JHOUR, JMIN, and JAMPM in the main program. The value of MTIME printed in line 4 of the main program is the value computed for L in the subroutine.

Note that in programs in both Figures 8-3 and 8-4, statement numbers 20 and 30 appear both in the main program and in the subprogram. This leads to no confusion whatsoever. The only way to transfer to a function subprogram is by use of the function in an expression. The only way to transfer to a subroutine is by the CALL statement. The only way to transfer from a function subprogram or a subroutine to the calling program is by the RETURN statement.

8-3. Role of Arguments

In each of the examples in the previous section, arguments are used to communicate information between the main program and the function or subroutine. In this section we examine this aspect in more detail.

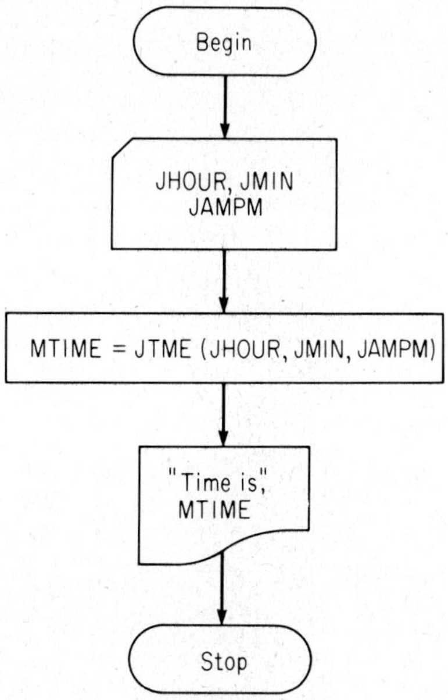

(a) Main program

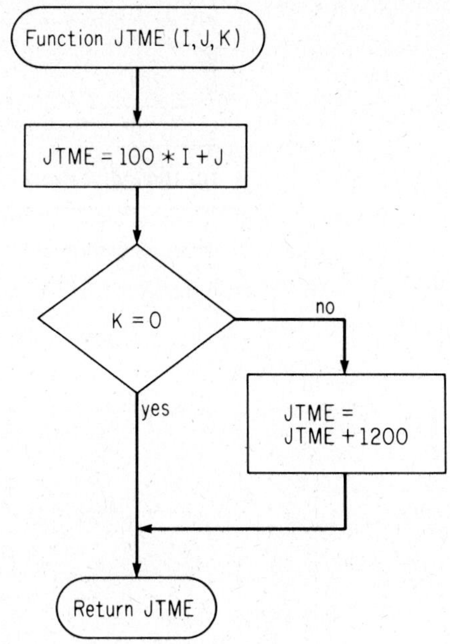

(b) Function subprogram

```
      READ(5,20)JHOUR,JMIN,JAMPM
20    FORMAT(3I5)
      MTIME=JTME(JHOUR,JMIN,JAMPM)
      WRITE(6,30)MTIME
30    FORMAT(' TIME IS',I5)
      STOP
      END

      FUNCTION JTME(I,J,K)
      JTME=100*I+J
      IF(K)20,20,30
30    JTME=JTME+1200
20    RETURN
      END
```

(c) Program

```
4    27    1
```

(d) Input data

```
TIME IS 1627
```

(e) Output

Figure 8-3. Example of a function subprogram

Values of variables used as arguments can be communicated to and from subprograms in one of two ways

1. Call by address
2. Call by value

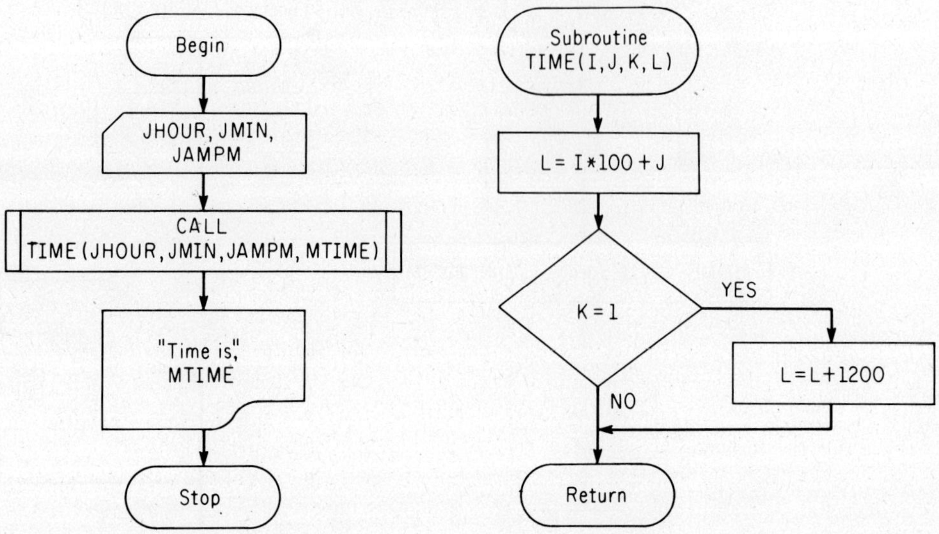

(a) Main program *(b) Subroutine*

```
          READ(5,20)JHOUR,JMIN,JAMPM
     20   FORMAT(3I5)
          CALL TIME(JHOUR,JMIN,JAMPM,MTIME)
          WRITE(6,30)MTIME
     30   FORMAT(' TIME IS',I5)
          STOP
          END

          SUBROUTINE TIME(I,J,K,L)
          L=100*I+J
          IF(K)20,30,30
     30   L=L+1200
     20   RETURN
          END
```

(c) Program

```
4    27    1
```

(d) Input data

```
TIME IS 1627
```

(e) Output

Figure 8-4. Example of a subroutine

We shall examine each of these using the function subprogram in Figure 8-3 and the subroutine in Figure 8-4 as the basis for our discussion. We shall first explain these two approaches, and then discuss their advantages and disadvantages.

Call by Value. In this approach, the actual numerical value is transferred from the storage location in the main program to a storage location in the subprogram. For the function subprogram in Figure 8-3, storage locations are reserved in the main program for variables JHOUR, JMIN, and JAMPM, and separate storage locations are reserved for variables I, J, and K in the subprogram. At the time the function is called, the current values stored in JHOUR, JMIN, and JAMPM are transfered to the storage locations for I, J, and K. However, upon execution of the RETURN statement, the reverse transfer of values is *not* made. Therefore, if the value of variable I, J, or K is changed in the subprogram, this change is not reflected in the corresponding variable in the main program. Therefore, if call by value is used for the subroutine in Figure 8-4, the value of L is not available in the main program.

Call by Address. In this approach, the address of each of the variables used as arguments in the calling statement is transferred to the subprogram and used for the respective variables in the argument list in the subprogram. For example, in the subroutine in Figure 8-4, the address of the storage location for JHOUR is transferred to the subprogram for use as the address for variable I. The other arguments are treated similarly. Therefore, if the value of variable I is changed in the subprogram, the value of variable JHOUR changes in the main program, since its address is being used for variable I in the subprogram. The subroutine in Figure 8-4 functions properly only if call by address is used.

Example. As an example of the difference between call by address and call by value, suppose we have written the function subprogram in Figure 8-5 that computes the electrical resistance for the following equation:

$$R = 1.2 + .047\ T - 0.00056T^2$$

where T is in °C. We have written our function so that it accepts temperatures in either °C or °F. The scale is designated by the second argument J (0 = °C; 1 = °F). Suppose we use the following statement to call RES:

R = RES(TEMP,1)

Since the value of the second argument is 1, the value of TEMP is in °F. Therefore, when the subprogram is executed, a new value is computed for T in the second statement in the subprogram.

If call by value is used, a separate location is reserved for T in the subprogram, and changing its value in the subprogram in no way changes the value of TEMP in the calling program.

However, if call by address is used, the address of TEMP in the calling program is used as the address for T in the subprogram, and changes to T in the subprogram are changes to TEMP in the main program. In effect, variable T is a dummy: no storage location is reserved for it. After execution of the function subprogram in Figure 8-5, the value of TEMP in the main program is changed from °F to °C.

Advantages and Disadvantages. Call by address and call by value have the advantages and disadvantages listed on page 198:

```
FUNCTION RES(T,J)
IF(J.EQ.1)T=(T-32.)/1.8
RES=1.2+T*(0.047-0.00056*T)
RETURN
END
```

Figure 8-5. Function subprogram to compute resistance

1. Call by address is meaningless when expressions are used as arguments in the main program. For example, suppose the following statement is used for the function RES in Figure 8-5:

   R = RES(TEMP−273.,0)

   Since the first argument is not a variable, no storage location is reserved in the calling program for this argument in this form. Call by value is best for this argument.
2. Use of call by address is not appropriate when a constant is used as an argument. For example, consider the statement

   R = RES(0.,1)

   This statement evaluates the resistance at 0°F. If call by address is used, the address of the storage location for the constant 0. in the main program is used for variable T in the subprogram. The second statement in the subprogram in Figure 8-5 changes the value from 0. to −17.8. Since the address for the constant 0. in the main program is used for T, the constant 0. is now −17.8. If 0. appears in any subsequent statement in the main program, −17.8 is used instead: the results will be disastrous. Use of call by value avoids this problem.
3. Call by value cannot be used for arguments such as MTIME in the subroutine in Figure 8-4 unless an extra step is taken: transferring values from the locations in the subprogram to the corresponding locations in the main program. However, with the addition of this extra step, call by value has the same disadvantages as call by address in the previous two situations.
4. Call by address is more efficient for arrays. Suppose an entire array A, containing 100 elements, is to be available to the subprogram. If call by value is used, 100 storage locations must be reserved in the subprogram in *addition* to the 100 storage locations reserved for A in the calling program. Furthermore, the values of each of the 100 elements must be copied from the storage locations in the calling program to the corresponding storage locations in the subprogram. When call by address is used, *only* the address of the first storage location in the array must be transferred to the subprogram, making call by address attractive for arrays.

Summary. Unfortunately, the choice between call by address and call by value varies from system to system; this prevents us from being explicit here. The choice between call by address and call by value can be summarized as follows:

1. All systems use call by address for arrays.
2. Call by address is used for all arguments of subroutines. Some systems do not accept expressions as arguments in subroutine call statements. In other systems, the compiler creates a storage location for the result of the expressions, and transfers this value to the subprogram. This makes the statement

```
CALL SUB(X+2.,Y,Z)
```

appear to be compiled as

```
XA = X+2.
CALL SUB(XA,Y,Z)
```

If the compiler does not accept expressions as arguments of subroutines, the programmer must insert the extra statement. Better compilers insert these steps when constants are used as arguments, thereby avoiding the pitfall outlined in step 2, above. Unfortunately, not all compilers do this, so many experienced programmers avoid the use of constants as arguments.

3. Some systems use call by address when simple variables are used as arguments of function subprograms; others use call by value. The difference is that if the value of a variable used as an argument in the subprogram is changed within the subprogram, these changes are *not* reflected in the corresponding variable in the calling program when call by value is used but *are* reflected when call by address is used. In this manual, we assume that call by address is used, but on this point programmers should consult manuals specific to their system.

8-4. The Statement Function

Rules regarding the statement function are as follows:

1. The statement function must be defined by a single statement, although the continuation feature can be used as for other statements.

2. The statement function is itself a non-executable statement in that it only defines the function; it is not executed until it is called.

3. The statement function must appear prior to any executable statements in the program.

4. The name of the statement function must conform to the general rules of the naming of variables. That is, the name must consist of from one to six characters, the first of which must be a letter. If the result of the functional evaluation is an integer, the name must begin with one of the letters I through N. For example, the name of the statement function

```
JTME(I,J,K) = I * 100 + J + 1200 * K
```

in Figure 8-2 begins with the letter J, which defines the result as an integer. Alternatively, the name can be declared integer in the INTEGER statement as illustrated by the following example:

```
INTEGER TIME
TIME(I,J,K) = I * 100 + J + K * 1200
```

Real functions are treated analogously.

5. A statement function must have at least one argument. If it contains more than one argument, arguments are separated by commas.

6. The statement function may include library functions, function subprograms, or other previously defined statement functions.

7. The arguments of the statement function are dummies in that no storage locations are reserved. In fact, variables used as arguments may be subsequently used as variables elsewhere within the program.

8. The statement function may include variables other than those used as arguments. For example, consider the function

```
RES(T) = A + T * (B + C * T)
```

Variable T is a dummy, but variables A, B, and C are not. When this function is called, the current values of variables A, B, and C are used in computing the function.

```
 1           F(X)=(X+4.7)**2/(SQRT(X)+X**2+1.)
 2           WRITE(6,1)
 3       1   FORMAT(3X,3('X',5X,'F(X)',6X))
 4           DO2I=2,20,2
 5           X=I-2
 6           FX=F(X)
 7           Y=X+20.
 8           FY=F(Y)
 9           Z=X+40.
10           FZ=F(Z)
11       2   WRITE(6,3)X,FX,Y,FY,Z,FZ
12       3   FORMAT(1X,3(F4.0,F10.4,2X))
13           STOP
14           END
```

(a) Program

X	F(X)	X	F(X)	X	F(X)
0.	22.0900	20.	1.5046	40.	1.2431
2.	6.9985	22.	1.4558	42.	1.2311
4.	3.9837	24.	1.4155	44.	1.2202
6.	2.9022	26.	1.3817	46.	1.2103
8.	2.3779	28.	1.3530	48.	1.2013
10.	2.0746	30.	1.3283	50.	1.1930
12.	1.8785	32.	1.3068	52.	1.1853
14.	1.7420	34.	1.2880	54.	1.1783
16.	1.6417	36.	1.2713	56.	1.1717
18.	1.5651	38.	1.2564	58.	1.1656

(b) Output

Figure 8-6. Use of a statement function

One example of the use of a statement function is in the following program. Suppose we would like to create a table of values for the function

$$f(X) = \frac{(X + 4.7)^2}{\sqrt{X} + X^2 + 1}$$

for values of X between zero and fifty-eight in increments of two. The program in Figure 8-6 prints this table in three columns. The statement function is defined in the first line of the program, and it is then called from lines 6, 8, and 10.

8-5. The Function Subprogram

Rules regarding the use of the function subprogram are as follows:

1. The first statement in the function subprogram must be a FUNCTION statement. As illustrated in Figure 8-3, this statement consists of the word FUNCTION followed by the name of the function subprogram followed by the arguments enclosed in parentheses and separated by commas.
2. The function subprogram must have at least one argument.
3. The function subprogram name conforms to the normal rules for the naming of variables. That is, the name consists of from one to six characters, the first of which must be a letter. If the value associated with the function subprogram is integer, the name must

begin with one of the letters I through N. If real, the name must begin with any other letter. The use of type declarations to override this convention is illustrated in a subsequent example.

4. The value associated with the function subprogram and used in evaluating the expression in which the function itself appears is the value of the variable in the function subprogram that is identical to the name of the function itself. Note the use of variable JTME in function JTME in Figure 8-3.

5. A function subprogram must have at least one RETURN statement. It may have more than one, and it may also include one or more STOP statements.

6. Array names may be used as arguments in the FUNCTION statement but must not be written with subscripts.

7. The function subprogram may call library functions, other function subprograms, or subroutines.

8. Expressions may be used as arguments of the function subprogram in the calling program.

As an example of a function subprogram, suppose we prepare a subprogram to find the largest number (called the greatest common divisor) that evenly divides two other numbers. Although there are more efficient approaches, we shall use the approach of trying successive numbers starting with 2 and continuing until the smaller of the two numbers is reached. The function subprogram and a short calling program are given in Figure 8-7. Since the value returned by the function subprogram is an integer, a name

```
      READ(5,1)N1,N2
    1 FORMAT(2I5)
      N=NGCD(N1,N2)
      WRITE(6,2)N1,N2,N
    2 FORMAT(' GCD UF',I5,' AND',I5,' IS',I5)
      STCP
      END

      FUNCTION NGCD(N,M)
      K=N
      IF(M.LT.K)K=M
      NGCD=1
      DO1J=2,K
      IF((N/J)*J.NE.N)GOTO1
      IF((M/J)*J.NE.M)GOTO1
      NGCD=J
    1 CONTINUE
      RETURN
      END
```

(a) Program

```
1528 5748
```

(b) Input data

```
GCD OF 1528 AND 5748 IS    4
```

(c) Output

Figure 8-7. Use of a function subprogram to determine the greatest common divisor

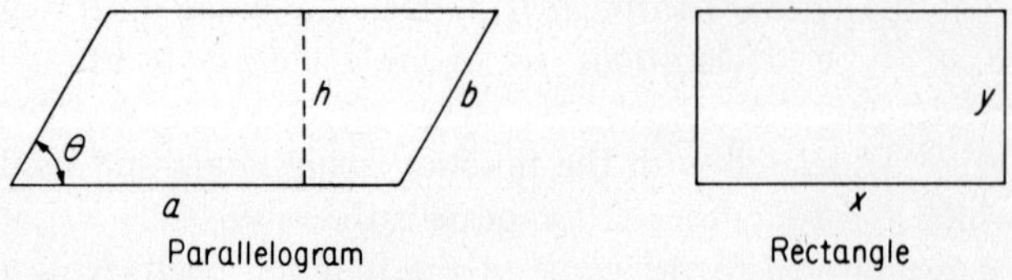

(a) Figures

```
      READ(5,1)A,B,THETA
    1 FORMAT(3F10.0)
      X=RECT(A,B,THETA,Y)
      WRITE(6,2)A,B,THETA,X,Y
    2 FORMAT(1X,3F10.2/1X2F10.2)
      STOP
      END

      FUNCTION RECT(A,B,T,Y)
      H=B*SIN(T/57.2)
      RECT=(A+B+SQRT((A+B)**2-4.*A*H))/2.
      Y=A*H/RECT
      RETURN
      END
```

(b) Program

```
8.          5.          26.
```

(c) Input data

```
  8.00        5.00        26.00
 11.47        1.53
```

(d) Output

Figure 8-8. Use of a function subprogram

beginning with N is chosen. Also note the use of NGCD as a variable in the function subprogram.

As a second example, suppose we have the parallelogram illustrated in Figure 8-8a. The angle θ and sides a and b are known. Suppose we would like to determine the sides x and y of a rectangle whose area and perimeter are the same as the parallelogram. The equations are as follows:

$$h = b \sin \theta$$
$$A = a \cdot h = x \cdot y$$
$$P = 2 \cdot (a + b) = 2 \cdot (x + y)$$

The equations for x and y are as follows:

$$x = \frac{(a+b) + \sqrt{(a+b)^2 - 4ah}}{2}$$
$$y = ah/x$$

Using a function subprogram for this problem is complicated by the fact that two values, one for x and one for y, are to be returned. One can be associated with the function name. If the computer system uses call by address for arguments of a function, the function subprogram can be written as in Figure 8-8b. The value of y is transferred back to the main program via the fourth argument. For systems that use call by value for function arguments, this program is not acceptable. Alternatively, COMMON can be used for Y, or a subroutine can be used instead of a function subprogram.

The next example of the use of a function subprogram is in interpolating between a set of data points. Specifically, suppose the following data are available:

x	y
45	1.7
50	1.9
55	2.2
60	2.4
65	3.1
70	4.2
75	5.8
80	7.2
85	10.5
90	14.7
95	19.2
100	26.5

```
$JOB               1105.50003
          DIMENSION Y(12)
          DATA Y/1.7,1.9,2.2,2.4,3.1,4.2,5.8,7.2,10.5,14.7,19.2,26.5/
          READ(5,1)X
    1     FORMAT(F5.0)
          YX=TER(X,Y)
          WRITE(6,2)X,YX
    2     FORMAT(' X =',F8.2,5X,'Y =',F6.2)
          STOP
          END

          FUNCTION TER(X,Y)
          DIMENSION Y(12)
          IF(X.LT.45.)GOTO1
          IF(X.GT.100.) GOTO2
          F=(X-40.)/5.
          J=F
          F=F-FLOAT(J)
          TER=Y(J)+F*(Y(J+1)-Y(J))
          RETURN
    1     WRITE(6,3)X
    3     FORMAT(' X =',F10.2,' IS BELOW 45')
          STOP
    2     WRITE(6,4)X
    4     FORMAT(' X =',F10.2,' EXCEEDS 100')
          STOP
          END
```

(a) Program

```
67.4
```

(b) Input data

```
X =    67.40         Y =    3.63
```

(c) Output

Figure 8-9. Use of a function subprogram to interpolate

For a given value of x, we would like to interpolate between the values of y using a straight-line approximation. The resulting function subprogram is shown in Figure 8-9. Note that the array Y appears in a DIMENSION statement in both the main program and the function subprogram. Since the entire array Y is to be available to the function subprogram, the name of the array written without a subscript appears in the calling statement. As we shall see in a subsequent example, an array written with a subscript in the calling statement causes transfer of a single number to the subprogram.

The function subprogram may change elements of an array used as argument. For example, the function subprogram in Figure 8-10 computes the arithmetic average of array Y and then subtracts the average from each of the elements. Since call by address is always used for arrays, the subprogram is actually changing the values in the array in the calling program.

```
          DIMENSION Y(20)
          READ(5,1)N,(Y(I),I=1,N)
     1    FORMAT(I5/(F5.0))
          A=AVG(Y,N)
          WRITE(6,2)A,(I,Y(I),I=1,N)
     2    FORMAT(' A =',F10.2/'     I',7X,'Y'/(1X,I3,F10.2))
          STOP
          END

          FUNCTION AVG(X,N)
          DIMENSION X(20)
          SUM=0.
          DO1I=1,N
     1    SUM=SUM+X(I)
          AVG=SUM/FLOAT(N)
          DO2I=1,N
     2    X(I)=X(I)-AVG
          RETURN
          END
```

(a) Program

```
    5
19.5
4.8
45.22
13.4
20.11
```

(b) Input data

```
A =       20.61
  I         Y
  1      -1.11
  2     -15.81
  3      24.61
  4      -7.21
  5      -0.50
```

(c) Output

Figure 8-10. Function subprogram to compute the average of the elements in an array

As a final example of the use of a function subprogram, note that in the enciphering program in Figure 7-5, a block of code to perform the lookup in the index table appears in two locations: once for the keyword, once for the message. Use of the function subprogram INDEX in Figure 8-11 permits the same block of code to be used for both these lookups. However, the array SYM must be defined by a DATA statement in both the main program and the function subprogram. As we shall see shortly, this can be circumvented by the use of COMMON.

At the beginning of this section, we mentioned that type statements could be used to alter the usual integer-real convention for function names. The program in Figure 8-12 is identical to the one in Figure 8-7, except that GCD is used as the function name instead of NGCD. This requires the use of the word INTEGER in the FUNCTION statement, defining the function as an integer function and defining variable GCD in the function subprogram as an integer variable. In addition, an INTEGER type statement is required in

```
      INTEGER KEY(8),MSG(16),SYM(27),NKEY(8),CRYP(16)
      DATA SYM/' ','A','B','C','D','E','F','G','H','I','J','K',
     1 'L','M','N','O','P','Q','R','S','T','U','V','W','X','Y','Z'/
      READ(5,1)KEY,MSG
    1 FORMAT(8A1/16A1)
      DO2J=1,8
    2 NKEY(J)=INDEX(KEY(J))
      J=0
      DO5L=1,16
      J=J+1
      IF(J.EQ.9)J=1
      M=INDEX(MSG(L))+NKEY(J)+1
      M=M-27*(M/27)
    5 CRYP(L)=SYM(M+1)
      WRITE(6,9)CRYP
    9 FORMAT('0CRYPTOGRAM IS ',16A1)
      STOP
      END

      FUNCTION INDEX(IC)
      INTEGER SYM(27)
      DATA SYM/' ','A','B','C','D','E','F','G','H','I','J','K',
     1 'L','M','N','O','P','Q','R','S','T','U','V','W','X','Y','Z'/
      DO1J=1,27
      IF(IC.EQ.SYM(J))GOTO2
    1 CONTINUE
      WRITE(6,3)
    3 FORMAT(' INVALID CHARACTER')
      STOP
    2 INDEX=J-1
      RETURN
      END
```

(a) Program

```
COMPUTER
HE HAD A BAD DAY
```

(b) Input data

```
CRYPTOGRAM IS UCWGEGOHM XCDGPZ
```

(c) Output

Figure 8-11. Use of a function subprogram in the enciphering problem

the calling program to declare the name GCD as integer. Since GCD is used as a function, this defines function GCD as integer in the main program.

8-6. Subroutines

Rules that apply to subroutines are as follows:

1. The first statement in the subroutine is the SUBROUTINE statement, an example of which is

```
SUBROUTINE TIME (I,J,K,L)
```

The word SUBROUTINE is followed by the subroutine name which is followed by the arguments enclosed in parentheses.

2. The name of the subroutine is restricted to six characters, the first of which must be alphabetic. Since no value is associated with the subroutine name, there is no integer-real distinction.

3. As illustrated by the example in Figure 8-4, the subroutine is called by a CALL statement

```
CALL TIME(JHOUR,JMIN,JAMPM,MTIME)
```

The word CALL is followed by the name of the subroutine to be called, which in turn is followed by the arguments. As pointed out in an earlier section, some systems do not permit expressions to be used for arguments in the CALL statement.

4. The subroutine may have no arguments; this generally occurs only when COMMON is used.

5. Transfer from the subroutine to the main program is by the RETURN statement. The subroutine may contain more than one RETURN statement, but unlike the function subprogram, it is not necessary that it contain a RETURN statement. STOP statements are permitted in subroutines.

As an example, we shall prepare a program using a subroutine to accomplish the same objective as the program in Figure 8-8. We need only add another argument (X) to the function subprogram in Figure 8-8, replace the function call with a subroutine CALL statement, and change the FUNCTION statement to a SUBROUTINE statement, giving the program in Figure 8-13. All communication between the main program and the subroutine is by the argument list. The values of A, B, and THETA are available to the subroutine since they appear in the argument list. Similarly, the values of X and Y are available to the main program. However, variable H in the subprogram does not appear in the argument list and is not available to the main program.

Although in many cases the use of a function subprogram as opposed to a subroutine or vice versa is purely a matter of personal choice, problems are not suitable for a function subprogram if there is no one value that can be designated as the functional value. An example of this situation occurs if a subroutine is used to perform the inventory update described in Figure 5-9.

If a subroutine to update the inventory is prepared, it can be used for items received and items shipped, provided negative values are used for the latter. In the program in Figure 8-14, array STOCK, array QUAN, variable STKNO, and variable NREC are available to the subroutine. Its primary objective is to update array QUAN, which appears as an argument. This routine is such that no functional value appears, and thus a subroutine is preferred over a function subprogram.

```
      INTEGER GCD
      READ(5,1)N1,N2
    1 FORMAT(2I5)
      N=GCD(N1,N2)
      WRITE(6,2)N1,N2,N
    2 FORMAT(' GCD OF',I5,' AND',I5,' IS',I5)
      STOP
      END

      INTEGER FUNCTION GCD(N,M)
      K=N
      IF(M.LT.K)K=M
      GCD=1
      DO1J=2,K
      IF((N/J)*J.NE.N)GOTO1
      IF((M/J)*J.NE.M)GOTO1
      GCD=J
    1 CONTINUE
      RETURN
      END
```

(a) Program

```
1528 5748
```

(b) Input data

```
GCD OF 1528 AND 5748 IS    4
```

(c) Output

Figure 8-12. Use of specification statements for a function

```
      READ(5,1)A,B,THETA
    1 FORMAT(3F10.0)
      CALL RECT(A,B,THETA,X,Y)
      WRITE(6,2)A,B,THETA,X,Y
    2 FORMAT(1X,3F10.2/1X2F10.2)
      STOP
      END

      SUBROUTINE RECT(A,B,T,X,Y)
      H=B*SIN(T/57.2)
      X=(A+B+SQRT((A+B)**2-4.*A*H))/2.
      Y=A*H/X
      RETURN
      END
```

(a) Program

```
8.        5.        26.
```

(b) Input data

```
  8.00      5.00     26.00
 11.47      1.53
```

(c) Output

Figure 8-13. Use of a subroutine

```
      INTEGER STOCK(20),QUAN(20),STKNO
      READ(5,1)ITEMS,(STOCK(J),QUAN(J),J=1,ITEMS)
    1 FORMAT(I5/(2I5))
    4 READ(5,2)STKNO,NREC
    2 FORMAT(2I5)
      IF(NREC.EQ.0)GOTO3
      CALL UPDATE(STOCK,QUAN,STKNO,ITEMS,NREC)
      GOTO4
    3 READ(5,2)STKNO,NSHP
      IF(NSHP.EQ.0)GOTO6
      NSHP=-NSHP
      CALL UPDATE(STOCK,QUAN,STKNO,ITEMS,NSHP)
      GOTO3
    6 WRITE(6,5)(STOCK(J),QUAN(J),J=1,ITEMS)
    5 FORMAT('0FINAL INVENTORY'/'0 ITEM',5X,'QUANTITY'/(1X,I5,I12))
      STOP
      END

      SUBROUTINE UPDATE(STOCK,QUAN,STKNO,ITEMS,N)
      INTEGER STOCK(20),QUAN(20),STKNO
      DO1J=1,ITEMS
      IF(STOCK(J).EQ.STKNO)GOTO2
    1 CONTINUE
      WRITE(6,3)STKNO
    3 FORMAT(' NO ITEM NUMBER',I6)
      RETURN
    2 QUAN(J)=QUAN(J)+N
      RETURN
      END
```

(a) Program

7	
1519	19
1206	5
1317	9
1802	3
1988	17
1012	15
1303	8
1802	5
1012	20
1206	15
1802	14
1012	7
0	0
1805	6
1012	5
1317	3
1012	3
1303	1
1317	5
0	0

(b) Input data

NC ITEM NUMBER 1805

FINAL INVENTORY

ITEM	QUANTITY
1519	19
1206	20
1317	1
1802	22
1988	17
1012	34
1303	7

(c) Output

Figure 8-14. Use of a subroutine in the inventory problem

```
      INTEGER KEY(16),MSG(16),SYM(27),CRYP(16)
      DATA SYM/' ','A','B','C','D','E','F','G','H','I','J','K',
     1 'L','M','N','O','P','Q','R','S','T','U','V','W','X','Y','Z'/
      READ(5,1)(KEY(J),J=1,8),MSG
    1 FORMAT(8A1/16A1)
      CALL INDEX(KEY,8)
      CALL INDEX(MSG,16)
      J=0
      DO5L=1,16
      J=J+1
      IF(J.EQ.9)J=1
      M=MSG(L)+KEY(J)+10
      M=M-27*(M/27)
    5 CRYP(L)=SYM(M+1)
      WRITE(6,9)CRYP
    9 FORMAT('0CRYPTOGRAM IS ',16A1)
      STOP
      END

      SUBROUTINE INDEX(C,N)
      INTEGER C(16),SYM(27)
      DATA SYM/' ','A','B','C','D','E','F','G','H','I','J','K',
     1 'L','M','N','O','P','Q','R','S','T','U','V','W','X','Y','Z'/
      DO1J=1,N
      DO2K=1,27
      IF(SYM(K).EQ.C(J))GOTO1
    2 CONTINUE
      WRITE(6,4)
    4 FORMAT(' INVALID CHARACTER')
      STOP
    1 C(J)=K-1
      RETURN
      END
```

(a) Program

```
$ENTRY
COMPUTER
HE HAD A BAD DAY
```

(b) Input data

```
CRYPTOGRAM IS UCWGEGOBM XCDGPZ
```

(c) Output

Figure 8-15. Use of a subroutine in the enciphering problem

Another case in which a subroutine is preferred over a function subprogram occurs if an array is computed in the subprogram. Only simple variables, not arrays, can be treated as functional values. As an example of such a situation, suppose we modify our approach in solving the enciphering process by using a subroutine INDEX to replace the alphabetic characters in the vectors for the keyword and the message by their respective indices. The resulting program is given in Figure 8-15. In this way, the vector of numeric indices is the result of the computation in the subprogram. This makes the subroutine a logical choice over the function subprogram.

8-7. COMMON

In all previous examples in this section, communication between the calling program and the subprogram has been exclusively via arguments. In some cases this leads to long argument lists. Furthermore, as will be pointed out in the next chapter, use of COMMON leads to computational efficiency.

The COMMON statement causes the system to create a set of storage locations (called the COMMON block) that is accessible to all programs and subprograms containing the COMMON statement. This is Fortran's counterpart to the global declaration of other programming languages. For example, the statement

```
COMMON G,A,K,A4
```

creates a COMMON block consisting of four storage locations.

The COMMON statement can be used to define arrays. For example, the statement

```
COMMON A(4,5),J,X,I(7)
```

creates a COMMON block consisting of twenty-nine storage locations. Alternatively, the following two statements can be used:

```
DIMENSION A(5,4),I(7)
COMMON A,J,X,I
```

Either alternative is acceptable, but the same variable must not be declared as an array in both the DIMENSION and the COMMON statements. REAL and INTEGER can be used similarly. For example, the statements

```
REAL J(7),IX
COMMON G,IX,J,K(8)
```

are equivalent to the statements

```
REAL J,IX
COMMON G,IX,J(7),K(8)
```

Either case creates a COMMON block consisting of seventeen storage locations.

As an example, we shall use COMMON in place of the fourth argument in the subprogram in Figure 8-8. As illustrated in Figure 8-16, we only add the statement

```
COMMON Y
```

to both the main program and the subprogram, and we delete the fourth argument. This causes a single location to be created for Y in the COMMON block, and this location is available to both the main program and the subprogram.

In the subroutine in Figure 8-13, COMMON can be used to remove all the arguments from the argument list as illustrated by the program in Figure 8-17. In the main program the COMMON block is defined by the statement

```
COMMON A,B,THETA,X,Y
```

In the subroutine the COMMON block is defined by the statement

```
COMMON A,B,T,X,Y
```

```
      COMMON Y
      READ(5,1)A,B,THETA
    1 FORMAT(3F10.0)
      X=RECT(A,B,THETA)
      WRITE(6,2)A,B,THETA,X,Y
    2 FORMAT(1X,3F10.2/1X2F10.2)
      STOP
      END

      FUNCTION RECT(A,B,T)
      COMMON Y
      H=B*SIN(T/57.2)
      RECT=(A+B+SQRT((A+B)**2-4.*A*H))/2.
      Y=A*H/RECT
      RETURN
      END
```

(a) Program

```
8.          5.          26.
```

(b) Input data

```
 8.00       5.00        26.00
11.47       1.53
```

(c) Output

Figure 8-16. Use of COMMON declaration

```
      COMMON A,B,THETA,X,Y
      READ(5,1)A,B,THETA
    1 FORMAT(3F10.0)
      CALL RECT
      WRITE(6,2)A,B,THETA,X,Y
    2 FORMAT(1X,3F10.2/1X2F10.2)
      STOP
      END

      SUBROUTINE RECT
      COMMON A,B,T,X,Y
      H=B*SIN(T/57.2)
      X=(A+B+SQRT((A+B)**2-4.*A*H))/2.
      Y=A*H/X
      RETURN
      END
```

(a) Program

```
8.          5.          26.
```

(b) Input data

```
 8.00       5.00        26.00
11.47       1.53
```

(c) Output

Figure 8-17. Use of COMMON

Each of these statements defines a COMMON block of five storage locations. The address of the first storage location is used for variable A both in the main program and in the subroutine. Similarly, the addresses of the second, fourth, and fifth storage locations are used for variables B, X, and Y, respectively, in both main program and subroutine. In the main program the address of the third location is used for variable THETA, but in the subprogram this same storage location is used for variable T. This makes variable THETA in the main program synonymous with variable T in the subprogram.

The COMMON statement only defines the addresses of certain variables as being storage locations in the COMMON block. In establishing a COMMON block, the programmer can select whatever variable names are most convenient. As illustrated in the example in Figure 8-17, the same names do not have to be used in the main program and in the subprogram.

For the sake of illustration, suppose that an array of four elements is most convenient for the main program, but that in the subprogram the use of simple variables for these four storage locations is more convenient. To implement this, the main program should contain the statement

```
COMMON X(4)
```

and the subprogram should contain the statement

```
COMMON A,G,YA,Z
```

In this case, the first location in COMMON is the first element of array X in the main program and is simple variable A in the subprogram, the second location is the second element of array X in the main program and is simple variable G in the subprogram, etc.

Although it is possible to change the variable names associated with COMMON storage locations between the main program and subprogram, it is not permissible to use an integer variable for a storage location in the main program and a real variable in the subprogram for the same storage location, or vice versa. That is, changing variable types is not permissible.

As a final example of COMMON, we shall use COMMON for array SYM in the program in Figure 8-15. In this program, array SYM is needed in both the main program and the subprogram. In Figure 8-15, separate storage locations are reserved for SYM in the main program and in the subprogram. By use of COMMON as illustrated in Figure 8-18, the same storage locations can be used for SYM in both the main program and the subprogram. However, many systems do not permit the DATA statement to assign initial values to storage locations in COMMON. In Figure 8-18, the elements of SYM are read into memory. This can be avoided by using the BLOCK DATA subprogram described in Section 8-10.

Most systems permit the length of the COMMON block in the calling program to be longer than the COMMON block in the subprogram.

Multiple COMMON statements may be used. Subsequent COMMON statements are treated as continuations of the first COMMON statement; together they define a single COMMON block. For example, the statements

```
COMMON X(8),J,K(7)
COMMON A,B,C(2,4)
```

are equivalent to the single statement

```
COMMON X(8),J,K(7),A,B,C(2,4)
```

In programs with several subprograms, the labeled COMMON feature can be used to

```
      INTEGER KEY(16),MSG(16),SYM(27),CRYP(16)
      COMMON SYM
      READ(5,1)(KEY(J),J=1,8),MSG,SYM
    1 FORMAT(8A1/16A1/27A1)
      CALL INDEX(KEY,8)
      CALL INDEX(MSG,16)
      J=0
      DO5L=1,16
      J=J+1
      IF(J.EQ.9)J=1
      M=MSG(L)+KEY(J)+10
      M=M-27*(M/27)
    5 CRYP(L)=SYM(M+1)
      WRITE(6,9)CRYP
    9 FORMAT('0CRYPTOGRAM IS ',16A1)
      STOP
      END

      SUBROUTINE INDEX(C,N)
      INTEGER C(16),SYM(27)
      COMMON SYM
      DO1J=1,N
      DO2K=1,27
      IF(SYM(K).EQ.C(J))GOTO1
    2 CONTINUE
      WRITE(6,4)
    4 FORMAT('  INVALID CHARACTER')
      STOP
    1 C(J)=K-1
      RETURN
      END
```

(a) Program

```
COMPUTER
HE HAD A BAD DAY
 ABCDEFGHIJKLMNOPQRSTUVWXYZ
```

(b) Input data

```
CRYPTOGRAM IS UCWGEGOBM XCDGPZ
```

(c) Output

Figure 8-18. Use of COMMON for array SYM in the enciphering program

define different COMMON blocks. The label, enclosed in slashes, follows the word COMMON, as illustrated by the following example:

COMMON /JACK/A,G(16)

The name used as a label is generally restricted to six characters, the first of which must be alphabetic. A few systems do not permit the name used as a label in a COMMON statement to be used as a variable elsewhere in the program. Unlabeled COMMON is referred to as blank COMMON.

Labeled COMMON enables the programmer to define certain variables as in COMMON between one program or subprogram and another subprogram, while other variables are in COMMON between the same program or subprogram and a third subprogram. The same program may contain blank COMMON along with one or more labeled COMMON blocks. However, the same variable may not appear in more than one COMMON block.

8-8. EQUIVALENCE

Within a given program or subprogram, a unique variable has been associated with each available storage location in all discussions up to this point. Using COMMON, a storage location within the COMMON block can be associated with one variable in the main program and another variable in the subprogram. But within the main program this storage location was associated with a single variable name.

Using the EQUIVALENCE statement permits two or more variables to be associated with the same storage location. For example, the statement

```
EQUIVALENCE (JACK,K)
```

causes the same storage location to be used for variables JACK and K. In effect, these two variables are identical.

The EQUIVALENCE statement may be used to cause any number of variables to be associated with a given storage location. Furthermore, equivalencing may be accomplished for more than one storage location within the same EQUIVALENCE statement, as illustrated by the following statement:

```
EQUIVALENCE (JACK,K,LAMP),(X,G)
```

Elements in an array may also be included in an EQUIVALENCE statement:

```
EQUIVALENCE (AK,X(4))
```

This statement causes the fourth storage location within array X to be used for variable AK.

Since arrays are always stored in consecutive storage locations, entire arrays can be equivalenced by equivalencing single elements. For example, the statements

```
DIMENSION G(14),X(9)
EQUIVALENCE (X(1),G(1))
```

cause the first nine storage locations for array G to be used for array X. In addition to equivalencing X(1) and G(1), we have also equivalenced X(2) and G(2), X(3) and G(3), etc.

Equivalencing may be desirable for several reasons

1. The name used for a variable in one section of the program is changed, erroneously, in another section of the program. The EQUIVALENCE statement corrects this situation without changing the statements.

2. The use of subscripted variables entails more computational overhead than the use of simple variables: the address of the element must be computed from the value of the subscript and the address of the first element reserved for the array. For simple variables, the address is available directly. Therefore, if a specific element of an array, X(4), appears explicitly in several statements within the program, it is more efficient to use

```
EQUIVALENCE (X(4),X4)
```

and replace the subscripted variable X(4) with the simple variable X4 throughout the program. Some compilers effectively do this automatically.

3. The EQUIVALENCE statement can be used to conserve storage in large programs. For example, suppose variable A is used only in one section of the program, variable B is used only in another section, and outside these sections these variables are not needed for any purpose. In this case, the statement

```
EQUIVALENCE (A,B)
```

reduces the storage requirements by one. Of course, equivalencing arrays produces greater reductions than equivalencing simple variables.

The use of the EQUIVALENCE statement in conjunction with the COMMON statement produces interesting results. For example, the statements

```
DIMENSION X(4)
EQUIVALENCE (X(1),A),(X(2),B),(X(3),C),(X(4),D)
```

equivalences X(1) with A, X(2) with B, X(3) with C, and X(4) with D. This can also be accomplished as follows:

```
DIMENSION X(4)
COMMON A,B,C,D
EQUIVALENCE (X(1),A)
```

The COMMON statement defines a COMMON block consisting of four storage locations reserved for variables A, B, C, and D. The EQUIVALENCE statement defines the first location in the COMMON block as the first element in array X. Since the COMMON statement specifies that the storage location reserved for B immediately follows the storage location reserved for A, and since elements in an array are always stored in consecutive storage locations, it follows that these statements have equivalenced X(2) and B, X(3) with C, and X(4) with D.

In the above example, the statement

```
EQUIVALENCE (X(1),A)
```

can be replaced by any one of the following statements:

```
EQUIVALENCE (X(2),B)
EQUIVALENCE (X(3),C)
EQUIVALENCE (X(4),D)
```

The EQUIVALENCE statement may also be used to extend the COMMON block. For example, consider the following statements:

```
DIMENSION X(4)
COMMON A,B,C,D
EQUIVALENCE (X(1),D)
```

The COMMON block is defined as consisting of the four storage locations for variables A, B, C, and D. However, the location for D is then defined by the EQUIVALENCE statement as being the first element of a four-element array. Therefore, the COMMON block consists of seven storage locations, since three additional consecutive storage locations are reserved for the array in addition to the four locations explicitly reserved by the COMMON statement.

While it is quite acceptable to extend COMMON by using the EQUIVALENCE statement to attach storage locations to the end of the explicitly defined COMMON block, it is not acceptable to attach locations to the front of the COMMON block. For example, the statements

```
DIMENSION X(4)
COMMON A,B,C,D
EQUIVALENCE (X(4),A)
```

equivalence A with the fourth element of array X. For this to be possible, the three storage locations preceding A must be available for array X. Fortran does not permit COMMON blocks to be extended in this manner.

8-9. Adjustable Dimensions

In the enciphering programs in Figures 8-15 and 8-18, the array KEY is defined to consist of sixteen elements when only eight are used. This is because array C in subroutine INDEX is defined for sixteen elements in order to accommodate array MSG. In reality, the increase in the size of KEY is not necessary because no storage locations in the subprogram are reserved for C: it is used as an argument. However, some systems require that consistent array sizes be defined in both the calling program and the subprogram.

On these systems, increasing the sizes of the arrays can be avoided by using the adjustable dimension feature. Since no storage locations are reserved for the subprogram arguments, the compiler need not know how large the array will be, provided it knows that it will be specified when the subprogram is called. A variable may be used in the DIMENSION statement in the subprogram in these cases. The restrictions are as follows:

1. The variable specifying the size of the array in the subprogram appears as an argument. Placing this variable in COMMON is not acceptable.
2. The name of the array must also be an argument in the subprogram. Arrays not appearing as arguments must be defined as usual in the DIMENSION statement since storage locations must be reserved for them.

Figure 8-19 presents an example of the use of adjustable dimensions in the enciphering program.

8-10. BLOCK DATA

In earlier sections it was pointed out that some systems do not permit DATA statements to assign initial values to variables in COMMON. In these cases, a subprogram beginning with the statement

```
BLOCK DATA
```

can contain such DATA statements. This subprogram may not contain any executable statements; it may only contain the following statements:

```
      INTEGER KEY(8),MSG(16),SYM(27),CRYP(16)
      DATA SYM/' ','A','B','C','D','E','F','G','H','I','J','K',
     1 'L','M','N','O','P','Q','R','S','T','U','V','W','X','Y','Z'/
      READ(5,1)KEY,MSG
    1 FORMAT(8A1/16A1)
      CALL  INDEX(KEY,8)
      CALL  INDEX(MSG,16)
      J=0
      DO5L=1,16
      J=J+1
      IF(J.EQ.9)J=1
      M=MSG(L)+KEY(J)+10
      M=M-27*(M/27)
    5 CRYP(L)=SYM(M+1)
      WRITE(6,9)CRYP
    9 FORMAT('0CRYPTOGRAM IS ',16A1)
      STOP
      END

      SUBROUTINE  INDEX(C,N)
      INTEGER C(N),SYM(27)
      DATA SYM/' ','A','B','C','D','E','F','G','H','I','J','K',
     1 'L','M','N','O','P','Q','R','S','T','U','V','W','X','Y','Z'/
      DO1J=1,N
      DO2K=1,27
      IF(SYM(K).EQ.C(J))GOTO1
    2 CONTINUE
      WRITE(6,4)
    4 FORMAT('  INVALID CHARACTER')
      STOP
    1 C(J)=K-1
      RETURN
      END
```

(a) Program

```
COMPUTER
HE HAD A BAD DAY
```

(b) Input data

```
CRYPTOGRAM IS UCWGEGOBM XCDGPZ
```

(c) Output

Figure 8-19. Use of adjustable dimensions

1. DIMENSION, INTEGER, or REAL statements
2. COMMON statements
3. EQUIVALENCE statements
4. DATA statements
5. An END statement

An example of the use of the BLOCK DATA subprogram is illustrated in Figure 8-20 for the enciphering program.

```
      INTEGER KEY(16),MSG(16),SYM(27),CRYP(16)
      COMMON SYM
      READ(5,1)(KEY(J),J=1,8),MSG
    1 FORMAT(8A1/16A1)
      CALL INDEX(KEY,8)
      CALL INDEX(MSG,16)
      J=0
      DO5L=1,16
      J=J+1
      IF(J.EQ.9)J=1
      M=MSG(L)+KEY(J)+10
      M=M-27*(M/27)
    5 CRYP(L)=SYM(M+1)
      WRITE(6,9)CRYP
    9 FORMAT('0CRYPTOGRAM IS ',16A1)
      STOP
      END

      SUBROUTINE INDEX(C,N)
      INTEGER C(16),SYM(27)
      COMMON SYM
      DO1J=1,N
      DO2K=1,27
      IF(SYM(K).EQ.C(J))GOTO1
    2 CONTINUE
      WRITE(6,4)
    4 FORMAT(' INVALID CHARACTER')
      STOP
    1 C(J)=K-1
      RETURN
      END

      BLOCK DATA
      INTEGER SYM(27)
      COMMON SYM
      DATA SYM/' ','A','B','C','D','E','F','G','H','I','J','K',
     1 'L','M','N','O','P','Q','R','S','T','U','V','W','X','Y','Z'/
      END
```

(a) Program

```
COMPUTER
HE HAD A BAD DAY
```

(b) Input data

```
CRYPTOGRAM IS UCWGEGOBM XCDGPZ
```

(c) Output

Figure 8-20. Use of BLOCK DATA

8-11. The EXTERNAL Statement

The names appearing in the EXTERNAL type statement are subprogram names to be used as arguments in a subprogram call. Suppose for one call the subprogram should use ALOG while for another the subprogram should use ALOG10. The proper statements are

```
C     MAIN PROGRAM
      EXTERNAL ALOG10,ALOG
      :
      CALL SUB(. . . ,ALOG, . . . )
      :
      CALL SUB( . . . ,ALOG10, . . . )
      :
      END
      SUBROUTINE SUB( . . . ,FLOG, . . . )
      :
      RESULT = FLOG(ARG)
      :
      RETURN
      END
```

8-12. Multiple ENTRY and RETURN

The normal entry into either a SUBROUTINE or a FUNCTION subprogram occurs when the CALL statement references the subprogram name. Entry into the subprogram is at the first executable statement following the FUNCTION or SUBROUTINE statement. In some cases, this is not always desirable. For example, suppose there is to be some initialization the first time a subprogram is called. Thereafter, this initialization is unnecessary. Thus, all entries except the first can be at some point other than the first executable statement following the FUNCTION or SUBROUTINE statement.

Multiple entry points in the subprograms are created by using the ENTRY statement of the form

$$\text{ENTRY } name(a_1,a_2, \ldots ,a_n)$$

where *name* is the name of the entry point. Rules for ENTRY names are the same as for FUNCTION and SUBROUTINE names. $a_1, a_2, \ldots, a_n$ are arguments analogous to the arguments in a FUNCTION or SUBROUTINE statement.

The ENTRY statement is nonexecutable, and the entry into the subprogram is at the first executable statement following the ENTRY statement. Entry cannot be made within the range of the DO. Some systems require that the arguments in the ENTRY statement be identical to the arguments in the FUNCTION or SUBROUTINE statement, although others relax this requirement.

As an example, suppose we wish to prepare a function subprogram to calculate the resistance as a function of temperature from an equation of the form $a+bT+cT^2$. Also suppose that the first time the function subprogram is called, the values of a, b, and c must be read and the value of $a+bV+cV^2$ returned to the calling program. The subprogram can be as follows:

```
      FUNCTION RESIS(T)
      READ (5,10)A,B,C
10    FORMAT (3F10.0)
      ENTRY RES(T)
```

```
      RESIS = A + T * (B + C * T)
      RETURN
      END
```

The value returned at the exit from a function subprogram is the value last assigned to the FUNCTION name or any ENTRY name. However, if the last value assigned to an ENTRY name differs in type from the current ENTRY name, the returned value is undefined. That is, it is possible to change types between ENTRY names, but the type of the returned value must be consistent with the type of the current ENTRY name.

A calling sequence for the above subprogram is

```
C     MAIN PROGRAM
      .
      .
      .
      P = V ** 2/RESIS(TEMP)
      .
      .
      .
      V = CURNT * RES(TA)
```

The first time the function is called, entry is at the READ statement. Thereafter, it is at the arithmetic statement for calculating RESIS.

Just as it may be desirable to enter a subprogram at different points, it may also be desirable to return to some statement other than the statement following the SUBROUTINE call (multiple return only applies to SUBROUTINE subprograms). For example consider the following sequence:

```
C     MAIN PROGRAM
      .
      .
      .
      CALL SUB(A,X,Z,&4,Q,&8)
    3 B = A * X
      .
      .
      .
    4 X = X + A
    8 X = X + Q
      .
      .
      .
      END
      SUBROUTINE SUB(B,C,D, *, Z, *)
      .
      .
      .
      IF (F)8,19,30
    8 RETURN 2
   19 RETURN
   30 RETURN 1
      END
```

Notice that the RETURN statement is of the form

RETURN *i*

where i is an integer constant or variable whose value denotes the location of the statement number in the argument list at which return to the main program is to be made. Note that statement numbers in the CALL statement are preceded by &, and the corresponding arguments in the SUBROUTINE statement consist only of an *. In the above example, return is as follows:

$F > 0$, return to statement 4
$F = 0$, return to statement 3
$F < 0$, return to statement 8

Perhaps the multiple return illustrated above can be best explained by comparison with the computed GO TO. The return is the same as for the following sequence:

```
C     MAIN PROGRAM
      .
      .
      .
      CALL SUB(A,X,Z,Q,J)
      GO TO (3,4,8),J
      .
      .
      .
      END
      SUBROUTINE SUB(A,X,Z,Q,J)
      .
      .
      .
      IF (F)8,19,30
    8 J = 3
      RETURN
   19 J = 1
      RETURN
   30 J = 2
      RETURN
      END
```

This could also be accomplished with an assigned GO TO.

EXERCISES‡

†**8-1.** Exercise 5-17 describes the use of interval halving to locate roots of polynomials. Reprogram this exercise using a statement function for evaluating $f(x)$.

8-2. Exercise 5-18 describes Newton's method for locating roots of polynomials. Reprogram this exercise using statement functions to evaluate $f(x)$ and $f'(x)$.

8-3. Exercise 5-19 describes an iterative procedure for solving nonlinear equations. Reprogram this exercise using statement functions to evaluate the two functions. Run program for k equal to 0.5 and 1.0.

†**8-4.** Reprogram Exercise 7-9 using a statement function to evaluate $f(x)$.

‡Solutions to Exercises marked with a dagger † are given in Appendix E.

8-5. Reprogram Exercise 5-14 using a statement function to evaluate $f(x)$.

8-6. Reprogram Exercise 5-15 using a statement function to evaluate $f(x)$.

†8-7. Reprogram Exercise 5-16 using a statement function to evaluate $f(x)$.

8-8. Reprogram Exercise 5-20 using a statement function to evaluate the derivative.

8-9. Reprogram Exercise 5-21 using a statement function to evaluate $dc(t)/dt$.

†8-10. Reprogram Exercise 5-22 using a statement function to evaluate $dc(t)/dt$.

8-11. Prepare a function subprogram SIN2 (X) to compute $\sin^2(x)$. Use the series representation in Exercise 5-13, truncated after 100 terms. Prepare a main program to check the results against the computer's SIN function for $x = 2$.

8-12. Prepare a function subprogram IBINOM to evaluate the binomial coefficients as discussed in Exercise 7-2. This subprogram should use a subprogram IFAC to compute factorials. Use these subprograms to program Exercise 7-11.

8-13. Prepare a function subprogram to compute the cube root $\sqrt[3]{x} = \dfrac{|x|^{4/3}}{x}$ of a number. Prepare a program using this subprogram to compute the cube roots of 5.6 and −7.2.

†8-14. Let $f(x) = a_n x^n + a_{n-1} x^{n-1} + \cdots + a_1 x + a_0$. The coefficients are stored in a one-dimensional array A, a_0 being stored in A(1), a_1 in A(2), etc. Prepare a function subprogram FUNC (A,N,B) to evaluate $f(b)$. Also prepare a main program to read n, the coefficients of $f(x)$ beginning with a_0, and b; to call FUNC; and to print b and $f(b)$ with appropriate labeling. The maximum value of n is fifty. Evaluate $f(x) = x^4 + 1.2x^3 + 1.7x^2 - 1.9x + 0.8$ at $x = 2.2$.

8-15. A number of interesting exercises can be devised around the effect of computational precision upon numerical techniques. For example, the series e^x is represented as follows:

$$e^x = 1 + x + \frac{x^2}{2} + \frac{x^3}{3!} + \frac{x^4}{4!} + \cdots$$

where the ith term is $x^i/i!$. In computing this series, the best approach is to compute the ith term by multiplying the previous term by x/i.

To determine the effect of computational precision, first write a function subprogram to limit the precision of a number to three significant digits, using rounding for the last digit. For example, 127568.2 is 128000. to three significant digits and 0.0012743 is 0.00127. The ALOG10 function can be used for this purpose.

In evaluating the above series, the function ROUND should be inserted after every addition, subtraction, etc. For example, the statement

```
TERM = TERM * X/FLOAT(I)
```

should be programmed as follows:

```
TERM = ROUND (ROUND(TERM * X)/FLOAT(I))
```

Compute $e^{-5.5}$ directly according to the above series using three digits precision. Terminate the computation of the series whenever an additional term changes the value of the summation by less than 0.001 percent. Compare to the value of $e^{-5.5}$ computed by the EXP function. Then compute $e^{-5.5}$ by noting that

$$e^{-5.5} = 1/e^{5.5}$$

and evaluate $e^{5.5}$ by the above series. Compare the value of $e^{-5.5}$ computed in this manner to the value obtained above.

†**8-16.** Prepare a function subprogram SUM (A, N, M) to evaluate

$$\sum_{i-1}^{N} A(I)$$

where A is a one-dimensional array of M elements (M ⩾ N). Use this subprogram to solve Exercise 7-15.

8-17. Prepare a function subprogram SPGRAV to perform the table lookup for Exercise 6-23, and reprogram this exercise using this subprogram. Use a DATA statement in the subprogram to enter the table as in Exercise 7-14.

8-18. Prepare a function subprogram called ANORM with arguments (A,N) to compute the norm of the $n \times 1$ vector a. Also prepare a main program to read n and a, compute the norm, and print the result. See Exercise 5-54 for a more detailed discussion. The maximum value for n is fifty.

8-19. Modify the function subprogram in the previous exercise so that the vector is normalized (see Exercise 5-55). The main program should print the normalized vector in addition to the norm of the original vector.

†**8-20.** Prepare a function subprogram DOT to compute the dot product of vectors a and b. Use this subprogram to program Exercise 5-57. Transfer the number of components in the vectors as an argument.

8-21. Use the function subprogram ANORM developed for Exercise 8-18 and the subprogram DOT developed for Exercise 8-20 to program Exercise 5-58.

8-22. Prepare a subroutine to interchange column I with column J in an $n \times n$ matrix A. The CALL statement should transfer I, J, A, N (the order of A), and M (the dimensioned size of A). Prepare a program calling the above subroutine to switch columns 2 and 4 in the following matrix:

$$\begin{bmatrix} 1 & 2 & 1 & 4 \\ 4 & 1 & 2 & 2 \\ 0 & 3 & 1 & -9 \\ 7 & 5 & 0 & 2 \end{bmatrix}$$

This program should read N, A, I, and J as data, and print the final result in a columnar fashion.

†**8-23.** Prepare a subroutine called SCALAR to multiply an $n \times 1$ vector by a scalar quantity. Do not destroy original vector. Use this subroutine along with the function subprogram DOT in Exercise 8-20 to program Exercise 5-59.

8-24. Prepare a subroutine to normalize the $n \times 1$ vector a. Use this subroutine to program Exercise 5-55.

8-25. Prepare a subroutine to add an $n \times 1$ vector a to an $n \times 1$ vector b to obtain an $n \times 1$ vector c. Use this subroutine to program Exercise 5-56.

†**8-26.** Prepare a subroutine called TRANS to take the transpose of the $n \times n$ matrix A. Use this subroutine to program Exercise 6-24. Let the maximum value of n be twenty.

8-27. Prepare a subroutine called MTXSUM to add matrices A and B of order $n \times m$ to obtain matrix C. Use this subroutine to program Exercise 6-25.

8-28. Prepare a subroutine to multiply an $n \times m$ matrix A by an mth-order vector b to obtain nth-order vector c. Use this subroutine to program Exercise 6-26.

†**8-29.** Prepare a subroutine to multiply an $n \times m$ matrix A by an $m \times k$ matrix B to obtain an $n \times k$ matric C. Use this subroutine to solve Exercise 7-26.

8-30. Prepare a subroutine called SOLVE (A, B, X, N, M), where M is the dimensional size of A, B, and X, to solve the set of equations given in Exercise 6-16. Also prepare a main program using this subroutine to solve the same set of equations as in Exercise 6-16.

8-31. Exercise 6-17 discusses the Gauss reduction technique for solving sets of linear algebraic equations. Prepare a subroutine called GAUSS (A, B, N, M), where M is the dimensional size of A and B, to perform the Gauss reduction. Prepare a main program to perform the same objectives as required in Exercise 6-17.

†**8-32.** Repeat Exercise 6-18 using the two subroutines prepared for the above two examples. Use an input similar to that of Exercise 7-26.

8-33. Prepare a subroutine named CONV to convert a complex number to a magnitude and an angle. Using this subroutine along with an appropriate program, convert the following complex numbers and print the results:

$$\begin{array}{r} 1 + i2 \\ -3 - i5 \\ -3 + i2 \\ 2 - i3 \end{array}$$

Use two arguments, one for the real part and one for the imaginary part, to communicate the complex number to the subroutine.

8-34. Prepare a subroutine to perform the least-squares analysis as performed by the program in Figure 5-4. The main program should read the observations into arrays X and Y. The subroutine should compute the regression coefficients which should then be printed by the main program.

8-35. Prepare a subroutine to plot points as does the program in Figure 7-3. The points should be read into arrays X and Y by a main program. This program should also read maximum and minimum values for the coordinates of the axes. The number of rows and columns should be fixed at forty and fifty, respectively.

9

Efficient Programming in Fortran‡

A number of techniques can be used to decrease the running time and memory space requirements for Fortran programs. The usage of these depends upon the characteristics of a particular compiler and system.

Real mastery of a problem-oriented language implies the ability to describe a job so that it will be done efficiently, i.e. with a minimum of unnecessary extra operations. At present, concern for program efficiency is considered archaic by many people. However, it assumes renewed importance with the advent of the many small computers which can execute problem-oriented languages, in particular Fortran. It does not take much of a Fortran program to tax the capabilities of these small machines. Therefore, efficiency can make the difference between being able to run such a program in a straightforward manner, or, on the other hand, having to segment the program, resort to machine language, or look for a larger computer—all of which are inconvenient.

The measures that are necessary to improve program efficiency depend upon how optimally each type of Fortran statement is handled by a given compiler. In general, the compilers for the smaller machines do less well in this respect, so that more attention is required from the programmer to obtain optimal code. Therefore, the programmer must know the characteristics of the particular compiler which he uses. Because of the variety of compilers now available and the rate at which new ones are being introduced, it is not practical to give those characteristics here. They can be ascertained by examination of the machine language output produced by the compiler from some benchmark programs. (Ideally, such information should be provided by the computer manufacturers.)

Normally, the measures discussed in this paper save both running time and memory space. (It is the latter that normally limits the size of problem that can be run on a small computer.) Where a trade-off between the two is involved, that will be noted.

‡Charles Erwin Cohn, Argonne National Laboratory, Argonne, Illinois. Reprinted by permission from *Software Age,* Vol. 2, No. 5 (June 1968), pp.22–31. Work performed under the auspices of the U.S. Atomic Energy Commission.

Although the discussion in this paper is in terms of Fortran, it applies in general to any problem-oriented language. The points discussed may seem trivial, but it is the author's experience that many "professional" programmers and practically all "amateur" programmers are unaware of them. They are not covered in most texts.

9-1. Arithmetic Expressions and Replacement Statements

Arithmetic expressions and replacement statements can be optimized by eliminating the repeated calculation of redundant subexpressions. In the statement

```
Z = (A * B/C) * SIN(A * B/C)
```

the redundant subexpression (A * B/C), although appearing twice, should be calculated only once and the result saved until it is needed again. Most compilers will do this automatically if the redundant subexpression is set in parentheses, as shown here.

If a particularly rudimentary compiler does not optimize this case automatically, the programmer must do it as follows:

```
TEMP1 = A * B/C
Z = TEMP1 * SIN(TEMP1)
```

Practically no compilers, except the most sophisticated, will optimize subexpressions that are redundant between two or more arithmetic replacement statements. These must invariably be optimized by the programmer. For example, the statements

```
X = SIN(A * B/C)
Y = COS(A * B/C)
```

should instead be written

```
TEMP1 = A * B/C
X = SIN(TEMP1)
Y = COS(TEMP1)
```

In both cases, additional running time and memory space are required for the instructions that store the result of the redundant subexpression in the memory location assigned to the variable TEMP1. This extra time and space is outweighed, however, by the savings resulting from elimination of the instructions required to calculate the subexpression a second time. The net savings become greater, of course, as the subexpression becomes more complicated and as it is used a greater number of times. The saving in time is especially noteworthy, as floating-point operations are unduly time-consuming on small computers that do not have floating-point hardware. The memory space consumed by the temporary storage variable TEMP1 can be used most efficiently by using the same name wherever temporary storage is required.

If a loop contains an expression whose variables do not change value during the course of the loop, time (but not space) may be saved by evaluating the expression once, outside the loop, and holding the result until needed. For example, the loop

```
      DO 14 I = 1,N
14    Y(I) = A * B * X(I)/C
```

can be rewritten as

```
      TEMP1 = A * B/C
      DO 1 4I = 1,N
14    Y(I) = TEMP1 * X(I)
```

The latter version may incur a slight space penalty from the extra instructions needed to store and retrieve the result of the expression.

Arithmetic operations on whole numbers are best done in integer mode, with the results converted to real where needed.

9-2. Constants

Where mixed mode arithmetic is allowed, it is best to write constants in the dominant mode of the expression to avoid needless conversions. For the expression 2 * A, most compilers will store the 2 as an integer and convert it to real each time the expression is evaluated. With the expression in the form 2. * A (i.e. with the decimal point shown) the constant is stored as real and the conversion is eliminated.

Arithmetic operations on constants should be performed by the programmer before writing an expression. In the expression 4. * A/3., the two constants are stored separately by most compilers, and the division is performed each time the expression is evaluated. It should instead be written 1.333333 * A. This and other transcendental constants should be written to as many significant figures as the computer handles in its arithmetic, so that full advantage is taken of the computer's precision. There is no penalty for the additional digits.

Some compilers store constants only as magnitudes. When a negative constant is used as a subprogram argument, extra instructions to negate the constant are inserted. Where the same negative constant is used in more than one argument list, it is efficient in such a system to assign the value to a variable and use the variable name in the argument lists. For example, instead of

```
CALL SUBRA(W,X,-3)
.
.
.
CALL SUBRB(Y,Z,-3)
```

you would write

```
M3 = -3
.
.
.
CALL SUBRA(W,X,M3)
.
.
.
CALL SUBRB(Y,Z,M3)
```

9-3. Powers

In many compilers the use of the "**" notation calls upon a special subroutine in the library. If only small whole-number powers are to be calculated, the time and space required for this subroutine can be saved by avoiding the "**" notation. For example, for X ** 2 write X * X, for X ** 3 write X * X * X, and for X ** 4 write (X * X) * (X * X) (with the redundant subexpression (X * X) handled as described above).

When the use of the "**" notation is appropriate, the mode of the exponent can make a difference. That is because many systems use different library subroutines for real or integer exponents of real arguments. If such a program already contains a real exponent, memory space can be saved by making whole number exponents real, thus eliminating any need for the integer exponent subroutine. Other systems have a subroutine for real exponents only, and convert all integer exponents to real before calling the subroutine. There, the exponents might as well be shown as real to begin with, thus eliminating the conversion step.

9-4. Polynomials

Optimization of polynomials is useful for any compiler. For a polynomial of the form

```
Y = A + B * X + C * X ** 2 + D * X ** 3
```

calculation requires three additions, three multiplications, and two exponentiations. There is a saving if the polynomial is instead written in *nested* form as

```
Y = A + X * (B + X * (C + X * D))
```

which is obviously equivalent. The additions and multiplications remain but the exponentiations have been eliminated. It is straightforward to put any polynomial into this optimal form.

Special treatment is needed when one of the terms carries a minus sign. Since, in the nested form, the minus sign multiplies all subsequent terms, the next term must also carry a minus sign to cancel the effect of the previous minus. Thus, for example, the polynomial

```
Z = A + B * X - C * X ** 2 + D * X ** 3 + E * X ** 4
```

would be written in nested form as

```
Z = A + X * (B - X * (C - X * (D + X * E)))
```

Care must be taken, of course, to close the expression with the correct number of parentheses. The coefficients, shown here as single variables, may be expressions enclosed in parentheses, with any redundancies handled as described above.

9-5. Statement Numbers

Ordinarily there is no penalty for attaching a number to a statement even when it is not needed for reference by another statement. However, such a penalty can arise under two special circumstances.

First, some small machine compilers are very limited in the size of programs that they can compile because of limited memory space for the assignment tables that keep track of variables, statement numbers, etc. There, elimination of unneeded statement numbers will reduce the burden on the available space.

Second, some compilers perform limited optimization on sequences of arithmetic replacement statements. In particular, a variable needed in one statement may not have to be fetched from memory if it is already in a register as the result of a previous statement. This optimization is done only if none of the statements has a number, indicating that the sequence is never entered in the middle. If the last statement in the sequence ends the range of a DO, its number can be removed and attached to a CONTINUE statement following. There is never a penalty for the use of a CONTINUE statement.

9-6. IF Statements

When the quantity calculated in the expression embedded in an IF statement, or any part of it, is also used earlier or later in the program, the unnecessary repeated calculations of that quantity should be avoided as described above for redundant subexpressions. For example, the program segment

```
      X = A * B + E
      IF(A * B - C * D)1,2,2
1     Y = C * D + F
2     . . .
```

can be optimized as

```
      TEMP1 = A * B
      TEMP2 = C * D
      X = TEMP1 + E
      IF (TEMP1 - TEMP2)1,2,2
1     Y = TEMP2+F
2     . . .
```

(Note that two variables are needed for temporary storage.)

The Fortran logical IF statement is not handled efficiently by some compilers. These set up an intermediate logical variable according to the results of the relational operations specified, and then test this logical variable to determine the outcome of the IF statement. With such a compiler it is more efficient to replace the logical IF statement with one or more three-branch IF statements as required.

9-7. Subscripted Variables

Retrieval or storage of subscripted variables always requires more work than the retrieval or storage of unsubscripted variables. This is because the address of the datum must be calculated from the subscript combination. In more advanced systems, this arithmetic is done through indexing so no additional time or space is required that can readily be eliminated. However, less advanced compilers insert additional instructions to perform address arithmetic wherever a subscripted variable is referenced. Here, it helps to cut down on such references.

In the statement

```
C(I) = C(I) + X
```

there are two references to the same subscripted variable. A well-designed compiler will perform the necessary address arithmetic only once and save the result until needed. If a compiler is not so optimized, nothing can be done here, because the two references to the subscripted variable are on opposite sides of the equals sign.

In the statement

```
Z = C(I) * SIN(C(I) * D)
```

the compiler should again do the address arithmetic only once for the two references. If that is not the case, the two references can here be treated as redundant subexpressions as explained previously, because they appear on the same side of the equal sign.

When the same subscripted variable is referenced in two or more statements, these references may be handled as redundant subexpressions, provided that the values of the subscripts do not change through the sequence. The statements

```
   DO 1 I = 1,M
   IF (INDEX(I,1) - INDEX(I,2))2,1,2
2  JROW = INDEX(I,1)
   JCOLUM = INDEX(I,2)
1  CONTINUE
```

may be optimized as

```
   DO 1 I = 1,M
   ITEMP1 = INDEX(I,1)
   ITEMP2 = INDEX(I,2)
   IF (ITEMP1 - ITEMP2)2,1,2
2  JROW = ITEMP1
   JCOLUM = ITEMP2
1  CONTINUE
```

When the value of a subscripted variable is formed in one statement and used in a subsequent statement, the extra reference may be eliminated similarly. The statements

```
   DO 4 I = 1,N
   C(I) = A(I) + B(I)
4  WRITE (5,1000)A(I),B(I),C(I)
```

may be changed to

```
   DO 4 I = 1,N
   TEMP1 = A(I)
   TEMP2 = B(I)
   TEMP3 = TEMP1 + TEMP2
   C(I) = TEMP3
4  WRITE (5,100)TEMP1,TEMP2,TEMP3
```

However, if one of the statements has the subscripted variable on both sides of the equals sign, such a change might not save anything if the compiler would do the address arithmetic only once for the statement in any case.

Subscripted variable references with constant subscripts need not be handled in this way. Most compilers will perform the address arithmetic during compilation, so that the subscript reference incurs no penalty. For those systems which leave even this address arithmetic until program execution, an unsubscripted variable name may be made equivalent to the element in question and used in all references. Thus, the coding

```
      DIMENSION B(38)
      .
      .
      .
      B(14) = . . .
```

may be replaced by

```
      DIMENSION B(38)
      EQUIVALENCE (B14,B(14))
      .
      .
      .
      B14 = . . .
```

Sometimes a two- or three-dimensional array may be handled more efficiently by making it equivalent to a one-dimensional array. The initialization of a matrix to zero is usually written as

```
      DIMENSION A(20,10)
      .
      .
      .
      DO 3 J = 1,10
      DO 3 I = 1,20
    3 A(I,J) = 0.
```

This may be done more efficiently with any compiler by

```
      DIMENSION A(20,10),AA(200)
      EQUIVALENCE (A,AA)
      . . .
      DO 3 I = 1,200
    3 AA(I) = 0.
```

which saves address arithmetic as well as the instructions for the inner DO loop. This approach clearly offers an advantage only in those special cases, such as the one shown, in which computation of the subscript is not necessary.

The use of subscripts with any variable is justified only if the values so saved will actually be needed later in the program. In the DO loop

```
      DO 1 I = 1,N
      .
      .
      .
      A(I) = . . .
    1 WRITE (4,2)I,A(I), . . .
```

the variable A should carry subscripts only if the values assigned to it will be needed again after the loop has been completed. If that information will not be needed later, time and space will be saved by dropping the subscripts, handling A as a simple variable.

9-8. Input-Output Statements

The input or output of an entire array may be specified either by a DO-implying loop over the array or by mention of the name of the array with no qualification. In many systems, the latter saves space by causing fewer instructions to be compiled, and also saves central processor time.

In many systems there is a space penalty for specifying additional input-output modes, since each mode requires its own subroutine from the library. For example, consider a program whose primary output is a printer. If the programmer decides to include monitor output on the console typewriter for the convenience of the operator, the space penalty incurred may include the typewriter output subroutine in addition to the coding for the output statements. If memory space is critical, it might be best to forego the monitor output or take it on the printer.

9-9. Subprograms

Use of subprogram organization incurs a time and space penalty because of the linkage instructions. The space penalty is more than made up, however, if the subprogram is called from more than one place in the main program, because the coding to perform the subprogram's functions need not be repeated at each place it is needed. If a subprogram is called from only one place in the main program, it is most efficient to eliminate its separate identity as a subprogram and incorporate it directly into the main program. Where a subprogram is a function that can be executed in one replacement statement, it may best be included in the main program as an arithmetic statement function (but see below).

Attention must also be paid to the manner of linking variables between a main program and a subprogram. There are two ways of doing this, through argument lists and through COMMON statements, and each has its proper role. There is a time and space penalty associated with the use of argument lists. The subprogram must contain coding that will fetch the address of an argument from the main program and plant that address where it is accessible to those instructions in the subprogram that require it. With COMMON linkage, on the other hand, there is no penalty.

Therefore, we may state the following rule: when a variable in the subprogram always corresponds to the same variable in the main program at every call of the subprogram, then the linkage should be through COMMON (or parameters, for an arithmetic statement function). On the other hand, when a variable in the subprogram corresponds to different variables in the main program at different calls of the subprogram, then the linkage should be through the argument list. (Of course, a reference to a function subprogram must always have at least one argument so that the compiler may distinguish it from a reference to an ordinary variable.)

There is a time penalty and there may be a space penalty associated with each additional reference to an argument within a subprogram. Therefore, if an unsubscripted variable is referenced more than once in a subprogram, it could be worthwhile to use a local variable in its stead. The local variable is made equal to the argument, or vice versa, at the beginning or end of the subprogram, depending upon whether the argument is an input or output variable. Examples are as follows:

```
      FUNCTION POLY(X)
      COMMON A,B,C,D
      XA = X
      POLY = A + XA * (B + XA * (C + XA * D))
      RETURN
      END
      SUBROUTINE SUM(TOTAL,X,N)
      DIMENSION X(N)
      TEMP = 0.
      DO 1 I = 1,N
    1 TEMP = TEMP + X(I)
      TOTAL = TEMP
      RETURN
      END
```

(For an array, this substitution would require a DO loop. It may or may not be worthwhile, depending upon the length of the array and the number of times it is referenced in the subprogram.)

Some compilers handle arithmetic statement functions like open subroutines or macros, repeating the instructions for the function at each place where it is called in the program. This saves a little time (by eliminating linkage) at the cost of much space. (If a program on such a system is space-limited, the arithmetic statement functions should be replaced with function subprograms.

COMMON storage has an important use in addition to the linkage of variables. In most systems, variables declared as COMMON (blank COMMON for Fortran IV) are assigned to the memory area that is occupied by the loader during object-program loading. This space is otherwise unavailable to the Fortran programmer. Therefore, a program that taxes memory can obtain some relief by use of COMMON storage, even when subprogram linkage is not in question. For best use to be made of this feature, enough arrays and unsubscripted variables should be declared COMMON to fill the loader area.

9-10. In Summary

We have seen how the efficiency of a Fortran program can be improved through a number of measures, depending on the properties of the compiler and system. The saving from each of these measures is small individually, but throughout a program their sum total can be significant. If applied to all the production programs in a computer installation, a worthwhile reduction can be made in the installation's workload.

Appendix **A**

Types of Variables

Up to this point only real and integer variables and constants have been considered. Fortran IV will also recognize double-precision, complex, and logical variables. Although most programmers find only occasional need for these, their advantages in certain applications make their study worthwhile. For example, problems in electrical engineering are considerably facilitated by using complex variables, and logical variables are used advantageously for problems in Boolean algebra. Double precision is often necessary for matrix inversion, solution of simultaneous equations, etc.

A-1. Complex Variables

A single complex variable is in reality two floating-point (real) variables: one is the real part and the other is the imaginary part of the complex number. To denote which variables are to be treated as complex, the type statement COMPLEX is used in the following manner:

```
COMPLEX A,I,B(20),J(2,3,5)
```

Note that a complex variable may also be subscripted.

The real advantage in using complex variables in Fortran is that the five arithmetic operations of addition, subtraction, multiplication, division and exponentiation (complex variable raised to *integer* exponent only) are defined as usual. The permissible operations with complex variables are shown in Figure A-1. In addition, the complex functions are defined as follows ($i = \sqrt{-1}$):

$$\begin{aligned}
\text{CABS}\,(a+ib) &= \sqrt{a^2+b^2}\\
\text{CEXP}\,(a+ib) &= e^a(\cos b + i\sin b)\\
\text{CLOG}\,(a+ib) &= 1/2\log(a^2+b^2) + i\tan^{-1}(b/a)\\
\text{CSIN}\,(a+ib) &= \sin(a\cosh b) + i\cos(a\sinh b)\\
\text{CCOS}\,(a+ib) &= \cos(a\cosh b) - i\sin(a\sinh b)\\
\text{CONJG}\,(a+ib) &= a - ib
\end{aligned}$$

These complex functions are used in the same manner as the real functions described previously, with the exception that the argument of all must be complex and the result, except for CABS, is also complex. A complete list is given in Appendix C.

The value of a complex variable can be assigned by either a READ statement, an arithmetic statement, or a DATA statement. The arithmetic assignment statement makes use of the CMPLX function as illustrated below

```
C = CMPLX(A,B)
```

where C is a complex variable, and A and B are real variables, constants, or expressions.

Addition, Subtraction, Multiplication, Division

+ − * /	Real	Integer	Complex	Double-Precision	Logical
Real	Yes	Machine-dependent	Yes	Yes	No
Integer	Machine-dependent	Yes	No	No	No
Complex	Yes	No	Yes	No	No
Double-precision	Yes	No	No	Yes	No
Logical	No	No	No	No	No

Exponentiation

Base \ Exponent	Real	Integer	Complex	Double-Precision	Logical
Real	Yes	Yes	No	Yes	No
Integer	No	Yes	No	No	No
Complex	No	Yes	No	No	No
Double-precision	Yes	Yes	No	Yes	No
Logical	No	No	No	No	No

Relational Operators

.GT. .GE. .LT. .LE. .EQ. .NE.	Real	Integer	Complex	Double-Precision	Logical
Real	Yes	No	No	Yes	No
Integer	No	Yes	No	No	No
Complex	No	No	No	No	No
Double-precision	Yes	No	No	Yes	No
Logical	No	No	No	No	No

Figure A-1. Permissible operations for the types of variables

The result is C = A + *i*B. On input, two real variables, the first being the real part and the second being the imaginary part, are read for each complex variable. For example, if C is a complex variable, the READ and FORMAT statements are

```
      READ (5,3)C
    3 FORMAT (1X,F10.3,E20.2)
```

A similar situation exists for output. A complex variable appearing in a DATA statement also requires two constants

```
      DATA C/10.-1.0/
```

Arithmetic statements involving complex variables do *not* permit a change of variable type across the equals sign. That is, the results of a complex expression must be stored in a complex variable. However, it is permissible (see Figure 8-1) to add, subtract, multiply, and divide complex and real variables, the result being in the complex mode.

To illustrate these points, consider the evaluation of the following expression:

$$a + ib = \frac{c(d + if)\exp(ic)}{g + ih} - (g + ih)$$

The program reads c, $d + if$, and $g + ih$, calculates $a + ib$, and prints the results as shown in Figure A-2. The use of the COMPLEX type statement‡ in line 1 and the functions CEXP and CMPLX in line 4 should be noted.

A-2. Double Precision

On most computers the real variable is accurate to about seven or eight significant figures, depending on the word length of the machine. In some cases these are simply not enough digits for sufficient accuracy. In such cases the double-precision feature of Fortran IV is used, at least doubling the number of significant digits. The double-precision variable is designated by the DOUBLE PRECISION type statement, an example of which is

DOUBLE PRECISION A, J, C(12,12)

Note that a double-precision variable may also be subscripted.

A set of functions have also been developed for double-precision variables, the more common functions being

```
1              COMPLEXA,D,G,CEXP,CMPLX
2              READ(5,2)C,D,G
3         2    FORMAT(F10.0/(2F10.0))
4              A=C*D*CEXP(CMPLX(0.,C))/G-G
5              WRITE(6,3)A
6         3    FORMAT(14H1REAL PART IS ,F10.3/19H IMAGINARY PART IS ,F10.3)
7              STOP
10             END
```

(a) Program

```
2.1
-1.7         1.2
0.2          -0.7
```

(b) Input data

```
REAL PART IS           5.410
IMAGINARY PART IS           -1.436
```

(c) Output

Figure A-2. Illustration of the use of complex variables

‡In some versions of Fortran, the functions CEXP and CMPLX must also be included in the type statement.

DABS	absolute value
DSQRT	square root
DSIN	sine
DCOS	cosine
DATAN	arctangent
DEXP	exponentiation
DLOG	natural logarithm

The argument as well as the result of each of these functions is in double precision.

The double-precision variable may be assigned a value by either an arithmetic statement, a READ statement, or a DATA statement. An example of an arithmetic statement is

```
A = 1.71D2
```

where the D is the double-precision equivalent of E. On input and output, the FORMAT field specification corresponding to a double-precision variable is the D field, which is analogous to the E field. For example, a READ statement for A is

```
   READ (5,5)A
5  FORMAT (D20.8)
```

The output is handled in a similar fashion. The DATA statement also follows similarly, an example being

```
DATA A/1.71D2/
```

Change of mode across the equals sign in arithmetic statements is permissible. Integer to double precision, double precision to integer, real to double precision, and double precision to real are all legal. Double-precision and real variables may also be mixed in an arithmetic statement. Figure A-1 gives the permissible operations using double-precision variables.

As an example of the use of double precision, consider the solution of the equations

$$x + 2y = 1$$
$$1.0017262x + 1.9991278y = 1$$

These equations can be solved for x and y by double precision. The equations

$$a_1x + b_1y = c_1$$
$$a_2x + b_2y = c_2$$

have solutions

$$y = (c_1a_2 - c_2a_1)/(b_1a_2 - b_2a_1)$$
$$x = (c_1 - b_1y)/a_1$$

The program and the results are shown in Figure A-3. Solution of large sets of simultaneous equations is one application frequently requiring double precision, and one of the exercises at the end of this chapter treats the Gauss reduction in double precision.

```
          DOUBLE PRECISION AD(2),BD(2),CD(2),XD,YD
          READ(5,2)(AD(I),BD(I),CD(I) ,I=1,2)
  2       FORMAT(3D8.0)
          YD=(CD(1)*AD(2)-CD(2)*AD(1))/(BD(1)*AD(2)-BD(2)*AD(1))
          XD=(CD(1)-BD(1)*YD)/AD(1)
          WRITE(6,4)XD,YD
  4       FORMAT(25H DOUBLE PRECISION RESULTS/5H X = D30.16/5H Y = D30.16)
          STOP
          END
```

(a) Program

```
  1.D00    1.D00    1.D00
1.71D-8 2.78D00 1.45D-4
```

(b) Input data

```
DOUBLE PRECISION RESULTS
X =              0.9999478478773771D 00
Y =              0.5215212262295011D-04
```

(c) Output

Figure A-3. Illustration of the use of double precision

A-3. Logical Operations

In Chapter 4 the use of the logical IF was introduced along with a few logical expressions. Entire logical equations can be programmed so that the computer can solve Boolean algebra or other problems involving logic. The logical variables can assume only the values true or false, and a logical constant is either .TRUE. or FALSE.. A logical variable must be specified in a LOGICAL type statement such as the following:

```
LOGICAL A,J,K(10)
```

Again subscripting is permitted.

A logical variable may be assigned values by either a logical assignment statement (analogous to the arithmetic assignment statement), the DATA statement, or the READ statement. An example of the logical assignment statement is

```
J = .TRUE.
```

which sets J to be true. Similarly, the DATA statement is used as follows:

```
DATA J/.TRUE./
```

The input and output of logical information is by the L field. Consider the following input statements:

```
    READ (5,5) J
5   FORMAT (L5)
```

Although the width of the L field is five columns the scan routine looks at only the first nonblank character in the field. If it is a T, J is set true; if an F or if the field is completely blank, J is set false; if neither, a read error occurs. The remaining columns are completely ignored, and may contain anything. On output, a T or an F depending on the value of the logical variable, is inserted in the rightmost column of the L field (right justified).

In Chapter 4 the relational operator .LT., .LE., .EQ., .NE., .GT. and .GE. were defined along with logical operators .AND., .OR. and .NOT.. Figure 8-1 gives the permissible operations using .LT., .LE., .EQ., .NE., .GT. and .GE.. Using these operators, logical assignment statements can be constructed as follows:

```
J = A.GT.B
```

If A > B, J is .TRUE.; otherwise, J is .FALSE.. Combinations of logical operators and relational operators to form logical expressions are also permissible, the rules regarding their use being

1. Use of parentheses in a logical expression to control order of execution is analogous to their use in an arithmetic expression.
2. The precedence of execution is

Order of Precedence	*Operation*
1 (highest)	Any arithmetic operations appearing in the logical expression
2	The relational operators .GT., .GE., .LT., .LE., .EQ., and .NE.
3	.NOT.
4	.AND.
5 (lowest)	.OR.

According to these rules, the logical expression

```
A.LT.B + C.AND..NOT.I.EQ.J.OR.K.LE.M
```

is equivalent to

```
((A.LT.(B + C)).AND.(.NOT.(I.EQ.J))).OR.(K.LE.M)
```

The use of the logical IF in the following fashion is sometimes advantageous:

```
LOGICAL TEST
TEST = A.GT.B
IF (TEST)C = D + G
IF (.NOT.TEST)C = ALOG10(D)
```

That is, logical variables can be used directly in the logical IF.

To illustrate the use of logical expressions, consider programming the computer to solve the logic circuit corresponding to the binary half-adder in Figure A-4. For all possible combinations of states for A and B (the inputs to the circuit), the states of C and D (the outputs) are to be determined. The results from the program should be as follows:

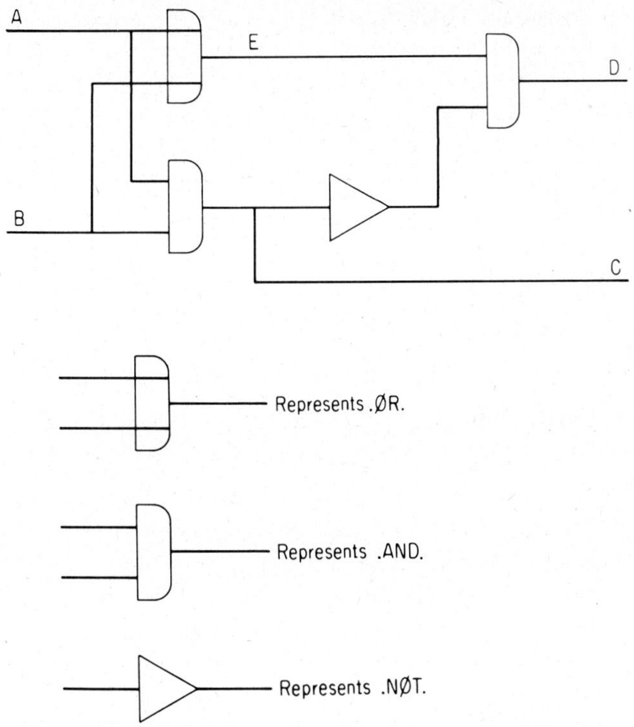

Figure A-4. Binary half-adder

A	*B*	*C*	*D*
.FALSE.	.FALSE.	.FALSE.	.FALSE.
.FALSE.	.TRUE.	.FALSE.	.TRUE
.TRUE.	.FALSE.	.FALSE.	.TRUE.
.TRUE.	.TRUE.	.TRUE.	.FALSE.

The program reads the values of A and B, computes C and D, and prints the results. The construction of the table with this program is illustrated in Figure A-5.

A-4. Type Statements for the IBM System 360

On the IBM System 360 and comparable machines of other manufacturers, the standard word length is thirty-two bits (binary digits). These words are said to consist of four bytes (eight binary digits). The programmer has various options for modifying the standard convention, as shown below:

Variable Type	*Standard Length*	*Optional Length*
INTEGER	4 bytes (32 bits)	2 bytes (16 bits)
REAL	4 bytes (32 bits)	8 bytes (64 bits)
COMPLEX	8 bytes (64 bits)	16 bytes (128 bits)
LOGICAL	4 bytes (32 bits)	1 byte (8 bits)

```
        LOGICAL A,B,C,D,E
        DO2I=1,4
        READ(5,3)A,B
      3 FORMAT(2L5)
        E=A.OR.B
        C=A.AND.B
        D=E.AND..NOT.C
      2 WRITE(6,4)A,B,C,D
      4 FORMAT(1X,4L5)
        STOP
        END
```

(a) Program

```
F    F
F    T
T    F
T    T
```

(b) Input data

```
F    F    F    F
F    T    F    T
T    F    F    T
T    T    T    F
```

(c) Output

Figure A-5. Illustration of the use of logical variables

These types may be selected by either Fortran conventions (standard length), by explicit type statements (REAL, COMPLEX, INTEGER, LOGICAL), or by the IMPLICIT statement. The results of arithmetic operations involving the various modes are given in Figure A-6. Note that mixed mode is permitted.

The REAL statement is essentially the same as described in the previous section except as illustrated in the following examples:

REAL * 4 I,J,C(10)
REAL * 8 A(15)

The number following the asterisk is the number of bytes to be used. The second example is equivalent to the DOUBLE PRECISION statement described in Section A-2.

This convention is directly extendable to the other explicit type statements. One notable feature is that the statement

COMPLEX * 16 AX(5)

causes the array AX to consist of double-precision complex variables.

It is also worth noting that the DATA statement and the explicit type statement may be combined. For example, the statement

INTEGER B(2)/'INVERSE'/

causes this alphanumeric information to be stored in this array.

All the type statements discussed previously can only change the type of the variables included in the list. The IMPLICIT statement is used to modify the standard

+ − * /	INTEGER * 2	INTEGER * 4	REAL * 4	REAL * 8	COMPLEX * 8	COMPLEX * 16
INTEGER * 2	INTEGER * 2	INTEGER * 4	REAL * 4	REAL * 8	COMPLEX * 8	COMPLEX * 16
INTEGER * 4	INTEGER * 4	INTEGER * 4	REAL * 4	REAL * 8	COMPLEX * 8	COMPLEX * 16
REAL * 4	REAL * 4	REAL * 4	REAL * 4	REAL * 8	COMPLEX * 8	COMPLEX * 16
REAL * 8	REAL * 8	REAL * 8	REAL * 8	REAL * 8	COMPLEX * 16	COMPLEX * 16
COMPLEX * 8	COMPLEX * 8	COMPLEX * 8	COMPLEX * 8	COMPLEX * 16	COMPLEX * 16	COMPLEX * 16
COMPLEX * 16	COMPLEX * 16	COMPLEX * 16	COMPLEX * 16	COMPLEX * 16	COMPLEX * 16	COMPLEX * 16

Exponent

BASE

**	INTEGER * 2	INTEGER * 4	REAL * 4	REAL * 8	COMPLEX * 8	COMPLEX * 16
INTEGER * 2	INTEGER * 2	INTEGER * 4	REAL * 4	REAL * 8	*no*	*no*
INTEGER * 4	INTEGER * 4	INTEGER * 4	REAL * 4	REAL * 8	*no*	*no*
REAL * 4	REAL * 4	REAL * 4	REAL * 4	REAL * 8	*no*	*no*
REAL * 8	REAL * 8	REAL * 8	REAL * 8	REAL * 8	*no*	*no*
COMPLEX * 8	COMPLEX * 8	COMPLEX * 8	*no*	*no*	*no*	*no*
COMPLEX * 16	COMPLEX * 16	COMPLEX * 16	*no*	*no*	*no*	*no*

Figure A-6. Type of result of arithmetic operations on the IBM System 360

Fortran convention (i.e., variables beginning with I through N are integer, others real). For example, the statement

IMPLICIT INTEGER * 2(I − N), REAL * 8(O − Y), COMPLEX * 8(C,Z)

causes variables beginning with I through N to be treated as two-byte integer variables, variables beginning with O through Y as double-precision real variables, and variables beginning with C and Z as complex variables. All other variables are treated as usual. It is also noteworthy that the statement

IMPLICIT REAL * 8(A − H,O − Z,$)

would convert a normal single-precision to a double-precision program. Some compilers in this category would also automatically retype any functions if necessary. The IMPLICIT statement must be the first statement in a main program or the second statement in a subprogram.

Appendix **B**

Various System Configurations

	ASA Basic	*ASA*	*ASI 6000 Series*	*Bur-roughs B5500*	*Com-puter Control DDP-24, 116 124,224*	*CDC 1604 3600 3800*	*CDC 1700*	*CDC 6000 Series*	*PDP-6*	*EA I 640*	*EA I 8400*	*GE 200 Series*	*GE 400 Series*	*GE 600 Series*
Maximum statement number	9999	99999	99999	99999	99999	99999	99999	99999	99999	99999	32767	32767	32767	99999
Maximum continuation cards	5	19	No limit	9	No limit	No limit	5	No limit	19	19	19	No limit	No limit	19
Specification statements must precede first executable statement	*	*	*		*	*	*	*	*	*		*		*
INTEGER constant, maximum digits			7	11	7	14	5	18	11	5	5	6	7	11
INTEGER maximum magnitude			$2^{23}-1$	$2^{39}-1$	$2^{23}-1$	$2^{47}-1$	$2^{15}-1$	$2^{59}-1$	$2^{35}-1$	$2^{15}-1$	$2^{15}-1$	$2^{19}-1$	$2^{23}-1$	$2^{35}-1$
REAL constant, maximum digits			11	11	7	11	7	15	8	7	7	9	8	9
DOUBLE PRECISION constant, digits					14	25		29	16	14	14	18		19
REAL, DOUBLE PRECISION magnitude			10^{76}	10^{69}	10^{76}	10^{308}		10^{308}	10^{38}	10^{38}	10^{38}	10^{76}	10^{127}	10^{38}
Variable name maximum characters	5	6	6	6	6	8	6	8	No limit	6	6	12	6	6
Mixed mode arithmetic permitted			*			*		*	*	*	*	*		
Assigned GO TO		*	*	*	*	*	*	*	*	*	*	*	*	*
Logical IF, relations		*	*	*	*	*	*	*	*	*	*	*		*
DOUBLE PRECISION operations		*			*	*		*	*	*	*	*		*
COMPLEX operations		*			*	*		*	*	*	*	*		*
LOGICAL operations		*	*	*	*	*	*	*	*	*	*	*		*
Dimension data in type statements		*		*	*		*		*	*	*	*	*	*
Labeled COMMON		*		*	*	*	*	*	*	*	*			*
Maximum array dimensions	2	3	3	3	3	3	3	3	3	3	7	63	3	7
Adjustable dimensions		*	*	*	*	*		*	*		*	*		*
Zero and negative subscripts									*		*			
Subscripts may be any expression, with subscripted variables permitted				*		*		*				*		
Subroutine multiple entries and/or nonstandard returns								*						*
DATA statement		*	*	*	*	*	*	*	*	*	*	*	*	*
Object time FORMAT		*	*		*	*	*	*	*	*	*	*	*	*

Source: D. D. McCracken, *A Guide to Fortran IV Programming.* Wiley, New York, 1965, with updating by authors.

Honey-well 200	*Honey-well 800 1800*	*IBM 1130 1800*	*IBM 1401 1440 1460*	*IBM 1410 7010*	*IBM 7040 7044 (16-32K)*	*IBM 7090 7094*	*IBM 360/370 D level E level*	*IBM 360 H level*	*NCR Century Series*	*RCA Spectra 70 Size A*	*RCA Spectra 70 Size B*	*SDS Sigma 2*	*SDS Sigma 5 & 7*	*Univac 111*	*Univac 1107*
99999	32767	99999	99999	99999	99999	32767	99999	99999	99999	99999	99999	99999	99999	32767	32767
9	19	5	9	9	9	19	19	19	19	19	19	No limit	No limit	9	19
*	*	*		*			*		*	*		*			
20	13	5	20	20	11	11	10	10	10	10	10	5	10	6	11
$2^{119}-1$	$2^{44}-1$	$2^{15}-1$	$10^{20}-1$	$10^{20}-1$	$2^{35}-1$	$2^{35}-1$	$2^{31}-1$	$2^{31}-1$	$2^{31}-1$	$2^{31}-1$	$2^{31}-1$	$2^{15}-1$	$2^{31}-1$	$10^{6}-1$	$2^{35}-1$
20	12	7	20	18	9	9	7	7	7	7	7	7	7	10	9
	20				16	16	16	16	16	16	16		16		17
10^{99}	10^{76}		10^{99}	10^{99}	10^{38}	10^{38}	10^{75}	10^{75}	10^{75}	10^{75}	10^{75}		10^{75}	10^{50}	10^{38}
6	6	5	6	6	6	6	6	6	8	6	6	6	No limit	6	6
		*					*	*	*	*	*		*		*
*	*				*	*		*	*		*		*	*	*
*	*		*	*	*	*		*	*		*		*	*	*
	*				*	*	*	*	*	*	*		*		*
	*				*	*		*	*		*		*		*
*	*		*		*	*		*	*		*		*	*	*
*	*	*			*	*	*	*	*	*	*		*	*	*
*	*	1800			*	*		*	*		*		*	*	*
3	3	3	3	3	3	7	3	7	No limit	3	7	3	No limit	3	7
	*		*		*	*		*	*		*		*	*	*
									*						
									*						*
						*		*			*		*		* *
*	*	1800	*		*	*		*	*		*	*	*	*	*
*	*		*		*	*		*	*		*	*	*	*	*

Appendix **C**

Fortran IV Library Functions

The functions in the following list are common to most Fortran IV systems. However, specific installations often add to the basic list as their needs warrant.

Integer functions

Function name	*Type of argument*	*Number of arguments*	*Examples*	*Explanation*
IABS	Integer	1	I = IABS (J)	Absolute value of argument
INT	Real	1	I = INT (A)	Convert floating-point to fixed-point
IFIX	Real	1	I = IFIX (A)	(same as INT)
IDINT	Double-precision	1	I = IDINT (D)	Convert double-precision to fixed-point
MOD	Integer	2	I = MOD (J,K)	Remaindering: arg 1 − [arg 1/arg 2] arg 2, where [*X*] = integral part of *X*
MAX0	Integer	⩾2	I = MAX0 (J,K,L, . . .)	Largest of set of arguments
MAX1	Real	⩾2	I = MAX1 (X,Y,Z, . . .)	(same as MAX0)
MIN0	Integer	⩾2	I = MIN0 (J,K,L, . . .)	Smallest of set of arguments
MIN1	Real	⩾2	I = MIN1 (X,Y,Z, . . .)	(same as MIN0)
ISIGN	Integer	2	I = ISIGN (J,K)	Sign of arg 2 × arg 1
IDIM	Integer	2	I = IDIM (J,K)	Positive difference: arg 1 − min (arg 1, arg 2)

Real functions

Function name	*Type of argument*	*Number of arguments*	*Examples*	*Explanation*
ABS	Real	1	X = ABS (Y)	Absolute value of argument
AINT	Real	1	X = AINT (Y)	Truncation: sign of argument times absolute value of the largest integer in argument
AMOD	Real	2	X = AMOD (Y,Z)	Remaindering: arg 1 − [arg 1/arg 2] arg 2, where [*X*] = integral part of *X*
AMAX0	Integer	⩾2	X = AMAX0 (I,J,K, . .)	Largest value of arguments
AMAX1	Real	⩾2	X = AMAX1 (R,S,T, . .)	(same as AMAX0)
AMIN0	Integer	⩾2	X = AMIN0 (I,J,K, . .)	Smallest value of arguments
AMIN1	Real	⩾2	X = AMIN1 (R,S,T, . .)	(same as AMIN0)
FLOAT	Integer	1	X = FLOAT (I)	Convert fixed point to floating point

Real functions (Continued)

Function name	*Type of argument*	*Number of arguments*	*Examples*	*Explanation*
SIGN	Real	2	X = SIGN (Y,Z)	Transfer of sign: sign of arg 2 times arg 1
DIM	Real	2	X = DIM (Y,Z)	Positive difference: arg 1 − min (arg 1, arg 2)
SNGL	Double-precision	1	X = SNGL (D)	Convert double precision to single precision
REAL	Complex	1	X = REAL (C)	Obtaining real part of a complex number
AIMAG	Complex	1	X = AIMAG (C)	Obtaining the imaginary part of a complex number
SQRT	Real	1	X = SQRT (Y)	$x = \sqrt{y}$: the square root
EXP	Real	1	X = EXP (Y)	$x = e^y$: the natural antilogarithm of y
ALOG	Real	1	X = ALOG (Y)	$x = \ln y$: the natural logarithm of y
ALOG 10	Real	1	X = ALOG10 (Y)	$x = \log_{10} (y)$: the common logarithm of y
SIN	Real	1	X = SIN (Y)	$x = \sin(y)$: the trigonometric sine
COS	Real	1	X = COS (Y)	$x = \cos(y)$: the trigonometric cosine
ATAN	Real	1	X = ATAN (Y)	$x = \tan^{-1} (y)$, the arctangent of y: result is placed in first two quadrants depending upon sign of y
ATAN2	Real	2	X = ATAN2 (Y,Z)	$x = \tan^{-1} (y/z)$: same as ATAN except that result is placed in proper quadrant
ARSIN	Real	1	X = ARSIN (Y)	$x = \sin^{-1} (y)$: the arcsine of y
ARCOS	Real	1	X = ARSIN (Y)	$x = \cos^{-1} (y)$: the arcsine of y
TANH	Real	1	X = TANH (Y)	$x = \tanh (y)$: the hyperbolic tangent
CABS	Complex	1	X= CABS (C)	Magnitude of a complex number: $x = \sqrt{a^2 + b^2}$, where $c = a + ib$

Double-precision functions

Function name	*Type of argument*	*Number of arguments*	*Examples*	*Explanation*
DABS	Double-precision	1	D = DABS (DA)	Absolute value of argument
DMAX1	Double-precision	⩾2	D = DMAX1 (DA, DB, . . .)	Largest of set of arguments
DMIN1	Double-precision	⩾2	D = DMIN1 (DA, DB, . . .)	Smallest of set of arguments
DSIGN	Double-precision	2	D = DSIGN (DA, DB)	Transfer of sign: sign of arg 2 times arg 1

Double-precision functions (Continued)

Function name	*Type of argument*	*Number of arguments*	*Examples*	*Explanation*
DBLE	Real	1	D = DBLE (X)	Convert single-precision to double-precision
DMOD	Double-precision	2	D = DMOD (DA, DB)	Remaindering: arg 1 − [arg 1/arg 2] arg 2, where [X] = integral part of X
DSQRT	Double-precision	1	D = DSQRT (DA)	Double-precision equivalent of SQRT
DEXP	Double-precision	1	D = DEXP (DA)	Double-precision equivalent of EXP
DLOG	Double-precision	1	D = DLOG (DA)	Double-precision equivalent of ALOG
DLOG 10	Double-precision	1	D = DLOG10 (DA)	Double-precision equivalent of ALOG10
DSIN	Double-precision	1	D = DSIN (DA)	Double-precision equivalent of SIN
DCOS	Double-precision	1	D = DCOS (DA)	Double-precision equivalent of COS
DATAN	Double-precision	1	D = DATAN (DA)	Double-precision equivalent of ATAN
DATAN2	Double-precision	1	D = DATAN2 (DA)	Double-precision equivalent of ATAN2

Complex functions

Function name	*Type of argument*	*Number of arguments*	*Examples*	*Explanation*
CMPLX	Real	2	C = CMPLX (X,Y)	Express two arguments in complex form, $C = X + iY$
CONJG	Complex	1	C = CONJG (CA)	Obtain complex conjugate of argument
CSQRT	Complex	1	C = CSQRT (CA)	Complex square-root function
CEXP	Complex	1	C = CEXP (CA)	Complex exponential
CLOG	Complex	1	C = CLOG (CA)	Complex natural logarithm
CSIN	Complex	1	C = CSIN (CA)	Complex sine
CCOS	Complex	1	C = CCOS (CA)	Complex cosine

Appendix **D**

American Standard Flowchart Symbols‡

Any text or notes may be placed inside or beside these symbols:

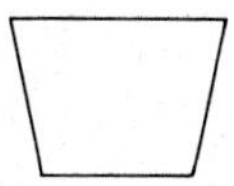
Basic Input-Output Symbol (represents an input or output operation if one of the special symbols is not used)

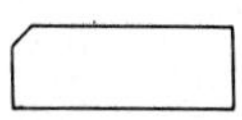
Punched-card Input or Output

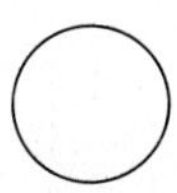
Magnetic Tape Input or Output

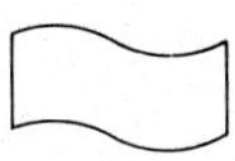
Punched Paper Tape Input or Output

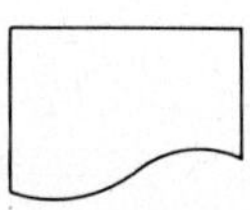
Printed Output (document)

Manual Input (keyboard)

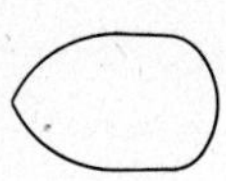
Display Output (video devices, etc.)

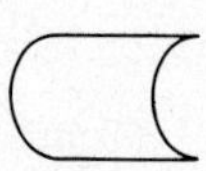
On-line Storage (magnetic drums, discs, etc.)

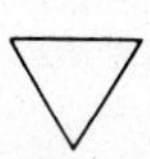
Off-line Storage

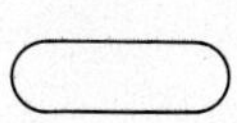
Terminal Symbol (stop or start)

Communication Link (direct connection between remote locations)

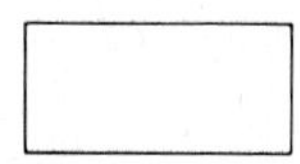
Processing Symbol (arithmetic operations)

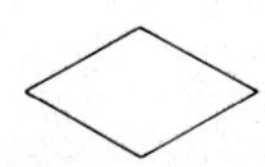
Decision Symbol

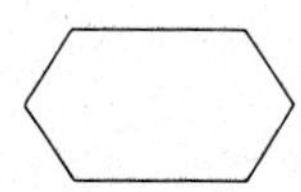
Predefined Process (subroutine)

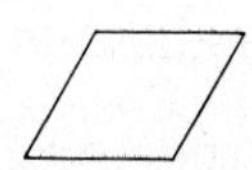
Manual Operation

Auxiliary Operation of Off-line Equipment

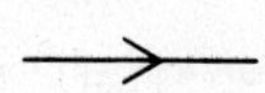
Direction of Flow (with or without arrowheads)

Connector or Junction (to be used when the flow direction is broken)

Annotation Symbol (can be used to annotate the flow chart with additional comments)

‡These symbols are substantially those recommended by the X6 Committee to the United States of America Standards Institute, New York City.

Appendix **E**

Solutions to Selected Exercises

Chapter 2

2-1.

```
(C) -16   (D)86487
```

2-3.

```
(E)8.2E-6
```

2-4.

```
(A)-27281.0
```

2-5.

```
(C)EXPONENTIAL PRESENT AND NORMALLY TOO LARGE
```

2-6.

```
(C)IMBEDDED COMMA
```

2-7.

```
(B)NORMALLY TOO LARGE
```

2-8.

```
(C)IMBEDDED COMMA AND NO DECIMAL
```

2-9.

```
(B)REAL   (E)UNACCEPTABLE   (I)REAL
```

2-10.

```
(B)UNACCEPTABLE    (E)UNACCEPTABLE    (J)INTEGER
```

2-11.

```
(A)(A+B)/(C+D)   (D)A*B/(C+10.0)
```

2-12.

```
(B)(A+B)/(C+D/E)   (E)A/B+C*D/(E*F*G)
```

2-13.

```
(D)(P*R/S)**(T-1.0)
```

2-14.

```
(A)3   (E)0
```

2-15.

```
(B)0.0   (F)4.3333333
```

2-16.

```
(B)X=COS(Y)+X*SIN(Z)   (F)X=Y*SIN(3.1416/Z)
```

2-17.

```
(B)X=ABS((1.0+COS(Y))/(1.0-COS(Y)))
(E)X=ALCG10(ABS(SIN(Y)/CCS(Y)))
```

2-18.

```
(B)X=Y**0.5*Z**(I+1)*EXP(-Y)
(F)X=ALCG10(ABS(1.0/SQRT(COS(Y))))*ALOG10(ABS(EXP(-X)))
```

2-19.

```
(C)TWO ADJACENT ARITHMETIC OPERATIONS
(F)MIXED MODE. 3 IS AN INTEGER AND Y IS REAL.  SHOULD READ
   (Y+3.0)**2
```

2-20.

```
(C)INVALID VARIABLE NAME ON LEFT OF EQUATION. MULTIPLICATION
   SIGN CANNOT BE USED IN VARIABLE NAME.
(F)MIXED MCDE.
```

Chapter 3

3-1(c).

```
   READ(5,25)X,J,YES
25 FORMAT(F10.2,I10,F10.2)
```

or

```
READ,X,J,YES
```

3-2(d).

```
    READ(5,101)CONST,OUKID,A,J
101 FCRMAT(3F10.2,I10)
```

or

```
READ,CONST,CUKID,A,J
```

3-5(a).

```
   WRITE(6,13)A,B,CAT,CO,ANS
13 FORMAT(1X,5(E20.7,3X))
```

3-5(b).

```
   WRITE(6,51)I,J,KID,ANS
51 FORMAT(1X,3(I10,3X),E20.7)
```

3-5(c).

```
    WRITE(6,130)X,J,YES,ANS
130 FORMAT(1X,E20.7,3X,I10,3X,E20.7,3X,E20.7)
```

3-5(d).

```
   WRITE(6,33)A,SIMPLE,GO,I,ANS
33 FORMAT(1X,3(E20.7,3X),I10,3X,E20.7)
```

3-8.

```
C         INPUT
C
          READ(5,1)A,B,C,S
C
C         CALCULATE T
C
          T=A*COS(S)+B*SIN(S)+C*TAN(S)
C
C         OUTPUT
C
          WRITE(6,2)A,B,C,S,T
          STOP
C
C         FORMAT STATEMENTS
C
        1 FORMAT(4F10.2)
        2 FORMAT(1X,4F10.2,E20.7)
          END
```

Input

```
5.0        6.92        1.73        1.0472
```

Output

```
5.00       6.92        1.73        1.05          0.1148936E 02
```

3-12.

```
C         INPUT
C
          READ(5,1)A,B,C
C
C         CALCULATE A1
C
          DUM1=1.0+A*B*C
          DUM2=1.0+(A**2/(B*C))**(1.0/3.0)
          A1=1.0/(1.0-DUM1/DUM2)
```

```
C
C     CALCULATE A2
C
      A2=TAN(A1)+ALOG(ABS(A1))
C
C     OUTPUT
C
      WRITE(6,2)A,B,C,A1,A2
      STOP
C
C     FORMAT STATEMENTS
C
    1 FORMAT(3F10.2)
    2 FORMAT(1X,3F10.2,2F20.7)
      END
```

Input

```
3.0       5.0    0.33333
```

Output

```
3.00      5.00      0.33      -0.8486789E 00      -0.1299377E 01
```

3-15.

```
C     INPUT
C
      READ(5,1)X,Y,Z
C
C     CALCULATION OF A1, A2, AND A3
C
      A1=X**3+X**2+X+1.0
      A2=Y**3+Y**2+Y+1.0+A1
      A3=Z**3+Z**2+Z+1.0+A2
C
C     OUTPUT
C
      WRITE(6,2)X,Y,Z,A1,A2,A3
      STOP
C
C     FORMAT STATEMENTS
C
    1 FORMAT(3F10.2)
    2 FORMAT(1X,3F10.2/1X,3E20.7)
      END
```

Input

```
-17.5      8.0      3.
```

Output

```
-17.50     8.00      3.00
  -0.5069625E 04      -0.4484625E 04      -0.4444625E 04
```

3-18.

```
C     INPUT
C
      READ(5,1)R,S,T,U,X,Y
```

```
C
C       CALCULATIONS
C
        UP=R-S+T-U+X-Y
        DOWN=R+S+T+U+X+Y
        FIRST=R+T+X
        SEC=S+U+Y
        FINAL=EXP(UP)+SQRT(DOWN)+COS(FIRST)
C
C       ABSOLUTE VALUE OF UP MUST BE
C       LESS THAN 88.029
C
C       OUTPUT
C
        WRITE(6,2)R,S,T,U,X,Y,UP,DOWN,FIRST,SEC,FINAL
        STOP
C
C       FORMAT STATEMENTS
C
      1 FORMAT(2F10.2/2F10.2/2F10.2)
      2 FORMAT(1X,6F10.2/1X,3E20.7/1X,E20.7,30X,E20.7)
        END
```

Input

```
10.        9.
 8.        7.
 6.        5.
```

Output

```
10.00       9.00       8.00       7.00       6.00       5.00
  0.3000000E 01          0.4500000E 02          0.2400000E 02
  0.2100000E 02                                          0.2721788E 02
```

Chapter 4

4-1(c).

```
C       INPUT
C
     10 READ(5,1)X,Y,Z
C
C       CALCULATION OF A1, A2, AND A3
C
        A1=X**3+X**2+X+1.0
        A2=Y**3+Y**2+Y+1.0+A1
        A3=Z**3+Z**2+Z+1.0+A2
C
C       OUTPUT
C
        WRITE(6,2)X,Y,Z,A1,A2,A3
C
C       TRANSFER CONTROL TO READ NEXT SET
C       OF DATA.
C
        GO TO 10
C
C       FORMAT STATEMENTS
```

```
C
      1 FORMAT(3F10.2)
      2 FORMAT(1X,3F10.2/1X,3E20.7)
        END
```

Input

```
-17.5       8.0       3.
 15.0       8.0       3.0
 15.0       9.        3.
 17.5       9.        3.00
```

Output

```
-17.50      8.00      3.00
  -0.5069625E 04      -0.4484625E 04      -0.4444625E 04
 15.00      8.00      3.00
   0.3616000E 04       0.4201000E 04       0.4241000E 04
 15.00      9.00      3.00
   0.3616000E 04       0.4436000E 04       0.4476000E 04
 17.50      9.00      3.00
   0.5684125E 04       0.6504125E 04       0.6544125E 04
```

4-3.

```
C     CALCULATION OF CALORIC INTAKE REQUIREMENTS
C     DEPENDENT ON AGE
C
C     INPUT OF AGE AND OTHER DATA
C
  100 READ(5,1)AGE,...
    1 FORMAT(F10.1,...)
C
C     ASSIGN INTEGER VALUES TO REPRESENT THE
C     AGE GROUPS
C
      AGE=AGE-0.001
      NAGE=AGE/10.0
      NAGE=NAGE+1
C
C     COMPUTED GO TO FOR BRANCH SELECTION
C
      GO TO (10,11,12,13,14,15,16,17,18,19),NAGE
C
C     BRANCHES
C
   10 CALCULATIONS FOR 0-10 AGE GROUP AND OUTPUT OF RESULTS
      GO TO 100
C
   11 CALCULATIONS FOR 11-20 AGE GROUP AND OUTPUT OF RESULTS
      GO TO 100
C
   12 CALCULATIONS FOR 21-30 AGE GROUP AND OUTPUT OF RESULTS
      GO TO 100
C
   13 CALCULATIONS FOR 31-40 AGE GROUP AND OUTPUT OF RESULTS
      GO TO 100
C
   14 CALCULATIONS FOR 41-50 AGE GROUP AND OUTPUT OF RESULTS
      GO TO 100
C
```

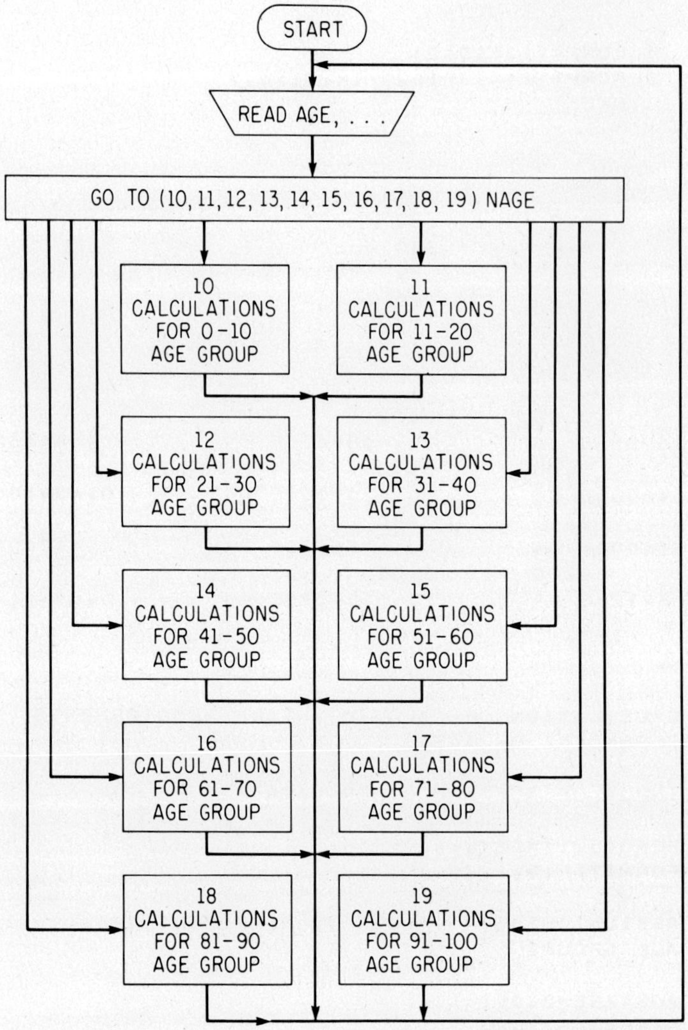


```
   15 CALCULATIONS FOR 51-60 AGEGROUP AND OUTPUT OF RESULTS
      GO TO 100
C
   16 CALCULATIONS FOR 61-70 AGE GROUP AND OUTPUT OF RESULTS
      GO TO 100
C
   17 CALCULATIONS FOR 71-80 AGE GROUP AND OUTPUT OF RESULTS
      GO TO 100
C
   18 CALCULATIONS FOR 81-90 AGE GROUP AND OUTPUT OF RESULTS
      GO TO 100
C
   19 CALCULATIONS FOR 91-100 AGE GROUP AND OUTPUT OF RESULTS
      GO TO 100
      END
```

4-6.

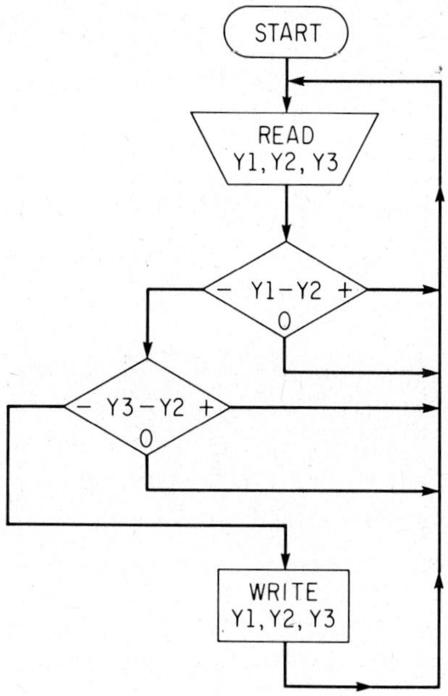


```
C       INPUT
C
   101  READ(5,102)Y1,Y2,Y3
C
C       ARITHMETIC IF TO CHECK FOR LOCAL MAXIMUM
C       AND TRANSFER CONTROL TO INPUT IF NONE EXISTS
C       IN PRESENT SET OF DATA
C
        IF(Y1-Y2)110,101,101
   110  IF(Y3-Y2)120,101,101
C
C       IF LOCAL MAX. EXISTS, WRITE THE 3 ORDINATES,
C
C       OUTPUT
C
   120  WRITE(6,102)Y1,Y2,Y3
C
C       TRANSFER CONTROL TO READ NEXT SET
C       OF DATA.
C
        GO TO 101
C
C       FORMAT STATEMENTS
C
   102  FORMAT(1X,3F10.2)
        END
```

Input

```
 0.      3.      9.
 3.      9.     12.
 9.     12.      7.
12.      7.      5.
 7.      5.     10.
 5.     10.      6.
10.      6.      0.
 6.      0.      0.
 0.      0.      8.
 0.      8.      3.
```

Output

```
9.00     12.00      7.00
5.00     10.00      6.00
0.00      8.00      3.00
```

4-12.

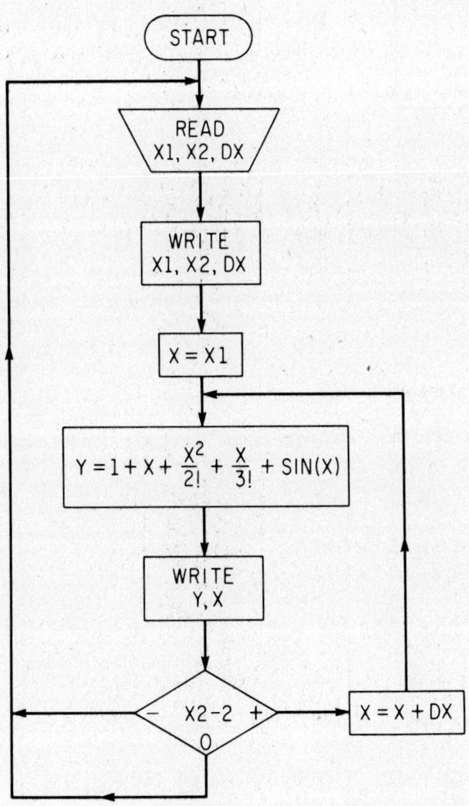


```
      C          INPUT
      C
        1        READ(5,2)X1,X2,DX
      C
      C          OUTPUT
      C
```

```
      WRITE(6,3)X1,X2,DX
C
C     ASSIGN INITIAL VALUE OF X
C
      X=X1
C
C     CALCULATE Y
C
   10 Y=1+X+X**2/2.+X**3/6.+SIN(X)
C
C     OUTPUT
C
      WRITE(6,4)Y,X
C
C     TEST FOR VALUE OF X LESS THAN X2
C
      IF(X2-X)50,50,20
C
C     INCREMENT X
C
   20 X=X+DX
      GO TO 10
C
C     TRANSFER CONTROL TO READ NEXT SET
C     OF DATA.
C
   50 GO TO 1
C
C     FORMAT STATEMENTS
C
    2 FORMAT(3F10.2)
    3 FORMAT(1X,3F10.2)
    4 FORMAT(1X,E15.5,F10.2)
      END
```

Input

```
  1.        15.        1.5
  2.        10.         2.
 75.       500.        25.
```

Output

```
   1.00      15.00       1.50
 0.35081E 01       1.00
 0.98276E 01       2.50
 0.22910E 02       4.00
 0.48649E 02       5.50
 0.90324E 02       7.00
 0.14878E 03       8.50
 0.22712E 03      10.00
 0.33123E 03      11.50
 0.46509E 03      13.00
 0.62966E 03      14.50
 0.82738E 03      16.00
   2.00      10.00       2.00
 0.72426E 01       2.00
 0.22910E 02       4.00
 0.60721E 02       6.00
 0.12732E 03       8.00
 0.22712E 03      10.00
  75.00     500.00      25.00
```

```
0.73201E 05      75.00
0.17177E 06     100.00
0.33346E 06     125.00
0.57390E 06     150.00
0.90872E 06     175.00
0.13535E 07     200.00
0.19240E 07     225.00
0.26357E 07     250.00
0.35042E 07     275.00
0.45453E 07     300.00
0.57745E 07     325.00
0.72074E 07     350.00
0.88597E 07     375.00
0.10747E 08     400.00
0.12885E 08     425.00
0.15289E 08     450.00
0.17975E 08     475.00
0.20959E 08     500.00
```

4-15.

```
C       DEFINE COUNTER
C
        K=1
C
C       INPUT
C
  101   READ(5,102)Y1,Y2,Y3
C
C       ARITHMETIC IF TO CHECK FOR LOCAL MAXIMUM
C       AND TRANSFER CONTROL TO INPUT IF NONE EXISTS
C       IN PRESENT SET OF DATA
C
        IF(Y1-Y2)110,104,104
  110   IF(Y3-Y2)120,104,104
C
C       IF LOCAL MAX. EXISTS, WRITE THE 3 ORDINATES.
C
C       OUTPUT
C
  120   WRITE(6,102)Y1,Y2,Y3
C
C       TEST COUNTER
C
  104   IF(K-7)105,11,11
C
  105   K=K+1
C
C       TRANSFER CONTROL TO READ NEXT SET
C       OF DATA.
C
        GO TO 101
   11   STOP
C
C       FORMAT STATEMENTS
C
  102   FORMAT(1X,3F10.2)
        END
```

Input

```
 3.        9.       12.
 9.       12.        7.
12.        7.        5.
 7.        5.       10.
 5.       10.        6.
10.        6.        0.
 6.        0.        0.
```

Output

```
9.00      12.00      7.00
5.00      10.00      6.00
```

4-19.

```
C      INPUT
C
 101   READ(5,102)Y1,Y2,Y3,N
C
C      ARITHMETIC IF TO CHECK FOR LOCAL MAXIMUM
C      AND TRANSFER CONTROL TO INPUT IF NONE EXISTS
C      IN PRESENT SET OF DATA
C
       IF(Y1-Y2)110,101,101
 110   IF(Y3-Y2)120,101,101
C
C      IF LOCAL MAX. EXISTS, WRITE THE 3 ORDINATES,
C
C      OUTPUT
C
 120   WRITE(6,102)Y1,Y2,Y3
C
C      CHECK FOR END OF DATA
C
       IF(N)150,108,150
 108   CONTINUE
C
C      TRANSFER CONTROL TO READ NEXT SET
C      OF DATA.
C
       GO TO 101
 150   STOP
C
C      FORMAT STATEMENTS
C
 102   FORMAT(1X,3F10.2,I5)
       END
```

Input

```
 0.        3.        9.
 3.        9.       12.
 9.       12.        7.
12.        7.        5.
 7.        5.       10.
 5.       10.        6.
10.        6.        0.
```

```
6.          0.          0.
0.          0.          8.
0.          8.          3.      1
```

Output

```
9.00       12.00        7.00
5.00       10.00        6.00
0.00        8.00        3.00
```

Chapter 5

5-2.

```
      C    DEFINE PRODUCT COST, PLANT COST, AND PRODUCTION RATE
           C=1.50
           B=900000.
           P=200000.
      C    ITERATE ON VALUES OF PRODUCT VALUE
           DO1I=275,325,5
           Z=I
      C    COMPUTE PAY-OUT TIME
           V=Z/100.
           PNET=P*(V-C)
           PROF=.48*PNET
           TIME=B/PROF
      C    WRITE RESULTS
        1  WRITE(6,2)V,TIME
        2  FORMAT(1X,2F10.2)
           STOP
           END
```

Input—none

Output

```
2.75       7.50
2.80       7.21
2.85       6.94
2.90       6.70
2.95       6.47
3.00       6.25
3.05       6.05
3.10       5.86
3.15       5.68
3.20       5.51
3.25       5.36
```

5-7.

```
      C    DO FOR 25 YEARS
           DO1N=1,25
      C    COMPUTE CAPITAL RECOVERY FACTOR
           CRF=.08*(1.08)**N/((1.08)**N-1.)
      C    WRITE RESULTS
        1  WRITE(6,2)N,CRF
```

```
  2     FORMAT(1X,I5,F10.5)
        STOP
        END
```

Input—none

Output

```
    1   1.08000
    2   0.56077
    3   0.38803
    4   0.30192
    5   0.25046
    6   0.21632
    7   0.19207
    8   0.17401
    9   0.16008
   10   0.14903
   11   0.14008
   12   0.13270
   13   0.12652
   14   0.12130
   15   0.11683
   16   0.11298
   17   0.10963
   18   0.10670
   19   0.10413
   20   0.10185
   21   0.09983
   22   0.09803
   23   0.09642
   24   0.09498
   25   0.09368
```

5-10.

```
C       SET SUM TO ZERO AND PRODUCT TO 1,
        SUM=0.0
        PROD=1.0
C       READ NUMBER OF POINTS
        READ(5,1)N
  1     FORMAT(I5)
C       READ DATA AND COMPUTE SUMS AND PRODUCT
        DO3I=1,N
        READ(5,2)VALUE
  2     FORMAT(F5.1)
        PROD=PROD*VALUE
  3     SUM=SUM+VALUE
C       COMPUTE MEANS
        TERM=N
        AMEAN=SUM/TERM
        GMEAN=PROD**(1./TERM)
C       WRITE RESULTS
        WRITE(6,5)AMEAN,GMEAN
  5     FORMAT(1X,2F6.1)
        STOP
        END
```

Input

```
      7
   12.2
    7.9
   20.2
   13.5
   49.4
    2.1
    5.8
```

Output

```
   15.9   10.7
```

5-13.

```
C      READ X
C
       READ(5,1)X
       TSOL=SIN(X)**2
C
C      BEGIN SUMMATION
C
       TERM=X**2
       SUM=TERM
       DO 2I=2,100
       AI=2*I*(2*I-1)
C      THE FOLLOWING STATEMENT IS TO AVOID EXPONENT UNDERFLOWS
       IF(ABS(TERM).LT.1.E-50)TERM=0.
       TERM=-TERM*(2.*X)**2/AI
       SUM=SUM+TERM
    2  IF(I.EQ.5.OR.I.EQ.10.OR.I.EQ.50.OR.I.EQ.100)
      *WRITE(6,3)I,SUM,TSOL
       STOP
C
C      FORMAT STATEMENTS
C
    1  FORMAT(F5.0)
    3  FORMAT(1X,I5,2F15.4)
       END
```

Input

```
   2.
```

Output

```
      5          0.8429         0.8268
     10          0.8268         0.8268
     50          0.8268         0.8268
    100          0.8268         0.8268
```

5-14.

```
C      READ THE NUMBER OF INCREMENTS
C
    1  READ(5,2)NINC
C
C      CONVERT TO FLOATING POINT AND DETERMINE
```

```
      C     SIZE CF INCREMENT.
      C
            ANINC=NINC
            DELX=2./ANINC
      C
      C     NUMERICALLY INTEGRATE
      C
            X=0.
            SUM=0.
            DO3I=1,NINC
            FX=1.+X**2
            SUM=SUM+FX*DELX
        3   X=X+DELX
      C
      C     WRITE RESULTS
      C
            WRITE(6,4)NINC,SUM
            GOTO1
      C
      C     FORMAT STATEMENTS
      C
        2   FORMAT(I5)
        4   FORMAT(1X,I5,F15.4)
            END
```

Input

```
    4
   10
   20
   50
  100
 1000
```

Output

```
    4        3.7500
   10        4.2800
   20        4.4700
   50        4.5872
  100        4.6267
 1000        4.6622
```

5-17.

```
      C     READ INPUT
      C
            READ(5,1)A,B
      C
      C     INITIALIZE BY HALVING INTERVAL
      C
            C=(A+B)/2.
            DO2I=1,20
            FC=((C-1.)*C-1.)*C-1.9
            IF(FC)3,4,5
      C
      C     IF FC NEGATIVE, REPLACE LEFT VALUE OF
      C     THE INTERVAL BY C.
      C
        3   A=C
            GO TO 2
```

```
C
C      IF FC PCSITIVE, REPLACE RIGHT VALUE OF
C      THE INTERVAL BY C
C
   5   B=C
   2   C=(A+B)/2.
C
C      THE RCOT IS FCUND
C
   4   WRITE(6,7)C
       STCP
C
C      FORMAT STATEMENTS
C
   1   FORMAT(2F10.0)
   7   FORMAT(1X,F15.4)
       ENC
```

Input

```
0.        5.
```

Output

```
1.9856
```

5-19.

```
C      INPUT FCR B,EPS,AND AK
C
       READ(5,1)BO,EPS
   5   READ(5,2)AK
       B=BC
       WRITE(6,3)B,EPS,AK
C
C      PERFORM 20 ITERATIONS IF NECESSARY
C
       DO4I=1,20
C
C      COMPUTE Y1,Y2, AND DELTA. COMPARE TC EPS.
C
       Y1=1.-EXP(-B)
       Y2=B*ABS(B)
       DELTA=Y1-Y2
       WRITE(6,6)B,Y1,Y2,DELTA
       IF(ABS(CELTA).LT.EPS)GOTO5
   4   B=B+AK*CELTA
       GOTC5
C
C      FCRMAT STATEMENTS
C
   1   FORMAT(2F10.0)
   2   FORMAT(F10.0)
   3   FORMAT(1X,3F12.3)
   6   FORMAT(1X,4E15.4)
       END
```

Input

```
1.       .001
.1
```

```
.5
1.
2.
```

Output

```
   1.000          0.001          0.100
0.1000E 01      0.6321E 00      0.1000E 01     -0.3679E 00
0.9632E 00      0.6183E 00      0.9278E 00     -0.3094E 00
0.9323E 00      0.6063E 00      0.8691E 00     -0.2628E 00
0.9060E 00      0.5959E 00      0.8208E 00     -0.2250E 00
0.8835E 00      0.5867E 00      0.7806E 00     -0.1939E 00
0.8641E 00      0.5786E 00      0.7467E 00     -0.1681E 00
0.8473E 00      0.5714E 00      0.7179E 00     -0.1465E 00
0.8326E 00      0.5651E 00      0.6933E 00     -0.1282E 00
0.8198E 00      0.5595E 00      0.6721E 00     -0.1126E 00
0.8086E 00      0.5545E 00      0.6538E 00     -0.9927E-01
0.7986E 00      0.5501E 00      0.6378E 00     -0.8776E-01
0.7899E 00      0.5461E 00      0.6239E 00     -0.7779E-01
0.7821E 00      0.5425E 00      0.6117E 00     -0.6910E-01
0.7752E 00      0.5394E 00      0.6009E 00     -0.6151E-01
0.7690E 00      0.5365E 00      0.5914E 00     -0.5486E-01
0.7635E 00      0.5340E 00      0.5830E 00     -0.4900E-01
0.7586E 00      0.5317E 00      0.5755E 00     -0.4383E-01
0.7543E 00      0.5296E 00      0.5689E 00     -0.3926E-01
0.7503E 00      0.5278E 00      0.5630E 00     -0.3520E-01
0.7468E 00      0.5261E 00      0.5577E 00     -0.3160E-01
   1.000          0.001          0.500
0.1000E 01      0.6321E 00      0.1000E 01     -0.3679E 00
0.8161E 00      0.5578E 00      0.6660E 00     -0.1081E 00
0.7620E 00      0.5333E 00      0.5806E 00     -0.4737E-01
0.7383E 00      0.5221E 00      0.5451E 00     -0.2302E-01
0.7268E 00      0.5165E 00      0.5282E 00     -0.1169E-01
0.7210E 00      0.5137E 00      0.5198E 00     -0.6062E-02
0.7179E 00      0.5122E 00      0.5154E 00     -0.3177E-02
0.7163E 00      0.5115E 00      0.5131E 00     -0.1674E-02
0.7155E 00      0.5111E 00      0.5119E 00     -0.8847E-03
   1.000          0.001          1.000
0.1000E 01      0.6321E 00      0.1000E 01     -0.3679E 00
0.6321E 00      0.4685E 00      0.3996E 00      0.6896E-01
0.7011E 00      0.5040E 00      0.4915E 00      0.1244E-01
0.7135E 00      0.5101E 00      0.5091E 00      0.9748E-03
   1.000          0.001          2.000
0.1000E 01      0.6321E 00      0.1000E 01     -0.3679E 00
0.2642E 00      0.2322E 00      0.6982E-01      0.1624E 00
0.5890E 00      0.4451E 00      0.3469E 00      0.9819E-01
0.7854E 00      0.5441E 00      0.6168E 00     -0.7278E-01
0.6398E 00      0.4726E 00      0.4094E 00      0.6323E-01
0.7663E 00      0.5353E 00      0.5872E 00     -0.5195E-01
0.6624E 00      0.4844E 00      0.4388E 00      0.4561E-01
0.7536E 00      0.5293E 00      0.5679E 00     -0.3860E-01
0.6764E 00      0.4916E 00      0.4575E 00      0.3403E-01
0.7445E 00      0.5250E 00      0.5542E 00     -0.2922E-01
0.6860E 00      0.4964E 00      0.4706E 00      0.2579E-01
0.7376E 00      0.5217E 00      0.5441E 00     -0.2233E-01
0.6930E 00      0.4999E 00      0.4802E 00      0.1972E-01
0.7324E 00      0.5192E 00      0.5364E 00     -0.1715E-01
0.6981E 00      0.5025E 00      0.4873E 00      0.1514E-01
0.7284E 00      0.5173E 00      0.5305E 00     -0.1321E-01
0.7019E 00      0.5044E 00      0.4927E 00      0.1166E-01
0.7253E 00      0.5158E 00      0.5260E 00     -0.1020E-01
0.7049E 00      0.5058E 00      0.4968E 00      0.8993E-02
0.7228E 00      0.5146E 00      0.5225E 00     -0.7877E-02
```

5-20.

```
C      READ NINC AND CALCULATE DT
C
       TSOL=1.-EXP(-1.)
   1   READ(5,4)NINC
       ANINC=NINC
       DT=1./ANINC
C
C      BEGIN NUMERICAL SOLUTION
C
       C=0.
       DO2I=1,NINC
   2   C=C+(1.-C)*DT
C
C      OUTPUT
C
       WRITE(6,3)NINC,C,TSOL
       GOTO1
C
C      FORMAT STATEMENTS
C
   4   FORMAT(I5)
   3   FORMAT(1X,I5,2F15.4)
       END
```

Input

```
    4
   10
   20
   50
  100
 1000
```

Output

```
    4        0.6836        0.6321
   10        0.6513        0.6321
   20        0.6415        0.6321
   50        0.6358        0.6321
  100        0.6340        0.6321
 1000        0.6323        0.6321
```

5-23.

```
C      READ NINC AND CALCULATE INCREMENT SIZE
C
   1   READ(5,2)NINC
       ANINC=NINC
       DT=4./ANINC
C
C      BEGIN SOLUTION
C
       C=0.
       Z=0.
       DO3I=1,NINC
       DC=Z
       DZ=1.-C-Z
       C=C+DC*DT
   3   Z=Z+DZ*DT
```

```
C
C     WRITE RESULTS
C
      WRITE(6,4)NINC,C
      GOTO1
C
C     FORMAT STATEMENTS
C
    2 FORMAT(I5)
    4 FORMAT(1X,I5,F15.4)
      END
```

Input

```
    4
   10
   20
   50
  100
 1000
```

Output

```
    4         2.0000
   10         1.2672
   20         1.2001
   50         1.1704
  100         1.1616
 1000         1.1538
```

5-30.

```
C
      DIMENSIONA(10),X(10),Y(10)
C
C     INPUT
C
      READ(5,11)(A(J),J=1,8)
C
C     CREATE A WORKING ARRAY AND FIND ABSOLUTE VALUES
C
      DO25J=1,8
      Y(J)=A(J)
   25 X(J)=ABS(A(J))
C
C     ORDER THE ARRAY BY ARRANGING ADJACENT NUMBERS
C
      DO75I=1,7
      DO75J=1,7
      IF(X(J).LE.X(J+1))GOTO75
      DX=X(J)
      DY=Y(J)
      X(J)=X(J+1)
      Y(J)=Y(J+1)
      X(J+1)=DX
      Y(J+1)=DY
   75 CONTINUE
C
C     OUTPUT
C
      WRITE(6,101)(Y(J),J=1,8)
```

```
      999   STCP
      C
      C     FCRMAT STATEMENTS
      C
       11   FCRMAT(9F5.1)
      101   FCRMAT(1X,9F5.1)
            END
```

Input

```
5.C-25.0 -130 -975 13.1 43.0    74
```

Output

```
0.0  5.0  7.4-13.0 13.1-25.0 43.0-97.5
```

5-32.

```
      C
            DIMENSICNA(10),B(10)
      C
      C     INPUT
      C
            DC5I=1,10
            N=11-I
        5   READ(5,11)A(I),B(N)
      C
      C     CALCULATE NORM
      C
            SUMAB=C.0
            DC20J=1,10
       20   SUMAB=SUMAB+A(J)*B(J)
            ABNCRM=SQRT(SUMAB)
      C
      C     OUTPUT
            WRITE(6,50)ABNORM
      999   STCP
      C
      C     FCRMAT STATEMENTS
      C
       11   FCRMAT(2F20.4)
       50   FCRMAT(1X,E20.7)
            ENC
```

Input

```
1.                  1.
2.                  2.
3.                  3.
4.                  4.
5.                  5.
6.                  6.
7.                  7.
8.                  8.
9.                  9.
10.                 10.
```

Output

```
0.1483240E 02
```

5-35.

```
      DIMENSION NO(50),BILL(50)
C     REAC BASE CHARGES
      DO1I=1,10
 1    READ(5,2)NO(I),BILL(I)
C     READ LONG CISTANCE CHARGES
 77   REAC(5,2)NUMBER,CHARGE
 2    FORMAT(I3,F6.2)
C     IS CARD BLANK
      IF(NUMBER.EQ.0)GOTO6
C     ACC TC APPROPRIATE BILL
      DO4I = 1,10
      IF(NUMBER.EQ.NO(I))BILL(I)=BILL(I)+1.1*CHARGE
 4    CONTINUE
      GOTC77
C     WRITE FINAL BILLS
 6    DO7I=1,10
 7    WRITE(6,8)NO(I),BILL(I)
 8    FORMAT(1X,I5,F10.2)
      STCP
      ENC
```

Input

```
  1  1.50
  2  1.29
  3  1.75
  4  1.75
  5  2.00
  6  1.10
  7  1.75
  8  1.75
  9  2.00
 10  1.75
  8  6.00
  7  3.12
  1  1.75
  4  5.60
  8  1.50
 10  4.20
(BLANK CARD)
```

Output

```
  1      3.43
  2      1.29
  3      1.75
  4      7.91
  5      2.00
  6      1.10
  7      5.18
  8     10.00
  9      2.00
 10      6.37
```

5-41.

```
C      RESERVE STORAGE FOR FIFTY ELEMENTS
C
       DIMENSION A(50)
C
C      READ INPUT
C
       READ(5,1) N,(A(J),J=1,N),A(N+1),B
C
C      INITIALIZE F TO COEFFICIENT OF HIGHEST POWER
       F=A(N+1)
C
C      USE LOOP TO GEN POWERS
C
       DO2J=1,N
C
C      MULTIPLY BY B AND ADD COEFFICIENT OF
C      NEXT POWER OF X  .
C
       K=N+1-J
     2 F=B*F+A(K)
C
C      WRITE RESULTS
C
       WRITE(6,3) B,F
C
C      FORMAT STATEMENTS
C
     1 FORMAT(I5/(F10.0))
     3 FORMAT(1X,F14.4)
       STOP
       END
```

Input

```
    5
1.
7.
-3.2
1.7
-0.06
-0.8
0.75
```

Output

```
0.7500
4.9584
```

5-45.

```
       DIMENSION A(16),B(16)
C
C      INPUT
C
    10 READ(5,11)(A(I),I=1,16)
C
C      CALCULATION OF B ARRAY
C
```

```
         I=1
   12    RI=I
         B(I)=RI*A(I)
         I=I+1
         IF(I.LT.17)GOTO12
C
C        OUTPUT
C
   13    WRITE(6,101)(A(I),B(I),I=1,16)
  999    STOP
C
C        FORMAT STATEMENTS
C
   11    FORMAT(4F10.2)
  101    FORMAT(1X,2F10.2)
         END
```

Input

```
1.00      2.00      3.00      4.00
5.00      6.00      7.00      8.00
9.00      1.00      2.00      3.00
4.00      5.00      6.00      7.00
```

Output

```
1.00      1.00
2.00      4.00
3.00      9.00
4.00     16.00
5.00     25.00
6.00     36.00
7.00     49.00
8.00     64.00
9.00     81.00
1.00     10.00
2.00     22.00
3.00     36.00
4.00     52.00
5.00     70.00
6.00     90.00
7.00    112.00
```

5-49.

```
         DIMENSION A(5),B(5),C(5)
C
C        INPUT
C
   10    READ(5,11)(A(I),B(I),I=1,5)
C
C        CALCULATE C ARRAY
C
         I=1
   20    IF(B(I).GE.A(I))GO TO 50
         C(I)=A(I)-B(I)
         GO TO 60
   50    C(I)=A(I)+B(I)
   60    I=I+1
         IF(I.LT.6)GOTO20
C
```

```
C     OUTPUT
C
  100 WRITE(6,101)(A(I),B(I),C(I),I=1,5)
  999 STOP
C
C     FORMAT STATEMENTS
C
   11 FORMAT(2F10.2)
  101 FORMAT(1X,3F10.2)
      END
```

Input

```
      0.         5.
     10.         7.
      6.         6.
7281.00         82.
  0.111      0.112
```

Output

```
     0.00      5.00      5.00
    10.00      7.00      3.00
     6.00      6.00     12.00
  7281.00     82.00   7199.00
     0.11      0.11      0.22
```

5-51.

```
      DIMENSION A(10),B(10),P(10),X(10)
C
C     READ INPUT
C
      READ (5,1)N,PT,T
      DO2I=1,N
    2 READ(5,3)X(I),A(I),B(I)
C
C     LET SUM BE SUM(RI*XI).INITIALIZE TO ZERO,
C     AND CALCULATE PI, RI, AND SUM
C
    6 SUM=0.
      DO4I=1,N
      P(I)=10.**(B(I)-0.05223*A(I)/T)
      R=P(I)/P(1)
    4 SUM=SUM+R*X(I)
C
C     CALCULATE PA AND TA
C
      PA=PT/SUM
      TA=0.05223*A(1)/(B(1)-ALOG10(PA))
C
C     CHECK
C
      IF(ABS(TA-T)/TA.LT.0.001)GOTO5
      T=TA
      GOTO6
C
C     SOLUTION IS FOUND
C
    5 WRITE(6,7)TA
      STOP
C
```

```
C     FORMAT STATEMENTS
C
    1 FORMAT(I2,2F10.0)
    3 FORMAT(3F10.0)
    7 FORMAT(1X,F12.3)
      END
```

Input

```
2     2000.       273.
        .5     23450.      7.395
        .5     27691.      7.558
```

Output

```
313.861
```

5-53.

```
      DIMENSION A(50)
C
C     READ N
C
      READ(5,1)N
C
C     READ ELEMENTS OF VECTOR AND COMPUTE NORM
C
      SUM=0.
      DO2I=1,N
      READ(5,3)A(I)
    2 SUM=SUM+A(I)**2
      SUM=SQRT(SUM)
C
C     DIVIDE EACH ELEMENT BY NORM AND PRINT
C
      DO4I=1,N
      A(I)=A(I)/SUM
    4 WRITE(6,5)A(I)
      STOP
C
C     FORMAT STATEMENTS
C
    1 FORMAT(I3)
    3 FORMAT(F10.0)
    5 FORMAT(1X,F12.4)
      END
```

Input

```
4
       2.
       1.
       0.
       3.
```

Output

```
0.5345
0.2673
0.0000
0.8018
```

5-55.

```
      DIMENSION A(50)
C
C     READ N
C
      READ(5,1)N
C
C     READ VECTOR A
C
      DO2I=1,N
    2 READ(5,3)A(I)
C
C     READ VECTOR B AND COMPUTE DOT PRODUCT.
C
      DOT=0.
      DO4I=1,N
      READ(5,3)B
    4 DOT=DOT+B*A(I)
C
C     PRINT RESULT
C
      WRITE(6,5)DOT
      STOP
C
C     FORMAT STATEMENTS
C
    1 FORMAT(I3)
    3 FORMAT(F10.0)
    5 FORMAT(1X,F12.4)
      END
```

Input

```
  4
      4.
      0.
      7.
      2.
     -1.
      2.
      1.
     -2.
```

Output

```
-1.0000
```

Chapter 6

6-1(c). Subscript must be an integer variable; Subscript must not be a subscripted variable; K * 3 should be 3 * K.

6-2(b). Subscript must be an integer.

(f). As J = 5, subscript exceeds size specified in dimension statement.

6-3.

```
      DIMENSION DATA(5,4),TAVG(4),SAVG(5)
C
C     READ INPUT DATA
C
      READ(5,1) ((DATA(I,J),J=1,4),I=1,5)
    1 FORMAT(4F10.1)
C
C     COMPUTE TEST AVERAGE
C
      DO2I=1,4
      SUM=0.
      DO3J=1,5
    3 SUM=SUM+DATA(J,I)
    2 TAVG(I)=SUM/5.
C
C     COMPUTE STUDENT AVERAGE
C
      SUMA=0.
      DO4I=1,5
      SUM=0.
      DO5J=1,4
    5 SUM=SUM+DATA(I,J)
      SAVG(I)=SUM/4.
    4 SUMA=SAVG(I)+SUMA
      AVG=SUMA/5.
C
C     WRITE RESULTS
C
      WRITE(6,6) TAVG
      WRITE(6,6) SAVG
      WRITE(6,6) AVG
    6 FORMAT(1X,5F10.2)
      STOP
      END
```

Input

```
48.6      30.0      62.8      23.4
40.1      40.0      60.1      29.6
63.4      50.0      63.7      31.2
56.2      60.0      58.2      27.3
71.0      70.0      67.3      26.4
```

Output

```
55.86     50.00     62.42     27.58
41.20     42.45     52.07     50.42     58.67
48.96
```

6-8.

```
C
      DIMENSION A(25,25),B(25),X(25)
C
C     INPUT
C
```

```
      READ(5,11)N,((A(I,J),J=1,N),I=1,N),(B(K),K=1,N)
C
C     CALCULATION OF X ARRAY
C
      X(1)=B(1)/A(1,1)
      DO15J=2,N
      K=J-1
      SUM=0.0
      DO25I=1,K
   25 SUM=SUM+A(J,I)*X(I)/A(J,J)
   15 X(J)=B(J)/A(J,J)-SUM
C
C     OUTPUT
C
      WRITE(6,30)(X(K),K=1,N)
C
C     FORMAT STATEMENTS
C
   11 FORMAT(I5/(10F7.2))
   30 FORMAT(1X,5E15.5)
      STOP
      END
```

Input

```
    7
  500                                                          350   -740
                                       111   -420    918
           50    100   -250    380                                     17   1200
  630     490   -850                         1300                555   -202    800
 1605            301    301      5              8                 65    720   2500
 2350    2200   2000   1500   1200   1000
```

Output

```
 0.50000E 01    -0.81081E 00     0.14210E 01     0.57535E 01     0.15605E 01
-0.38473E 01    -0.91436E-01
```

6-11.

```
      INTEGER AGAIN(2,2,3)
      K=2
      DO6J=1,2
      DO6L=1,3
      DO6N=1,2
      AGAIN(J,N,L)=K
    6 K=K+2
      WRITE(6,7)(((I,J,K,AGAIN(I,J,K),I=1,2),J=1,2),K=1,3)
    7 FORMAT(1X,4I5)
      STOP
      END
```

Input—none

Output

```
    1    1    1    2
    2    1    1   14
    1    2    1    4
    2    2    1   16
    1    1    2    6
    2    1    2   18
```

```
1   2   2    8
2   2   2   20
1   1   3   10
2   1   3   22
1   2   3   12
2   2   3   24
```

6-14.

```
      DIMENSION A(3,5),B(5,3)
C
C     INPUT
C
      READ(5,11)((A(I,J),J=1,5),I=1,3)
C
C     INVERSION OF A-MATRIX
C
      I=1
  100 J=1
  101 B(J,I)=A(I,J)
      J=J+1
      IF(J.LT.6)GOTO101
      I=I+1
      IF(I.LT.4)GOTO100
C
C     OUTPUT
C
   20 WRITE(6,21)((B(J,I),I=1,3),J=1,5)
  999 STOP
C
C     FORMAT STATEMENTS
C
   11 FORMAT(5F10.2)
   21 FORMAT(1X,3F10.2)
      END
```

Input

```
11.50     -17.80     22.4               17.90
 -9.8      39.7       5.2      22.7     -39.
 -7.07     16.20     70.40    -14.01     36.040
```

Output

```
 11.50     -9.80     -7.07
-17.80     39.70     16.20
 22.40      5.20     70.40
  0.00     22.70    -14.01
 17.90    -39.00     36.04
```

6-17.

```
      DIMENSION A(20,20),B(10)
C
C     INPUT
C
      READ(5,1)N
      DO2I=1,N
      DO2J=1,N
    2 READ(5,3)A(I,J)
      DO4I=1,N
```

```
    4 READ(5,3)B(I)
C
C     NCTE THAT N-1 RCWS MUST BE RECALCULATED
C
      NN=N-1
      DO5I=1,NN
C
C     MULTIPLICATION FACTOR FOR EQUATION J
C     IS A(K,J)/A(JJ) WHEN SUBTRACTING FROM
C     EQUATION K
C
      J=N+1-I
C
C     J-1 EQUATIONS MUST BE OPERATED ON
C
      L=J-1
      DO6K=1,L
      FACT=A(K,J)/A(J,J)
C
C     THERE ARE J NONZERO TERMS IN EACH EQUATION
C
      DO7M=1,J
    7 A(K,M)=A(K,M)-FACT*A(J,M)
C
C     DO NOT FORGET CONSTANT TERM
C
    6 B(K)=B(K)-FACT*B(J)
    5 CONTINUE
C
C     OUTPUT
C
      DO8I=1,N
      DO8J=1,N
    8 WRITE(6,9)A(I,J)
      DO1^I=1,N
    1 WRITE(6,9)F(I)
      STOP
C
C     FORMAT STATEMENTS
C
    1 FORMAT(I5)
    3 FORMAT(F1^,^)
    9 FORMAT(1X,F12,4)
      END
```

Input

```
3
   3.
   4.
   1.
   1.
   4.
  -2.
   2.
   1.
   1.
   4.
   0.
   1.
```

Output

```
-1.5000
-0.0000
-0.0000
 5.0000
 6.0000
-0.0000
 2.0000
 1.0000
 1.0000
 2.0000
 2.0000
 1.0000
```

6-22.

```
C       ARRAY C IS INTERMEDIATE STORAGE, WHEN THIS
C       PROGRAM IS COMBINED WITH THE PROGRAM IN
C       THE PREVIOUS PROBLEM, ARRAYS C AND X MAY
C       BE THE SAME ARRAY TO CONSERVE STORAGE
C
        DIMENSION A(210),B(20),X(20),C(20)
C
C       READ N AND FIRST EQUATION
C
        READ(5,1)N
        DO2I=1,N
    2   READ(5,3)A(I)
        READ(5,3)B(1)
        I=N
C
C       MUST DO FOR REMAINING ROWS
C
        DO4J=2,N
C
C       INPUT
C
        DO5K=1,N
    5   READ(5,3)C(K)
        READ(5,3)B(J)
C
C       J-1 PREVIOUS ROWS, M IS INDEX IN ARRAY A
C
        L=J-1
        M=1
        DO6K=1,L
        FACT=C(K)/A(M)
        M=M+1
C
C       REMAINING ELEMENTS IS N-K, BEGIN AT K+1
C
        NN=K+1
        DO7JJ=NN,N
        C(JJ)=C(JJ)-FACT*A(M)
    7   M=M+1
    6   B(J)=B(J)-FACT*B(K)
C
C       SHIFT C TO A.
```

```
C
      DO4K=J,N
      I=I+1
    4 A(I)=C(K)
C
C     OUTPUT
C
      DO10J=1,I
   10 WRITE(6,12)A(J)
      DO11J=1,N
   11 WRITE(6,12)B(J)
      STOP
C
C     FORMAT STATEMENTS
C
    1 FORMAT(I5)
    3 FORMAT(F10.0)
   12 FORMAT(1X,F12.4)
      END
```

Input

```
3
      3.
      4.
      1.
      4.
      1.
      4.
     -2.
      0.
      2.
      1.
      1.
      1.
```

Output

```
    3.0000
    4.0000
    1.0000
    2.6667
   -2.3333
   -1.1250
    4.0000
   -1.3333
   -2.5000
```

6-25.

```
      DIMENSION A(10,4),B(4),C(4)
C
C     READ N
C
      READ(5,1)N
C
C     READ MATRIX A
C
      DO2I=1,N
    2 READ(5,3)A(I,1),A(I,2),A(I,3),A(I,4)
C
```

```
C       READ MATRIX B(ONE ROW AT A TIME),COMPUTE
C       THE CORRESPONDING ROW OF C, AND WRITE
C       RESULTS,
C
        DO4I=1,N
        READ(5,3)B(1),B(2),B(3),B(4)
        DO5J=1,4
   5    C(J)=A(I,J)+B(J)
   4    WRITE(6,6)C(1),C(2),C(3),C(4)
        STOP
C
C       FORMAT STATEMENTS
C
   1    FORMAT(I3)
   3    FORMAT(4F10.0)
   6    FORMAT(1X,4F12.4)
        END
```

Input

```
3
      2.         1.        -2.         0.
      7.         8.        -6.         5.
      0.         7.         1.        -3.
     -4.         4.         0.         3.
      2.         7.        -3.         1.
      0.         0.         2.         0.
```

Output

```
 -2.0000      5.0000     -2.0000      3.0000
  9.0000     15.0000     -9.0000      6.0000
  0.0000      7.0000      3.0000     -3.0000
```

6-28.

```
        DIMENSION D(4,4)
C
C       READ INPUT
C
        DO1I=1,4
   1    READ(5,2)D(I,1),D(I,2),D(I,3),D(I,4)
C
C       BEGIN GAUSS REDUCTION
C
        DO4I=1,3
        K=I+1
        DO4J=K,4
        AMUL=-D(J,I)/D(I,I)
        D(J,I)=0.
        DO4L=K,4
   4    D(J,L)=D(J,L)+AMUL*D(I,L)
C
C       EVALUATE DETERMINANT
C
        DET=D(1,1)
        DO3I=2,4
   3    DET=DET*D(I,I)
C
C       OUTPUT
```

```
C
      WRITE(6,5)DET
      STOP
C
C     FORMAT STATEMENTS
C
    2 FORMAT(4F10.0)
    5 FORMAT(1X,F15.4)
      END
```

Input

```
  5.        3.        1.        7.
  2.        3.        0.        5.
 -1.        2.       -9.        1.
  7.       -4.        0.        2.
```

Output

```
649.9993
```

Chapter 7

7-3.

```
C     DATA STATEMENT
C
      DATA DENSW,HT,DIA,WTCON/62.4,0.75,0.333,1.04/
C
C     INPUT
C
      READ(5,1)WTDRY,WTWET
      VOID=(WTWET-WTDRY)/DENSW
      VOL=3.1416*HT*(0.5*DIA)**2
      VOID FR=VOID/VOL
      DENS=(WTDRY-WTCON)/(VOL-VOID)
      WRITE(6,2)DIA,HT,WTCON,WTDRY,WTWET,VOIDFR,DENS
      STOP
C
C     FORMAT STATEMENTS
C
    1 FORMAT(2F10.0)
    2 FORMAT('1DIMENSIONS OF CONTAINER -'/6X,'DIAMETER',F15.4,' FT'/
     1 6X,'HEIGHT',F15.4,' FT'/6X,'WEIGHT',F15.4,' LB'/
     2 ' WEIGHT WITHOUT WATER',F15.4/' WEIGHT WITH WATER',F15.4/
     3 '0VOID FRACTION',F15.4/'0DENSITY OF MATERIAL',F15.4,
     4 ' LBS/CU. FT.')
      END
```

Input

```
7.12      8.30
```

Output

```
DIMENSIONS OF CONTAINER -
     DIAMETER            0.3330 FT
     HEIGHT            0.7500 FT
     WEIGHT            1.0400 LB
WEIGHT WITHOUT WATER          7.1200
WEIGHT WITH WATER          8.3000

VOID FRACTION            0.2895

DENSITY OF MATERIAL        131.0096 LBS/CU. FT.
```

7-5.

```
C     WRITE HEADINGS
C
      WRITE(6,1)
    1 FORMAT(7X,4HTIME,3X,8HRESPONSE/)
C
C     COMPUTE AND PRINT VALUES
C
      T=0.
      DO2I=1,21
      FT=1.-EXP(-T)
      WRITE(6,3)T,FT
    2 T=T+.2
    3 FORMAT(1XF10.2,F10.4)
      STOP
      END
```

Input—none

Output

```
TIME   RESPONSE

0.00   -0.0000
0.20    0.1813
0.40    0.3297
0.60    0.4512
0.80    0.5507
1.00    0.6321
1.20    0.6988
1.40    0.7534
1.60    0.7981
1.80    0.8347
2.00    0.8647
2.20    0.8892
2.40    0.9093
2.60    0.9257
2.80    0.9392
3.00    0.9502
3.20    0.9592
3.40    0.9666
3.60    0.9727
3.80    0.9776
4.00    0.9817
```

7-11.

```
      DATAX/1./
C
C     READ N AND A AND WRITE HEADINGS. FIRST COEFFICIENT IS 1.
C
      READ(5,1)N,A
    1 FORMAT(I5,F5.0)
      WRITE(6,2)N,A,N,X
    2 FORMAT(25H1COEFFICIENTS OF (X+A)**N/6X3HN =I6/6X3HA =,
     1   F10.4/11H0POWER OF X,5X,11HCOEFFICIENT//1X,I8,F18.4)
C
C     CALCULATE N FACTORIAL AND INITIALIZE CALCULATION OF
C     BINARY COEFFICIENTS
C
      NFACT=1
      DO3I=2,N
    3 NFACT=NFACT*I
      JFACT=1
      JNFACT=NFACT
C
C     CALCULATE COEFFICIENTS
C
      DO4I=1,N
      IXP=N-I
      JFACT=JFACT*I
      JNFACT=JNFACT/(N+1-I)
      C=NFACT/(JFACT*JNFACT)
      C=C*A**I
    4 WRITE(6,5)IXP,C
    5 FORMAT(1X,I8,F18.4)
      STOP
      END
```

Input

```
10  1.2
```

Output

```
COEFFICIENTS OF (X+A)**N
     N =      10
     A =      1.2000

POWER OF X      COEFFICIENT

       10            1.0000
        9           12.0000
        8           64.7999
        7          207.3598
        6          435.4553
        5          627.0559
        4          627.0559
        3          429.9810
        2          193.4915
        1           51.5977
        0            6.1917
```

7-14.

```
      DIMENSION T(6,5)
C
C     DATA STATEMENT
C
      DATA T/1.023,1.068,1.113,1.158,1.202,1.247,
     *       1.018,1.061,1.104,1.148,1.192,1.235,
     *       1.010,1.052,1.094,1.137,1.181,1.224,
     *       0.993,1.035,1.077,1.120,1.162,1.205,
     *       0.980,1.022,1.064,1.107,1.149,1.191/
      WRITE(6,2)((T(I,J),J=1,5),I=1,6)
    2 FORMAT(24X,18HTEMPERATURE, DEG F//16X,2H50,6X,2H86,
     *5X,3H122,
     *5X,3H176,5X,3H212//11X,1H*,4X,5(1H*,7X)//8X,4H2   *,
     *F7.3,4F8.3//
     *8X,4H6   *,F7.3,4F8.3/4H PER/7X,5H10   *,F7.3,4F8.3/5H CENT/
     *7X,5H14   *,F7.3,4F8.3/5H NAOH/7X,5H18   *,F7.3,4F8.3//7X,5H22   *,
     *F7.3,4F8.3//13X,38H(SOURCE - INT. CRIT. TABLES, VOL. III,/
     *16X,8HPAGE 79))
      STOP
      END
```

Input—none

Output

```
                    TEMPERATURE, DEG F

           50       86      122      176      212

      *    *        *        *        *        *

  2   *  1.023    1.018    1.010    0.993    0.980

  6   *  1.068    1.061    1.052    1.035    1.022
PER
 10   *  1.113    1.104    1.094    1.077    1.064
CENT
 14   *  1.158    1.148    1.137    1.120    1.107
NAOH
 18   *  1.202    1.192    1.181    1.162    1.149

 22   *  1.247    1.235    1.224    1.205    1.191

     (SOURCE - INT. CRIT. TABLES, VOL. III,
        PAGE 79)
```

7-17.

```
      DIMENSION F(11),FN(11)
C
C     CALCULATE MAXIMUM VALUE OF F(X)
C
      X=0.0
      N=1
      DO1I=1,11
      F(I)=X**2*SIN(3.1416*X)
```

```
      IF(F(I).GT.F(N))N=I
    1 X=X+0.1
C
C     CALCULATE NORMALIZED VALUES
C
      DO2I=1,11
    2 FN(I)=F(I)/F(N)
C
C     OUTPUT
C
      WRITE(6,3)
    3 FORMAT(28H1F(X) = X**2 * SIN(3.1416*X)//7X,1HX7X,4HF(X),
     *5X8HNOR F(X))
      X=0.
      DO4I=1,11
      WRITE(6,5)X,F(I),FN(I)
    5 FORMAT(1X3F10.4)
    4 X=X+0.1
      STOP
      END
```

Input—none

Output

```
F(X) = X**2 * SIN(3.1416*X)

      X        F(X)     NOR F(X)
    0.0000    0.0000     0.0000
    0.1000    0.0031     0.0078
    0.2000    0.0235     0.0593
    0.3000    0.0728     0.1837
    0.4000    0.1522     0.3839
    0.5000    0.2500     0.6306
    0.6000    0.3424     0.8637
    0.7000    0.3964     1.0000
    0.8000    0.3762     0.9489
    0.9000    0.2503     0.6314
    1.0000   -0.0000    -0.0000
```

7-20.

```
      DIMENSION A(51)
C
C     READ INPUT
C
    9 READ(5,1) N,(A(I),I=1,N),A(N+1)
    1 FORMAT(I5/(F5.3))
C
C     OUTPUT
C
      IF(N-1)2,3,4
    4 M=N-1
      DO5I=1,M
      K=N+1-I
    5 WRITE(6,6)A(I),K
    6 FORMAT(2H (F6.3,5H) X**I3,2H +)
    3 WRITE(6,7)A(N)
    7 FORMAT(2H (F6.3,3H) X,6X,1H+)
    2 WRITE(6,8)A(N+1)
    8 FORMAT(2H (F6.3,1H)/1H1)
      GOTO9
      END
```

Input

```
    1
 1712
 1000
    4
 5917
 1722
-1001
 0022
 1000
    2
 1000
 1222
-1710
```

Output (rule designates new page)

```
( 1.712) X       +
( 1.000)
-------------------
( 5.917) X**   4 +
( 1.722) X**   3 +
(-1.001) X**   2 +
( 0.022) X       +
( 1.000)
-------------------
( 1.000) X**   2 +
( 1.222) X       +
(-1.710)
```

7-22.

```
C       READ INPUT AND WRITE HEADERS
C
        READ(5,1)X,XO
   1    FORMAT(2F10.0)
        WRITE(6,2)X,XO
   2    FORMAT(36H EVALUATION OF F(X) = SIN(2X) AT X =F6.3/
       *39H FROM TAYLOR SERIES EXPANSION ABOUT X =F6.3/
       *10H0NUMBER OF,3X 11HAPPROXIMATE3X5HEXACT/
       *3X5HTERMS,8X5HVALUE,5X5HVALUE)
C
C       INITIALIZE
C
        TRUE=SIN(2.*X)
        DEL=X-XO
        FX=SIN(2.*XO)
        COEF=1.
        DO3I=1,10
C
C       UPDATE COEFFICIENT
C
        AI=I
        COEF=COEF*2.*DEL/AI
C
C       TEST FOR I EVEN OR ODD
C
        TST=I/2
        ITST=TST
        IF(I.EQ.2*ITST)FX=FX+COEF*(-1.)**(I/2)*SIN(2.*XO)
        IF(I.NE.2*ITST)FX=FX+COEF*(-1.)**((I-1)/2)*COS(2.*XO)
   3    WRITE(6,4)I,FX,TRUE
   4    FORMAT(1XI5,F16.5,F11.5)
        STOP
        END
```

Input

```
1.1          1.
```

Output

```
EVALUATION OF F(X) = SIN(2X) AT X = 1.100
FROM TAYLOR SERIES EXPANSION ABOUT X = 1.000

NUMBER OF    APPROXIMATE    EXACT
  TERMS         VALUE       VALUE
    1          0.82607     0.80850
    2          0.80788     0.80850
    3          0.80844     0.80850
    4          0.80850     0.80850
    5          0.80850     0.80850
    6          0.80850     0.80850
    7          0.80850     0.80850
    8          0.80850     0.80850
    9          0.80850     0.80850
   10          0.80850     0.80850
```

7-25.

```
      DIMENSION XX(3),YY(3),A(3)
      DATA A/3*0./
C     READ PHI,CALCULATE EXTREMITIES OF AXES,AND PRINT
C
      READ(5,1)PHI
    1 FORMAT(F10.0)
      WRITE(6,2)PHI
    2 FORMAT(39H1***** THREE-DIMENSIONAL PLOTTING *****//
     19X,5HPHI = F8.2,8H DEGREES//6X,19HEXTREMITIES OF AXES
     26X,2HXP,8X,2HYP/)
      PHI=PHI/57.3
      XA=COS(PHI)
      YA=SIN(PHI)
      DO3I=1,3
      A(I)=4.
      XX(I)=A(1)-A(3)*XA
      YY(I)=A(2)-A(3)*YA
    3 A(I)=0.
      WRITE(6,4)(XX(I),YY(I),I=1,3)
    4 FORMAT(21X,1HX,F13.3,F10.3/21X,1HY,F13.3,F10.3/21X1HZF13.3,
     *F10.3//10X,1HX,14X,1HY,14X,1HZ,14X,2HXP,13X,2HYP/)
C
C     CALCULATE POINTS
C
      X=0.0
      DO5I=1,31
      Y=(X+1.)**1.2
      Z=X**2/(X+2.)
      XP=X-Z*XA
      YP=Y-Z*YA
      WRITE(6,6)X,Y,Z,XP,YP
    6 FORMAT(1X,5F15.5)
    5 X=X+.1
      STOP
      END
```

Input

```
35.
```

Output

```
***** THREE-DIMENSIONAL PLOTTING *****

      PHI =    35.00 DEGREES

   EXTREMITIES OF AXES        XP          YP

                    X         4.000      -0.000
                    Y        -0.000       4.000
                    Z        -3.277      -2.294
```

X	Y	Z	XP	YP
0.00000	1.00000	0.00000	-0.00000	1.00000
0.10000	1.12117	0.00476	0.09610	1.11844
0.20000	1.24456	0.01818	0.18511	1.23414
0.30000	1.37003	0.03913	0.26795	1.34759
0.40000	1.49745	0.06667	0.34539	1.45922
0.50000	1.62671	0.10000	0.41808	1.56935
0.60000	1.75770	0.13846	0.48658	1.67828
0.70000	1.89033	0.18148	0.55133	1.78625
0.80000	2.02454	0.22857	0.61276	1.89345
0.90000	2.16025	0.27931	0.67120	2.00005
1.00000	2.29740	0.33333	0.72694	2.10622
1.10000	2.43592	0.39032	0.78026	2.21205
1.20000	2.57577	0.45000	0.83137	2.31768
1.30000	2.71690	0.51212	0.88048	2.42317
1.40000	2.85925	0.57647	0.92777	2.52863
1.50000	3.00281	0.64286	0.97338	2.63410
1.60000	3.14751	0.71111	1.01747	2.73966
1.70000	3.29333	0.78108	1.06015	2.84535
1.80000	3.44024	0.85263	1.10154	2.95122
1.89999	3.58820	0.92564	1.14173	3.05731
1.99999	3.73718	1.00000	1.18082	3.16364
2.09999	3.88716	1.07560	1.21888	3.27026
2.19999	4.03812	1.15238	1.25599	3.37718
2.29999	4.19001	1.23023	1.29222	3.48443
2.39999	4.34283	1.30908	1.32762	3.59202
2.49999	4.49656	1.38888	1.36225	3.69998
2.59999	4.65116	1.46956	1.39616	3.80831
2.69999	4.80663	1.55105	1.42940	3.91704
2.79999	4.96294	1.63332	1.46201	4.02616
2.89999	5.12007	1.71632	1.49402	4.13569
2.99999	5.27801	1.79999	1.52548	4.24565

7-27.

```
      DIMENSION IA(80)
      DATA ICOM,IPER,IBLK/','.'.',' '/
      READ(5,1)IA
    1 FORMAT(80A1)
      N=0
      DO 2 I=1,80
      IF(IA(I).EQ.IPER) GO TO 3
```

```
      IF(IA(I).EQ.ICOM.OR.IA(I).EQ.IBLK) GO TO 2
      N=N+1
    2 CONTINUE
    3 WRITE(6,4)N
    4 FORMAT(' SENTENCE CONTAINS',I3,' CHARACTERS')
      STOP
      END
```

Input

```
AN IMPORTANT CHARACTERISTIC OF DIGITAL COMPUTERS IS THEIR INCREDIBLE SPEED.
```

Output

```
SENTENCE CONTAINS 65 CHARACTERS
```

7-34.

```
      DIMENSION IA(800),N(12)
      DATA N/12*0/
      DATA IBLK,IPER,ICOM/' ','.',','/
      READ(5,1)IA
 1    FORMAT(80A1)
      I=1
 3    IF(I.GT.800)GOTO4
      IF(IA(I).NE.IBLK)GOTO2
      I=I+1
      GOTO3
 2    NC=1
 6    I=I+1
      IF(IA(I).EQ.IBLK)GOTO5
      IF(IA(I).EQ.IPER)GOTO5
      IF(IA(I).EQ.ICOM)GOTO5
      NC=NC+1
      GOTO6
 5    IF(NC.GT.12)NC=12
      N(NC)=N(NC)+1
      I=I+1
      GOTO3
 4    WRITE(6,7) (I,N(I),I=1,12)
 7    FORMAT('1WORD LENGTH DISTRIBUTION'/'0CHS,/WORD      OCCURRENCES'/
     $ 11(1X,I5,I16/),1X,I5,' OR MORE',I8)
      STOP
      END
```

Input

```
     INSTEAD OF PROCESSING A SINGLE SENTENCE, SUPPOSE WE PROCESS A
PARAGRAPH.  THE PARAGRAPH WILL BE PUNCHED ON A MAXIMUM OF TEN CARDS AS
ILLUSTRATED IN THE ACCOMPANYING FIGURE.  A BLANK CHARACTER ALWAYS FOLLOWS THE
DECIMAL POINT, AND NO HYPHENATED WORDS WILL BE USED.  FOR THIS EXERCISE, THE
PARAGRAPH SHOULD BE READ INTO A SINGLE ARRAY OF EIGHT HUNDRED ELEMENTS, ONE
CHARACTER TO THE ELEMENT.  COMPUTE THE AVERAGE NUMBER OF WORDS IN THE SENTENCES
IN THE PARAGRAPH AND PRINT THE ANSWER TO TWO DECIMAL PLACES.
```

Output

```
WORD LENGTH DISTRIBUTION

CHS./WORD       OCCURRENCES
    1                5
    2               16
    3               15
    4                6
    5                8
    6                8
    7               12
    8                3
    9                7
   10                2
   11                1
   12 OR MORE        1
```

7-35.

```
          DIMENSION IA(80)
          DATA IBLK,IPER/' ','.'/
          NWDS=0
          NSEN=0
          DO 7 I=1,10
          READ(5,1) IA
    1     FORMAT(80A1)
          JW=0
          J=1
    5     IF(IA(J).NE.IPER) GO TO 2
          IF(JW.NE.0) NWDS=NWDS+1
          NSEN=NSEN+1
          GO TO 3
    2     IF(IA(J).EQ.IBLK) GO TO 4
          JW=1
          GO TO 3
    4     IF(JW.EQ.1) NWDS=NWDS+1
          JW=0
    3     J=J+1
          IF(J.LE.80) GO TO 5
    7     IF(JW.EQ.1) NWDS=NWDS+1
          AVG=FLOAT(NWDS)/FLOAT(NSEN)
          WRITE(6,6) AVG
    6     FORMAT('0AVERAGE WORDS PER SENTENCE =',F10.2)
          STOP
          END
```

Input

```
     INSTEAD OF PROCESSING A SINGLE SENTENCE, SUPPOSE WE PROCESS A
PARAGRAPH.  THE PARAGRAPH WILL BE PUNCHED ON A MAXIMUM OF TEN CARDS AS
ILLUSTRATED IN THE ACCOMPANYING FIGURE.  A BLANK CHARACTER ALWAYS FOLLOWS THE
DECIMAL POINT, AND NO HYPHENATED WORDS WILL BE USED.  FOR THIS EXERCISE, THE
PARAGRAPH SHOULD BE READ INTO A SINGLE ARRAY OF EIGHT HUNDRED ELEMENTS, ONE
CHARACTER TO THE ELEMENT.  COMPUTE THE AVERAGE NUMBER OF WORDS IN THE SENTENCES
IN THE PARAGRAPH AND PRINT THE ANSWER TO TWO DECIMAL PLACES.
```

Output

```
AVERAGE WORDS PER SENTENCE =      17.80
```

7-41.

```
      DIMENSION IDIG(10),IA(80)
      DATA IBLK,IDIG,IPLS,IMIN/' ','0','1','2','3','4','5','6','7','8','
     19','+','-'/
      READ(5,1) IA
    1 FORMAT(80A1)
      IDG=0
      NUM=0
      J=0
    3 J=J+1
      IF(J.GT.80) GO TO 2
      IF(IA(J).EQ.IBLK) GO TO 3
      IS=+1
      IF(IA(J).NE.IMIN) GO TO 4
      IS=-1
      J=J+1
      GO TO 5
    4 IF(IA(J).EQ.IPLS) J=J+1
    5 IF(J.GT.80) GO TO 6
      DO 7 I=1,10
      IF(IA(J).EQ.IDIG(I)) GO TO 8
    7 CONTINUE
      IF(IA(J).NE.IBLK) GO TO 9
      IF(IDG.EQ.0) GO TO 9
   12 NUM=NUM*IS
      WRITE(6,10) NUM
   10 FORMAT('0VALUE =',I10)
      STOP
    2 WRITE(6,11)
   11 FORMAT('0BLANK CARD')
      STOP
    6 IF(IDG.NE.0) GO TO 12
    9 WRITE(6,13) IA,J
   13 FORMAT(6X,80A1/6X,'INVALID CHARACTER NEAR COLUMN',I3)
      STOP
    8 NUM=NUM*10+I-1
      IDG=1
      J=J+1
      GO TO 5
      END
```

Input

```
+154678
```

Output

```
VALUE =     154678
```

Chapter 8

8-1.

```
C       DEFINITION OF F(X)
C
        F(X)=((X-1.)*X-1.)*X-1.9
C
C       READ LIMITS
C
        READ(5,1)A,B
C
C       ITERATION TO LOCATE ROOT
C
        C=(A+B)/2.
        DO2I=1,20
        IF(F(C))3,4,5
   3    A=C
        GOTO2
   5    B=C
   2    C=(A+B)/2.
C
C       ROOT IS FOUND
C
   4    WRITE(6,7)C
        STOP
C
C       FORMAT STATEMENTS
C
   1    FORMAT(2F10.0)
   7    FORMAT(1X,F15.4)
        END
```

Input

```
0.          5.
```

Output

```
1.9856
```

8-4.

```
C       DEFINE F(X). WRITE HEADINGS,
C
        F(X)=X**2
        WRITE(6,1)
   1    FORMAT(39H0APPROXIMATION OF DERIVATIVE OF F(X) =
       *14HX**2 AT X = 1./
       *6X,26HTRUE DERIVATIVE = 2*X = 2./9X,1HH6X,
       *12HAPPROX, DER.)
C
C       READ H AND CALCULATE APPROXIMATION
C
   4    READ(5,2)H
   2    FORMAT(F5.0)
        DER=(F(1.+H)-F(1.))/H
```

```
           WRITE(6,3)H,DER
      3    FORMAT(5X,F8.4,F14.5)
           GOTO4
           ENC
```

Input

```
   1.
  0.5
  0.2
  0.1
 0.05
 0.02
 0.01
0.001
```

Output

```
APPRCXIMATION CF CERIVATIVE CF F(X) = X**2 AT X = 1.
     TRUE CERIVATIVE = 2*X = 2.
        H         APPROX. DER.
     1.0000         3.00000
     0.5000         2.50000
     0.2000         2.19999
     0.1000         2.09998
     0.0500         2.04996
     0.0200         2.01993
     0.0100         2.00977
     0.0010         1.99986
```

8-7.

```
C         DEFINE F(X)
C
          F(X)=1.+X**2
C
C         READ NUMBER OF INCREMENTS AND CALCULATE
C         STEP SIZE
C
     1    READ(5,2)NINC
          DELX=2./FLCAT(NINC)
C
C         NUMERICAL INTEGRATION
C
          SUM=(F(0.)+F(2.))*DELX/2.
          X=CELX
          DO3I=2,NINC
          SUM=SUM+F(X)*CELX
     3    X=X+DELX
C
C         WRITE RESULTS
C
          WRITE(6,4)NINC,SUM
          GOTO1
C
C         FORMAT STATEMENTS
C
     2    FORMAT(I5)
     4    FORMAT(1X,I5,F15.4)
          ENC
```

Input

```
   4
  10
  20
  50
 100
1000
```

Output

```
   4        4.7500
  10        4.6800
  20        4.6700
  50        4.6672
 100        4.6667
1000        4.6662
```

8-10.

```
C     DEFINE DC(C)
C
      DC(C)=1.-C
C
C     READ NINC AND CALCULATE DT
C
      TSOL=1.-EXP(-1.)
    1 READ(5,4)NINC
      DT=1./FLOAT(NINC)
C
C     NUMERICAL INTEGRATION
C
      C=0.
      DO2I=1,NINC
      AK1=DC(C)
      AK2=DC(C+DT*AK1/2.)
      AK3=DC(C+DT*AK2/2.)
      AK4=DC(C+DT*AK3)
    2 C=C+DT*(AK1+2.*AK2+2.*AK3+AK4)/6.
C
C     OUTPUT
C
      WRITE(6,3)NINC,C,TSOL
      GOTO1
C
C     FORMAT STATEMENTS
C
    4 FORMAT(I5)
    3 FORMAT(1XI5,2F15.4)
      END
```

Input

```
   4
  10
  20
  50
 100
1000
```

Output

```
   4         0.6321         0.6321
  10         0.6321         0.6321
  20         0.6321         0.6321
  50         0.6321         0.6321
 100         0.6321         0.6321
1000         0.6321         0.6321
```

8-14.

```
      DIMENSION A(51)
C
C     READ INPUT,CALL FUNC,AND WRITE RESULTS
C
      READ(5,1)N,(A(I),I=1,N),A(N+1),B
    1 FORMAT(I5/(F10.0))
      R=FUNC(A,N,B)
      WRITE(6,2)B,R
    2 FORMAT(3H0F(F10.4,3H) =F15.4)
      STOP
      END

      FUNCTION FUNC(A,N,B)
C
C     EVALUATION OF F(B)
C
      DIMENSION A(51)
      FUNC=A(1)
      DO1I=1,N
    1 FUNC=FUNC+A(I+1)*B**I
      RETURN
      END
```

Input

```
4
  1.0
  1.2
  1.7
  1.9
  0.8
  2.2
```

Output

```
F(     2.2000) =          50.8396
```

8-16.

```
      DIMENSION X(50),Y(50),XX(50),XY(50),PRED(50)
C
C     READ INPUT AND COMPUTE X*X AND X*Y
C
      READ(5,1)N,(X(I),Y(I),I=1,N)
    1 FORMAT(I5/(2F10.0))
      DO2I=1,N
      XX(I)=X(I)**2
    2 XY(I)=X(I)*Y(I)
C
C     COMPUTE CORRECTED SUMS AND CROSS PRODUCTS
C
```

```
      CSCP=SUM(XY,N,50)-SUM(X,N,50)*SUM(Y,N,50)/FLOAT(N)
      CSS=SUM(XX,N,50)-SUM(X,N,50)**2/FLOAT(N)
C
C     COMPUTE COEFFICIENTS AND PREDICTED VALUES
C
      B=CSCP/CSS
      A=(SUM(Y,N,50)-B*SUM(X,N,50))/FLOAT(N)
      DO7I=1,N
    7 PRED(I)=A+B*X(I)
C
C     OUTPUT
C
      WRITE(6,6)A,B,(I,X(I),Y(I),PRED(I),I=1,N)
    6 FORMAT(17X,17HLEAST SQUARES FIT// 8X,5HY = (1PE12.5,
     *5HX + (E12.5,1H)//6X,3HOBS,8X,1HX,12X,1HY,8X,9HPREDICTED
     *//(1X,I7,0P3F13.3))
      STOP
      END

      FUNCTION SUM(A,N,M)
C
C     SUMS AN ARRAY
C
      DIMENSION A(M)
      SUM=0.
      DO1I=1,N
    1 SUM=SUM+A(I)
      RETURN
      END
```

Input

```
5
  1.716      3.021
  5.911     10.819
  3.726      7.502
  9.123     17.801
  4.022      7.688
```

Output

```
                 LEAST SQUARES FIT

        Y = (-2.23407E-01X + ( 1.95722E 00)

      OBS          X            Y         PREDICTED

        1        1.716        3.021         3.135
        2        5.911       10.819        11.346
        3        3.726        7.502         7.069
        4        9.123       17.801        17.632
        5        4.022        7.688         7.649
```

8-20.

```
      DIMENSION A(50),B(50)
C     READ INPUT,CALL DOT,AND WRITE RESULTS
      READ(5,1)N,(A(I),I=1,N),(B(I),I=1,N)
      R=DOT(A,B,N)
      WRITE(6,2)R
    1 FORMAT(I5/(F10.0))
```

```
    2     FORMAT(14H0DOT PRODUCT =F15.7)
          STOP
          END

          FUNCTION DOT(A,B,N)
    C     COMPUTES DOT PRODUCT OF A AND B
          DIMENSION A(50),B(50)
          DOT=0.
          DO1I=1,N
    1     DOT=DOT+A(I)*B(I)
          RETURN
          END
```

Input

```
4
     4.
     0.
     7.
     2.
    -1.
     2.
     1.
    -2.
```

Output

```
DOT PRODUCT =         -1.0000000
```

8-23.

```
          DIMENSION A(50),B(50),C(50),D(50)
    C
    C     READ INPUT
    C
          READ(5,1)N,(A(I),I=1,N),(B(I),I=1,N),(C(I),I=1,N)
     1    FORMAT(I5/(F10.0))
    C
    C     COMPUTE D AND WRITE RESULTS
    C
          CALL SCALAR(C,DOT(A,B,N),D,N)
          WRITE(6,2)(I,D(I),I=1,N)
     2    FORMAT(14H0ELEMENTS OF D/(1XI10,F15.4))
          STOP
          END

          FUNCTION DOT(A,B,N)
    C
    C     COMPUTES DOT PRODUCT OF A AND B
    C
          DIMENSION A(50),B(50)
          DOT=0.
          DO1I=1,N
     1    DOT=DOT+A(I)*B(I)
          RETURN
          END

          SUBROUTINE SCALAR(A,C,B,N)
    C
    C     MULTIPLIES ARRAY A BY SCALAR C TO OBTAIN
    C     ARRAY B
```

```
      C
            DIMENSION A(50),B(50)
            DO1I=1,N
          1 B(I)=A(I)*C
            RETURN
            END
```

Input

```
4
   1.
   0.
   4.
   2.
   7.
  -3.
   2.
   1.
   2.
   2.
  -2.
   7.
```

Output

```
ELEMENTS OF D
          1          34.0000
          2          34.0000
          3         -34.0000
          4         119.0000
```

8-26.

```
            DIMENSION A(20,20)
      C
      C     READ INPUT,CALL TRANS,AND WRITE RESULTS
      C
            READ(5,1)N,((A(I,J),J=1,4),I=1,4)
          1 FORMAT(I5/(4F10.0))
            CALL TRANS(A,N)
            WRITE(6,2)((A(I,J),J=1,4),I=1,4)
          2 FORMAT(17H0TRANSPOSE MATRIX/(1H 4F15.4))
            STOP
            END

            SUBROUTINE TRANS(A,N)
      C
      C     TAKES TRANSPOSE OF A
      C
            DIMENSION A(20,20)
            NN=N-1
            DO3I=1,NN
            K=I+1
            DO3J=K,N
            TEMP=A(I,J)
            A(I,J)=A(J,I)
          3 A(J,I)=TEMP
            RETURN
            END
```

Input

```
4
      1.          2.          0.          5.
     -1.          3.          7.          1.
      0.         -5.          1.          4.
      8.         -9.          0.          0.
```

Output

```
TRANSPOSE MATRIX
          1.0000          -1.0000           0.0000           8.0000
          2.0000           3.0000          -5.0000          -9.0000
          0.0000           7.0000           1.0000           0.0000
          5.0000           1.0000           4.0000           0.0000
```

8-29.

```
            DIMENSION A(25,25),B(25,25),C(25,25),FMT(20)
      C
      C     READ INPUT
      C
            READ(5,1)N,K,M
        1   FORMAT(3I5)
            READ(5,2)FMT
        2   FORMAT(20A4)
            READ(5,FMT)((A(I,J),J=1,K),I=1,N)
            READ(5,2)FMT
            READ(5,FMT)((B(I,J),J=1,M),I=1,K)
      C
      C     MULTIPLY AND WRITE RESULTS
      C
            CALL MTXMPY(A,B,C,N,K,M)
            READ(5,2)FMT
            WRITE(6,FMT)((C(I,J),J=1,M),I=1,N)
            STOP
            END

            SUBROUTINE MTXMPY(A,B,C,N,K,M)
      C
      C     MULTIPLIES A AND B
      C
            DIMENSION A(25,25),B(25,25),C(25,25)
            DO5I=1,N
            DO5J=1,M
            C(I,J)=0.
            DO5L=1,K
        5   C(I,J)=C(I,J)+A(I,L)*B(L,J)
            RETURN
            END
```

Input

```
    3    4    2
(4F10.0)
          1.          0.         -2.          4.
          2.          1.          7.          3.
          5.         -2.          0.          0.
```

```
(2F10.0)
        1.        2.
        2.        0.
        0.        7.
        3.        6.
(1H 2F15.4)
```

Output

```
13.0000         12.0000
13.0000         71.0000
 1.0000         10.0000
```

8-32.

```
      DIMENSION A(20,20),B(20),X(20),FMT(20)
C
C     READ INPUT
C
      READ(5,1)N,FMT
    1 FORMAT(I5/20A4)
      READ(5,FMT)((A(I,J),J=1,N),I=1,N),(B(I),I=1,N)
C
C     GAUSS REDUCTION
C
      CALL GAUSS(A,B,N,20)
C
C     SOLUTION
C
      CALL SOLVE(A,B,X,N,20)
C
C     OUTPUT
C
      WRITE(6,2)(I,X(I),I=1,N)
    2 FORMAT(9H0SOLUTION/(3H X(I3,3H) =F15.4))
      STOP
      END

      SUBROUTINE SOLVE(A,B,X,N,MM)
C
C     SOLUTION OF EQUATIONS
C
      DIMENSION A(MM,MM),B(MM),X(MM)
      X(1)=B(1)/A(1,1)
      DO2I=2,N
      M=I-1
      SUM=B(I)
      DO3J=1,M
    3 SUM=SUM-A(I,J)*X(J)
    2 X(I)=SUM/A(I,I)
      RETURN
      END

      SUBROUTINE GAUSS(A,B,N,MM)
C
C     PERFORMS GAUSS REDUCTION
C
      DIMENSION A(MM,MM),B(MM)
```

```
          NN=N-1
          DO5I=1,NN
          J=N+1-I
          L=J-1
          DO6K=1,L
          FACT=A(K,J)/A(J,J)
          DO7M=1,J
    7     A(K,M)=A(K,M)-FACT*A(J,M)
    6     B(K)=B(K)-FACT*B(J)
    5     CONTINUE
          RETURN
          END
```

Input

```
    3
(3F10.0)
         3.          4.          1.
         1.          4.         -2.
         2.          1.          1.
         4.          0.          1.
```

Output

```
SOLUTION

X(   1) =         -1.3333
X(   2) =          1.4444
X(   3) =          2.2222
```

Appendix **F**

WATFOR and WATFIV

Users of computing equipment fall into two categories: expert programmers and poor programmers. Members of the second category are by far the more numerous, encompassing most computer users who view the comptuer only as a tool to obtain numerical solutions to numerical problems in their field of interest. To best serve their needs, the Fortran compilers should possess two characteristics: fast compilation, which means the computer center can potentially give them fast turnarounds (especially for debugging), and excellent error detection capabilities, both during compilation and during execution.

To meet these requirements a compiler named WATFIV, pronounced "what five," has been developed by the Department of Applied Analysis and Computer Science, University of Waterloo. Chronologically, WATFIV is an extension of WATFOR, pronounced "what for," which was developed in 1965 for the IBM 7040 and extended to the IBM 360 in 1967. WATFIV appeared in 1969, and essentially is a more powerful version of WATFOR. WATFIV has now almost completely replaced WATFOR, and WATFIV will receive our prime attention in this appendix. WATFIV is a Fortran IV compiler, but a few aspects of the basic language are especially useful. One of these, format-free input-output feature permits the READ, PRINT, and PUNCH statements to be used *without* a FORMAT statement.

This appendix seeks to accomplish three objectives: describe some aspects of WATFIV, discuss the control cards, and present the error codes for WATFIV.

F-1. Special Aspects

The items to be presented here are only those items which are not covered completely in the regular sequence of this text and which are thought to be most useful to beginning programmers. Except as noted, they apply to both WATFOR and WATFIV. For other facets of these compilers, the student should consult his computer center's reference manuals on these special compilers.

Format-Free Input-Output. Since one of the most perplexing features to the beginning student of Fortran is the FORMAT statement, the format-free input-output feature of the language is very useful. This is first introduced in Chapter 3. The format-free input-output feature permits the READ, PRINT, and PUNCH statements to be used *without* a FORMAT statement.

First consider the format-free READ statement, which takes the following form:

READ, *variable list*

Note that a comma separates the word READ from the variable list, and no FORMAT statement number or device number appears, the latter normally assumed to be a card reader. As an example, the statement

```
READ, A,B,N,C
```

would cause the reading of values for the variables A, B, N, and C. Execution of this READ statement would cause a card to be read and scanned for these values. The numerical values for these variables should be punched on this card or succeeding cards in the order in which they appear in the READ statement, i.e., the value for A followed by the value for B, etc. The values may be punched anywhere on the card, but successive values should be separated by one or more blanks or by a comma. If the values for all variables in the READ statement are not found on the first card, another card is read and scanned. This process is continued until all values have been read. This permits entry of data with one value per data card, if desired. Floating-point constants may be punched in either decimal or exponential format.

As an example, data for the previous READ statement may appear on one data card in any of the following ways:

```
1.7    0.0012    5    99.8
1.7,   0.0012,   5,   99.8
1.7,   1.2E-3    5,   9.98E1
1.7    12.E-4    5    99.8
```

Blank cards are completely ignored, and thus may be placed anywhere in the data deck.

Next, consider use of the format-free PRINT statement, whose general form is

PRINT, *variable list*

Again, only a comma follows the word PRINT. The values of the variables in the output list are printed across the page. Each value is printed to full precision with spaces inserted between values for clarity. Eight values are normally printed across the page, but this varies with computer installations. Real (floating-point) numbers are printed in exponential form with seven significant figures. For example, suppose the variables entered with the above READ statement are printed with the statements

```
PRINT, N,A
PRINT, B,C
```

The output would appear as follows:

```
             5     0.1700000 E 01
0.1200000E-02     0.9980000 E 02
```

If the PRINT statement contains more values than can be printed on one line, output is continued on the following line.

Rules for the PUNCH statement are analogous to those for the PRINT statement.

Expressions in Output Lists. The WATFOR and WATFIV compilers permit expressions to be used in output lists. Only the results of these expressions are printed. Functions may be freely used in these expressions. For example, the following statement is entirely valid:

```
PRINT, X,Y,I + J, A/SQRT(B)
```

Only four values are printed. One restriction must be observed: the expression must not begin with an open parenthesis.‡ That is, the expression (I + J)/2 must be written as + (I + J)/2, making the PRINT statement

```
PRINT, + (I + J)/2
```

It is also possible for constants to appear in output lists, for example

```
PRINT, 2
```

This statement causes the integer 2 to be printed. This feature is helpful in debugging.

WATFIV also permits explanatory messages to be written with format-free input-output statements. For example, the statement

```
PRINT, 'THE SQUARE ROOT OF' ,A, 'IS' ,SQRT (A)
```

gives the output

```
THE SQUARE ROOT OF 0.4000000E 01 IS 0.2000000E 01
```

Extended Assignment Statement. Statements of this type permit more than one variable to be assigned a value in a single Fortran statement. Examples are

```
SUMA = SUM = A = 0.
I = J = 1
A = B = C = D = SQRT(1. - X ** 2)
```

In the first example, the three variables SUMA, SUM, and A are all assigned the value of zero. The other two statements function analogously.

When mixed expressions of the type

```
X = I = Y = 2.4
```

appear, the manner in which the compiler treats this statement is important. For this example, this statement is equivalent to the three statements

```
Y = 2.4
I = Y
X = I
```

Note that X is assigned the value 2.0 rather than 2.4. Precision may also be lost when integers appear in statements of the type

```
M = A = N = 123456789
```

When A is in single precision, only about seven of the nine digits are retained.

Multiple Statements per Card. One of the notable extensions of WATFIV over WATFOR and other Fortran IV compilers is that several statements may be punched on a single card. For statements without statement numbers, the successive statements are simply separated by semicolons. For example, the program

‡This indicates an implied DO to the compiler.

```
READ, A,B
C = A * SQRT(B)
PRINT, C
STOP
END
```

could be punched on one card as follows:

```
READ, A,B;C = A * SQRT(B); PRINT, C;STOP;END
```

Only columns 7-72 are used, although the normal rules for continuation cards still apply.

When statement numbers are used, they must either appear in columns 1-5 as usual or be separated from the Fortran statement by a colon. For example, the statements

```
22      SUM = 0.
        DO 32 J = 2,M
32      SUM = SUM + X(J)
```

could be punched

```
22      SUM = 0.;DO 32 J = 2,M;32:SUM = SUM + X(J)
```

Statement numbers may not be split onto a continuation card. Nor can FORMAT statements be punched in this manner.

Comment cards must also be punched in the conventional manner.

F-2. Control Cards

The program deck when using the WATFOR or WATFIV compiler appears as follows:

$JOB
{*Fortran program*}
$ENTRY
{*Data cards*}

The $JOB and $ENTRY cards are known as *control cards.* Both cards must be punched beginning in column 1, with no blank spaces. The $JOB card signifies to the compiler the beginning of the Fortran program, and the $ENTRY card signifies that execution is to begin. Both of these cards are usually available prepunched on colored cards from the computer center. WATFIV permits certain options to be obtained with entries in the $JOB card, but again the computer center should be consulted about the use of these.

F-3. Error Codes

The WATFOR and WATFIV compilers may generate error messages during either compilation or execution. At compile time, the compiler checks for violations of the rules of Fortran. During execution it checks for unreasonable situations that usually mean programming errors. Examples of such situations include undefined variables, value of subscript exceeding dimensioned size of array, etc. Few other compilers detect error of this type.

During compilation, three types of error messages may appear

1. Extension. These messages flag each use (other than format-free input-output) of one of the extensions of these compilers, since it is unlikely that other compilers will accept these statements.
2. Warning. These messages flag situations in which the compiler has encountered ambiguous code but has taken a predetermined course of action to generate executable code. For example, upon encounter of a variable name with more than six characters, the first six are used as the variable name and a VA-2 warning message is generated.
3. Error. An error message flags code that cannot be interpreted by the compiler. The error message appears with the print-out of the program, designates a particular error code, and in some cases gives other information relating to the source of the error.

The error codes for WATFOR and WATFIV are somewhat different. Since virtually all computer centers now use the WATFIV compiler exclusively (over WATFOR), the WATFIV error codes are reproduced on the following pages for convenience.‡

WATFIV *compiler error messages*

```
'ASSEMBLER LANGUAGE SUBPROGRAMMES'
AL-0    'MISSING END CARD ON ASSEMBLY-LANGUAGE OBJECT DECK'
AL-1    'ENTRY-POINT OR CSECT NAME IN AN OBJECT DECK WAS PREVIOUSLY
        DEFINED.FIRST DEFINITION USED'

'BLOCK DATA STATEMENTS'
BD-0    'EXECUTABLE STATEMENTS ARE ILLEGAL IN BLOCK DATA SUBPROGRAMS'
BD-1    'IMPROPER BLOCK DATA STATEMENT'

'CARD FORMAT AND CONTENTS'
CC-0    'COLUMNS 1-5 OF CONTINUATION CARD ARE NOT BLANK.
        PROBABLE CAUSE:STATEMENT PUNCHED TO LEFT OF COLUMN 7'
CC-1    'LIMIT OF 5 CONTINUATION CARDS EXCEEDED'
CC-2    'INVALID CHARACTER IN FORTRAN STATEMENT.
         A '$' WAS INSERTED IN THE SOURCE LISTING'
CC-3    'FIRST CARD OF A PROGRAM IS A CONTINUATION CARD.
        PROBABLE CAUSE:STATEMENT PUNCHED TO LEFT OF COLUMN 7'
CC-4    'STATEMENT TOO LONG TO COMPILE (SCAN-STACK OVERFLOW)'
CC-5    'A BLANK CARD WAS ENCOUNTERED'
CC-6    'KEYPUNCH USED DIFFERS FROM KEYPUNCH SPECIFIED ON JOB CARD'
CC-7    'THE FIRST CHARACTER OF THE STATEMENT WAS NOT ALPHABETIC'
CC-8    'INVALID CHARACTER(S) ARE CONCATENATED WITH THE FORTRAN KEYWORD'
CC-9    'INVALID CHARACTERS IN COLUMNS 1-5.STATEMENT NUMBER IGNORED.
        PROBABLE CAUSE:STATEMENT PUNCHED TO LEFT OF COLUMN 7'

'COMMON'
CM-0    'THE VARIABLE IS ALREADY IN COMMON'
CM-1    'OTHER COMPILERS MAY NOT ALLOW COMMONED VARIABLES TO BE INITIALIZED IN
        OTHER THAN A BLOCK DATA SUBPROGRAM'
CM-2    'ILLEGAL USE OF A COMMON BLOCK OR NAMELIST NAME'
```

‡WATFIV error codes have been reproduced by permission from "/360 WATFIV Implementation Guide," Department of Applied Analysis and Computer Science, University of Waterloo, Waterloo, Ontario, Sepetember 1969.

WATFIV *compiler error messages (Continued)*

```
'FORTRAN TYPE CONSTANTS'
CN-0    'MIXED REAL*4,REAL*8 IN COMPLEX CONSTANT:REAL*8 ASSUMED FOR BOTH'
CN-1    'AN INTEGER CONSTANT MAY NOT BE GREATER THAN 2,147,483,647 (2**31-1)'
CN-2    'THE EXPONENT OF A REAL CONSTANT IS GREATER THAN 99,THE MAXIMUM'
CN-3    'A REAL CONSTANT HAS MORE THAN 16 DIGITS.IT WAS TRUNCATED TO 16'
CN-4    'INVALID HEXADECIMAL CONSTANT'
CN-5    'ILLEGAL USE OF A DECIMAL POINT'
CN-6    'CONSTANT WITH E-TYPE EXPONENT HAS MORE THAN 7 DIGITS, D-TYPE ASSUMED'
CN-7    'CONSTANT OR STATEMENT NUMBER GREATER THAN 99999'
CN-8    'AN EXPONENT OVERFLOW OR UNDERFLOW OCCURRED WHILE CONVERTING A CONSTANT
        IN A SOURCE STATEMENT'

'COMPILER ERRORS'
CP-0    'A COMPILER ERROR WAS DETECTED IN DECK LANDR'
CP-1    'COMPILER ERROR.LIKELY CAUSE:MORE THAN 255 DO STATEMENTS'
CP-2    'A COMPILER ERROR WAS DETECTED IN DECK ARITH'
CP-4    'COMPILER ERROR - INTERRUPT AT COMPILE TIME,RETURN TO SYSTEM'

'CHARACTER VARIABLE'
CV-0    'A CHARACTER VARIABLE IS USED WITH A RELATIONAL OPERATOR'
CV-1    'LENGTH OF A CHARACTER VALUE ON RIGHT OF EQUAL SIGN EXCEEDS THAT ON
        LEFT. TRUNCATION WILL OCCUR'

'DATA STATEMENT'
DA-0    'REPLICATION FACTOR IS ZERO OR GREATER THAN 32767.
        IT IS ASSUMED TO BE 32767'
DA-1    'MORE VARIABLES THAN CONSTANTS'
DA-2    'ATTEMPT TO INITIALIZE A SUBPROGRAM PARAMETER IN A DATA STATEMENT'
DA-3    'OTHER COMPILERS MAY NOT ALLOW NON-CONSTANT SUBSCRIPTS IN DATA
        STATEMENTS'
DA-4    'NON-AGREEMENT BETWEEN TYPE OF VARIABLE AND CONSTANT'
DA-5    'MORE CONSTANTS THAN VARIABLES'
DA-6    'A VARIABLE WAS PREVIOUSLY INITIALIZED.THE LATEST VALUE IS USED.
        CHECK COMMONED AND EQUIVALENCED VARIABLES'
DA-7    'OTHER COMPILERS MAY NOT ALLOW INITIALIZATION OF BLANK COMMON'
DA-8    'A LITERAL CONSTANT HAS BEEN TRUNCATED'
DA-9    'OTHER COMPILERS MAY NOT ALLOW IMPLIED DO-LOOPS IN DATA STATEMENTS'

'DEFINE FILE STATEMENTS'
DF-0    'THE UNIT NUMBER IS MISSING'
DF-1    'INVALID FORMAT TYPE'
DF-2    'THE ASSOCIATED VARIABLE IS NOT A SIMPLE INTEGER VARIABLE'

'DIMENSION STATEMENTS'
DM-0    'NO DIMENSIONS ARE SPECIFIED FOR A VARIABLE IN A DIMENSION STATEMENT'
DM-1    'THE VARIABLE HAS ALREADY BEEN DIMENSIONED'
DM-2    'CALL-BY-LOCATION PARAMETERS MAY NOT BE DIMENSIONED'
DM-3    'THE DECLARED SIZE OF ARRAY EXCEEDS SPACE PROVIDED BY CALLING ARGUMENT'

'DO LOOPS'
DO-0    'THIS STATEMENT CANNOT BE THE OBJECT OF A DO-LOOP'
DO-1    'ILLEGAL TRANSFER INTO THE RANGE OF A DO-LOOP'
DO-2    'THE OBJECT OF THIS DO-LOOP HAS ALREADY APPEARED'
DO-3    'IMPROPERLY NESTED DO-LOOPS'
DO-4    'ATTEMPT TO REDEFINE A DO-LOOP PARAMETER WITHIN THE RANGE OF THE LOOP'
DO-5    'INVALID DO-LOOP PARAMETER'
DO-6    'ILLEGAL TRANSFER TO A STATEMENT WHICH IS INSIDE THE RANGE OF A DO-LOOP'
DO-7    'A DO-LOOP PARAMETER IS UNDEFINED OR OUT OF RANGE'
DO-8    'BECAUSE OF ONE OF THE PARAMETERS,THIS DO-LOOP WILL TERMINATE AFTER THE
        FIRST TIME THROUGH'
DO-9    'A DO-LOOP PARAMETER MAY NOT BE REDEFINED IN AN INPUT LIST'
DO-A    'OTHER COMPILERS MAY NOT ALLOW THIS STATEMENT TO END A DO-LOOP'
```

WATFIV *compiler error messages (Continued)*

```
'EQUIVALENCE AND/OR COMMON'
EC-0   'EQUIVALENCED VARIABLE APPEARS IN A COMMON STATEMENT'
EC-1   'A COMMON BLOCK HAS A DIFFERENT LENGTH THAN IN A PREVIOUS
       SUBPROGRAM:GREATER LENGTH USED'
EC-2   'COMMON AND/OR EQUIVALENCE CAUSES INVALID ALIGNMENT.
       EXECUTION SLOWED.REMEDY:ORDER VARIABLES BY DECREASING LENGTH'
EC-3   'EQUIVALENCE EXTENDS COMMON DOWNWARDS'
EC-4   'A SUBPROGRAM PARAMETER APPEARS IN A COMMON OR EQUIVALENCE STATEMENT'
EC-5   'A VARIABLE WAS USED WITH SUBSCRIPTS IN AN EQUIVALENCE STATEMENT BUT HAS
       NOT BEEN PROPERLY DIMENSIONED'

'END STATEMENTS'
EN-0   'MISSING END STATEMENT:END STATEMENT GENERATED'
EN-1   'AN END STATEMENT WAS USED TO TERMINATE EXECUTION'

'EQUAL SIGNS'
EQ-0   'ILLEGAL QUANTITY ON LEFT OF EQUALS SIGN'
EQ-1   'ILLEGAL USE OF EQUAL SIGN'
EQ-2   'OTHER COMPILERS MAY NOT ALLOW MULTIPLE ASSIGNMENT STATEMENTS'
EQ-3   'MULTIPLE ASSIGNMENT IS NOT IMPLEMENTED FOR CHARACTER VARIABLES'

'EQUIVALENCE STATEMENTS'
EV-0   'ATTEMPT TO EQUIVALENCE A VARIABLE TO ITSELF'
EV-2   'A MULTI-SUBSCRIPTED EQUIVALENCED VARIABLE HAS BEEN INCORRECTLY
       RE-EQUIVALENCED.REMEDY:DIMENSION THE VARIABLE FIRST'

'POWERS AND EXPONENTIATION'
EX-0   'ILLEGAL COMPLEX EXPONENTIATION'
EX-1   'I**J WHERE I=J=0'
EX-2   'I**J WHERE I=0, J.LT.0'
EX-3   '0.0**Y WHERE Y.LE.0.0'
EX-4   '0.0**J WHERE J=0'
EX-5   '0.0**J WHERE J.LT.0'
EX-6   'X**Y WHERE X.LT.0.0, Y.NE.0.0'

'ENTRY STATEMENT'
EY-0   'ENTRY-POINT NAME WAS PREVIOUSLY DEFINED'
EY-1   'PREVIOUS DEFINITION OF FUNCTION NAME IN AN ENTRY IS INCORRECT'
EY-2   'THE USAGE OF A SUBPROGRAM PARAMETER IS INCONSISTENT WITH A PREVIOUS
       ENTRY-POINT'
EY-3   'A PARAMETER HAS APPEARED IN A EXECUTABLE STATEMENT BUT IS NOT A
       SUBPROGRAM PARAMETER'
EY-4   'ENTRY STATEMENTS ARE INVALID IN THE MAIN PROGRAM'
EY-5   'ENTRY STATEMENT INVALID INSIDE A DO-LOOP'

'FORMAT'
   SOME FORMAT ERROR MESSAGES GIVE CHARACTERS IN WHICH ERROR WAS DETECTED
FM-0   'IMPROPER CHARACTER SEQUENCE OR INVALID CHARACTER IN INPUT DATA'
FM-1   'NO STATEMENT NUMBER ON A FORMAT STATEMENT'
FM-2   'FORMAT CODE AND DATA TYPE DO NOT MATCH'
FM-4   'FORMAT PROVIDES NO CONVERSION SPECIFICATION FOR A VALUE IN I/O LIST'
FM-5   'AN INTEGER IN THE INPUT DATA IS TOO LARGE.
         (MAXIMUM=2,147,483,647=2**31-1)'
FM-6   'A REAL NUMBER IN THE INPUT DATA IS OUT OF MACHINE RANGE (1.E-78,1.E+75)'
FT-0   'FIRST CHARACTER OF VARIABLE FORMAT IS NOT A LEFT PARENTHESIS'
FT-1   'INVALID CHARACTER ENCOUNTERED IN FORMAT'
FT-2   'INVALID FORM FOLLOWING A FORMAT CODE'
FT-3   'INVALID FIELD OR GROUP COUNT'
FT-4   'A FIELD OR GROUP COUNT GREATER THAN 255'
FT-5   'NO CLOSING PARENTHESIS ON VARIABLE FORMAT'
FT-6   'NO CLOSING QUOTE IN A HOLLERITH FIELD'
```

WATFIV *compiler error messages (Continued)*

```
FT-7    'INVALID USE OF COMMA'
FT-8    'FORMAT STATEMENT TOO LONG TO COMPILE (SCAN-STACK OVERFLOW)'
FT-9    'INVALID USE OF P FORMAT CODE'
FT-A    'INVALID USE OF PERIOD(.)'
FT-B    'MORE THAN THREE LEVELS OF PARENTHESES'
FT-C    'INVALID CHARACTER BEFORE A RIGHT PARENTHESIS'
FT-D    'MISSING OR ZERO LENGTH HOLLERITH ENCOUNTERED'
FT-E    'NO CLOSING RIGHT PARENTHESIS'
FT-F    'CHARACTERS FOLLOW CLOSING RIGHT PARENTHESIS'
FT-G    'WRONG QUOTE USED FOR KEY-PUNCH SPECIFIED'
FT-H    'LENGTH OF HOLLERITH EXCEEDS 255'

'FUNCTIONS AND SUBROUTINES'
FN-1    'A PARAMETER APPEARS MORE THAN ONCE IN A SUBPROGRAM OR STATEMENT
        FUNCTION DEFINITION'
FN-2    'SUBSCRIPTS ON RIGHT-HAND SIDE OF STATEMENT FUNCTION.
         PROBABLE CAUSE:VARIABLE TO LEFT OF EQUAL SIGN NOT DIMENSIONED'
FN-3    'MULTIPLE RETURNS ARE INVALID IN FUNCTION SUBPROGRAMS'
FN-4    'ILLEGAL LENGTH MODIFIER'
FN-5    'INVALID PARAMETER'
FN-6    'A PARAMETER HAS THE SAME NAME AS THE SUBPROGRAM'

'GO TO STATEMENTS'
GO-0    'THIS STATEMENT COULD TRANSFER TO ITSELF'
GO-1    'THIS STATEMENT TRANSFERS TO A NON-EXECUTABLE STATEMENT'
GO-2    'ATTEMPT TO DEFINE ASSIGNED GOTO INDEX IN AN ARITHMETIC STATEMENT'
GO-3    'ASSIGNED GOTO INDEX MAY BE USED ONLY IN ASSIGNED GOTO AND ASSIGN
        STATEMENTS'
GO-4    'THE INDEX OF AN ASSIGNED GOTO IS UNDEFINED OR OUT OF RANGE,OR INDEX OF
        COMPUTED GOTO IS UNDEFINED'
GO-5    'ASSIGNED GOTO INDEX MAY NOT BE AN INTEGER*2 VARIABLE'

'HOLLERITH CONSTANTS'
HO-0    'ZERO LENGTH SPECIFIED FOR H-TYPE HOLLERITH'
HO-1    'ZERO LENGTH QUOTE-TYPE HOLLERITH'
HO-2    'NO CLOSING QUOTE OR NEXT CARD NOT A CONTINUATION CARD'
HO-3    'UNEXPECTED HOLLERITH OR STATEMENT NUMBER CONSTANT'

'IF STATEMENTS (ARITHMETIC AND LOGICAL)'
IF-0    'AN INVALID STATEMENT FOLLOWS THE LOGICAL IF'
IF-1    'ARITHMETIC OR INVALID EXPRESSION IN LOGICAL IF'
IF-2    'LOGICAL,COMPLEX OR INVALID EXPRESSION IN ARITHMETIC IF'

'IMPLICIT STATEMENT'
IM-0    'INVALID DATA TYPE'
IM-1    'INVALID OPTIONAL LENGTH'
IM-3    'IMPROPER ALPHABETIC SEQUENCE IN CHARACTER RANGE'
IM-4    'A SPECIFICATION IS NOT A SINGLE CHARACTER.THE FIRST CHARACTER IS USED'
IM-5    'IMPLICIT STATEMENT DOES NOT PRECEDE OTHER SPECIFICATION STATEMENTS'
IM-6    'ATTEMPT TO DECLARE THE TYPE OF A CHARACTER MORE THAN ONCE'
IM-7    'ONLY ONE IMPLICIT STATEMENT PER PROGRAM SEGMENT ALLOWED. THIS ONE
        IGNORED'

'INPUT/OUTPUT'
IO-0    'I/O STATEMENT REFERENCES A STATEMENT WHICH IS NOT A FORMAT STATEMENT'
IO-1    'A VARIABLE FORMAT MUST BE AN ARRAY NAME'
IO-2    'INVALID ELEMENT IN INPUT LIST OR DATA LIST'
IO-3    'OTHER COMPILERS MAY NOT ALLOW EXPRESSIONS IN OUTPUT LISTS'
IO-4    'ILLEGAL USE OF END= OR ERR= PARAMETERS'
IO-5    'INVALID UNIT NUMBER'
IO-6    'INVALID FORMAT'
IO-7    'ONLY CONSTANTS,SIMPLE INTEGER*4 VARIABLES,AND CHARACTER VARIABLES ARE
        ALLOWED AS UNIT'
```

WATFIV *compiler error messages (Continued)*

```
'JOB CONTROL CARDS'
JB-0    'CONTROL CARD ENCOUNTERED DURING COMPILATION;
        PROBABLE CAUSE:MISSING $ENTRY CARD'
JB-1    'MIS-PUNCHED JOB OPTION'

'JOB TERMINATION'
KO-0    'SOURCE ERROR ENCOUNTERED WHILE EXECUTING WITH RUN=FREE'
KO-1    'LIMIT EXCEEDED FOR FIXED-POINT DIVISION BY ZERO'
KO-2    'LIMIT EXCEEDED FOR FLOATING-POINT DIVISION BY ZERO'
KO-3    'EXPONENT OVERFLOW LIMIT EXCEEDED'
KO-4    'EXPONENT UNDERFLOW LIMIT EXCEEDED'
KO-5    'FIXED-POINT OVERFLOW LIMIT EXCEEDED'
KO-6    'JOB-TIME EXCEEDED'
KO-7    'COMPILER ERROR - EXECUTION TIME:RETURN TO SYSTEM'
KO-8    'TRACEBACK ERROR. TRACEBACK TERMINATED'

'LOGICAL OPERATIONS'
LG-0    '.NOT. WAS USED AS A BINARY OPERATOR'

'LIBRARY ROUTINES'
LI-0    'ARGUMENT OUT OF RANGE DGAMMA OR GAMMA. (1.382E-76 .LT. X .LT. 57.57)'
LI-1    'ABSOLUTE VALUE OF ARGUMENT .GT. 174.673, SINH,COSH,DSINH,DCOSH'
LI-2    'SENSE LIGHT OTHER THAN 0,1,2,3,4 FOR SLITE OR 1,2,3,4 FOR SLITET'
LI-3    'REAL PORTION OF ARGUMENT .GT. 174.673, CEXP OR CDEXP'
LI-4    'ABS(AIMAG(Z)) .GT. 174.673 FOR CSIN, CCOS, CDSIN OR CDCOS OF Z'
LI-5    'ABS(REAL(Z)) .GE. 3.537E15 FOR CSIN, CCOS, CDSIN OR CDCOS OF Z'
LI-6    'ABS(AIMAG(Z)) .GE. 3.537E15 FOR CEXP OR CDEXP OF Z'
LI-7    'ARGUMENT .GT. 174.673, EXP OR DEXP'
LI-8    'ARGUMENT IS ZERO, CLOG, CLOG10, CDLOG OR CDLG10'
LI-9    'ARGUMENT IS NEGATIVE OR ZERO, ALOG, ALOG10, DLOG OR DLOG10'
LI-A    'ABS(X) .GE. 3.537E15 FOR SIN, COS, DSIN OR DCOS OF X'
LI-B    'ABSOLUTE VALUE OF ARGUMENT .GT. 1, FOR ARSIN, ARCOS, DARSIN OR DARCOS'
LI-C    'ARGUMENT IS NEGATIVE, SQRT OR DSQRT'
LI-D    'BOTH ARGUMENTS OF DATAN2 OR ATAN2 ARE ZERO'
LI-E    'ARGUMENT TOO CLOSE TO A SINGULARITY, TAN, COTAN, DTAN OR DCOTAN'
LI-F    'ARGUMENT OUT OF RANGE DLGAMA OF ALGAMA. (0.0  .LT. X .LT. 4.29E73)'
LI-G    'ABSOLUTE VALUE OF ARGUMENT .GE. 3.537E15, TAN, COTAN, DTAN, DCOTAN'
LI-H    'LESS THAN TWO ARGUMENTS FOR ONE OF MIN0,MIN1,AMIN0,ETC.'

'MIXED MODE'
MD-0    'RELATIONAL OPERATOR HAS LOGICAL OPERAND'
MD-1    'RELATIONAL OPERATOR HAS COMPLEX OPERAND'
MD-2    'MIXED MODE - LOGICAL OR CHARACTER WITH ARITHMETIC'
MD-3    'OTHER COMPILERS MAY NOT ALLOW SUBSCRIPTS OF TYPE COMPLEX,LOGICAL OR
        CHARACTER'

'MEMORY OVERFLOW'
MO-0    'INSUFFICIENT MEMORY TO COMPILE THIS PROGRAM.REMAINDER WILL BE ERROR
        CHECKED ONLY'
MO-1    'INSUFFICIENT MEMORY TO ASSIGN ARRAY STORAGE. JOB ABANDONED'
MO-2    'SYMBOL TABLE EXCEEDS AVAILABLE SPACE.JOB ABANDONED'
MO-3    'DATA AREA OF SUBPROGRAM EXCEEDS 24K -- SEGMENT SUBPROGRAM'
MO-4    'INSUFFICIENT MEMORY TO ALLOCATE COMPILER WORK AREA OR WATLIB BUFFER'

'NAMELIST STATEMENTS'
NL-0    'NAMELIST ENTRY MUST BE A VARIABLE,NOT A SUBPROGRAM PARAMETER'
NL-1    'NAMELIST NAME PREVIOUSLY DEFINED'
NL-2    'VARIABLE NAME TOO LONG'
NL-3    'VARIABLE NAME NOT FOUND IN NAMELIST'
NL-4    'INVALID SYNTAX IN NAMELIST INPUT'
NL-6    'VARIABLE INCORRECTLY SUBSCRIPTED'
NL-7    'SUBSCRIPT OUT OF RANGE'
```

WATFIV *compiler error messages (Continued)*

```
'PARENTHESES'
PC-0    'UNMATCHED PARENTHESIS'
PC-1    'INVALID PARENTHESIS NESTING IN I/O LIST'

'PAUSE, STOP STATEMENTS'
PS-0    'OPERATOR MESSAGES NOT ALLOWED:SIMPLE STOP ASSUMED FOR STOP,
        CONTINUE ASSUMED FOR PAUSE'

'RETURN STATEMENT'
RE-1    'RETURN I, WHERE I IS OUT OF RANGE OR UNDEFINED'
RE-2    'MULTIPLE RETURN NOT VALID IN FUNCTION SUBPROGRAM'
RE-3    'VARIABLE IS NOT A SIMPLE INTEGER'
RE-4    'A MULTIPLE RETURN IS NOT VALID IN THE MAIN PROGRAM'

'ARITHMETIC AND LOGICAL STATEMENT FUNCTIONS'
    PROBABLE CAUSE OF SF ERRORS - VARIABLE ON LEFT OF = WAS NOT DIMENSIONED
SF-1    'A PREVIOUSLY REFERENCED STATEMENT NUMBER APPEARS ON A STATEMENT
        FUNCTION DEFINITION'
SF-2    'STATEMENT FUNCTION IS THE OBJECT OF A LOGICAL IF STATEMENT'
SF-3    'RECURSIVE STATEMENT FUNCTION DEFINITION:NAME APPEARS ON BOTH SIDES OF
        EQUAL SIGN.LIKELY CAUSE:VARIABLE NOT DIMENSIONED'
SF-4    'A STATEMENT FUNCTION DEFINITION APPEARS AFTER THE FIRST EXECUTABLE
        STATEMENT'
SF-5    'ILLEGAL USE OF A STATEMENT FUNCTION NAME'

'SUBPROGRAMS'
SR-0    'MISSING SUBPROGRAM'
SR-1    'SUBPROGRAM REDEFINES A CONSTANT,EXPRESSION,DO-PARAMETER OR ASSIGNED
        GOTO INDEX'
SR-2    'THE SUBPROGRAM WAS ASSIGNED DIFFERENT TYPES IN DIFFERENT PROGRAM
        SEGMENTS'
SR-3    'ATTEMPT TO USE A SUBPROGRAM RECURSIVELY'
SR-4    'INVALID TYPE OF ARGUMENT IN REFERENCE TO A SUBPROGRAM'
SR-5    'WRONG NUMBER OF ARGUMENTS IN A REFERENCE TO A SUBPROGRAM'
SR-6    'A SUBPROGRAM WAS PREVIOUSLY DEFINED. THE FIRST DEFINITION IS USED'
SR-7    'NO MAIN PROGRAM'
SR-8    'ILLEGAL OR MISSING SUBPROGRAM NAME'
SR-9    'LIBRARY PROGRAM WAS NOT ASSIGNED THE CORRECT TYPE'
SR-A    'METHOD FOR ENTERING SUBPROGRAM PRODUCES UNDEFINED VALUE FOR
        CALL-BY-LOCATION PARAMETER'

'SUBSCRIPTS'
SS-0    'ZERO SUBSCRIPT OR DIMENSION NOT ALLOWED'
SS-1    'YOU ALREADY HAVE THE MESSAGE'
SS-2    'INVALID SUBSCRIPT FORM'
SS-3    'SUBSCRIPT IS OUT OF RANGE'

'STATEMENTS AND STATEMENT NUMBERS'
ST-0    'MISSING STATEMENT NUMBER'
ST-1    'STATEMENT NUMBER GREATER THAN 99999'
ST-2    'STATEMENT NUMBER HAS ALREADY BEEN DEFINED'
ST-3    'UNDECODEABLE STATEMENT'
ST-4    'THIS STATEMENT SHOULD HAVE A STATEMENT NUMBER'
ST-5    'STATEMENT NUMBER IN A TRANSFER IS A NON-EXECUTABLE STATEMENT'
ST-6    'ONLY CALL STATEMENTS MAY CONTAIN STATEMENT NUMBER ARGUMENTS'
ST-7    'STATEMENT SPECIFIED IN A TRANSFER STATEMENT IS A FORMAT STATEMENT'
ST-8    'MISSING FORMAT STATEMENT'
ST-9    'SPECIFICATION STATEMENT DOES NOT PRECEDE STATEMENT FUNCTION DEFINITIONS
        OR EXECUTABLE STATEMENTS'

'SUBSCRIPTED VARIABLES'
SV-0    'THE WRONG NUMBER OF SUBSCRIPTS WERE SPECIFIED FOR A VARIABLE'
```

WATFIV *compiler error messages (Continued)*

```
SV-1    'AN ARRAY OR SUBPROGRAM NAME IS USED INCORRECTLY WITHOUT A LIST'
SV-2    'MORE THAN 7 DIMENSIONS ARE NOT ALLOWED'
SV-3    'DIMENSION OR SUBSCRIPT IS TOO LARGE (MAXIMUM 10**-1)'
SV-4    'A VARIABLE USED WITH VARIABLE DIMENSIONS IS NOT A SUBPROGRAM PARAMETER'
SV-5    'A VARIABLE DIMENSION IS NOT ONE OF:SIMPLE INTEGER VARIABLE,SUBPROGRAM
        PARAMETER,IN COMMON'

'SYNTAX ERRORS'
SX-0    'MISSING OPERATOR'
SX-1    'EXPECTING OPERATOR'
SX-2    'EXPECTING SYMBOL'
SX-3    'EXPECTING SYMBOL OR OPERATOR'
SX-4    'EXPECTING CONSTANT'
SX-5    'EXPECTING SYMBOL OR CONSTANT'
SX-6    'EXPECTING STATEMENT NUMBER'
SX-7    'EXPECTING SIMPLE INTEGER VARIABLE'
SX-8    'EXPECTING SIMPLE INTEGER VARIABLE OR CONSTANT'
SX-9    'ILLEGAL SEQUENCE OF OPERATORS IN EXPRESSION'
SX-A    'EXPECTING END-OF-STATEMENT'

'TYPE STATEMENTS'
TY-0    'THE VARIABLE HAS ALREADY BEEN EXPLICITLY TYPED'
TY-1    'THE LENGTH OF THE EQUIVALENCED VARIABLE MAY NOT BE CHANGED.
        REMEDY: INTERCHANGE TYPE AND EQUIVALENCE STATEMENTS'

'I/O OPERATIONS'
UN-0    'CONTROL CARD ENCOUNTERED ON UNIT 5 AT EXECUTION.
        PROBABLE CAUSE:MISSING DATA OR INCORRECT FORMAT'
UN-1    'END OF FILE ENCOUNTERED (IBM CODE IHC217)'
UN-2    'I/O ERROR (IBM CODE IHC218)'
UN-3    'NO DD STATEMENT WAS SUPPLIED (IBM CODE IHC219)'
UN-4    'REWIND,ENDFILE,BACKSPACE REFERENCES UNIT 5, 6 OR 7'
UN-5    'ATTEMPT TO READ ON UNIT 5 AFTER IT HAS HAD END-OF-FILE'
UN-6    'AN INVALID VARIABLE UNIT NUMBER WAS DETECTED (IBM CODE IHC220)'
UN-7    'PAGE-LIMIT EXCEEDED'
UN-8    'MISSING DEFINE FILE STATEMENT OR ATTEMPT TO DO SEQUENTIAL I/O ON A
        DIRECT ACCESS FILE (IBM CODE IHC231)'
UN-9    'WRITE REFERENCES 5 OR READ REFERENCES 6 OR 7'
UN-A    'ATTEMPT TO DO DIRECT ACCESS I/O ON A SEQUENTIAL FILE (IBM CODE IHC235)'
UN-B    'RECORD SIZE IN DEFINE FILE STATEMENT IS TOO LARGE(MAX=32768),OR EXCEEDS
        DD STATEMENT SPECIFICATION (IBM CODE IHC233,IHC237)'
UN-C    'FOR DIRECT ACCESS I/O THE RELATIVE RECORD POSITION IS NEGATIVE,ZERO,OR
        TOO LARGE (IBM CODE IHC232)'
UN-D    'AN ATTEMPT WAS MADE TO READ MORE INFORMATION THAN LOGICAL RECORD
        CONTAINS (IBM CODE IHC236)'
UN-E    'FORMATTED LINE EXCEEDS BUFFER LENGHT'
UN-F    'I/O ERROR - SEARCHING LIBRARY DIRECTORY'
UN-G    'I/O ERROR - READING LIBRARY'
UN-H    'ATTEMPT TO DEFINE THE OBJECT ERROR FILE AS A DIRECT ACCESS FILE
        (IBM CODE IHC234)'
UN-I    'RECFM OTHER THAN V(B) IS SPECIFIED FOR I/O WITHOUT FORMAT CONTROL
        (IBM CODE IHC214)'
UN-J    'MISSING DD CARD FOR WATLIB.NO LIBRARY ASSUMED'
UN-K    'ATTEMPT TO READ OR WRITE PAST THE END OF CHARACTER VARIABLE BUFFER'

'UNDEFINED VARIABLES'
UV-0    'VARIABLE IS UNDEFINED'
UV-3    'SUBSCRIPT IS UNDEFINED'
UV-4    'SUBPROGRAM IS UNDEFINED'
UV-5    'ARGUMENT IS UNDEFINED'
UV-6    'UNDECODABLE CHARACTERS IN VARIABLE FORMAT'
```

WATFIV *compiler error messages (Continued)*

```
'VARIABLE NAMES'
VA-0    'A NAME IS TOO LONG.IT HAS BEEN TRUNCATED TO SIX CHARACTERS'
VA-1    'ATTEMPT TO USE AN ASSIGNED OR INITIALIZED VARIABLE OR DO-PARAMETER IN A
        SPECIFICATION STATEMENT'
VA-2    'ILLEGAL USE OF A SUBROUTINE NAME'
VA-3    'ILLEGAL USE OF A VARIABLE NAME'
VA-4    'ATTEMPT TO USE THE PREVIOUSLY DEFINED NAME AS A FUNCTION OR AN ARRAY'
VA-5    'ATTEMPT TO USE A PREVIOUSLY DEFINED NAME AS A SUBROUTINE'
VA-6    'ATTEMPT TO USE A PREVIOUSLY DEFINED NAME AS A SUBPROGRAM'
VA-7    'ATTEMPT TO USE A PREVIOUSLY DEFINED NAME AS A COMMON BLOCK'
VA-8    'ATTEMPT TO USE A FUNCTION NAME AS A VARIABLE'
VA-9    'ATTEMPT TO USE A PREVIOUSLY DEFINED NAME AS A VARIABLE'
VA-A    'ILLEGAL USE OF A PREVIOUSLY DEFINED NAME'

'EXTERNAL STATEMENT'
XT-0    'A VARIABLE HAS ALREADY APPEARED IN AN EXTERNAL STATEMENT'
```

Index

A

B

C

Printer and Binder: The Murray Printing Company

83 84 85 86 10 9 8 7